COMPUTER CONCEPTS AND PROGRAMMING IN C

THEORY, PROBLEMS AND APPLICATIONS

"We want that education by which character is formed, strength of mind is increased, the intellect is expanded, and by which one can stand on one's own feet..."

... Swami Vivekananda

"The meaning of education is to encourage in people a sense of self-introspection, the ability to grasp and to develop the capacity for constructive works..."

... Dr. S. Radhakrishnan

"Always surround yourself with the kind of people who can make you believe that you can do it..."

... R. S. Salaria

"Treat others the way you wish to be treated..."

... R. S. Salaria

"May the blessings of the almighty go with this book to one and all..."

... R. S. Salaria

COMPUTER CONCEPTS AND PROGRAMMING IN C

THEORY, PROBLEMS AND APPLICATIONS

Thoroughly Revised according to the model curriculum designed by AICTE

for Windows & Linux/Unix platforms

Prof. R. S. Salaria
Alumnus of IIT, Delhi.
Certified Software Quality Professional, Govt. of India.
SUN Certified Programmer, SUN Microsystems, USA.
SUN Certified Trainer, SUN Microsystems, USA.

Former Head
Department of Computer Science & Engineering
Thapar University, PATIALA-147004.

Assisted by
Anita Salaria

KHANNA BOOK PUBLISHING CO. (P) LTD.
Publisher of Engineering and Computer Books
4C/4344, Ansari Road, Darya Ganj, New Delhi-110002
Phone : 011-23244447-48 **Mobile:** +91-9910909320
E-mail : contact@khannabooks.com
Website : www.khannabooks.com

Dear Readers,

To prevent the piracy, this book is secured with HIGH SECURITY HOLOGRAM on the front title cover. In case you don't find the hologram on the front cover title, please write us to at contact@khannabooks.com or whatsapp us at +91-99109 09320 and avail special gift voucher for yourself.

Specimen of Hologram on front Cover title:

Moreover, there is a SPECIAL DISCOUNT COUPON for you with EVERY HOLOGRAM.

How to avail this SPECIAL DISCOUNT:

Step 1: Scratch the hologram
Step 2: Under the scratch area, your "coupon code" is available
Step 3: Logon to www.khannabooks.com
Step 4: Use your "coupon code" in the shopping cart and get your copy at a special discount
Step 5: Enjoy your reading!

Price: ₹ 450.00

ISBN: 978-93-86173-78-2

Computer Concepts and Programming in C
by R.S. Salaria

First Edition: 2018
Reprint: 2020, **2024**

To view complete list of books, Please scan the QR Code:

Published by:
Khanna Book Publishing Co. (P) Ltd.
CIN: U22110DL1998PTC095547

Visit us at: **www.khannabooks.com**
Write us at: **contact@khannabooks.com**

Printed in India by: Vaibhav Products, Delhi.

Dedication

Our Dearest Parents,
Daughters Surbhi & Mehak,
Beloved Readers,

AND

Our Country Men/Women at Large.

My Slogan for My Fellow Citizens

India . . .

. . . is a Great Country

AND

Indians . . .

. . . are Outstanding.

Preface to First Edition

This book is designed to serve as textbook for the students of BCA, BSc (Computer Science), BSc (IT), PGDCA, MSc (Computer Science), MSc (IT), BE/BTech and MCA of different Indian universities and deemed universities.

While writing the book, special emphasis is given to keep the language very simple and lucid; level of presentation is kept simple and illustrative so that even an average reader can grasp the subject matter with quite ease. Practically this book will provide you every thing you need on the subject of "*Computer Concepts and Programming in C*".

The areas of strength of this book are in terms of that

- It provides a comprehensive coverage of the subject in a very lucid manner.
- It demonstrates the development of programs in a good programming style, as inline with the industry standards.
- It provides large number of ready to run example programs, for reference.
- It provides challenging review exercises to test your knowledge about the subject learned.
- It also provides large number of challenging programming exercises to test your programming skills acquired.

I am certain that you will enjoy reading this book. I do need a little favour from your side in the form of your response about the book. Your free and frank comments, suggestions, and positive criticism will help me to improve the book further to meet your expectations.

. . . R. S. Salaria
Email: *rssalaria@yahoo.com*

Preface to Revised Edition

Continuing with the tradition of providing rich content, the present edition lays more emphasis on the overall layout of the subject matter so as to make it more appealing and attractive. I am certain that the present edition will help the students in inculcating the habit of reading and self-learning.

Most of the topics are thoroughly revised and presented in a kind of manner with visuals where ever possible so that the students can grasp them with quite each.

Plenty of programming exercises are added to provide an intellectual challenge to the students, and the students are advised to convert this challenge to an opportunity and at the end of the day, you will be a very satisfied person.

In addition, new topics are added to provide comprehensive coverage of the subject as per the requirements of the model curriculum designed by AICTE for Under Graduate programme in Engineering & Technology.

I am hopeful that this edition will go beyond your expectations. Do keep on writing, as your valuable feedback and suggestions will help me in tuning the book to your expectations.

. . . R. S. Salaria

Acknowledgement

It is my pleasure to take this opportunity to sincerely thank all the teachers who have adopted my book and introducing it to their students. I am also thankful for their appreciations that I have been receiving from them in the form of emails and letters.

I would be failing in my duty if go without appreciating the response and interest shown by the students in my books. They are always a source of inspiration for me and I feel honoured because of their faith in me.

Finally, I must thank my publisher for their aggressive marketing and thus establishing the book as one of the best books on *Computer Concepts and Programming in C.*

. . . R. S. Salaria

Word of Advice for Teachers

Dear friends, let us remind ourselves that teachers can be categorized as follows:

Mediocre Teacher Tells
Good Teacher Explains
Superior Teacher Demonstrates
Great Teacher Inspires

Now you are to find out where you fit-in and where you want to be.

We believe that in addition to academic qualifications, a teacher must possess the following essential qualifications:

- Capability of providing inspirational leadership,
- Desire to teach,
- Knowledge of the subject and its relationship to other subjects, and
- Ability to transfer the knowledge to the students so that it is alive and meaningful.

If you possess all of the above essential qualifications, hats-off to you. Even if you lack in one or more of the above essential qualifications, but make a commitment to yourself to acquire those, we are certain that sooner you can become a great teacher.

For those who neither possess the above essential qualifications and nor prepared to acquire them, we pray the almighty to find a suitable place for them in some other profession.

We also want to share with you our views about the (holistic) education. Holistic education has two aspects:

- First aspect of it teaches us how to make living, and
- Second aspect of it teaches us how to live life.

We, as teachers, have to shoulder the responsibility of imparting both aspects of education so that we can contribute our share in the development of the country by producing individuals who are globally competent in their respective disciplines and are well equipped with morals and values of joyful life (*honesty*, *sincerity*, *integrity*, *loyalty*, *commitment*, . . .).

We sincerely advise you to treat your every student as your own child, the best in you will automatically come out - you know every parent want to give *the best* to their child.

As rightly said,

"A Teacher is a Nation builder"
and
"Teaching is a noble profession"

Enjoy your profession . . .

Wish you a nice time ahead.

. . . R. S. Salaria

Word of Advice for Students

My beloved students, we would like to remind you that we can categorize people as:

People who watch the things happening,
People who look into how things are happening, and
People who make the things happen.

Now you are to find out where you fit-in and where you want to be.

We firmly believe that youth of our country is second to none, and this fact is recognized world wide.

Our honorable former president Late Dr. APJ Kalam (first and may be the last president known as *people's president*) has been saying at all the platform that in India there is no dearth of resources and talent, only thing we need to change is *the mindset* (we have to shed *chalta hai* attitude). He has set a vision for us to see India a developed country by 2020, and the basis for his vision is the talent of our youth.

Take some time to discover yourself and try to assess how much talent you possess. Utilize your period of study to harness that talent. I can assure you that you will have a great future.

We want to share a popular game with you which all of us used to play in our childhood. The game is of burning a peace of paper using a lens under the sun. When the lens and the paper are held stationery, it starts burning in a few seconds. However, if you keep moving either the paper or the lens, the paper will never burn. *Why it happens so?* The answer is simple – the light energy emitted by the sun is not focused. The same is with us. We have enough energy in ourselves, but we don't focus it, rather we waste it in meaningless acts. The next question arises is – *where to focus our energy?* The natural answer of this question should be – what you want to become in your life (that basically defines your goal). So you need to focus your entire energy on your goal, and surely you will achieve your goal.

We would also like to share with you a scene from the popular epic – *Mahabharta*. When Dronacharya, Guru of Pandvas, asked his disciples to aim at the eye of the sparrow placed on a tree. All his disciples, except Arjuna, replied in a same manner – *Guru ji, we see a sparrow*. However, when the turn of Arjuna came, his reply was – *Guru ji, I see only the eye*. That is the kind of the focus you also need to develop in your life.

The next point is that when you have identified your goal, you need to identify the steps that you need to follow in order to accomplish your goal. Once the goal and the steps to accomplish your goal are identified, write them nicely on a piece of a paper and paste that paper at a place which you visit regularly. Whenever you will visit that place, the writing on the paper will remind you about your goal and what you have to do to achieve your goal.

The final word, you may set any goal for yourself and that may be of becoming a successful doctor, an engineer, an administrator or a businessman, but you must also try to be a *nice human being*. You know a nice human being is like a fruit of all seasons, and is welcome every where, anytime. We believe, the basic mantra to become a nice human being is too simple and can be stated as

"Treat the others the way you want to be treated, in other words, don't do anything with others which you wish others shouldn't do with you."

Enjoy your student life and make best use of it . . .

Wish you good luck and a nice time ahead.

. . . R. S. Salaria

Contents at a Glance

Table of Contents

Chapter 1

Introduction to Computers

Learning Objectives

After reading this chapter, students will be able to

- describe a computer and its operations
- differentiate hardware and software
- differentiate between data and information
- explain characteristics of a computer
- elaborate on the evolution of early computing devices
- explain the functional diagram of a computer
- explain the function of each functional unit
- explain the concept of booting and its types
- classify computers into various categories
- broad areas of applications of a computer

1.1 INTRODUCTION

The human civilization has seen many revolutions, which changed its life style many times. With the discovery of fire, man started eating cooked food. The invention of steam engine led to the industrial revolution and invention of telephone led to the communication revolution. Now, we are already going through information revolution brought about by the wonder machine known as a *Computer.* At present everyone is talking about computer as every one is getting benefits of it directly or indirectly.

In this chapter, we will discuss about basic aspects of computers - *the wonderful machine.*

1.2 WHAT IS A COMPUTER?

Computer is an electronic machine that performs tasks or computations according to a set of instructions called *programs.*

The first fully electronic computers, introduced in the 1940s, were huge machines that required teams of people to operate. Compared to those early machines, today's computers are amazing - they are thousands of times faster and can fit on your desk, in your lap, or even in your pocket.

A computer, in general, is capable of

- Receiving the data and instructions in various forms,
- Storing the data and instructions in its memory,
- Retrieving the data already stored on secondary storage,
- Performing arithmetic and logical operations, according to the specified instructions, with very high speed and greater accuracy,
- Producing the results in many forms, and
- Communicating with other computers.

1.2.1 Hardware and Software

Computers work through an interaction of *hardware* and *software.*

Hardware refers to the parts of a computer that you can see and touch, including the case and everything inside it. The most important piece of hardware is a tiny rectangular chip inside your computer called the *microprocessor.* It's the "brain" of your computer—the part that translates instructions and performs calculations. Hardware items such as your monitor, keyboard, mouse, printer, and other components are often called *hardware devices*, or *devices.*

Software refers to the instructions, or programs, that tell the hardware what to do. A word processing program using which you can write letters on your computer is a type of software. The most important example of software is an *operating system* (OS) that manages all the resources (such as memories, input/output devices, etc.) of your computer system, and provides an interface using which the user can interact with the computer to perform various tasks. Two well-known operating systems are Windows and Linux.

1.2.2 Data and Information

The terms *data* and *information* have been used to mean the same thing. But actually information is more than just data.

Data – The term *data* simply refers to a value or set of values. These values may represent some observations from an experiment, some figures collected during some survey (such as *census*, *exit polls*, etc.), marks obtained by a student in an examination, etc.

Information – In simple terms, information is a processed data. Data is just a collection of values (raw data), from which no conclusions can be drawn. Thus, data as such is not useful for decision making. When the data is processed, by applying certain rules, new generated data becomes information. This new generated data (information) conveys some meaning and hence can be used for decision-making. For more clarity, consider the next example.

An agricultural scientist wants to study the effect of a particular pesticide on a new variety of wheat. He uses a different amount of pesticide for different fields of wheat and notes down the yield of wheat in each field. Here, the amount of pesticide used and yield of wheat in each field represents data.

As such these values do not convey anything regarding the effect of pesticide on the yield. Next he applies the technique of correlation analysis to determine the correlation coefficient whose value lies in the range -1 to $+1$. This coefficient, which is also a value, conveys valuable information about the effect of pesticide on yield of wheat. If correlation coefficient is greater than 0, it means increased amount of pesticide has positive effect on the yield. If correlation coefficient is less than 0, it means increased amount of pesticide has negative effect on the yield. If correlation coefficient is equal to 0, it means increased amount of pesticide has no effect on the yield.

1.3 CHARACTERISTICS OF A COMPUTER

A computer is a very powerful and versatile machine. The key characteristics of a computer include the following:

Speed - A computer can perform arithmetic as well logical operations at very high speed. The speed of a computer is usually measured in Million Instructions Per Second (MIPS) or Millions of Floating-point Operations Per Second (MFLOPS). For example, a simple microcomputer (also known as PC) can have a speed of about 1 MFLOPS, where as a super computer can have a speed more than 80 MFLOPS.

An average computer executes instructions at 20 MIPS. Even such a high unit to measure the speed of computers, becomes so small for very high speed parallel computers. For example, an ordinary computer can add two 18 digits numbers in just 3×10^{-4} seconds.

Accuracy - If the data and instructions given are correct, computers will always give the correct results. The errors in the calculations are due to humans, who either don't give the correct data or instructions to the computer or ignore the data handling limitations of the computer.

Capacity - Information is useful only if it is available on time and computer is the only solution for it. Computer can handle very large amount of data. Whole encyclopedia, which is on many volumes of books, can be stored on a single disk of computer and any information can be accessed in seconds by just a push of button.

Reliability - Being a machine, computers never get tired or bored. Computer can perform millions of similar type of operations without getting bored or tired, for number of days together without showing any sign of fatigue. It does not require even tea or lunch break. Computer is made of mostly electronic components, which don't have any wear and tear; therefore computer can work for years with requiring any maintenance.

Versatility - The basic operation of computer is to receive the data, process it and produce the accurate result at a very high speed. This quality makes the computer a very versatile device which can be used for number of applications like word-processing, accounting, scientific calculations, designing, training, controlling and entertainment.

Automatic - Computer works automatically without any aid from the humans. It requires the data and instructions only in the beginning, later it works automatically according to the instructions.

Communication - Computers can communicate with each other using telephones and modems. This enables the computer to share the information and resources at much lower price. The large problems can be distributed among the various computers to have fast processing of data.

Diligence - A computer is free from tiredness, lack of concentration, fatigue, etc. It can work for hours without creating any error. It does not require any tea breaks. If millions of calculations are to be performed, a computer will perform every calculation with the same accuracy. Due to this capability, it overpowers human being in routine type of work.

No IQ - Computer is a dumb machine and it cannot do any work without instruction from the user. It performs the instructions at tremendous speed and with accuracy. It is you to decide what you want to do and in what sequence. So a computer cannot take its own decision as you can.

No Feeling - It does not have feelings or emotion, taste, knowledge and experience. Thus, it does not get tired even after long hours of work. It does not distinguish between users.

1.4 LIMITATIONS OF A COMPUTER

The only limitation of the computer is that it does not have any intelligence of its own. It can't work on its own. It can't learn from its mistakes or previous experiences. It can't think or innovate. The research is going on to render artificial intelligence to computers.

1.5 EVOLUTION OF COMPUTERS

History of computers could be traced back to the effort of man to count large numbers. This process of counting of large numbers generated various systems of numeration like Babylonian system of numeration, Greek system of numeration, Roman system of numeration and Indian system of numeration. Out of these the Indian system of numeration has been accepted universally. It is the basis of modern decimal system of numeration (0, 1, 2, 3, 4, 5, 6, 7, 8, and 9). You will be surprised to know that the computer does not understand the decimal system and uses binary system of numeration for processing.

In this section, we will briefly discuss some of the path-breaking inventions in the field of computing devices.

Abacus

Abacus was discovered by the Mesopotamians somewhere around 3000 BC. It basically consists of beads on movable rods which are divided into two parts. Various basic arithmetic operations such as addition, subtraction, multiplication and division of numbers can be done by using the place value of digits of the numbers and position of beads in an abacus.

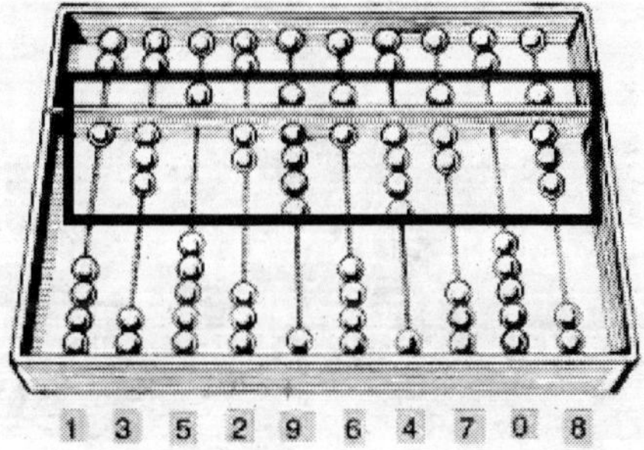

Figure 1.1: ABACUS

Napier's Logs and Bones

Napier is best known for the idea of using logarithms in 1614 to make arithmetic easier. He devised a set of numbering rods known as Napier's Bones through which both multiplication and
division could be performed.

Every number has a logarithm and adding logarithms is the same a multiplying the original values. If you have two numbers that you want to multiply you look up their logs, add the logs together and then look up the antilog. Similarly dividing is just a matter of subtraction.

Logs make multiplication and division easy - but only if you have suitable tables in which to look up the logs and anti-logs.

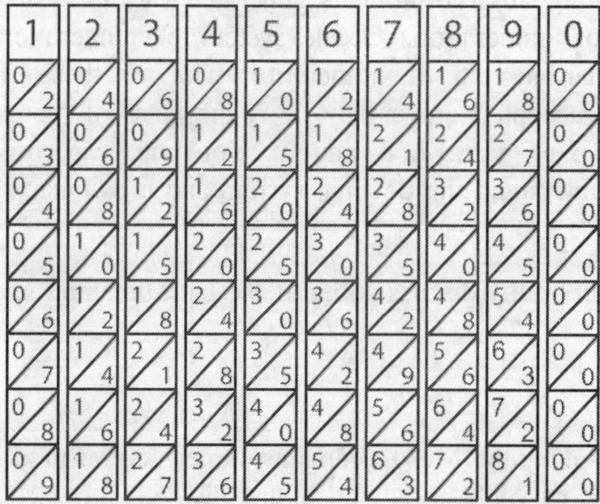

Figure 1.2: Napier's Logs and Bones

Pascal's Calculator or Pascaline

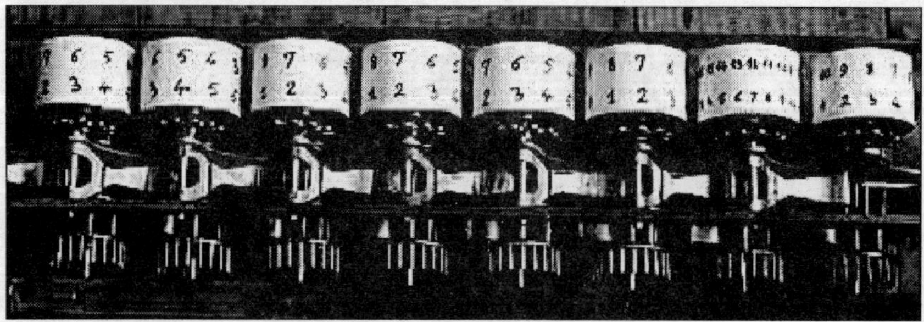

Figure 1.3: Pascal's Calculator

Pascal's Calculator, also known as Pascaline, was developed by Blasie Pascal in the year 1642, at the age of 19 that could add and subtract. It consists of wheels, gears and cylinders.

Slide Rule

The slide rule is a mechanical analog computer. It is used primarily for multiplication and division, and also for functions such as exponents, roots, logarithms and trigonometry.

Figure 1.4: Slide rule

It is actually made of three bars that are fixed together. The sliding center bar is sandwiched by the outer bars which are fixed with respect to each other. The metal "window" is inserted over the slide rule to act as a place holder. A cursor is fixed in the center of the "window" to allow for accurate readings.

Leibnitz's Calculating Machine

The German philosopher and mathematician Gottfried Wilhelm von Leibnitz built a calculating machine called the Step Reckoner in the year 1673. It expanded on Pascal's ideas and did multiplication by repeated addition and shifting.

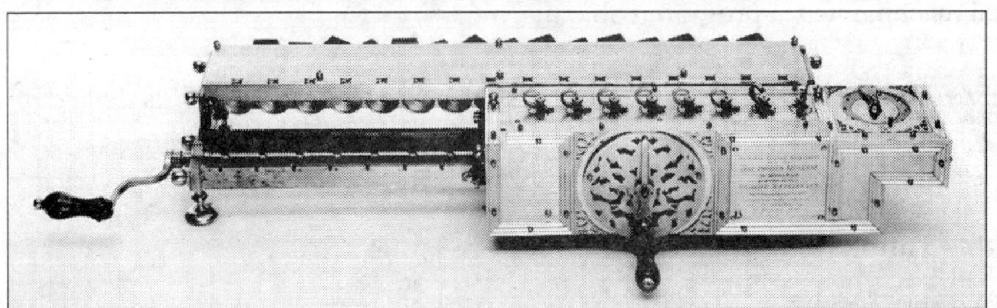

Figure 1.5: Leibnitz's Calculating Machine

Babbage's Difference Engine and Analytical Engine

It was in the year 1823 that a famous English man Charles Babbage built a mechanical machine to do complex mathematical calculations, called *difference engine*.

Figure 1.6: Babbage's Difference Engine

Figure 1.7: Babbage's Analytical Engine

It is an automatic mechanical calculator designed to tabulate polynomial functions. The name derives from the method of divided differences, a way to interpolate or tabulate functions by using a small set of polynomial coefficients. Most mathematical functions commonly used by engineers, scientists and navigators, including logarithmic and trigonometric functions, can be approximated by polynomials, so a difference engine can compute many useful tables of numbers.

Later he developed a general-purpose calculating machine called an analytical engine. The analytical machine was a programmable machine.

Because of his pioneer work, Charles Babbage is known as *father of Modern Computers.*

Hollerith's Tabulating Machine

In the late 19th century punched cards were commercially used. The inventor of punched card tabulating machine, Herman Hollerith founded the Tabulating Machine Company in 1896.

They were widely used in the 1970s, and with the arrival of interactive display terminals these became obsolete. The punch card was a slightly larger than the size of a post card. It was used to store one line of data. The programs were in the form of a pack of punch cards. Hollerith's tabulator became so successful that he started his own firm to market the device; this company eventually became International Business Machines (IBM).

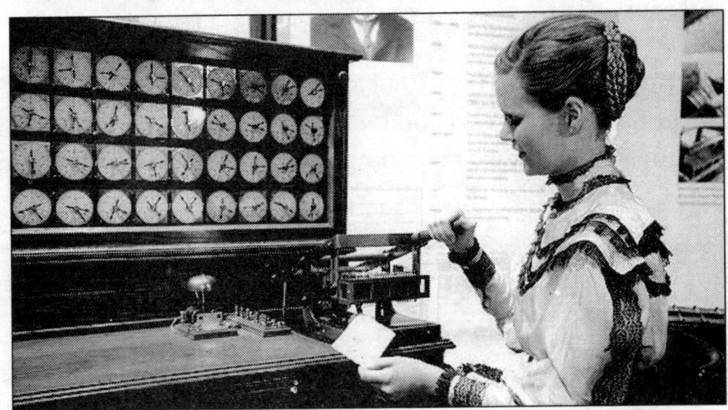

Figure 1.8: Hollerith;s Tabulating Machine

Howard Mark I

By the late 1930s punched-card machine techniques had become so well established and reliable that Howard Aiken, in collaboration with engineers at IBM, undertook construction of a large automatic digital computer based on standard IBM electromechanical parts. The result was Aiken's machine, called the Howard I, in the year 1944. It handled arithmetic operations, special built-in programs, subroutines, to handle logarithms and trigonometric functions.

Figure 1.9: Harvard Mark I

ENIAC

The first general purpose digital computer was ENIAC, invented in 1946. ENIAC stands for Electronic Numerical Integrator And Calculator. It was invented at University of Pennsylvania's Moore School of Electrical Engineering, and used by U.S. army forces to calculate ballistic tables. It took the team about one year to design the ENIAC and 18 months and 500,000 tax dollars to build it.

The ENIAC contained 17,468 vacuum tubes, along with 70,000 resistors, 10,000 capacitors, 1,500 relays, 6,000 manual switches and 5 million soldered joints. It covered 1800 square feet (167 square meters) of floor space, weighed 30 tons, and consumed 160 kilowatts of electrical power. In one second, the ENIAC (one thousand times faster than any other calculating machine to date) could perform 5,000 additions, 357 multiplications or 38 divisions.

Figure 1.10: ENIAC

EDVAC

Von Neumann, a Hungarian Mathematician in 1942, introduced Von Neumann's principle, which states that "*instructions and data are to be stored in some device and then from there instructions are fetched one by one and executed in sequence*", which led to the development of first stored-program computer, EDVAC (Electronic Discrete Variable Automatic Computer), in the year 1951.

Figure 1.11: EDVAC

1.6 FUNCTIONAL COMPONENTS OF A COMPUTER

A computer is a combination of hardware and software. Hardware represent the physical components of a computer like motherboard, memory devices, monitor, keyboard, etc., while software represents the set of programs or instructions. Both hardware and software together make the computer system function.

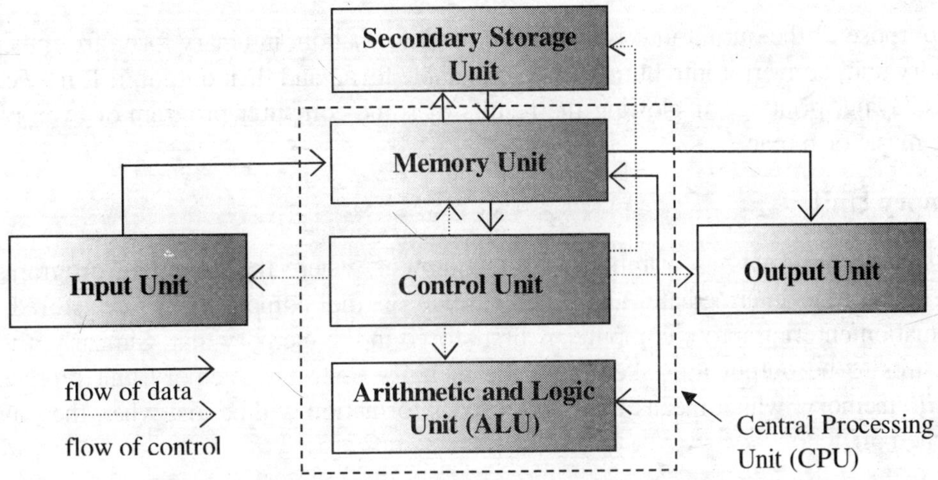

Figure 1.12: Functional components of a Computer

Every task given to a computer follows an Input- Process-Output Cycle (IPO cycle). It needs certain input, processes that input and produces the desired output. The input unit takes the input, the central processing unit does the processing of data and the output unit produces the output. The memory unit holds the data and instructions during the processing.

Let us have a look at the functional components of a computer.

Input Unit

The *input unit* consists of various input devices that can be connected to a computer, such as *keyboard*, *mouse*, *light pen*, *microphone*, etc. The standard input device is *keyboard*, which will come with every new computer. At any time, more than one input device can be connected to a computer.

The purpose of the input unit is to receive the information from the outside world, convert it into binary form, and then transfer it to the main memory. It may consist of entering data to be processed by some program, recording of speech, capturing of a scene or photograph, or selecting some objects on the display.

Output Unit

The *output unit* consists of various output devices that can be connected to a computer, such as *visual display unit* (VDU) or simply known as *monitor*, *printers*, *plotters*, *audio systems* etc. The standard output device is a *monitor*, which will come with every new computer. At any time, like input devices, more than one output device can be connected to a computer.

The purpose of the output unit is to receive the information, in binary form, from the main memory unit, convert it into human understandable form, and then output it. It may consist of displaying, printing, or plotting the results of some computer program or even playing some music or movie.

Memory Unit

The *memory unit* acts as warehouse of a computer, where the executing programs, the input data, the intermediate and final results of the computations are stored. The information entering into a computer is first stored in the memory unit. Similarly, the data or results to be output are taken from the memory unit. The memory unit represents a *volatile* memory, which means that the stored information will be lost when the power is switched off.

Arithmetic and Logic Unit

The arithmetic and logic unit (ALU), as its name implies, performs arithmetic and logical operations. Arithmetic operations include addition, subtraction, multiplication, and division. Logical operations are used to compare two data items, and include operations such as less than (<), less than or equal to (≤), greater than (>), greater than or equal to (≥), equal to (=), and not equal to (≠).

Control Unit

The control unit co-ordinates and controls all the other parts of the computer system. Under the direction of a program, the control unit performs four basic operations:

- *Fetch* - getting the next program instruction from the computer's memory.
- *Decode* - figuring out what the program is telling the computer to do?
- *Execute* - performing the requested action, such as adding two numbers or deciding whether one of them is larger.
- *Write-Back* - writing the results back to memory.

This four-step process is called *a machine cycle*, or *a processing cycle*, and consists of two phases: *the instruction cycle* (*fetch* and *decode*) and *the execution cycle* (*execute* and *write-back*).

Secondary Storage Unit

The *secondary storage unit* provides the long-term storage for important data for future use. The data for the secondary storage unit is transferred from the memory unit to the secondary storage unit. In order to process the data residing in secondary storage, it is transferred from the secondary storage to the memory. Please remember that data stored in secondary storage can not be processed directly in secondary storage itself. The data can only be processed if it is in the memory.

The various devices used in secondary storage unit are, also called *storage devices*, are *floppy disks*, *hard disks*, *tapes*, CDs. DVDs, pen drives, etc. The floppy disks, tapes, CDs, DVDs, pen drives are removable storage devices, where as hard disks are (mostly) fixed.

The device to read and write data onto a floppy disk is known as *floppy drive*, for tape it is *tape drive*, for CD it is CD drive, for DVD it is DVD drive, etc. The hard disk and its drive are embedded in a single unit, which is fixed inside the system box.

- The *control unit*, the *arithmetic and logic unit*, and the *main memory unit*, collectively, are known as *Central Processing Unit* (CPU).
- All the external devices, such as *input device* and *output devices*, connected to the computer are known by the common name as *peripherals*.

Figure 1.13 shows the block diagram of a personal computer (microcomputer). With the advancement in the field of materials and microelectronics, it became possible to embed the *control unit*, *arithmetic and logical unit*, and limited high speed memory in the form of few *registers*, inside the single *Very Large Scale Integration* (VLSI) chip, known as a *microprocessor*.

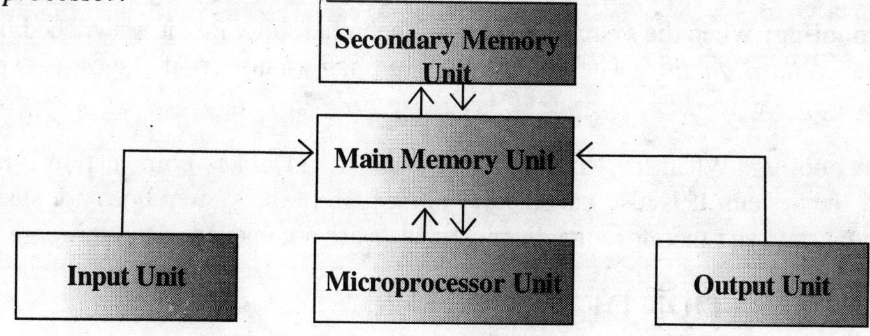

Figure 1.13: Functional diagram of a Personal Computer

Formally, a *microprocessor*, commonly referred as *processor*, is a general-purpose programmable device, which can receive the information in binary form, process it and transmit the results. It can be programmed to solve a wide variety of problems using the instructions that it understands. The set of all those instructions that it can understand is known as the *instruction set* of the processor.

The role of the other units remains the same as in the case of a general digital computer.

Majority of the present PCs including laptops are built around the *Intel* or *AMD* based microprocessors.

1.7 CONCEPT OF BOOTING

In simple terms, *booting* is a process in which your computer gets initialized. This process includes initializing all your hardware components in your computer and getting them to work together and to load your default operating system which will make your computer operational.

The technical details of booting process can be summarized as follows:

1. When the computer is switched on, a copy of boot program is brought from ROM into the main memory.
2. Then CPU runs a jump instruction that transfers to BIOS (Basic Input output System) and it starts executing.
3. The BIOS conducts a series of self diagnostic tests called POST (Power On Self Test). These tests include memory tests, configuring and starting video circuitry, configuring the system's hardware and checking other devices that help to function the computer properly.
4. Thereafter, the BIOS locates a bootable drive to load the boot sector. The Boot Strap Loader program loads and executes the operating system.

The booting process is of two types:

- **Cold booting:** When the system starts from the initial state, *i.e.*, it is switched on. It is also called *hard booting*. The system goes through a number of stages as explained above

- **Warm booting:** When the Reset button or Ctrl+Alt+Del key combination is used to restart the system. It is also called *soft booting*. Here the system does not start from the initial state and therefore the diagnostic tests are not carried out in this case.

1.8 CLASSIFICATION OF COMPUTERS

There is no single criteria according to which we can classify the computers. Hence, the computers are classified based on the

- electronic components used in the internal circuitry of the computer system,
- working principle,
- usage/applications, and
- size, cost, capacity, and speed.

1.8.1 Classification of Computers Based on Electronic Component Technology

Based on electronic components used in internal circuitry, computers can be classified as

- First generation computers,
- Second generation computers,
- Third generation computers, and
- Fourth generation computers.

This classification also tells us about the advances in evolution of computer systems to the present *state of the art* computer.

1.8.1.1 First Generation Computers (1940 - 1956)

The first generation started in 1940 and spans to the year 1956, approximately. The vacuum tubes were used in the internal circuitry of the computers and external wiring was used for making connections.

Main characteristics of computers belonging to this generation are:

- Large in size and generate lot of heat,
- Power consumption is more,
- Speed is Slower,
- Life is limited,
- Have slow and small internal memory made of magnetic core,
- Magnetic drums were used for secondary storage,
- Use machine and assembly languages for preparing instructions, and
- Used for scientific applications only.

Figure 1.14: Vacuum

Some examples of first generation computers are ENIAC, EDVAC, UNIVAC-I.

1.8.1.2 Second Generation Computers (1956 - 1963)

The second generation started in 1956 and spans to the year 1963, approximately. Instead of vacuum tubes, which are bulky in size, transistors were used in the internal circuitry of the computers belonging to this generation and *Printed Circuit Boards* (PCBs) to connect the various components of the circuit.

Figure 1.15: Transistors

Main characteristics of computers belonging to this generation are:

- Smaller in size as compared to first generation computers, and generate less heat as there is no heating element in transistors,
- Relatively faster, (speed measured in microseconds),
- Power consumption is drastically less,
- Relatively more internal storage,
- Use high level languages like FORTRAN & COBOL for preparing instructions in addition to machine and assembly languages.
- Used for scientific as well as commercial applications.

Some examples of second generation computers are IBM 1401, IBM 1620, IBM 7090, IBM 7094, CDC 1604.

1.8.1.3 Third Generation Computers (1964 - 1971)

The third generation started in the year 1964 and spans to the year 1971, approximately. Instead of using discrete components, such as transistors, resistors, capacitors, etc., *Integrated Circuits* (ICs) were used in the internal circuitry of the computers belonging to this generation. An IC contains many transistors and other components that are packed into a single silicon chip of size less than 5 mm square.

Main characteristics of computers belonging to this generation are:

- Smaller in size as compared to second generation computers,
- Relatively faster (speed measured in nanoseconds),
- Power consumption less,
- Uses increased semiconductor memory as internal storage
- Uses magnetic disks for secondary storage medium.
- Permits multiprogramming & on-line processing
- Use of the high-level languages, like COBOL, FORTRAN, etc., became common.

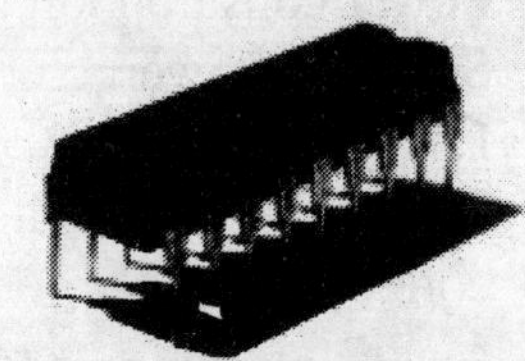

Figure 1.16: Integrated Circuit (IC)

Some examples of third generation computers are IBM 360/370 series, ICL's 1900 and 2900 series, CDC 6600, Burroughs B5500.

1.8.1.4 Fourth Generation Computers (1972 - Present)

The fourth generation started in the year 1972 and is continuing till date. With the advancement is material science and micro-electronics, we had various improved forms of ICs, such as MSI, LSI, VLSI. The original IC's started known as Small Scale Integration (SSI) which contains about 10-20 components per chip.

Figure 1.17: VLSI Chip

Medium Scale Integration (MSI) contains about 50 components per chip. Large Scale Integration (LSI) contains about 100 components per chip. Very Large Scale Integration (VLSI) contains about 150 components per chip.

With the advent of VLSI technology, it becomes possible to house the entire processor in a single chip. That resulting chip was given the name *microprocessor*. The computers in this generation are built around the microprocessor.

The main characteristics of computers belonging to this generation are:

- Very smaller in size. Can be placed on a desktop or even you can carry them along during your journey.
- Very cheap and are within the reach of an individual.
- Use of semiconductor memory for compactness and reliability.
- Used magnetic disks, cartages, CD-ROM, and DVDs for secondary storage.
- Uses variety of high-level languages, specialized user friendly packages/software.

Some examples of fourth generation computers are IBM PC and compatibles, Magnum from HCL, Landmark from Wipro, etc.

1.8.1.5 Fifth Generation Computers

Still research is going on and we are hearing about new developments such as quantum computers, biological computers, etc. We expect some big news will come sooner or later.

1.8.2 Classification of Computers Based on Working Principle

Based on working principle, the computers can be classified as

- analog computers,
- digital computers, and
- hybrid computers

Computers are made of large number of devices. In order to understand the working principle of the computer, we will try to understand the working of a single device used in these computers.

1.8.2.1 Analog Computers

In these computers, the various analog devices use physical relationships and are *measuring devices.* These are used to measure various quantities such as temperature, pressure, voltage, etc. An analog device works by setting up a model of the problem to be solved, representing the variables of the problem by the physical aspects of the device itself. The values of these variables are made proportional to these physical aspects. In order to fix the idea, consider the example of a mechanical watch, with which most of us are familiar.

The variable of the problem in hand is the *time*. The time is measured by the rotation of the wheels. There are separate wheels for measuring seconds, minutes and seconds. The wheels of the watch are its physical aspects, and the number of rotations determines the time measured. Here one rotation of wheel for measuring seconds is proportional to one second, sixty rotations of this wheel causes one rotation to the minutes wheel, which is set proportional to one minute, and sixty rotations of the minute wheel causes one rotation of the hours wheel, which is set proportional to one hour of time.

The other examples of popular analog devices are speedometer of an automobile, volt meter, barometer, thermometer, etc.

The speedometer of an automobile measures the voltage produced by the rotation of the wheels, which is set proportional to amount of deflection. The voltmeter measures the voltage across the circuit and the shows it as deflection of the needle. Similarly, the temperature is measured as a result of the expansion of the mercury, where the expansion of the mercury is set proportional to the temperature.

Analog computers are used by scientists and engineers, who interact with them directly to solve the various problems. The methods used here are *hit and trial* in nature, .*i.e.*, there are no fixed steps. The research and development is the main area of application of analog devices. These are also used in process control applications such as oil-refining, chemical processing, etc.

1.8.2.2 Digital Computers

In these computers, the various digital devices use numbers to represent the variables of the problem and are thus *counting devices.* All the variables of the problem are expressed as numbers and are manipulated according to the rules of arithmetic of a number system.

In order to under stand the working of a digital computer, let us understand the working of digital watch, with which most of us are familiar.

The variable of the problem in hand is the *time*. The time is shown by counting the seconds, minutes and seconds. After counting sixty seconds, a minute is counted and the seconds count is reset to zero. Similarly after counting sixty minutes, one hour is counted and the seconds count is reset to zero. Finally after counting twenty four hours, the hours count is reset to zero.

There are enormous examples of popular digital devices that include digital voltmeters, digital gasoline petrol pumps, etc.

Digital computers are used for many applications including research and development by scientists and engineers, commercial applications, entertainment applications, military applications, etc. There are definite steps to solve a problem on digital computer. The instruction for these steps are prepared by the user and then fed to the computer. The users don't have to interact with the computer once instructions are fed except inputting the desired data.

1.8.2.3 Hybrid Computers

These computers are made up of analog as well as of digital devices. In general, a hybrid computer is an analog computer whose overall function is controlled by a digital computer rather than a user. These computers are designed for applications where continuous monitoring is required and quick actions are to be taken in case some thing happens abnormal. The analog devices, *i.e.*, analog computer measures the various variables of the problem, these are converted to numbers and then fed to the digital computer, which analyses these numbers. If any of the numbers are not within the prescribed limits then it will send a alarming signal to the control room for immediate attention or will send the signals to the analog computer to change the values of the variables if there is a provision of automatic control.

To understand the working of hybrid computer let us take an example of Intensive Care Unit (ICU) in a modern hospital. The analog devices measure the pulse, temperature, pressure, etc., and these measurements are converted to numbers are then fed to the digital computer. The digital computer, according the prescribed instructions, analyses these measurements, and if any one or more of these measurements is/are beyond the prescribed limits, it will generate an alarming signal in the doctor's room.

The hybrid computers are mainly used in process control applications, where the continuous monitoring may not be feasible, for example due to health hazards in a nuclear power plant or expensive in terms of manpower.

1.8.3 Classification of Computers Based on Usage

Based on the usage, the computers can be classified as *special purpose computers* or *general purpose computers.*

1.8.3.1 Special Purpose Computers

As their name implies, these are computers, which are designed for handling specific problems. In these kinds of computers, the instructions are built into the hardware itself. One of the very popular examples of usage of special purpose computer is the *computerized STD*. In this application, the computer is given the instruction to monitor the incoming and outgoing calls. It records are the details of the calls made including the recipients telephone number, the time when call was made, the duration of the call, and the pulse rate at that time. Based on the recorded data it generates the billing slips. We can get the detail of any call later on, if required, and can also print the billing slip.

Other applications for which special purpose computer are designed includes the computerized home appliances, toys, military equipment, black boxes of the airplanes, etc.

The analog as well as hybrid computers fall in this category.

1.8.3.2 General Purpose Computers

As their name implies, these are computers, which can handle wide variety of problems. In these computers, you can feed new set of instructions to solve a new problem i.e. the set of instructions fed to the computer are alterable. The same computer can be used to solve some mathematical problem, to prepare salary slips of employees of an organization, to manage the inventory of an industrial house, to prepare a document, to play music or a movie, etc.

The digital computers fall in this category.

1.8.4 Classification of Computers Based their Cost, Speed, Capacity and Size

These terms are basically relative. Based on these relative terms, the computers, in order of decreasing of these terms, can be classified as

- Super computers
- Mainframe computers
- Mini computers
- Micro computers

1.8.4.1 Super Computers

They are the fastest and most expensive machines. They have high processing speed compared to other computers. They have also multiprocessing technique. One of the ways in which supercomputers are built is by interconnecting hundreds of microprocessors. Supercomputers are mainly being used for whether forecasting, biomedical research, remote sensing, aircraft design and other areas of science and technology.

Figure 1.18: Super computer

Few examples of supercomputers are CRAY X-MP-14, NEC SX-2, PARAM from India.

1.8.4.2 Mainframes Computers

Figure 1.19: Mainframe computer

Mainframe computer is a large, powerful, and expensive type of computer that can support many users at one time, can store vast amounts of data, and can perform many tasks at the same time. They operate at very high speed, and are generally used in centralized databases. They are also used as controlling nodes in Wide Area Networks (WANs).

Few examples of mainframe computers are CDC 6600, ICL 39, VAX 8842, DEC 10, IBM 4381.

1.8.4.3 Mini Computers

Minicomputers are smaller than a mainframe computer and larger than a microcomputer. This is designed to support more than one user at a time. It possesses large storage capacity and operates at a higher speed. The mini computer is used in multi-user system in which various users can work at the same time.

This type of computer is generally used for processing large volume of data in an organization. They are also used as servers in Local Area Networks (LANs).

Figure 1.19: Mini computer

Few examples of mini computers are PDP 11, CDC 1700, HP 3000 series, HCL's Magnum, Wipro's Landmark, etc.

1.8.4.4 Micro Computers

Microcomputer is at the lowest end of the computer range in terms of speed and storage capacity. Microcomputer is a small computer with enough power and storage capacity to meet the personal needs of different kind of users. These are also called personal computer (PC), home computer, or desktop computer.

Desktop Computer

Figure 1.20: Desktop PC

Desktop computers are designed for use at a desk or table. They are typically larger and more powerful than other types of personal computers. Desktop computers are made up of separate components. The main component, called the *system unit*, is usually a rectangular case that sits on or underneath a desk. Other components, such as the monitor, mouse, and keyboard, connect to the system unit.

Laptop Computer

Figure 1.21: Laptop Computer

Laptop computers, simply known as *laptops*, are lightweight mobile PCs with a thin screen. They are often called *notebook computers* because of their small size. Laptops can operate on batteries, so you can take them anywhere. Unlike desktops, laptops combine the CPU, screen, and keyboard in a single case. The screen folds down onto the keyboard when not in use.

Handheld Computer

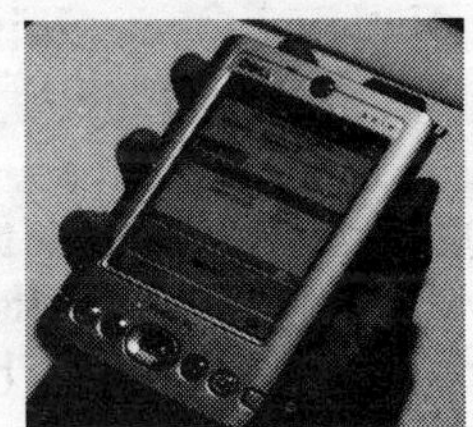

Figure 1.22: Handheld Computer

Handheld computers, also called *personal digital assistants (PDAs)*, are battery-powered computers small enough to carry almost anywhere. Although not as powerful as desktops or laptops, handhelds are useful for scheduling appointments, storing addresses and phone numbers, and playing games. Some have more advanced capabilities, such as making telephone calls or accessing the Internet. Instead of keyboards, handhelds have touch screens that you can use with your finger or a *stylus* (a pen-shaped pointing tool).

1.9 APPLICATIONS OF A COMPUTER

Today, no area of life is left where computers are not being used in one way and the other. In this section, we discuss few of them where computers have made significant contribution to our working.

1.9.1 Computers in Education

Computers are being used proficiently in various educational fields. Computers are used in running school and college administrations, during the admission procedures, storing of official and student records. They are also used in syllabus planning and decision-making, controlling, assisting instructions and simulation. Computers are helpful in directing aptitude tests and achievement tests, at the time of entrance exams. There is computer software designed to process performances related to teachers and employees promotion avenues. They also process records of salaries, examinations, schemes of examination, printing of papers and question papers, evaluation of answer sheets, mark sheets and certificates.

Computers are used in colleges, by the professors, to conduct special classes and enable their students to adopt a methodical way of study. Students take more interest in the documented programs, designed on different topics. Internet has provided a favourable means of pursuing courses from renowned universities, across the world. These facilities become available at a click of the mouse.

Indian Space Research Organisation (ISRO) launched the world's first dedicated education satellite called EDUcation SATellite (EDUSAT). EDUSAT resulted into virtual classrooms in the country. EDUSAT is a collaborative project of ISRO, the Union ministry of human resource development, state departments of education and the Indira Gandhi National Open University. EDUSAT is the first exclusive satellite for serving the educational sector in India.

Growing demand for an interactive satellite based distance education system through audio-visual medium, employing Direct To Home (DTH) quality broadcast prompted the government to launch it. The satellite has multiple regional beams covering different parts of India - five KU-band transponders with spot beams covering northern, north-eastern, eastern, southern and western regions of the country, a KU-band transponder with its footprint covering the Indian mainland region and six C-band transponders with their footprints covering the entire country. About seventeen state governments have so far sent proposals to the central government requesting setting up of EDUSAT Networks for Elementary Education. The experts can deliver lectures to the students or academician through teleconferencing with the combined efforts of Information Technology.

Distance Education

Formal education requires learner to attend the formal classes in the premises of a college or university. As students may be residing in the remote areas or serving in some organization, so it becomes difficult for them to attend the classes. To not to deprive of education, distance education came into existence and, now these days, is becoming very popular through out the country. Students enroll themselves under a university and get study material from the website. Every type of information pertaining to their course, class, examination, results etc, is present in the website. Students log onto their account and get the information of their choice.

1.9.2 Computers in Business

Computers are being used to run the businesses proficiently. Two important areas of applications in running the business are *e-Commerce* and *e-Business.*

E-Commerce, a subset of *e-Business*, is the purchasing, selling, and exchanging of goods and services over computer networks (such as the Internet) through which transactions or terms of sale are performed electronically. E-Commerce can be broken into four main categories: B2B, B2C, C2B, and C2C.

B2B (Business-to-Business)

This is model of commerce where one business house is transacting business with another business house.

B2C (Business-to-Consumer)

This is model of commerce where one business house is transacting business directly with the consumers.

C2B (Consumer-to-Business)

This is model of commerce where consumer is transacting business directly with the business house. A consumer posts his project with a set budget online and within hours, companies review the consumer's requirements and bid on the project. The consumer reviews the bids and selects the company that will complete the project. *Elance* empowers consumers around the world by providing the meeting ground and platform for such transactions.

C2C (Consumer-to-Consumer)

This is model of commerce where one consumer is transacting business directly with the other consumer. There are many sites offering free classifieds, auctions, and forums where individuals can buy and sell thanks to online payment systems like *PayPal*, where people can send and receive money online with ease. *eBay's* auction service is a great example of where consumer (person)-to-consumer transactions take place.

E-Business refers to commercial activities performed over computers and related technologies mainly through networks such as intranets, extranets, and the Internet to streamline, improve, and extend business operations. E-Business and e-Commerce are often viewed to be one and the same, however this is incorrect. E-Commerce is simply a part of e-Business, more specifically, the trading aspect of e-Business.

1.9.3 Computer in Governance

Today, Governments provides its services to the public using information technology. Government offices are interconnected with each other to share information, documents, etc. Many servers are uploaded with relevant information and where this information is provided further to the needful persons and government officials. For example, services like *e-Patvari*, *e-Suvidha*, etc., are provided by government to make the system fast, accurate, reliable. Indian Government's information is made available on the website *www.nic.net*.

G2G (Government-to-Government), G2E (Government-to-Employee), G2B (Government-to-Business), B2G (Business-to-Government), G2C (Government-to-Citizen), C2G (Citizen-to-Government) are other forms of e-commerce that involve transactions with the government from procurement to filing taxes to business registrations to renewing licenses. There are other categories of e-commerce out there, but they tend to be superfluous.

1.9.4 Computer in Entertainment

Today computers are being used heavily in entertainment industry. Many animation movies are being produced with the help of computers.

Similarly, special effects are being added to movies to make them entertaining and thrilling.

In the music aspect also, computers are playing significant role. For example, with the MP3 technology, it is possible to store hundreds of songs in a single CD or pen drive.

You must have seen how the computers are being used by the DJ's systems.

1.9.5 Computers in Medical and Health

Computers are significantly being used in medical field. Medical Transcription is one of the utmost application in which one keys in the names of medicines and diseases anywhere while one is traveling or sitting at home. These names of medicines and diseases are transformed into database for the future access by the doctors. This is worth mentioning here that this is another way to earn.

Computers also provides online platform to the doctors to use their expertise to benefit their colleagues, other doctors and patients at far off places, thereby, avoiding wastage of traveling time. *Robo Doc*, a robot for surgery, is another IT product in field of medical science.

1.9.6 Computers Facilitating Online Transaction

Imagine a situation when an applicant wants to apply for a job advertised by the university and applicant is to apply very on the form, which is available from the university's office. Such form becomes difficult to get for an applicant if he/she is too much far away from the university campus. There are two ways to get that form: by post and personally. But this is very difficult as both are time consuming and sometimes may not be feasible. Here online transaction works which means exchange of documents on the Internet. Special electronic formats of the forms of a university or a college are stored in the form of file having extension .PDF or .DOC on the website. Any one can download it and fill it. Cost of the form may be accumulated in the requisite fee.

E-Cash Payment and Deposits

E-cash payments can be made through credit card, visa-card or master card. Companies provide such facility of online payments through their websites links. You are to access the website and click on the appropriate link. Information about the credit card will be asked for. You are to fill up relevant columns with valid number and password and submit. You are to wait for a while and the amount gets transferred from your account to the company's account. Advantage of e-cash is that it has no threat of theft. For example, e-cash payments are usually made at big show rooms, cinemas, malls, etc.

E-Banking

Almost all banks are providing online services to their customers. Unlike traditional banks, customers need not to go to bank personally for the enquiry of account balance, cash withdrawal, drafts, etc. With help of IT, banks provide net banking and you can access your account through the bank website from your office or home. You can send online request to the bank to get your demand draft ready.

E-Booking

You can book your airway or railway tickets online by just sitting in the front of your PC. To avoid chaos or unwanted rush, bodies of religious places have launched their website to provide online number. After getting that number, pilgrims can schedule their journey accordingly. In metropolitan cities, most of the theaters provide online booking through credit cards to manage unwanted rush.

Stock and Share Markets

Another service of IT is that one can see the trend of share market online using a terminal at one's home. After noticing at the ups and down in the share market, one can sell or purchase one's shares online which saves a lot efforts and time.

1.9.7 Computers in Science and Engineering

Computers are being used scientifically to develop hypotheses, collect and analyze test data and exchange the same electronically with co-workers all over the world. Scientists can access remote databases without traveling. They can also use computers to simulate the complex events. Events may be natural like predicting the damages or causalities due to earthquakes, weather patterns due to pollution, etc.

While designing a product with the help of computer software (CAD), engineers can create electronic model by describing all three dimensions of the object. Computer software provides different views to the object with different perspective views.

1.9.8 Computers in Manufacturing

Software industry has given very sophisticated software (CAM), which are used to create different types models of the automobile vehicles. Some sophisticated software are used to generate different type of changes in the existing models. This leads to innovative effects in the model making the product more saleable and useful. Some factories are using computerized robotics arms to perform physical work that is hazardous. For example, automobile factories use robots to perform tasks like painting, welding and cutting and bending metal body parts.

1.9.9 Computer in Geographical Information Systems

Many devices are developed which are directly connected with satellite and communicates with transponders to exchange information. These devices get geographical information from the transponders and use it for intended purposes. For example, your mobile system shows the details of the location of where you are, if cell information service in the mobile system, is enabled.

1.9.10 Computers in Telecommunication

Many mobile and telephone companies make use of information technology to send SMSs to their subscribers to inform about the tariffs plans and rules. Not only this, some small companies utilize information technology in their business by sending SMSs to invite new customers for the upcoming proposals.

1.9.11 Computers in Space Craft Technology

Members on the earth communicate with crew members in the satellite with help of computers using wireless medium. Outer space exploration has become possible only with help of computers. Such space exploration or probes have brought a wealth of information about our solar system and the cosmos.

Computers are being put to various other uses apart from the ones discussed above online advertisements, e-marriages, BPO services, e-employments, etc. The list is endless which shows its worth in development of the nation.

EXERCISE

1. What is a computer? What are its characteristics?
2. Differentiate between
   (*a*) hardware and software
   (*b*) data and information
3. What is/are the limitation(s) of a computer?
4. Name at least five early calculating devices.
5. Name the first operational general purpose computer.
6. Who first proposed the concept of 'Stored Program Computer'?
7. Explain the Von Neumann Computer.
8. Explain the working of functional components of a computer with the help of a block diagram.
9. What are the functions of the control unit?
10. What are the functions of the memory unit?
11. When we say memory is volatile, what does it mean?
12. What are the functions of the secondary storage unit?
13. Define the IPO cycle.
14. What is a machine cycle?
15. Explain booting process and its types.
16. Compare the salient features of
    (*a*) first and second generation computers
    (*b*) second and third generation computers
17. Differentiate between
    (*a*) an analog computer and a digital computer
    (*b*) a general-purpose computer and a special-purpose computer
18. In which generation of computers, IC were used?
19. What role does memory play in a computer system?
20. How are computers are classified based on their working principle?
21. How are computers are classified based on their usage?

22. How are computers are classified based on their electronic components used in their circuitry?
23. What are hybrid computers?
24. What are various types of personal computers?
25. What are various models/types of E-Commerce?
26. How computer are being used in e-governance?
27. How computer are being used in medical and health?
28. How computer are being used in the field of education?
29. How computer are being used in the business?
30. How computer are being used in the conduct of online transactions?

❑ ❑ ❑

Chapter 2

Hardware Concepts

Learning Objectives

After reading this chapter, students will be able to

- explain inside & outside view of the system unit
- describe a microprocessor and its characteristics
- classify the microprocessors – RISC, CISC and EPIC
- explain various memory types
- explain various units of memory
- explain various input-output ports/connections
- explain the factors on which performance of the computer depends
- explain the meaning of specification of a computer system

2.1 INTRODUCTION

Hardware refers to the parts of a computer that you can see and touch, including the case and everything inside it. In this chapter, we will learn about various components of the computer system that constitutes its hardware.

2.2 SYSTEM UNIT

The system unit of the PC is the case that houses the computer's main components that includes the CPU and the memory.

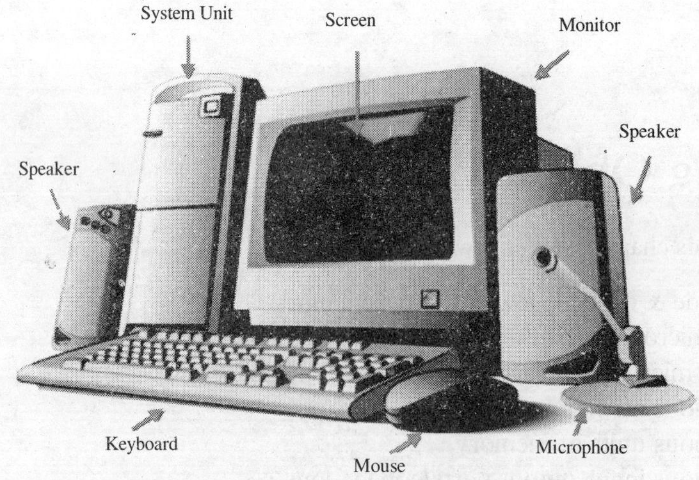

Figure 2.1: Typical home PC

2.2.1 Outside View

Figure 2.2: (*a*) Back panel of system (*b*) Front panel of system unit

- *Power Switch* – Sometimes this is located in the rear of the computer so you can't hit it by accident, which might cause you to lose your work.
- *Ports* – A port is a receptacle that enables you to plug in peripherals such as a printer, a keyboard, and mouse to the connectors, which are usually on the back of the computer.
- *Front Panel* – On most of the computer's you'll find *reset switch* that enables you to restart your computer in the event of a failure, a *drive activity light* (a light that tells when your hard disk is accessing data), and a *power-on light* (a light that tells you whether the power is on). You may also find a *key lock* that enables you to prevent others from operating the machine.

2.2.2 Inside View

- *Motherboard* – also called main board, is a large printed circuit board on which complex patterns of copper pathways have been created by means of an etching process. The pathways link the semiconductor chips, including the microprocessor and the chips that provide the computer's memory. They also link the motherboard's expansion slots, which are receptacles designed to fit expansion boards, also called *adapter cards*.

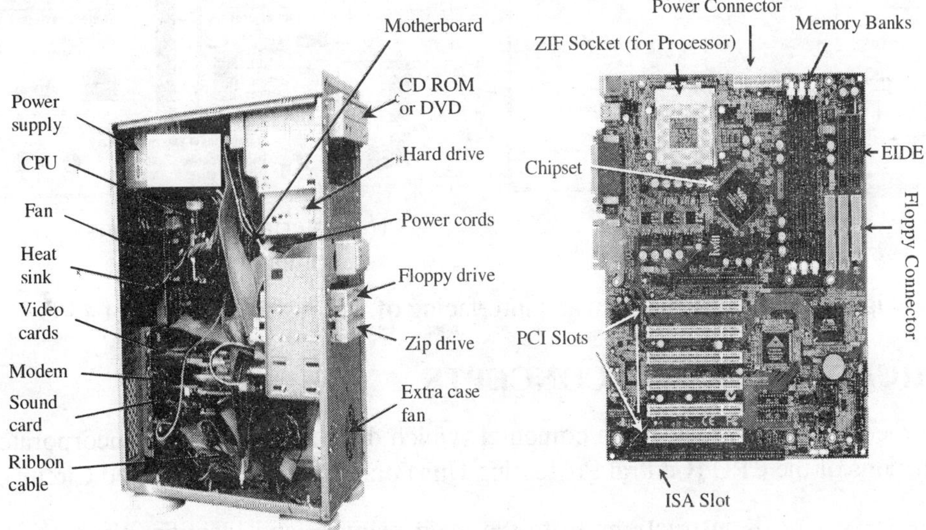

Figure 2.3: (*a*) Inside view of the system (*b*) Typical Motherboard

- *Power Supply* – it transforms alternating current into the direct current needed for the computer's operation and also steps the voltage down to the low voltage required by the motherboard.

- *Drive bays* – to accommodate the computer's *floppy disk drive, CD or DVD drive,* and a removable media drive such as a *Zip drive*. Some of the bays may be available for system upgrades.
- *Hard disk* – it may be mounted in a covered drive bay or deeper in the system unit.
- *Floppy disk drive* – it uses floppy disks, usually 3½-inch magnetic disks.
- *CD-ROM or DVD-ROM drive* – it uses optical CD or DVD discs.
- *Removable media drive* – it uses high-capacity removable disks.

Of all these components, by far the most important is the CPU, or microprocessor. As you've learned, in a strict sense, the CPU is the computer. More than any other factor, the CPU's characteristics determine the performance of the overall system.

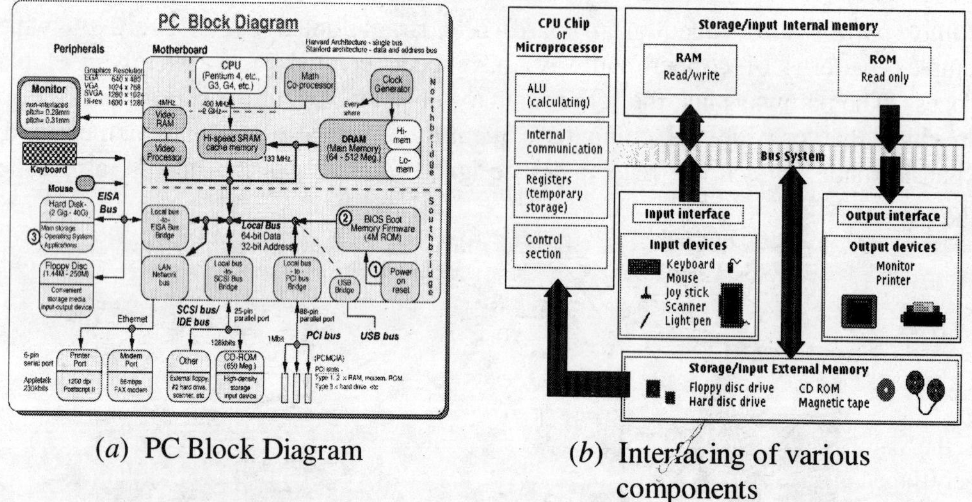

(*a*) PC Block Diagram (*b*) Interfacing of various components

Figure 2.5: Block diagram and interfacing of various components of a PC

2.3 MICROPROCESSOR CONCEPTS

Microprocessor is the brain of the computer, which does all the work. It incorporates all the functions of the CPU (Central Processing Unit) on a single IC (Integrated Circuit).

Microprocessor reads instructions from the main memory and identifies the tasks to be performed. The required data needed to complete the tasks is read from the memory and passed on the arithmetic and logic unit, which actually performs the desired operations. The results of the operations are stored back in the main memory for the future use.

In 1971, Intel Corporation fabricated the first microprocessor - 4004. It could do only add and subtract operations and that too it could process only 4 bits at a time.

Figure 2.6: Intel Core i7 Microprocessor

But Intel 4004 powered one of the first portable electronic calculators and since then the microprocessor technology has come a long way. Today we have processors with which can process upto 128 bits at a time at the speed of billion instructions per second.

2.3.1 Basic Characteristics of Microprocessors

There are few basic characteristics of microprocessors that define the power and capacity of the microprocessor. Let us have a look on these characteristics.

Instruction Set

It is the set of instructions that the microprocessor can understand.

Word Size

It is the number of bits a microprocessor can process in a single operations. The word size largely depends on size of internal registers, *i.e.*, how many bits an internal register can hold.

The word size is directly proportional to the processing power of the microprocessor.

During the processing, the internal general purpose registers hold the data. So if internal registers can hold data upto 8 bits, the word length is 8 bits. If it can process 16 bits at a time, then the internal registers can hold upto 16 bits at a time and so on. Hence, a 32 bit processor is about 4 times faster than an 8 bit processor.

Examples of typical word sizes are 16 bit, 32 bit, 64 bit and 128 bit.

Accordingly, terms 16-bit microprocessor, 16-bit microprocessor, 16-bit microprocessor and 128-bit microprocessor are used very often while talking about the microprocessors.

Now we know that these terms mean the maximum number of bits a given microprocessor can handle at a time.

Clock Speed

The clock speed, also called clock rate, is the speed at which microprocessor executes instructions. Every computer contains an internal clock called the *system clock*, that regulates the rate at which instructions are executed, and also synchronizes the operations of all the components of a computer.

The faster the clock, the more instructions a microprocessor can execute, i.e., clock speed is a major factor in determining the power of a microprocessor.

The clock speed is measured in units of cycles per second, which is called a Hertz (Hz). The clock speed of microprocessors is either measured in MHz (Mega Hertz) or GHz (Giga Hertz). 1 MHz is equal to 1 million cycles per second while 1 GHz is equal to 1 billion cycles per second.

Nowadays microprocessors have clock speed of several GHz.

2.3.2 Types of Microprocessors

Based on the instructions set of the microprocessors, the microprocessors can be classified as *CISC Processors* (Complex Instruction Set computing), *RISC Processors* (Reduced Instruction Set Computing), and EPIC Processors (Explicitly Parallel Instruction Computing).

CISC Processor

CISC stands for *Complex Instruction Set Computer*. This is a type of microprocessor design that contains a large set of computer instructions that range from very simple to very complex and specialized.

Main aim of the design was to compute complex instructions in the most efficient way. The major characteristics of CISC processors are

- Larger number of instructions.
- Larger number of addressing modes.
- Variable length of instruction formats.
- Several cycles may be required to execute one instruction.
- Micro programmed control unit.
- It consists of lesser number of registers.
- To access memory location, multiple mechanisms with complex addressing modes are used.

Few examples of CISC processors are Intel 386, 486, Pentium, Pentium Pro, Pentium II, Pentium III. Motorola's 68000, 68020, 68040, etc.

RISC Processor

RISC stands for *Reduced Instruction Set Computer.* This is a type of microprocessor design that aims to reduce the execution time by simplifying the instruction set of the computer. In RISC processors, each instruction requires only one clock cycle to execute.

The major characteristics of RISC processors are

- Lesser number of instructions.
- Few simple addressing modes.
- Fixed length instructions formats.
- Single cycle is required to execution one instruction.
- Hardwired control unit.
- It consists of larger number of registers.
- LOAD and STORE instructions are used to access the memory location.

Few examples of RISC processors are Intel P6, Pentium IV. DEC's Alpha 21064, AMD K6 K7, etc.

EPIC Processor

EPIC stands for *Explicitly Parallel Instruction Computing*. This is a type of microprocessor design in which features are provided to facilitate compiler enhancements of instruction-level parallelism (ILP) in all programs, while keeping hardware complexity relatively low.

Using ILP-enhancement techniques such as speculation and predication, the compiler identifies the operations that can execute in parallel in each cycle and communicates a plan of execution to the hardware.

The major characteristics of EPIC processors are

- Does not use fixed length instructions rather parallel as much as possible.
- Programs are written using sequential semantics with explicit laid out parallelism.
- Compiler plays the key role in designing the plan of execution.
- Architecture is designed to provide the requisite support to the compiler in designing the plan of execution.
- Architecture is designed to provides the requisite mechanism to communicate the compiler's plan of execution to the hardware.

Few examples of EPIC processors are Intel IA-64 and Itanium processor.

2.4 INPUT/OUTPUT DEVICES

Computers will of no use unless it can interact and communicate with the outside world. Input/output devices are attached (connected) to the computer so that it can interaction and communication with the outside world.

The Input/Output devices are also known as *peripherals* since they surround the CPU (processor) and memory of a computer system.

2.4.1 Input Devices

Input devices take the information from the outside world in human readable form, convert them into a form that a computer can understand (in 1s and 0s, i.e., binary form) and passes it to the computer for further processing. This may represent data to be processed by the computer or commands that are to be executed by the computer.

The typical input devices used in almost all computers are keyboard, mouse, microphone, and webcam, etc.

Keyboard

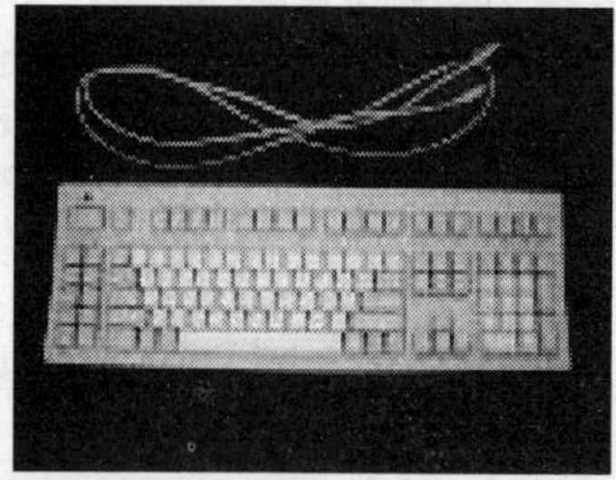

(*a*) Typical keyboard with QWERTY layout

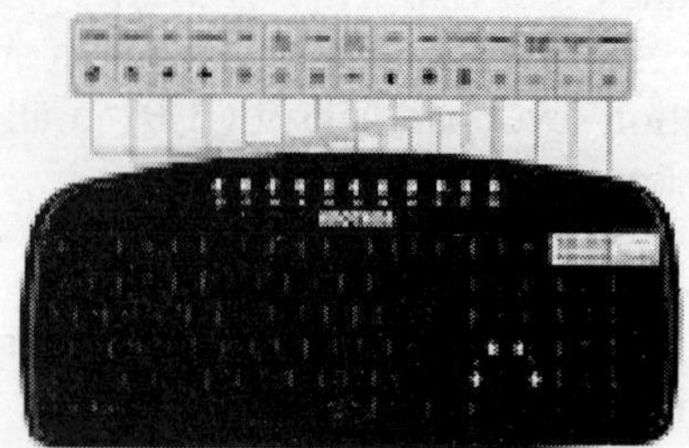

(*b*) Wireless keyboard

Figure 2.7: Different Models of keyboards

A keyboard is the most common input device. You will find keyboard with every computer. It is used to enter the numeric and textual information that may represent the data, instructions of thc computcr program or commands to the operating system.

In addition to the keys for *letters*, *numerals* and *punctuations characters*, all computer keyboards have additional keys that work some what differently.

Mouse

Mouse is a pointing device. It is used for many of the manipulations on computer that do not involve entering letters and numbers such as moving the cursor choosing options from menus in graphical user interface or drawing freehand lines and shapes.

The mouse is a palm-size device with a ball built into the bottom. The mouse may be connected to the computer by a cable and may have from one to four buttons (but usually two). The mouse may be mechanical or optical. Mice come in many shapes and sizes. When you move the mouse over a smooth surface the ball rolls and the pointer on the display screen moves in the same direction.

Figure 2.8: Mouse

On a PC running Windows or some other GUI, you can use the buttons in combination with movements to perform the following:

- *Point*: To point to an item means to move the mouse pointer so that it's touching the item.
- *Click*: Point to the item, then tap (press and release) the left mouse button.
- *Double-click*: Point to the item, and tap the left mouse button twice in rapid succession - click-click as fast as you can.
- *Right-click*: Point to the item, then tap the mouse button on the right.
- *Drag*: Point to an item, then hold down the left mouse button as you move the mouse. To *drop* the item, release the left mouse button.
- *Right-drag*: Point to an item, then hold down the right mouse button as you move the mouse. To *drop* the item, release the right mouse button.

Trackball

A trackball is like an upside-down mouse. Used similarly to the mouse, the trackball is frequently attached to or built into the keyboard. The main advantage of a trackball is that it requires less desk space than a mouse. Some individuals in the computer industry believe that the mouse will soon be replaced by devices that do not require as much space to use.

Figure 2.9: Track ball

Joystick

Joystick is another pointing device often used for playing games. The joystick has a gearshift-like lever that is used to move the pointer on the screen. On most joysticks, a button on the top is used to select options. In industry and manufacturing, joysticks are used to control robots. Flight simulators and other training simulators also use joysticks.

Figure 2.10: Joystick

Digitizing Tablet

It another important tool used in CAD applications and other graphics applications. A digitizing tablet (also known as *digitizer*) consists of a grid on which designs and drawing can be entered. Most digitizers are pressure sensitive and the user draws directly on the tablet using a special pen called a *stylus* (also called a *puck*). Digitizers are used to design such things as cars, buildings, medical devices, and robots, etc.

Figure 2.11: Digitizing tablet

Light Pen

A light pen is used is used by many engineers and architects. The light pen uses a photoelectric (light sensitive) cell to communicate the screen positions to the computer. The pen is operated by touching it to the screen light pens are frequently used for Computer Aided Design (CAD) applications.

(*a*) Typical light pen

(*b*) User interacting with the Application through light pen

Figure 2.12: Typical light pen and its usage

Barcode Reader

Of all the scanning devices used in business, you are probably most familiar with barcode readers. Many retail and grocery stores use some form of barcode reader to determine the item being sold and to retrieve the item price from a computer system. The bar code reader may be a handheld unit or embedded in a countertop. The barcode reader reads the Universal Product Code (UPC), a pattern of bars printed on merchandise.

Figure 2.13: Barcode

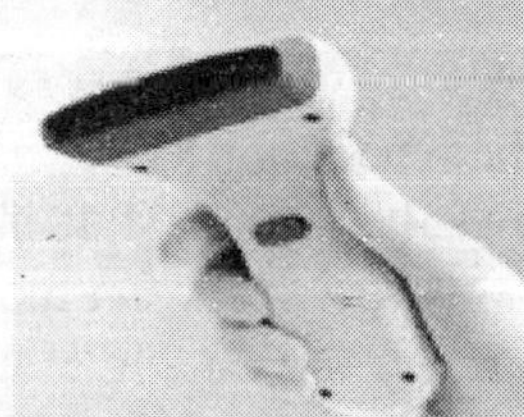

Figure 2.14: Barcode Reader

Optical Mark Reader

From taking exams you are already familiar with Mark Sense Character Recognition systems. Every time you take a test with a fill in the bubble Scranton form and use a #2 lead pencil you are creating input suitable for an Optical Mark Reader (OMR). A #2 lead pencil works best because of the number of magnetic particles in that weight lead.

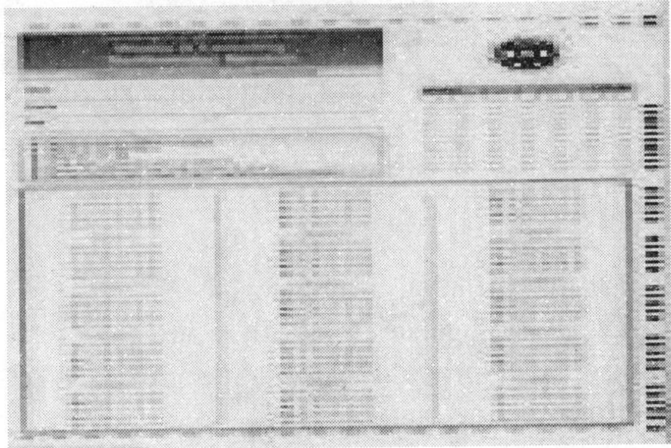

Figure 2.15: OMR Sheet

The OMR senses the magnetized marks enabling the reader to determine which responses are marked. OMR is also very helpful to researchers who need to tabulate responses to large surveys. Almost any type of survey or questionnaire can be designed for OMR devices.

Figure 2.16: Different models of OMRs

Magnetic Ink Character Reader

The banking industry developed one of the earliest scanning systems in the 1950s for processing checks. The Magnetic Ink Character Reader (MICR) system is used throughout the banking industry. The bank branch, account number, and check number are encoded on the check before it is sent to the customer. After the customer has used the check and it comes back to the bank all that needs to be entered manually is the amount. MICR has not been adopted by other industries because the character set has only fourteen symbols.

(*a*) MICR Cheque

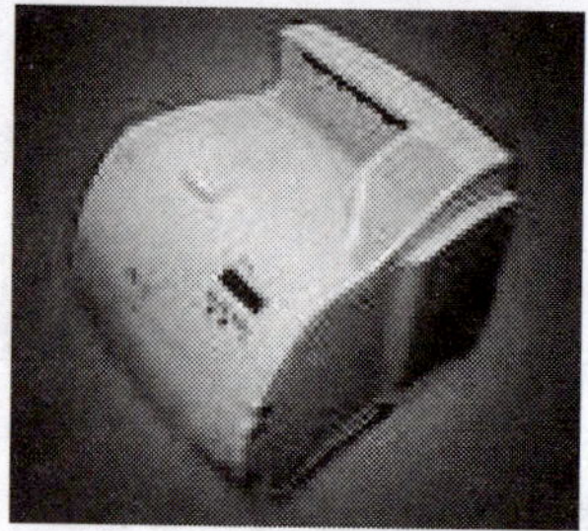

(*b*) Different models of MICRs

Figure 2.17

Microphone

Computer can't understand the meaning of human speech that would require artificial intelligence - but they are increasingly good at transcribing speech into text. Speech recognition requires a microphone and special speech recognition software and can transcribe speech with an accuracy rate of up to 98%. Speech recognition can take the place of keyboards for text entry. In addition some operating systems enable users to give vocal commands.

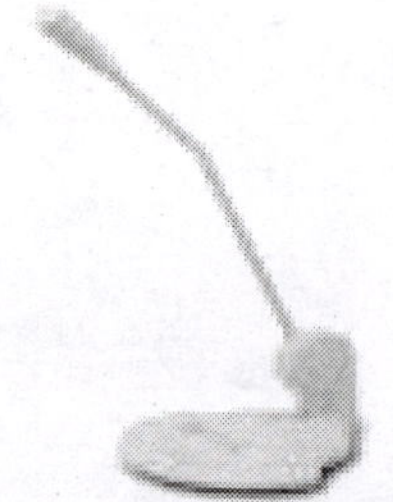

Figure 2.18: Microphone

Scanner

Scanners use Charge Coupled Devices (CCD) to digitize an image formed by a lens. Scanners are designed to copy anything that is printed on a sheet of paper including artwork, handwriting, printed documents or typed documents. Flatbed scanners work on a single sheet of paper at a time.

Sheet fed scanners draw in the sheets to be copied by means of a roller mechanism. Handheld scanners can be used to copy smaller originals such as photographs.

Figure 2.19: Scanner

Scanners have varying optical resolutions depending on the number of distinct light sensitive elements packed into the scanner's CCD. Scanners may use image enhancement techniques to simulate higher resolutions. Scanners also vary in bit depth, the number of bits used to represent each dot (pixel). A 24-bit scanner can capture up to 16.7 million colors.

Most scanners come with optical character recognition (OCR) software that automatically decodes imaged test into a text file. This technology has improved to the point that most printed or typed documents can be scanned into text files, eliminating the need to retype such documents to get them into the computer.

Web Camera

The web cameras provide you the facility to capture the video input. You can enter a full-motion recording into a computer and store the video on a hard disk or some other medium. Web Cameras are commonly used in video conferencing. A video conferencing is a meeting between two or more geographically separated individuals who use a network to transmit audio and video data.

Figure 2.20: Web Camera

Biometric Sensor

Utilizing biometrics for personal authentication is becoming convenient and considerably more accurate than current methods such as the utilization of passwords. Biometrics is the science of measuring physical properties of living beings. Biometric authentication is the automatic recognition of a living being using suitable body characteristics. These characteristics may be fingerprint, iris recognition, facial recognition, etc. Biometric sensor is a device that uses biometric authentication in place of manual controls to establish the genuineness of a user.

A basic biometric system is made up of a/an

- sensor to record the biometric trait
- computer unit to process and eventually save biometric trait
- application, for which the user's authentication is necessary

Figure 2.21: Biometric sensor

Touch Screen

A touch screen is a device, which allows users to control a computer by simply touching the display screen by finger or pin. This type of input is suitable for a large number of computing applications. Most systems use a touch screen as easily as other input devices such as track balls or touch pads.

Figure 2.22: Torch Screen

2.4.2 Output Devices

Output devices take the information from the computer in computer readable form, convert them into human readable form and pass onto the user in appropriate form (textual, graphical or multimedia) on a appropriate medium (display on screen, print on a paper, etc.).

The typical output devices used are visual display (monitor/screen), printer, plotter, and speaker, etc.

Display Devices

The most popular output device is the Visual Display Unit (VDU). It is also called the monitor. Monitor is used to display the output results on a screen.

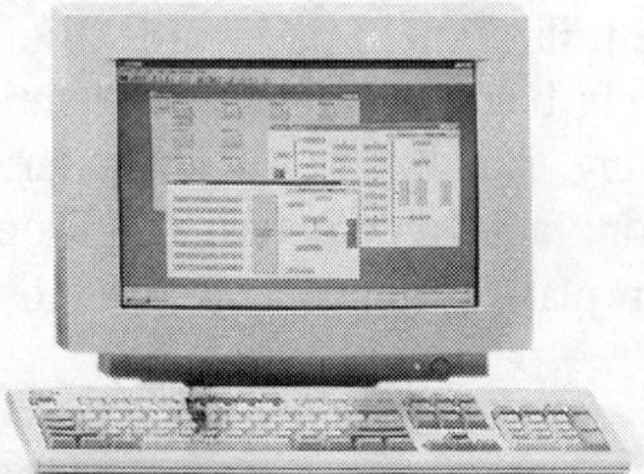

Figure 2.23: CRT monitor

Figure 2.24: LCD monitor

A monitor has its own box that is separated from the main computer system and is connected to the computer by cable. Some examples of display devices are:

- CRT Monitors
- LCD displays
- Gas plasma
- High-Definition Television

Printers

A most convenient and useful method by which the computer can deliver information is by means of printed characters. Printers in broader sense are categorized as *impact printers* and *non-impact printers*.

Impact printers make an impact on a ribbon that leaves an impression of text on the paper, where as impact printers make no impact. Impact printers can print one character at a time (speed is measured in characters per second) or one line at a time (speed is measured in lines per second) where as non-impact printers can print one page at time (speed is measured in pages per second).

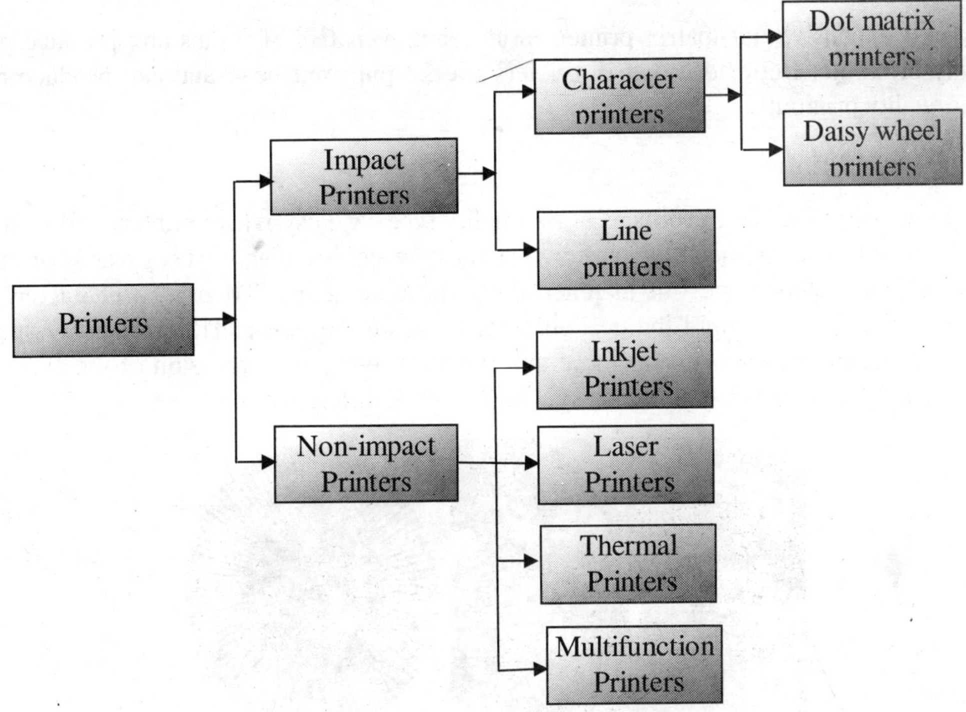

Figure 2.25: Classification of printers

Impact Printer

Impact printers press the paper to from the characters. These can produce a character, a line or a page at a time. Large organizations use line printers that can crank out hard copy at a rate of 3,000 lines per minute. Print quality is low but these printers are mainly used for printing backup copies of large amounts of data. Still used in some law offices are letter quality printers which closely resemble office typewriters.

Dot Matrix Printer

Dot-matrix printers are also popularly known as DMPs. If you use a magnifying glass to look at a report created with a dot-matrix printer, you can see the small dots forming each character.

Figure 2.26: Different models of dot matrix printers

The least expensive dot-matrix printers print using a matrix of 9 pins and produce poor quality printouts. Better dot-matrix printers use 24-pin print head and can produce near letter quality printouts.

Daisy Wheel Printer

It is a type of printer that produces letter-quality type. A daisy-wheel printer works on the same principle as a ball-head typewriter. The daisy wheel is a disk made of plastic or metal on which characters stand out in relief along the outer edge. To print a character, the printer rotates the disk until the desired letter is facing the paper. Then a hammer strikes the disk, forcing the character to hit an ink ribbon, leaving an impression of the character on the paper. You can change the daisy wheel to print different fonts.

Figure 2.27: Daisy wheel printer

Daisy-wheel printers cannot print graphics, and in general they are noisy and slow, printing from 10 to about 75 characters per second. As the price of laser and ink-jet printers has declined, and the quality of dot-matrix printers has improved, daisy-wheel printers have become obsolete.

Line Printer

A line printer is a high-speed printer capable of printing an entire line at one time. A fast line printer can print as many as 3,000 lines per minute. The disadvantages of line printers are that they cannot print graphics, the print quality is low, and they are very noisy.

Figure 2.29: Different models of line printers

Non-impact Printer

Because nothing presses on the page, a non-impact printer can't produce carbon copies. This is usually not a problem because it's easy to produce multiple originals but sometimes carbons are required for legal purposes. Non-impact printers are very quiet (makes no noise).

Because of their decreasing cost, non-impact printers are the most widely used printer for PCs today. Non-impact printer can produce both text and graphics. Some of the most popular non-impact printers are *laser printers* and *inkjet printers.*

Inkjet Printer

Inkjet printer (also called *bubble-jet printers*) are the least expensive (initial) non-impact printers. Like dot-matrix printers, inkjet printers work by forming an image that is composed of tiny dots, but the dots are much smaller and more numerous. The result is a printout that's difficult to distinguish from the fully formed characters printed by laser printer.

Figure 2.30: Different models of inkjet printers

Inkjet printers can also print in color which makes them popular choices for home users. Earlier inkjets had problems with smudging but new ink formulations have all but eliminated this problem. Although inkjet printers are inexpensive and produce excellent output they are slow and per-page costs may exceed the costs of running a laser printer due to the generally high cost of ink cartridge.

Laser Printer

Laser Printers work like copy machine. Under the printer's computerized control a laser beam creates electrical charges on a rotating print drum. These charges attract toner which is transferred to the paper and fused to its surface by a heat process. In contrast to inkjets laser printers print faster some can crank out 18 or more pages per minute. Although they are more expensive initially than inkjet printer's laser printer generally have lower per-page costs.

Figure 2.31: Different models of laser printers

Thermal Printer

Thermal printer produces a printed image by selectively heating coated thermal paper as it is commonly known, when the paper passes over the thermal print head. The coating turns black in the areas where it is heated, producing an image. Two-color direct thermal printers are capable of printing both black and an additional color (often red), by applying heat at two different temperatures. Thermal transfer printing is a related method that uses a heat-sensitive ribbon instead of heat-sensitive paper.

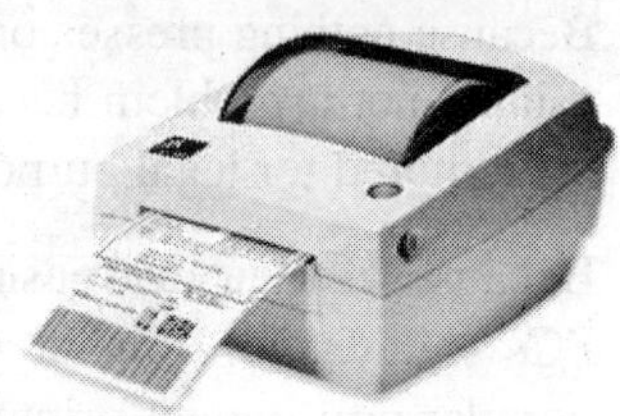

Figure 2.32: Thermal printer

Figure 2.33: Different models of multifunction printers

Multifunctional Printers

Multifunction printers combine inkjet or laser printer with a scanner, a fax machine, and a copier, enabling home and office users to obtain all these devices without spending a great deal of money.

Plotters

A plotter, like printer, produces hard copy output. Most of the plotters form an image by physically moving a pen over a sheet of paper. A continuous curve plotter is used to draw maps from stored data. Computer generated maps can be retrieved and plotted or used to show changes over time. Plotters are generally more expensive than printers.

Figure 2.34: Different Models of Plotters

Speakers

Increasingly found on new computer systems are sound cards and speakers the two accessories needed to listen to computer generated sound. Such sounds include various system beeps and warnings the output of recorded sound files and even synthesized speech. In speech synthesis a program reads a text file out loud. Speech synthesis enables people who are blind or have too low vision to access huge amounts of text based material that would otherwise be inaccessible to them.

Figure 2.35: Sound Blaster

Figure 2.36: Speakers

Like audio compact disk player sound cards can play the contents of digitized recordings such as much recorded in the Windows WAV or MPEG sound file formats. Quality enters into the picture must noticeable when the sound card reproduces files containing Musical Instrument Digital Interface (MIDI) information. MIDI files are text files that tell a synthesizer when and how to play individual musical notes. A synthesizer produces music by generating musical tones.

2.5 MEMORIES AND STORAGE DEVICES

As you know, by this time, that hardware and software are integral parts of a computer system. Software constitutes that part of a computer system that drives the hardware to get the task done. Also software is generic name for any kind of program(s). All the programs process the relevant data to generate the desired results.

The program(s) and the data need to be stored in the computer system before they can be used. For this purpose, the memory (called *main memory* or *primary memory*) contained in the memory unit of the CPU is utilized. However, this memory looses its contents when the power is switched off.

Since the program(s) are to be used in future too, they need to be stored a kind of memory that does not loose its contents when the power is switched off. Likewise, the data entered into the computer system and the results produced, if needed in future, also need to be stored in such memory. For this purpose, additional devices, called *storage devices* (such as hard disk, floppy disk, CD or DVD), are attached to the computer system which supplements the primary memory. The total memory that results from the various storage devices is called *secondary memory*.

However, computer neither can run the programs from secondary memory and nor can process the data, directly. These first need to be transferred to the main memory (or simply called memory), and then can be executed/processed.

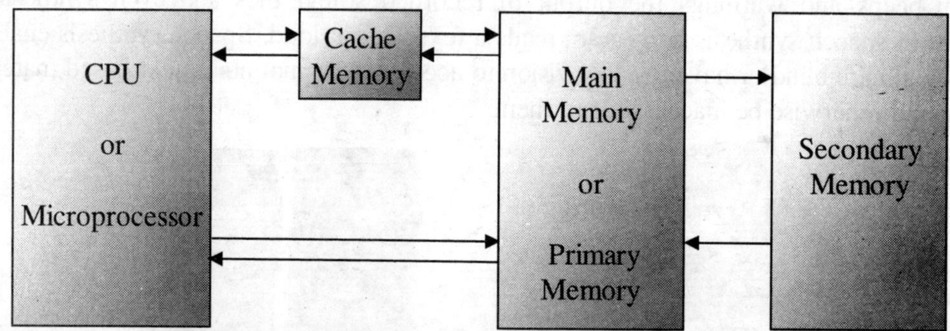

Figure 2.37: Connection of memories with the processor

2.5.1 Primary/Main Memory

Primary memory or main memory is a part of the CPU. It is used for storing data and instructions during the execution of the program.

As shown in Figure 2.38, main memory that is organized into words of fixed lengths. A given memory is divided into *N* words where each word is assigned an address in the memory. A word is generally more than 8 bits in length and the number of bits in a word is termed as *word size/length*. Computers with 32, 64 and 128 bit word lengths are available. The higher the word length, the more powerful a computer is.

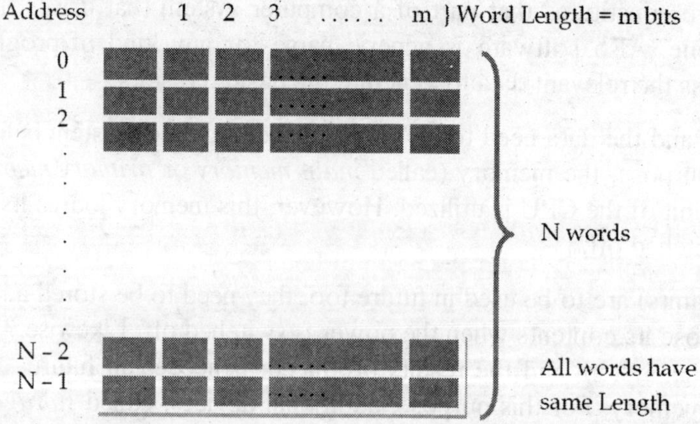

Figure 2.38: Organization of memory in words

Each word is assigned an address starting from 0 to the largest number that the computer can support. Each address uniquely specifies the memory location of a particular word. The total number of memory cells that can be uniquely addressed by CPU depends on the total number of address lines in an address bus. If there are n lines in the address bus then there are 2^n addressable locations in the memory.

Memories can be both read from and written to are called *read/write memories.* On the other hand memories that have data or program permanently stored onto them and hence can be only read from are called *read only memories.*

Broadly primary/main memory can be divided into two types

- Random Access Memory (RAM)
- Read Only Memory (ROM).

2.5.1.1 Random Access Memory

In random access memory, the memory cells can be accessed for storing or retrieving information from any desired location randomly. The process of locating a word in random access memory is the same and requires equal amount of time, and thus the name *random access.*

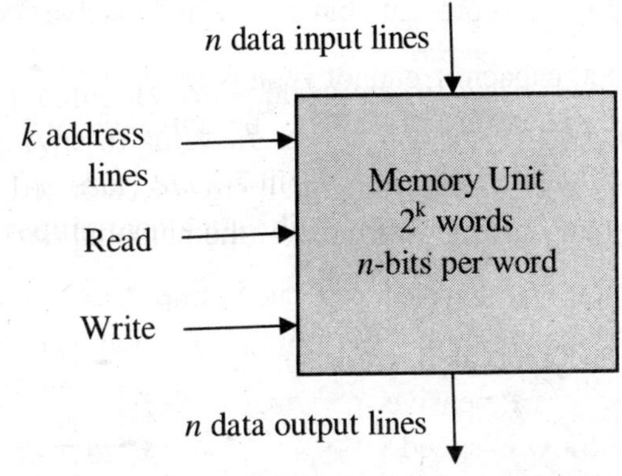

Figure 2.39: Block diagram of RAM

The communication between the random access memory and the processor is achieved through data input and output lines, address lines and control line (read and write) that specify the direction of transfer of information.

Working of the RAM as shown in the block diagram is as follows:

- n data input lines provide the information that is to be stored in memory,
- n data output lines provide the information that is read from the memory,
- k address line provide a number of k-bits that specify the address of a particular word chosen out of 2^k available words in memory,
- Read control line specify the read operation, as a result of which the contents of the selected word are placed on the data output lines, and
- Write control line specify the write operation, as a result of which the data available on the data input lines is stored (written) into the selected word.

The main drawback of RAM is that it is *volatile*, *i.e.*, its contents gets erased (lost) when the power goes off.

Types of RAM

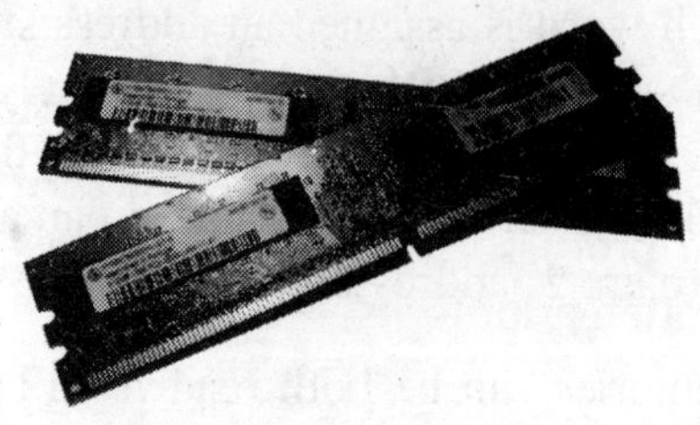

Figure 2.40: RAM Chips

The RAM can be of two types:

- Dynamic RAM (DRAM)
- Static RAM (SRAM)

Dynamic RAM

Each memory cell in a DRAM is made of one transistor and one capacitor, which store one bit of data. The bit is stored in the form of charge on capacitor. The charged state of capacitor represents binary 1 while discharged state represents binary 0.

Since capacitor cannot retains its charges, it starts losing its charge and hence data stored in it. Therefore, it needs to be refreshed, which takes up processor time.

However, due to the small size of each cell, one DRAM can have large number of cells. Primary memory of most of the personal computers is made of DRAM.

Major characteristics of DRAM are

- Memory cell size is small.
- Less expensive.
- Slow in speed.
- Need to be refreshed continuously.
- Mainly used as primary memory.

Static RAM

Each memory cell in SRAM is made of a flip flop that stores one bit. It doesn't need to be refreshed like DRAM. It also has shorter read-write cycles as compared to DRAM.

SRAM is a little more expensive, but faster and significantly consumes less power than DRAM. It is therefore used where either speed or low power, or both, are principal considerations.

Due to a more complex internal structure, SRAM is less dense than DRAM and is therefore not used for high-capacity, low-cost applications such as the main memory in personal computers.

Major characteristics of SRAM are

- Memory cell size is large.
- Expensive.
- Fast in speed.
- Need no refreshing.
- Mainly used as cache memory.

2.5.1.2 Read Only Memory

As the name suggests, Read Only Memory (ROM) is the memory than can only be read by the processor. New data cannot be written into ROM. Data to be stored into ROM is written prior to its use.

ROM contain data that does not need to be altered, like instructions for booting a computer, i.e., they used to record data and information that is permanent in nature. ROM is slower and hence cheaper than RAM. It retains its data even when power is switched off, *i.e.*, it is non-volatile.

Major characteristics of ROM are

- Data is not lose its contents when power goes off (non-volatile).
- Once data is stored, it can only be read, hence information stored on it can not be tampered with.
- Can store data for longer periods of time.
- Slow in speed as compared to RAM.
- Preferred memory to be used in special purpose computer.

Types of ROM

- *Programmable Read Only Memory (PROM)* – It is type of ROM that can programmed using a special hardware device called *PROM programmer* or *PROM burner*. Once the ROM chip has been programmed, its contents, *i.e.*, PROM becomes same as ROM.
- *Erasable Programmable Read Only Memory (EPROM)* – It is a type of ROM that can be erased and the chip can be reprogrammed to record new information. The chip is erased by exposing it to the ultraviolet light.
- *Electrically Erasable PROM (EEPROM)* - It is a type of ROM can be erased by electrical signals instead of exposure to ultraviolet light.

2.5.2 Cache Memory

Though RAM is quite fast but it is not fast enough to support the processing speeds of today's super-fast microprocessors. Therefore, to enable these microprocessors to function at maximum speed, computer designers use cache memory.

Cache (pronounced as cash) memory is a small piece of high speed memory (usually made of high speed SRAM) that temporarily stores frequently used data and/or information for fast processing by the processor.

The process of keeping some data and instructions in cache memory for faster access is called *caching*, and is done when a set of data or instructions is accessed again and again.

Whenever the processor needs any piece of data or instructions, it checks the cache first. If it is not found there, then the main memory and finally secondary memory is accessed. As cache has very high speed, time spent in accessing it every time is negligible as compared to time saved if data indeed is in the cache.

If the data or instruction is found in cache, it is called *cache hit*. The effectiveness of cache is measured by its *hit rate*.

There are two types of cache memory are available:

- The first type, called *primary cache*, or level 1 (L1) cache and is included inside the microprocessor chip.
- The second type, called *secondary cache*, or level 2 (L2) cache and is placed on the mother board very near to the microprocessor. To improve secondary cache performance the latest microprocessors are provided in plastic modules that contain special type of secondary cache, called *backside cache*. By keeping the secondary cache as close as possible to the processor, the performance improves.

2.5.3 Communication Between Processor and Main Memory

The contents of the main memory have to be accessed by the processor: *read* and *written*.

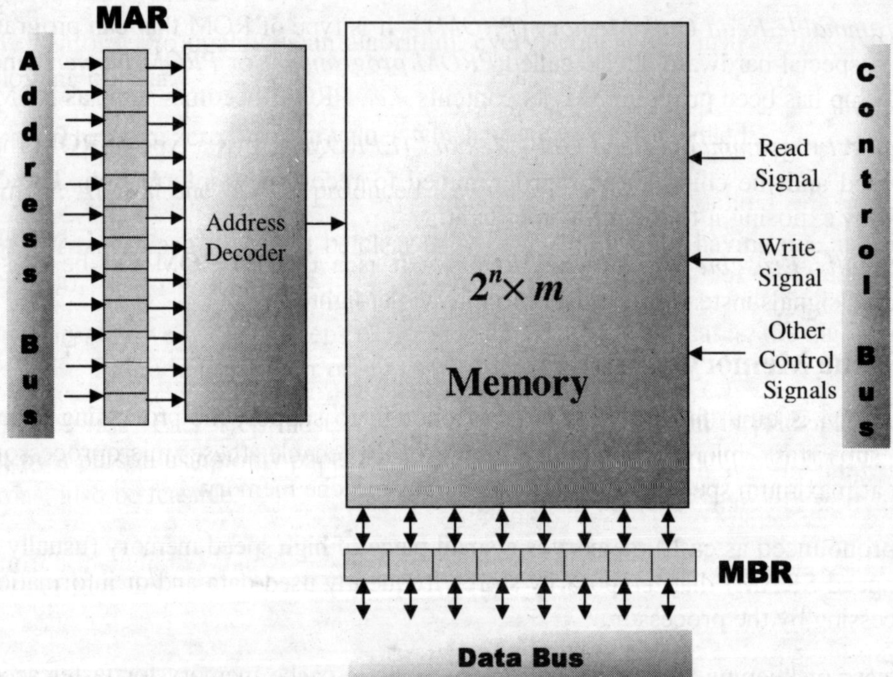

Figure 2.41: Simplest view of memory and its interfacing

The processor places an address in the address bus from where it gets loaded into a special-purpose register known as the Memory Address Register (MAR), and then sends a read control signal to the main memory to say "I want to do a memory read". Then the memory unit decodes that address to identify the memory location of the operand and then transfers that operand to the Memory Buffer Register (MBR). CPU takes the data from the MBR and uses it.

To write to memory, the CPU has to load the MAR with the address via address bus and the MBR with the data via data bus. Then it sends a write control to the main memory to say "I want to do a memory write". The memory unit decodes the address to identify the memory location and then copy the data from the MBR into the identified memory location.

The concept of *bus* is used to denote a set of parallel lines on which the individual binary signals travels simultaneously. Accordingly, there are three buses in computer system that carries different kind of information. The *address bus*, which is unidirectional, carries address information from the processor to memory and I/O devices. The *data bus*, which is bidirectional, carries data between processor, memory and I/O devices. The *control bus*, in which each line is independent and carries a different type of information, such *read* (RD), *write* (WR), *clock* (CLK), etc. These three buses together as a unit are referred to as *system bus*.

2.5.4 Secondary Memory

The major limitation of main/primary memory is that it has limited storage capacity and is volatile.

To overcome this limitation we have *secondary memory*. It is also called *external memory*. It refers to the various storage media on which a computer can store data and programs. It is an additional storage, not part of the main computer.

The secondary storage media can be *fixed* or *removable*.

- *Fixed storage media* is an internal storage medium that is fixed inside the system box. Examples are hard disk drive and CD/DVD drive.
- *Removable storage media* is a data storage medium that is portable and is outside the system box. Examples are pen drive and blue ray disk.

Following are some characteristics of secondary memory, which distinguish it from the primary memory –

- It is non-volatile, i.e., it retains data when power is switched off
- It is in large capacities to the tune of terabytes
- It is cheaper as compared to primary memory

Depending on whether secondary memory device is part of CPU or not, there are two types of secondary memory – fixed and removable.

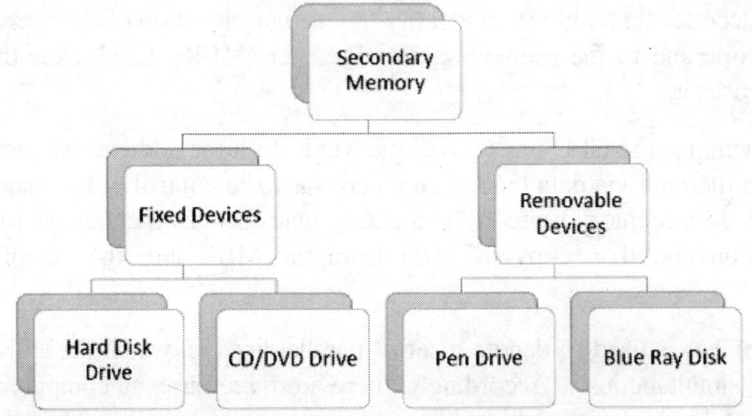

Figure 2.42: Classification of secondary memory

Let us look at some of the secondary memory devices available.

2.5.4.1 Hard Disk Drive

On almost all computers, the hard disk is the most important storage medium. It essentially stores the computer's operating system, applications and provides enough space for the user's data.

Figure 2.43: Cross sectional view of a hard disk drive

Hard disk drive is made up of a series of circular disks called *platters* arranged one over the other almost ½ inches apart around a *spindle*. Each disks is made of non-magnetic material like aluminium alloy and coated with 10-20 nm of magnetic material.

A *spindle* is a shaft that holds rotating platters in place.

The upper surface of the top most platter and the lower surface of the bottom platter is not used for recording data.

The surface of the platter is divided in concentric circles called *tracks*. Further, each track is divided into equal sized segments called *sectors*.

The set of corresponding tracks on each platter forms a *cylinder*.

Data is recorded by magnetizing (to store 1) or demagnetizing (to store 0) the magnetic coating. A magnetic reader arm which contains one read/write for every surface is used to read data from and write data to the disks.

A typical modern HDD has capacity in terabytes (TB).

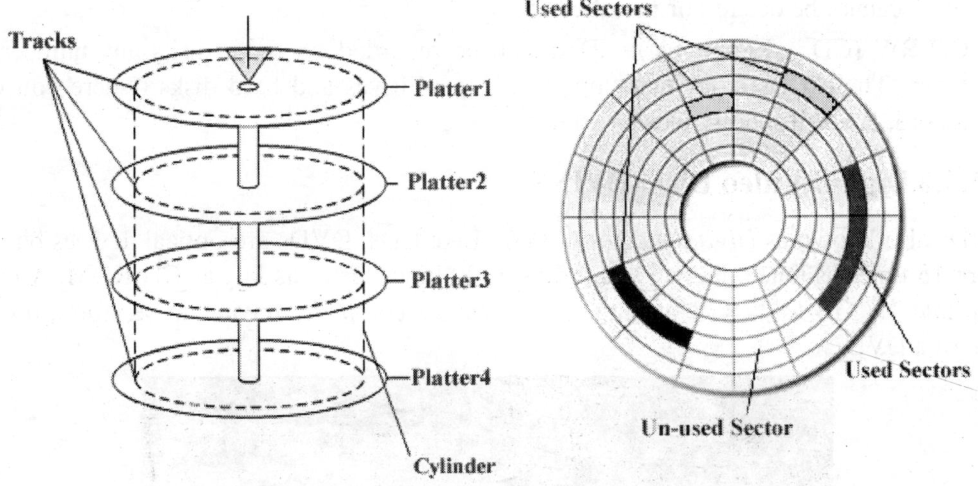

Figure 2.44: Concept of cylinders, tracks and sectors

2.5.4.2 Compact Disks (CDs)

CDs are circular disks that use optical rays, usually lasers, to read and write data. They are relatively cheap and have storage capacity upto 700 MB. CDs are inserted in CD drives built into CPU cabinet. They are portable as you can eject the drive, remove the CD and carry it with you.

Figure 2.45: CD and CD drive

There are three types of CDs –

- CD-ROM (CD – Read Only Memory) – The data on these CDs are recorded by the manufacturer. Proprietary Software, audio or video are released on CD-ROMs.
- CD-R (CD – Recordable) – The data on these CDs can be recorded only once. Later on, it cannot be deleted or modified.
- CD-RW (CD – Rewritable) – Data can be recorded on these disks any number of times. These CDs work like floppy disk, pen drives and hard disks, where you can record, erase or modify files any time.

2.5.4.3 Digital Video Disk (DVDs)

DVDs also known as *Digital Versatile Disk*. Like CDs, DVDs are optical devices but can store 15 times as much data and can transfer 20 times faster as fast as CD-ROM. A DVD can hold 4.7 GB to 17 GB of data. That means a complete movie can be stored on one side of a DVD.

Figure 2.46: DVD and DVD drive

From the outlook, you will not find any difference between CD and DVD, between CD drive and DVD drive, except labels on them.

Like CDs, there are three types of DVDs -

- DVD-ROM (DVD – Read Only Memory) – The data on these DVDs are recorded by the manufacturer. Proprietary Software, audio or video are released on DVD-ROMs.
- DVD-R (DVD – Recordable) – The data on these DVDs can be recorded by the user once. It can be read any number times, but cannot be deleted or modified later.
- DVD-RW (DVD – Rewritable) – The Data on these DVDs can be recorded any number of times. Like CDs, these DVDs also work like floppy disk, pen drives and hard disks, where you can record, erase or modify files any time.

2.5.4.4 Pen Drive

A *pen drive*, also known by names such as *flash drive*, *flash memory*, *thumb drive*, is a portable memory device that uses solid state memory rather than magnetic fields or lasers to record data. It uses a technology similar to RAM, except that it is non-volatile.

The drive gets its name from the fact that many have a retractable port connector like a ballpoint pen, and they are small enough to fit into a pocket.

Using a pen drive is simple: the user inserts one end of the drive, which is equipped with a USB connector, into the USB port on a desktop or laptop and activates it. Once the drive is active, files can be dragged and dropped or copied and pasted into the memory. The process is usually no more difficult than attaching files to an email or copying files onto a disk, mp3 player, or other storage device.

Figure 2.47: Pen drives of different brands

2.5.4.5 Blu-ray Disk

A *Blu-ray disk* (BD) is a high-capacity optical disk developed for recording, rewriting and playing back high definition video. It can store large amounts of data and was designed to replace the DVD.

Blu-ray was jointly developed by a group of personal computer and consumer electronics companies called the Blu-ray Disc Association (BDA). Blu-ray disks support higher resolutions and more advanced video and audio formats as compared to DVDs.

Figure 2.48: Blu-ray disk and Blu-ray disk drive

Blu-ray technology gets its name from the blue-violet laser that is used to read Blu-ray disks. Compared to a DVD's red laser, a blue laser, which has shorter wavelength, permits more information to be stored at a greater density.

For example, while a DVD can store 15 GB per layer, a Blu-ray disk can store 25 GB per layer, and dual-layer disks can hold up to 50 GB.

Compared to a DVD, Blu-ray also provides much higher resolution. While a DVD with standard definition can provide resolution of 720×480 pixels, a Blu-ray with high definition has a resolution of 1920×1080 pixels.

2.5.4.6 Complementary Metal-Oxidc Scmiconductor

The Complementary Metal-Oxide Semiconductor (CMOS) is a special type of memory used to store essential startup configuration options such as the amount of memory that has been installed in the computer. CMOS chips also track the time and date. CMOS requires battery power. If you see a dead battery warning when you start the computer or if your system suddenly loses the correct time and date, take your computer to a technician.

2.5.5 Memory Hierarchy

Memory hierarchy is a ranking of computer memory devices, with devices having the fastest access time at the top of the hierarchy, and devices with slower access times but larger capacity and lower cost at lower levels.

It is designed to take advantage of memory locality in computer programs. Each level of the hierarchy has the properties of higher bandwidth, smaller size, and lower latency than lower levels.

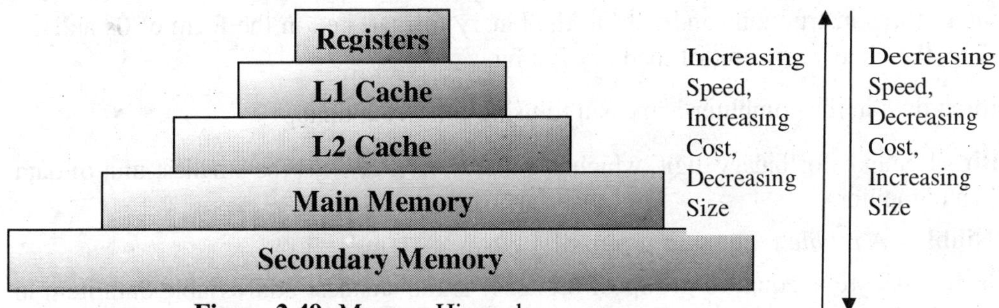

Figure 2.49: Memory Hierarchy

Levels of memory in a computer, from fastest to slowest are:

1. CPU registers
2. L1 cache
3. L2 cache
4. Main memory
5. Secondary memory

Most modern processors are so fast that for most program workloads, the locality of reference of memory accesses and the efficiency of the caching and memory transfer between different levels of the hierarchy are the practical limitation on processing speed. As a result, the processor spends much of its time idling, waiting for memory I/O to complete. This is sometimes called the space cost, as a larger memory object is more likely to overflow a small/fast level and require use of a larger/slower level.

The memory hierarchy in most computers is:

- *Processor registers* – fastest access (usually 1 CPU cycle), only hundreds of bytes in size
- *Level 1 (L1) cache* – often accessed in just a few cycles, usually tens of kilobytes
- *Level 2 (L2) cache* – higher latency than L1 by 2× to 10×, often 512 KB or more
- *Main memory* (DRAM) – may take hundreds of cycles, but can be multiple gigabytes. Access times may not be uniform, in the case of a NUMA machine.
- *Disk storage* – millions of cycles latency, but very large

Modern programming languages mainly assume two levels of memory - main memory and disk storage, though in assembly language, and in inline assembler in languages such as C, registers can be directly accessed. Taking optimal advantage of the memory hierarchy requires the cooperation of programmers, hardware, and compilers as well as underlying support from the operating system.

Programmers are responsible for moving data between disk and memory through file I/O operations. Hardware is responsible for moving data between memory and caches. Optimizing compilers are responsible for generating code that, when executed, will cause the hardware to use caches and registers efficiently.

2.5.6 Memory Units

Computer stores instructions and data in the binary format, i.e., in the form of 0s and 1s. Therefore, the elementary unit of memory is a bit.

The stored data in the computer is measured using following units.

(*i*) **Bit** - It stands for binary digit, which is either 0 or 1. A bit is the smallest unit of data in a computer.

(*ii*) **Nibble** - A *nibble* is equal to group of 4 bits.

(*iii*) **Byte** - A byte is equal to group of 8 bits. It is the smallest addressable data item in the computer because it is capable of representing an individual element of information, i.e., a single character (digit, letter, or a special character), from which bigger units of information can be formed.

(*iv*) **Word** - A word can be a group of 16 bits, 32 bits, 64 bits or even 128 bits. It depends upon the type of microprocessor.

(*v*) **Kilobyte** (KB) - One kilobyte is equal to 1024 bytes.

(*vi*) **Megabyte** (MB) - One megabyte is equal to 1024 kilobytes.

(*vii*) **Gigabyte** (GB) - One gigabyte is equal to 1024 megabytes.

(*viii*) **Terabyte** (TB) - One terabyte is equal to 1024 gigabytes.

(*ix*) **Petabyte** (PB) - One peabyte is equal to 1024 terabytes.

(*x*) **Exabyte** (EB) - One exabyte is equal to 1024 petabytes.

(*xi*) **Zettabyte** (ZB) - One zettabyte is equal to 1024 exabytes.

(*xii*) **Yottabyte** (YB) - One yottabyte is equal to 1024 zettabytes.

Table 2.1: Summary of memory units

SNo.	Units	Measurement	SNo.	Units	Measurement
1.	1 Bit	binary digit (0 or 1)	7.	1 TB	1024 GB = 2^{40} Bytes
2.	1 Nibble	4 Bits	8.	1 PB	1024 TB = 2^{50} Bytes
3.	1 Byte	8 Bits = 2 Nibbles	9.	1 EB	1024 PB = 2^{60} Bytes
4.	1 KB	1024 Bytes = 2^{10} Bytes	10.	1 ZB	1024 EB = 2^{70} Bytes
5.	1 MB	1024 KB = 2^{20} Bytes	11.	1 YB	1024 ZB = 2^{80} Bytes
6.	1 GB	1024 MB = 2^{30} Bytes			

2.6 INPUT OUTPUT PORTS/CONNECTIONS

A *port* is a connection point that acts as interface between the computer and the internal device or external device.

A port that connects internal device (such as hard disk drive, CD ROM or DVD drive, etc.) is known as *internal port*.

On the other hand, a port that connects an external device (such as monitor, mouse, printer. modem, etc.) is known as *external port*.

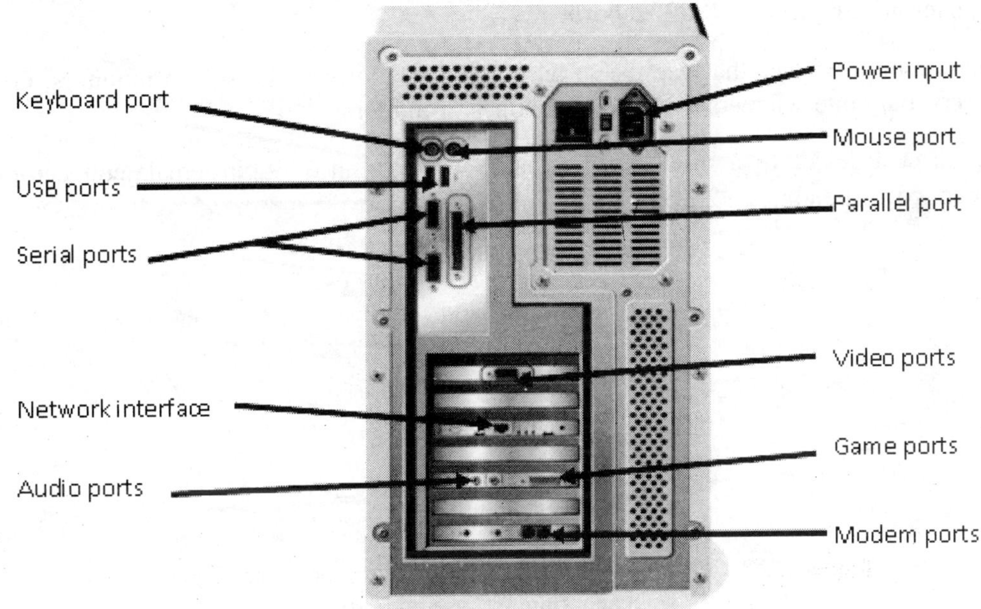

Figure 2.50: Back panel of system box showing various ports

Let us look at some of the most commonly used ports.

2.6.1 Serial Port

A *serial port* is a port that transmit data sequentially one bit at a time. So they need only one wire to transmit 8 bits.

The disadvantage is that it takes 8 times longer to transmit a byte.

Also it is necessary to send a start bit (to mark the beginning of the byte) before each byte of data, a stop bit (to mark the end of the byte) after each byte of data, and a parity bit to help check the integrity of data .

Figure 2.51: 25-pin and 9-pin male serial ports

Serial ports are usually 9-pin or 25-pin male connectors. They are also known as COM (communication) ports or RS323C ports.

Some common devices that use the serial port connection are flat screen monitors, GPS receivers, bar code scanners and satellite phones or modems.

To connect a device to a serial port, a cable with 25-pin or 9-pin female connector is required, corresponding to 25-pin or 9-pin male serial port.

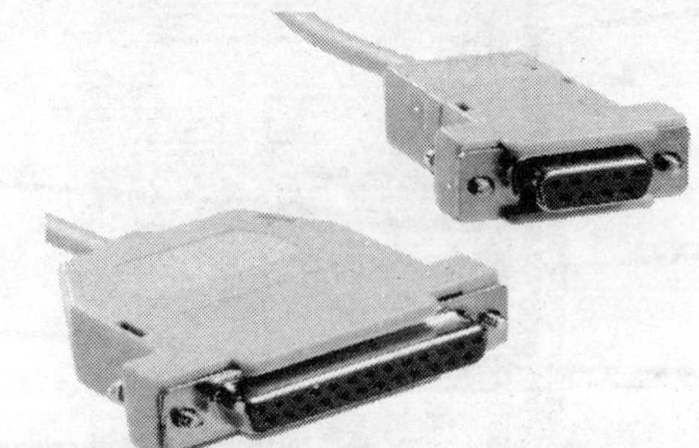

Figure 2.52: 25-pin and 9-pin female connectors for connecting to 25-pin and 9-pin male serial ports

2.6.2 Parallel Port

A *parallel port*, in contrast to serial port, is a port that can transmit 8 bits or 1 byte at a time. The main advantage of parallel port is that it transfers data much faster than a serial port. Parallel ports come in form of 25-pin female connectors.

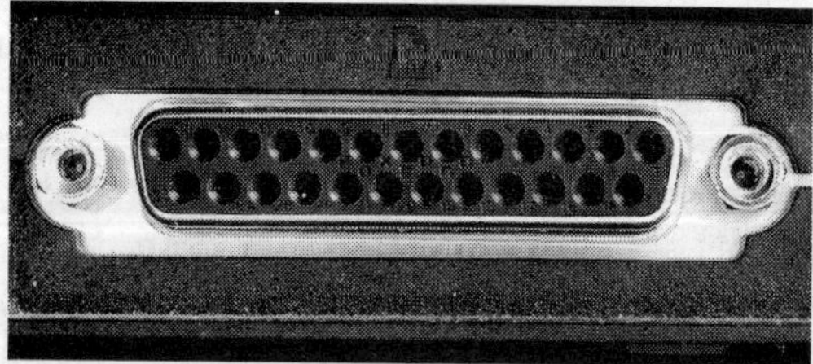

Figure 2.53: 25-pin female parallel port

The parallel port is virtually synonymous with being a printer port. Other devices that communicate with a parallel port are zip drives, scanners, joysticks, external hard drives and webcams.

To connect a device to a parallel port, a cable with 25-pin female connector is required.

Figure 2.54: 25-pin male connector for connecting to 25-pin female parallel port

Today, the parallel port has been replaced by the new USB port for connecting these same devices to the computer.

2.6.3 Universal Serial Bus Port

Universal Serial Bus (USB) is the most common type of computer port used in today's computers. It can be used to connect keyboard, mouse, game controller, printer, scanner, digital camera, and removable media drive, just to name a few.

USB is also faster than older ports, such as serial and parallel ports.

With the help of a few USB hubs, you can connect up to 127 peripherals to a single USB port and use them all at once.

Figure 2.55: USB port and cable

2.6.4 PS/2 (PS-2) Port

PS/2 stands for Personal System/2. PS/2 ports are round and consist of 6 pins. The purple PS/2 port is intended to be used by keyboard while green PS/2 port is to be used by mouse.

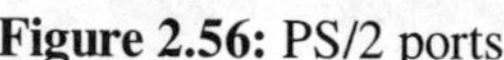

Figure 2.56: PS/2 ports

Figure 2.57: PS/2 connectors

The PS/2 standard had been *completely* replaced by the much faster, and more flexible, USB standard.

2.6.5 Infrared Port

Infrared port is a port that enables wireless exchange of data within a radius of 10 meters. Two devices that have infrared ports are placed facing each other so that beams of infrared lights can be used to share data.

Figure 2.58: Infrared port

We are already using Infrared (IR) to operate our TV, setup box, AC, and many more electric appliances which has Infrared port in it.

2.6.6 Bluetooth Port

Bluetooth is a wireless technology standard for exchanging data over short distances from fixed and mobile devices, and building personal area networks (PANs).

Bluetooth technology was primarily designed to support networking of portable consumer devices and peripherals that run on batteries, but Bluetooth support can be found in a wide range of devices including cell phones, wireless headsets, Wireless keyboards, printers, wireless speakers, computers, etc.

Two Bluetooth devices connect to each other by a process called *pairing*. When you press a button or select a menu option on the unit, a Bluetooth device initiates a new connection. The details of pairing process vary depending on the type of device.

Many mobile devices have Bluetooth radios embedded in them. PCs and other devices can also be enabled through the use of Bluetooth dongles.

Figure 2.59: A Bluetooth USB dongle

Bluetooth networks feature a dynamic topology called a *piconet*, which contains a minimum of two and a maximum of eight Bluetooth peer devices. Devices communicate using network protocols that are part of the Bluetooth specification.

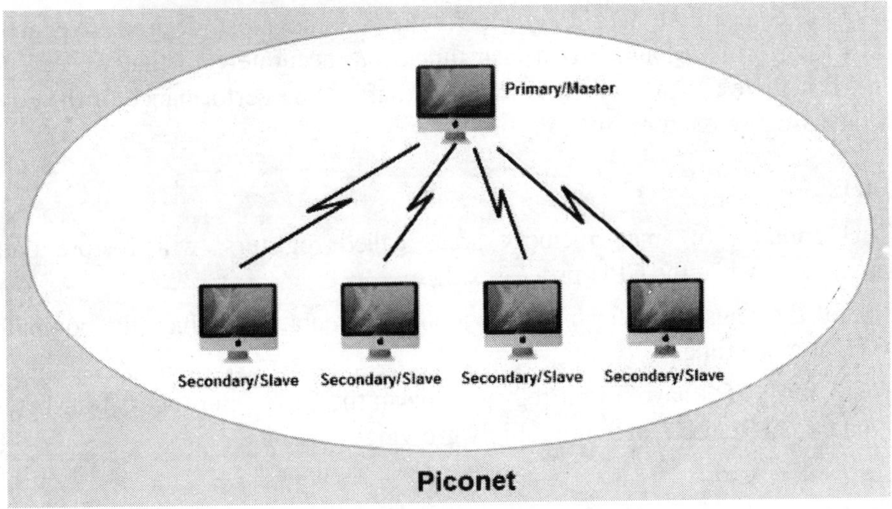

Figure 2.60: Example Piconet Network connecting Bluetooth enabled devices

A *piconet* is a network of devices connected using Bluetooth technology. The network ranges from two to eight connected devices. When a network is established, one device takes the role of the master while all the other devices act as slaves. Piconet gets its name from the word "pico", which means very small.

Radio signals that are transmitted with Bluetooth cover only short distances, typically up to 30 meters until the most recent standard 4.0.

2.6.7 FireWire Port

FireWire is Apple Computer's interface standard for enabling high speed communication using serial bus. It is also called IEEE 1394 and used mostly for audio and video devices like digital camcorders.

Figure 2.61: Firewire ports

Figure 2.62: Firewire connector

2.7 FACTORS AFFECTING THE PROCESSING SPEED OF COMPUTER

In the modern competitive world, quick results are the most desired. We are using computers to perform various certain task quickly & accurately so that we can get our work done. But there are many factors that could affect the performance of the computer system, which are discussed below:

- **Registers**
  - CPU contains of small memory areas called registers, which store data and instructions while the CPU processes them.
  - Size of the registers determines the amount of data with which the computer can work at a one time.
  - Today most PC's have 32-bit registers, mean the CPU can process four bytes data at one time. Register sizes are rapidly growing to 64 bits.

- **RAM**
  - Amount of RAM in a PC has a direct affect on the system's speed.
  - More RAM a PC has the more program instructions and data can be held in memory, which is faster than storage on disk.
  - If a PC does not have enough memory to run a program, it must move data between RAM and the hard disk frequently. This process called swapping can greatly slow a PC's performance.

- **System Clock**
  - Computer's system clock sets the pace the CPU by using a vibrating quartz crystal.
  - A single *tick* of the clock is the time required to turn a transistor off and back on. This is called a clock cycle.
  - Clock cycles are measured in Hertz(Hz), a measure of cycles per second. If a computer has a clock speed of 300 MHz, then its system clock *ticks* 300 million times every seconds.
  - Faster a PCs clock runs, the more instructions the PC can execute each second.

- **System Bus**
  - A bus is a path between the components of a computer. Data and instructions travel along these paths.
  - Data bus width determines how many bits can be transmitted between the CPU and other devices.
  - Address buss runs only between the CPU and RAM, and carries nothing but memory addresses for the CPU to use.
  - Peripheral devices are connected to the CPU by an expansion bus.

- **Cache Memory**
  - Cache memory is high-speed memory that holds the most recent data and instructions that have been loaded by the CPU.
  - Cache is located directly on the CPU or between the CPU and RAM, making it faster than normal RAM.
  - CPU-resident cache is called Level-1 (L1) cache. External cache is called Level-2 (L2) cache.
  - Amount of cache memory has a tremendous impact on the computer's speed.

2.8 SPECIFICATIONS OF A COMPUTER

The *specification* or *spec* is a list of the key components that make up the computer. It is helps the buyers to decide which PC, and which combination of features, they need.

When buying a PC, it is important to start by deciding what it is you want the PC to do. This then informs what specification you actually need. When reviewing a computer specification, the most important components to take account of are the processor, the amount of RAM and the size of the hard drive as these are central to the overall capability of the system.

In general, specifications of a computer include:

- Processor
- RAM
- Hard Drive
- Graphics processor/card
- Wireless (for laptops)
- Monitor
- Operating System
- Warranty

For example, following are the specifications of **Dell Inspiron 15 3542** Laptop:

- **Processor** – Intel core i5 (4th generation), 2.7 GHz
- **RAM** – 4 GB, DDR3, 1600 MHz
- **Hard Drive** – 1 TB, 5400 rpm
- **Graphics processor** – Intel HD Graphics 4400
- **Wireless** – WiFi, Bluetooth 4.0
- **Monitor** – 15.6", 1366 x 768, HD LED Backlit Display with Truelife
- **Operating System** – Windows 8.1 64 bit
- **Warranty** – 1 Year Accidental Damage Protection with 24x7 Phone Support -Retail

EXERCISE

1. What are the common factors that determines the performance of a micprocessor?
2. Define word length of a microprocessor.
3. What is the purpose of system clock?
4. Differentiate between CISC and RISC processors.
5. Explain random access memory.
6. Differentiate between static RAM and dynamic RAM.
7. What is cache memory? What is its purpose?
8. Distinguish between L1 and L2 cache.

9. Explain read only memory.
10. Describe various types of ROM.
11. What is secondary memory? Why is it needed?
12. RAM is volatile memory. What does it mean?
13. Why is it more appropriate to call RAM as Read-Write memory?
14. What are various units of measurement of memory?
15. Why do we use secondary storage? Name any two secondary storage devices.
16. Explain in brief the different ports and their purposes.
17. Distinguish between the following pairs:
    a. Primary memory and Secondary memory
    b. RAM and ROM
    c. Bluetooth and Infrared port
18. Explain the factors on which the speed/performance of a computer depends?
19. What do you mean by specifications of a computer system?

❑ ❑ ❑

9. Explain read only memory.
10. Describe various types of ROM.
11. What is secondary memory? Why is it needed?
12. RAM is volatile memory. What does it mean?
13. Why is it more appropriate to call RAM as Read Write memory?
14. What are various units of measurement of memory?
15. Why do we use secondary storage? Name any two secondary storage devices.
16. Explain in brief the different ports and their purpose.
17. Distinguish between the following pairs:
    a. Primary memory and secondary memory
    b. RAM and ROM
    c. Bluetooth and Infrared port
18. Explain the factors on which the speed/performance of a computer depends.
19. What do you mean by specifications of a computer system?

□ □ □

Chapter 3

Software Concepts

Learning Objectives

After reading this chapter, students will be able to

- describe a software and its types
- differentiate between various type of software
- describe a operating system, its functions and types
- describe commonly used operating systems
- explain the use of language translators
- describe various commonly used utility software
- describe various commonly used office and domain specific tools

3.1 INTRODUCTION

Software, in its most general sense, is a set of instructions or programs that tell the hardware what to do. Software can be difficult to describe because it is *virtual* not physical like computer hardware. Instead, software consists of lines of code (instructions) written by computer programmers that have been compiled into a computer program. Software programs are stored as binary data that is copied to a computer's hard drive, when it is installed. Since software is virtual and does not take up any physical space, it is much easier (and often cheaper) to upgrade than computer hardware.

The most important example of software is an *operating system* (OS) that manages the resources of the computer system, and provides an interface using which the user can interact with the computer to perform various tasks.

It is important to remember that hardware and software are integral parts of a computer system — *hardware is of no use without software and software cannot be used without hardware*. It is the software that drives hardware, i.e., it is the software that gives hardware its capability.

This chapter describes the various types of software, the role they play in efficient functioning of the computer system, and how it helps the user in solving their day-to-day problems.

3.2 TYPES OF SOFTWARE

Software can be broadly are categorized as

- **System software** – It is a type of software that is designed to run a computer's hardware and application programs. If we think of the computer system as a layered model, the system software is the interface between the hardware and user applications. The operating system and language translators (assembler, compiler and interpreter) are examples of system software.

- **Application software** – It is a type of software that is designed for a specific purpose and is used by end users. Word processor, database software, spreadsheet software, entertainment software, reservation software, inventory management software, etc., are examples of application software.

- **Utility software** – It is a type of software that is designed to help analyze, configure, optimize or maintain a computer. It is used to support the computer infrastructure. Antivirus software, compression tools, disk management tools, etc., are examples of utility software.

3.3 SYSTEM SOFTWARE

System Software is the software that is directly related to coordinating computer operations and performs tasks associated with controlling and utilizing computer hardware. These programs assist in running application programs and are designed to control the operation of a computer system.

System software can be further categorized into

- Operating System
- Compiler
- Interpreter
- Assembler

Compiler, interpreter and assembler are called language translators/processors. They translate source code (program written in assembly language or high-level language) to object code (machine language) which computer can understand and execute on hardware.

3.3.1 Operating System

The most important program on any computer is the *Operating System* or simply OS. The OS is a large program made up of many smaller programs. It acts as resource manager of the computer system and provides an interface between the users and the hardware. The resources of a computer system include processor, memories and I/O devices, users, etc. As a manager it coordinates the activities of various resources so as to provide the users with the required information.

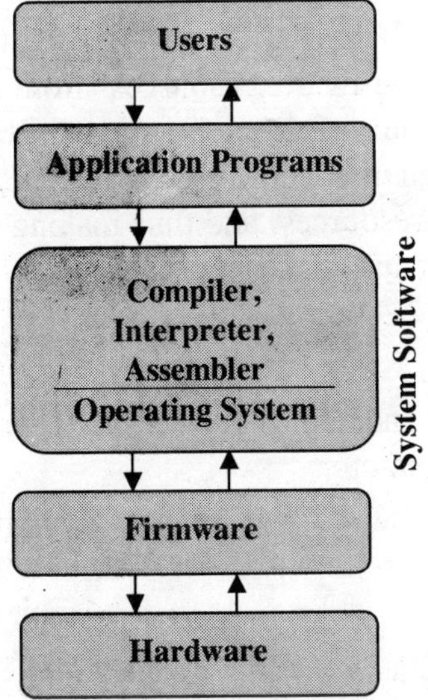

Figure 3.1: Layered architecture of a Computer System

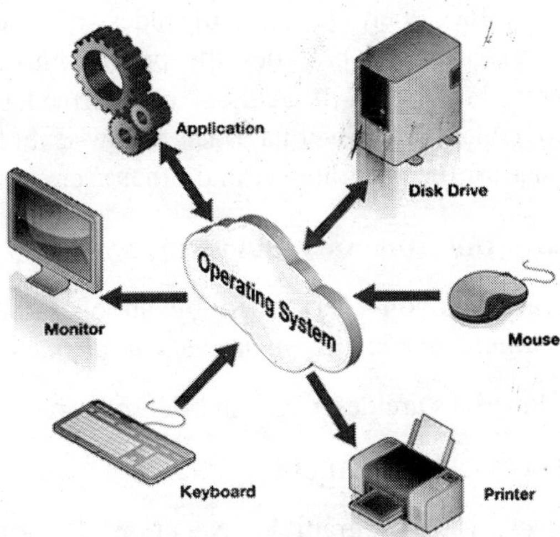

Figure3.2: Operating System managing various resources of a Computer System

Though, *firmware* is shown as a separate layer on the top of hardware for simplicity and clarity, actually it comprises software routines permanently embedded (stored) in hardware, and therefore, for all practical purposes, is treated as part of hardware of the computer system.

3.3.1.1 Need for Operating System

A computer would be useless without operating system because it cannot do anything on its own. It needs operating system to drive it and to make it do some task as desired by the user.

The following two objectives of operating systems justifies the need for operating system:

- ***Managing the resources of a computer system*** – The first important objective of the computer system is to manage various resources of the computer system. Two most important resources of a computer system are CPU (simply processor) and main memory.

  The task of managing the resources involves keeping track of who is using which resources, granting resource requests, accounting for resource usage and handling conflicting requests from different programs and users. The efficient and fair sharing of resources among programs and/or users is a key objective of an operating system.

- ***Making the computer system easy to use*** – As shown in Figure 3.1, an operating system is a layer of software on the top of bare hardware of the computer system that it manages all parts of the system and presents to the user an interface (or *virtual machine*) that is easy to program and use.

  Thus, the operating system hides the details of hardware resources from the programmer and provides the programmer with an interface that is convenient for using the system. It acts as an intermediary between the hardware and its users, providing a high-level interface to low-level hardware resources, and thus making it is easier for the programmer and other users to access and use those resources.

3.3.1.2 Functions of Operating System

The main functions performed by an operating system include *process management*, *memory management*, *file management*, *device management*, etc.

These functions are described, in brief, below:

- **Process Management**

A *process* is a program in execution. Process management functions deal with the allocation of processes to the processor.

Which process will get the turn for execution is decided on the basis of the scheduling policy. There exits many scheduling policies that can be used in different environments to improve the utilization of the processor. The component of OS responsible for this act is called *scheduler.*

❑ Memory Management

Memory management functions takes care of memory in use and memory available for use, i.e., free memory. These functions take care that a program gets desired amount of memory for its execution, and takes back the allocated memory once the program has finished its execution. Memory management functions also take care of, in case of multi-user OS, that different program don't interfere with each other and run in their own allocated memory.

❑ File Management

File management functions deal with storing the data information in files and folders. These functions include opening and closing of files, reading from files and writing to the files. These functions also take care of when the file was created and the last time it was modified. These functions also allow sharing of files and folders among related set of processes.

❑ Device Management

Device management functions deal with communicating with the various devices attached to the system via their respective drivers. These functions include keeping track of all devices connected to computer, and the component of the OS responsible for this is called *I/O controller.* These functions also decide on allocating the device to a process in an efficient way, for how long a process gets a device, and finally de-allocating devices so that they can be made available to other processes.

3.3.1.3 Types of Operating Systems

Within the broad family of operating systems, there are categorized into the following types depending on their capability of processing

❑ Interactive (GUI based) Operating System

An interactive operating system is one that allows the user to directly interact with the operating system while one or more programs are running. There will be an user interface in place to allow this to happen. It could be a *command line interface* (CLI) or it could be a *graphical user interface* (GUI).

Most of the modern operating systems provide a Graphic User Interface (GUI).

Through the Graphic User Interface (GUI) user can easily navigate and interact with the computer system. The computer responds almost immediately after an instruction has been entered, and the user can enter new instructions after seeing the results of the previous instructions.

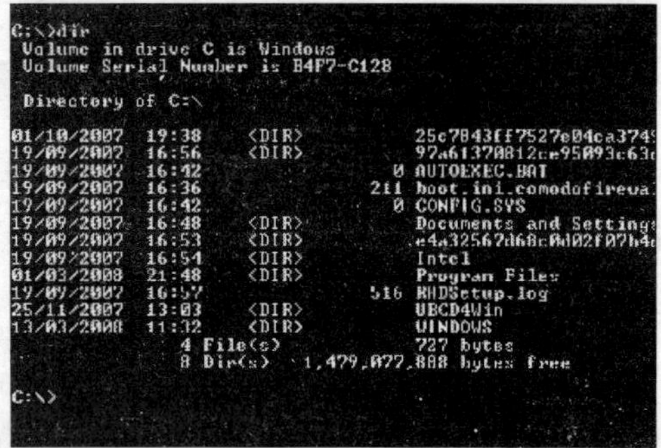

Figure 3.3: Command Line Interface (CLI)

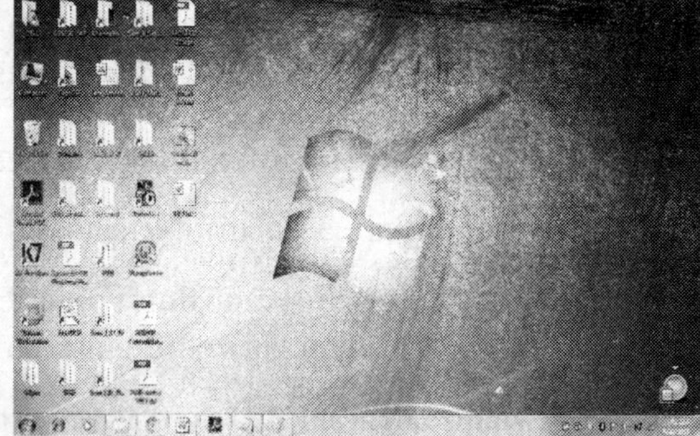

Figure 3.4: Graphic User Interface (GUI)

❑ Time Sharing Operating System

Time-sharing is a technique which enables many people, located at various terminals, to use a particular computer system at the same time. Processor's time which is shared (divided) among multiple users simultaneously is termed as time-sharing.

Multiple processes are executed by the CPU by switching between them. The switching between processes happens rapidly. Thus, the user can receive an immediate response.

The time sharing operating system uses CPU scheduling and multiprogramming to provide each user with a small portion of a time.

❑ Real Time Operating System

The real time operating system is designed to respond to the user commands in a predetermined fixed time frame. These are used to control machinery, scientific instruments and industrial systems. They typically have very little user-interface capability, and no end-user utilities, since the system will be a *sealed box* when delivered for use. A very important part of it is managing the resources of the computer so that a particular operation executes in precisely the same amount of time, every time it occurs.

There are two types of real-time operating systems - *hard real-time* and *soft real-time* systems.

Hard real-time systems guarantee that critical tasks complete on time, whereas soft real-time systems are less restrictive. Soft real-time systems have limited utility than hard real-time systems.

- **Distributed Operating System**

A *distributed system* is a system in which independent computers located on the network communicate and coordinate their actions by passing messages. The computers interact with each other in order to achieve a common goal.

Distributed operating system is designed to manage such a collection of independent computers and makes them appear to the users as if it were a single computer.

3.3.1.4 Commonly Used Operating Systems

Some of the commonly used operating systems are discussed below:

- **Unix** — It is a multi-user operating system. It was developed in the early 1970s at Bell Laboratories by Ken Thomson and Dennis Ritchie. It was the first operating system developed using C language.

  Unix operating system and its variants are very rich in features handling system security and networking. Because of these features, Unix is a natural choice for large computer systems and for managing servers providing critical services.

- **Linux** — Linux is a very popular open source operating system enhanced and backed by thousands of programmers worldwide. The name Linux was derived from its inventor Linus Torvalds. Linus, as a student, wrote the first version of Unix like operating system, as a toy project. Later, he posted the source code on Internet and asked the programmers across the world to help him build it into a working system, and as result the Linux was born. Linux has the ability to manage thousands of tasks at the same time.

  Like Unix, the Linux is also very rich in system security and networking features.

- **Windows** — Windows is an operating systems developed by Microsoft to overcome the limitations of its own operating system – *the MS DOS.*

  Windows operating system provides an easy to use graphical user interface (GUI). As part of the GUI, it shows a desktop where the various tasks are represented by small pictures, called *icons*. The user only needs to point at an icon and click into order to select and double click to launch the program/application.

  Microsoft launched Windows 1.0 operating system in 1985 and since then Windows has ruled the world's software market, and launched various versions of Windows line Windows 95, Windows 98, Window NT, Windows XP, Windows 7, Windows 8, and the latest being Windows 10 (at the time of publishing this book).

- **Solaris** SOLARIS — Solaris is a Unix based operating system originally developed by SUN Microsystems. In 2010, after SUN's acquisition by Oracle, it was renamed Oracle Solaris.

  It is known for its scalability. It supports SPARC-based and x86-based workstations and servers from Oracle and other vendors. Efforts are on to port to additional platforms.

- **BOSS (Bharat Operating System Solutions)** BOSS Bharat Operating System Solutions — It is a Linux distribution developed by C-DAC, Chennai, in order to benefit the usage of Free/Open Source Software in India. BOSS Linux, derived from Debian, is a key deliverable of National Resource Centre for Free/Open Source Software (NRCFOSS). It has enhanced Desktop Environment integrated with Indian language support and other software.

  It has been endorsed by the Government of India for adoption and implementation on a national scale.

Debian is a Unix-like operating system that is composed entirely of free software, most of which is under the GNU General Public License and packaged by a group of individuals participating in the Debian Project.

3.3.1.5 Mobile Operating Systems (Mobile OS)

A *mobile operating system*, also called a *mobile OS*, is an operating system that is specifically designed to run on mobile devices such as mobile phones, smart phones, PDAs, tablet computers and other handheld devices. It extends the features of a normal operating system for PCs so as to include the touch screen, Bluetooth, WiFi, GPS mobile navigation, camera, music player and many more.

Android and *Symbian* are two of the commonly used mobile operating systems.

- **Android** — Android is an open source and Linux-based mobile operating system for mobile devices such as smart phones and tablets.

  Android is one of the most user friendly, i.e., easy to use. Its user interface is mainly based on direct manipulation, using touch gestures that loosely correspond to real-world actions, such as swiping and tapping, to manipulate on-screen objects, along with a virtual keyboard for text input. Initially it was originally developed by Android Inc., and was later bought by Google in 2005.

- **iOS** — Originally iPhone OS, is a mobile operating system created and developed by Apple Inc., and distributed exclusively for Apple hardware. It is the operating system that presently powers many of the company's mobile devices, including the iPhone, iPad, and iPod touch. It is the second most popular mobile operating system in the world by sales, after Android.

- **Symbian** — Symbian is a mobile operating system targeted at mobile phones that offers a high-level of integration with communication and personal information management (PIM) functionality.

  It combines middleware with wireless communications through an integrated mailbox and the integration of Java and PIM functionality.

  Nokia has made the Symbian platform available under an alternative, open and direct model, to work with some Original Equipment Manufactures (OEMs) and the small community of platform development collaborators.

3.4 PROGRAMMING LANGUAGES

You are aware with the term language. A language is nothing but a means of communication. As you know, we communicate with each other either by speaking or by using gestures.

When we communicate by speaking, we are doing so by using languages that we know such as English, Punjabi, Hindi, etc. The languages spoken by the human beings are called *natural languages*.

When we communicate by gestures, we are doing so by the involvement of our physical organs. This language of communication is called *the body language*.

Similarly, the languages used for the purpose of instructing the computer to do a given task are called *computer programming languages* or simply as *programming languages*. Since the evolution of the computer, *a magical machine*, many programming languages have been developed.

3.4.1 Classification of Programming Languages

There are various classifications of programming languages. Although it is not possible to sort all languages into convenient groups, some attempt to categorize them is still possible and indeed helpful because some of them require very different programming techniques.

The oldest approach to classification of programming languages is according to the level of interaction and their dependence on the organization and architecture of the underlying processor. This approach divides programming languages into two major categories – *low-level languages* and *high-level languages.*

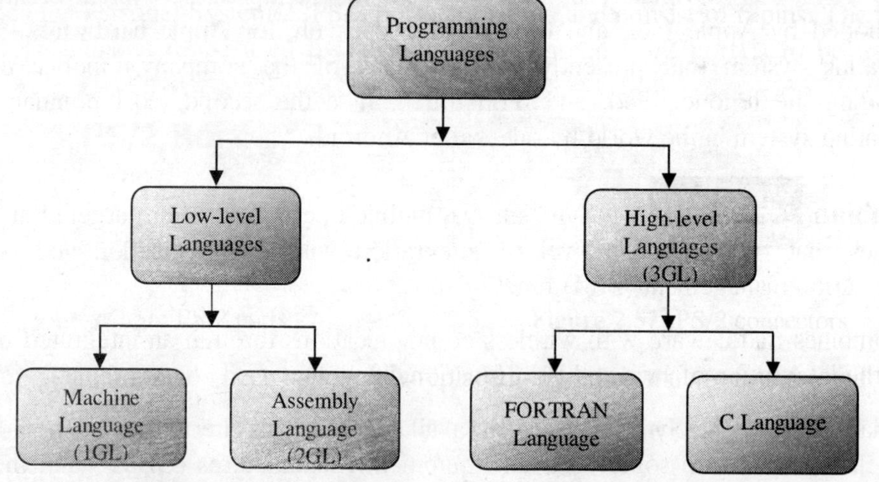

Figure 3.5: Classification of programming languages

3.4.1.1 Low-level Languages

Using low-level languages, you can have total control of the processor and can instruct the processor to perform all types of tasks that a processor can perform. However, to use low-level languages, you need to have through knowledge of the architecture of the processor, *i.e.*, internal functional blocks and set of instruction that they follow.

The low-level languages are further classified as follows:

- Machine Language
- Assembly Language

3.4.1.1.1 Machine Language

Machine language, as its name suggests, is the language that a machine (computer, hence *the processor*) can understand. Since, it was the first and the only language used when computer were invented, it was also known as first generation programming language (1GL).

The machine language involves expressing the instructions using 1s and 0s only. Each instruction can be divided into parts, where first part is used to instruct the computer *what to do*, called *the operation code*, and the remaining parts are used to represent the data on which the computer will perform the specified the operation.

Since, programming using machine language require an in-depth knowledge of the hardware, only people with sound knowledge in the disciplines of Physics, Electrical & Electronics Engineering were able to program the early computers.

Further, since the hardware design of the processor varies from manufacturer to manufacturer, each processor has its own machine language. For example, Intel processors from Intel Company, Motorola processors from Motorola Company, AMD processors from AMD Company, etc., have their own machine language.

Example 3.1: Instructions in machine language to find the average of numbers 10 and 50.

1011 1000 0001 0000 0000
0000 0101 0101 0000 0000
1101 0001 1110 1000

Advantages

1. Machine language instructions execute very fast as they are in the form that the processor understands.
2. The size of the programs is very small.
3. Ability to perform low-level operations, and thus gives a programmer total control of the hardware.

Disadvantages

1. Writing instructions in a machine language is very time-consuming and error-prone task. In addition, the programmer needs to have detailed knowledge of the hardware.
2. Program written in machine language is very difficult to read, understand and modify.
3. Machine language is dependent on the processor. Therefore, you can't use the same program on a computer with different processor, *i.e.*, machine language is not portable. You have to write it again from scratch, which a wastage of time and effort.
4. The programmer has to remember a lot of operation codes to write a program, which results in program errors.
5. High programming skill is required to do programming in machine language.
6. It is difficult to debug (locate and correct the errors) the program.

3.4.1.1.2 Assembly Language

Table 3.1: Common mnemonics used in assembly language

Mnemonic	Description
MOV	To assign (copy) source operand to destination operand.
ADD	To perform addition operation.
SUB	To perform subtraction operation.
DIV	To perform division operation.
MUL	To perform multiplication operation.
JMP	To transfer program control from one section of program to another section.
CMP	To perform the comparison operation for decision making.
SHR	To shift the bits of the operand from left to right.
SHL	To shift the bits of the operand from right to left.

The name given to this language is *the assembly language*. The use of mnemonics in preparing the instructions made the task of programming a much easy as compared to machine language. However, since computer can understand the machine language only, computer instructions written using assembly language need to be translated to the machine language. To do this translation, a translator program, called *assembler* was developed. The assembler will take the instructions written using assembly language and translates them to the machine language.

Note that, like the machine language, there is one and only one assembly language for a given computer.

Example 3.2: Instructions in assembly language to find the average of numbers 10 and 50.

```
MOV AX, 10
ADD AX, 50
SHR AX, 1
```

Advantages

1. The symbolic programming of assembly language is easier to understand and saves a lot of time and effort of the programmer.
2. It is easier to correct errors and modify program instructions.
3. Assembly language has the same efficiency of execution as the machine level language, because this is one-to-one correspondence between instruction in assembly language program and machine language.

Disadvantages

1. Assembly language is also machine dependent.
2. Even to do a simple task, you have to write a lot of instructions.
3. High programming skill is also required to do programming in assembly language.

3.4.1.2 High-level Languages

Though, the assembly language made the task of programming bit easy as compared to machine language, but still to work with assembly language you require deep knowledge of the computer hardware. Also, the assembly language is machine dependent, and hence the program written in assembly language can't be used on other computers.

Therefore, further need was felt to have programming languages, where you don't require the knowledge of computer hardware, and also the program once developed can be executed (run) almost on any computer. The quest to fulfill such a need lead to the development many languages which uses an English language like styles to express instructions. These languages were given the name of *high-level languages*.

Like, assembly language, the instructions expressed using high-level languages need to be translated into machine language. This translation can be done before the computer executes the instructions or during execution of the instructions. The translator that translates the instructions before they are executed is called *compiler*, and the translator that translates the instructions during execution is called *interpreter*.

You need separate compiler and/or interpreter for each high-level language, and for each computer. However, once you write a program in majority of high-level languages, it can be used on any computer without any modification or with minimum modifications, and thus it saves lot of valuable time and effort.

Example 3.3: Instruction in C, C++ and Java languages, to find the average of numbers 10 and 50.

```
average = ( 10 + 50 ) / 2;
```

Advantages

1. High-level languages are easy to learn and use. It is because that they are similar to the languages used by us in our day to day life.
2. The effort required to write instructions in high-level languages is very less as compared to machine language and assembly language.
3. High-level languages are machine independent, and thus programs written using high-level languages can be used on any computer.
4. Program written in high-level languages can be easily understood, and hence modification can be done with quite ease.

Disadvantages

1. Programs developed in high-level languages are large, and thus occupy more main memory and take more time to execute. It means high-level languages are less efficient.
2. Majority of the high-level language lack in features for performing low-level operations, with an exception of C/C++ languages.

Table 3.2 lists few high-level languages, along with the areas of usage/ applications.

Table 3.2: Description of some HLLs

Acronym	Expanded Name, if any	Targeted Application
BASIC	Beginner's Allpurpose Symbolic Instruction Code	Well suited for the beginner, and can be used for variety of tasks.
FORTRAN	FORmula TRANslation	Well suited for scientific and engineering applications.
COBOL	COmmon Business Oriented Language	Well suited for business applications.
C	–	Well suited for creating system programs such as operating systems, language translators, etc.

Table 3.2: Description of some HLLs ***contd...***

C++	–	Well suited for large and complex, and uses object-oriented approach manage size and complexity.
Java	–	Well suited for distributed applications, which runs on many computers located at different geographical locations.
LISP	LISt Processing	Well suited for artificial intelligence based applications.

3.4.1.3 Fourth Generation Languages (4GLs)

Though, high-level languages makes task of programming quite easy, still we have to develop a procedure (a set of instructions) to complete an entire task. Because of this, majority of the high-level languages fall into the category of what we call as *procedural languages*.

In order to handle the routine type of tasks, a need was felt to have a kind of languages where the user of the data don't have to write a detailed procedure, which lead to the development of non-procedural languages. One of the most popular languages with this capability is Structured Query Language (SQL). SQL allow the user to insert new data into the database, delete data from the database, and retrieve data from the database without writing the detailed procedure.

For example, the following simple statement in SQL

```
SELECT * FROM EMPLOYEE
```

will retrieve the information of all the employees from the table named *EMPLOYEE* in the given database.

Table in a database, in lay man's language, is something like a file containing the information of the employees in an organization. Database is something like collection of all the files containing information about the entire organization.

3.4.2 Language Translators

Language translators are also known as *language processors*. It is pertinent to mention here that while machine language requires no translation, the assembly language and high-level languages requires translators to translate instructions written in assembly language and machine language before they can be executed.

A program written using assembly language or high-level language is known as *source code*. The translated version of the source code is a program in machine language is known as *object code*.

The language translator for assembly language is known as an *assembler*, and the language translators for high-level languages are known as *compilers* and *interpreters*.

Assembler

An assembler is a program that translates a program in assembly language (*source code*) to machine language (*object code*).

As there is one-to-one correspondence between instructions in machine language and assembly language, the assembler translates each instruction in assembly language to corresponding instruction in machine language.

Compiler

A compiler is a program that translates (*compiles*) the program written in a high-level language (*source code*) to machine language (*object code*).

This process of translation is known as *compilation*. During compilation, compiler reads the source code, line by line, and checks for syntax errors. Note that any violation of the rules of the programming language (also known as the grammar of the language), is known as *syntax error*.

If there are syntax errors, then it displays the error messages identifying the error locations and prints a program listing that highlights the locations and the likely causes of the errors, and no translation takes place. However, if there are no syntax errors in the source code, the compiler re-reads the source code and does the translation and creates an object code which then it writes onto another file, usually with extension *obj* (for object).

Once translation is done, the compiler has no further role in the subsequent steps. However, if the source code is modified, we need to recompile it to incorporate the modification in the object code.

Interpreter

An interpreter is another type of translator used for translating high-level languages. However, interpreter doesn't produce object code. Instead, it translates one line of the source code at a time and executes the translated instruction. It continues till all the instructions are translated an executed. Note that if any instruction is to be executed repeatedly, it will be translated each time.

Note that once the source code is translated into the object code by the compiler, which is one time task, the object code is executed directly which result in faster execution of the program. However, the interpreter first does the translation and then executes the instruction, which lead to slow execution of the program. In addition, every time the program is executed using interpreter, the translation will be repeated.

Although interpreters run programs more slowly than programs compiled into object code, they are helpful tools for learning language for the beginners and also for debugging the programs. As the program executes line by line the programmer can see exactly what each line does.

Here it is important to mention that in order to execute a program using interpreter, first we need to run the interpreter, then only then we can instruct the interpreter the execute the user program.

Therefore, every time to run the program, you need to run the interpreter as well.

For most programming languages, a programmer can use both an interpreter and a compiler. The interpreter comes in handy during program development. When the program development is finished, it is compiled for efficient use.

Table 3.3: Comparison of Compiler and Interpreter

Compiler	Interpreter
It takes entire program as unit of translation and does not execute the program.	It translates one instruction at a time and executes it.
After translation, it writes the object code onto a disk file.	It translates instruction by instruction and does not create a permanent object code.
It does not execute the program after translation.	It executes every instruction after translation and continues doing so till all instructions are finished.
After translation, neither the source code nor the compiler is required for executing the program.	Both, interpreter as well the source code are required for execution of the program. In fact, first interpreter program is executed, and then it is instructed to execute the program under consideration.
It takes entire program as unit of translation and does not execute the program.	It translates one instruction at a time and executes it.
After translation, it writes the object code onto a disk file.	It translates instruction by instruction and does not create a permanent object code.
It does not execute the program after translation.	It executes every instruction after translation and continues doing so till all instructions are finished.
After translation, neither the source code nor the compiler is required for executing the program.	Both, interpreter as well the source code are required for execution of the program. In fact, first interpreter program is executed, and then it is instructed to execute the program under consideration.
Program execution is very fast since the object code is directly executed.	Program execution is slow since each instruction is translated first and then executed.
Compilers play almost no role in debugging, since after compilation, the compiler is not in picture and have no role during program execution.	Debugging is very easy since each instruction is executed one-by-one, programmer and/or user can see what each instruction does.
To execute the program on a different computer, you need to compile the program on that computer. It will be essential sometimes since it may have different machine language	However, if you have a interpreter on another machine, the program can be executed as such since translation takes place during execution, and will take place automatically.
Well suited for application where high performance is the need.	Well suited for the beginners who are just learning the particular high-level language.

3.5 PROGRAMMING ENVIRONMENTS

Programming environment is an environment in which programs are created and tested, and it has less influence on the design of the language that the operating environment on which the programs are expected to be run.

A programming environment consists of support tools and a command language (set of commands) to invoke them. Each support tool is another program that may be used by the programmer as an aid during one or more stages of creation of a program.

Typical tools in a programming environment include *editors*, *language translators*, *linkers*, *loaders*, *test data generators*, etc. Language translators are explained in the earlier section, the remaining tools are described here.

Editor – *Editor* is a program that allows creating and editing of files. Further, there are editors that allow working with text files only, and are called *text editors*. Examples of popular text editors are *notepad* and *edit* of *Windows* operating system, *vi* of *Unix* and *Linux* operating systems. Even popular word processing programs such as MS Word, allows to create text files in addition to word documents.

Linker – Note that the object code produced by the compiler is not in a form that can be executed by the computer. Some more information needed to be pumped into the object code to make it in a form that can be executed by the computer.

When you write a program, you may be referring to various library functions for doing input/output and for mathematical computation (*sqrt*, *sin*, *cos*, *abs*, *exp* to name a few frequently used mathematical library functions). The instructions defining the task to be performed by these library function are in the machine language (binary) form and are contained in system libraries (files with extension LIB) supplied with the compiler. Plus, you may be referring to some user-defined functions which are written in a separate program file, and whose object code is lying separately than the object code under consideration. Therefore, there is a need to combine the object code of the library as well as user-defined functions with the object code under consideration, and this task is accomplished by the program called *linker*.

Linker is a program that combines the object of the program with the object codes of the library and user-defined functions, in the desired manner, and writes the same in a separate program file with extension, usually EXE under Windows. This file produced by the linker is known as *executable file* or simply as *run file*, and is the file that is used to execute the program.

Loader – *Loader* is a program that is responsible for transferring the executable file from the secondary storage to memory. On execution, the loader, with the assistance of the operating system, first finds the free memory of the requisite amount and then transfers the executable file into that part of memory, takes appropriates steps such as address translation, and then initiates its execution. From that point onwards, the role of the loader is over, and the control is taken over by the program. The instruction of the program are executed to perform the desired task, but under the overall supervision of the operating system. As soon as the program finishes its execution, it is removed from the memory.

Debugger – All sort of errors that are encountered during program development (syntax errors, logical error and runtime/execution errors) are known as bugs, and the process of identifying those errors and fixing (correcting) them is known as *debugging*. The logical errors are most difficult to track. To catch logical errors, we need to observe the pattern in which the instructions of the program are executed and the intermediate and final results are produced. *Debugger* is a program that, in general, allows user to monitor the trace the execution of executable version of program.

Test Data Generator – *Test data generator* is a powerful and simple automatic tool that allows you to generate test data for testing a programs. The testing data is generating according to the internal structure of the program. Note that here by test data we mean that data for which the desired output is known. Testing is done to ensure that the program is performing its intended task.

Popular Integrated Developments Environments (IDEs), such as Turbo C/C++ and Borland C++, Visual Studio 6.0, Visual Studio .NET, integrate various tools (editor, compiler, linker, debugger, etc.) in a unified manner, so that a programmer can work with these tools with much ease and more productively.

3.6 UTILITY SOFTWARE

Utility software is a software designed to perform specific tasks related to the file management, file compression, disk management, virus protection, etc.

It is used to support the computer infrastructure in contrast to application software, which is aimed at directly performing tasks that benefit ordinary users.

Nowadays many utility software are part of the operating system itself.

Some of the commonly used utility software are *anti virus*, *file management tools*, *compression tools* and *disk management tools* such as *disk cleanup*, *disk defragmenter*, *backup*.

3.6.1 Anti Virus

Anti-virus software, as its name suggests, is software that is developed to protect your system against threats from malicious software (malware), called *viruses*.

Generally, good anti-virus software will have following components:

- ***Virus Guard*** **–** A component of anti-virus software that remains active in memory. As you connect new storage device with the computer, the virus guard immediately checks the storage device to see does it carry any known virus. If it finds any such virus, it generates a warning message. Some virus guards force the user to reboot the system (restart the system).
- ***Scanner*** **–** A component that scans the specified storage devices, connected to the system at that moment, folder-by-folder and file-by-file. It display the name of the virus(es) and the name of file being scanned.
- ***Healer*** **–** A component that removes the identified virus from the identified file. Healer usually works in tandem with the scanner. As and when virus is identified by the scanner, the healer is invoked to remove the virus. In case, healer is not able to remove the virus, it may ask the user for likely alternate action to be taken such as to delete the infected file or skip the infected file and continue with rest of the files.

Examples of some popular anti virus software are Norton, Kaspersky, Quick heal and McAfee.

3.6.2 File Management Tools

A *file management tool* is a program that provides a user with an interface in which he/she can organize files and folders on a storage device.

Windows Explorer in Windows operating system is an example of a file management tool.

3.6.3 File Compression Tools

File compression is the act of taking a file on your hard drive and making it so that it's size becomes smaller and therefore takes up less storage space and is faster to upload or download on a network or the Internet. A *file compressor tool* is a program that actually compresses file.

Examples of some popular file compressor tools are *Gzip*, *WinRar*, and *Winzip*.

3.6.4 Disk Management Tools

A *disk management* tool is utility that helps the user in storing, indexing, searching and sorting files and folders on the system. The most commonly used tool is the Windows Explorer and

❑ Disk Cleanup

Disk Cleanup is a utility included in Windows operating system designed to free up disk space on a computer's hard drive. The utility first searches and analyzes the hard drive for files that are no longer of any use, and then removes the unnecessary files.

Removing unnecessary files, including temporary files, can help to speed up and improve the performance of the computer.

❑ Disk Defragmenter

Disk Defragmenter is a utility in Windows operating system designed to increase access speed by rearranging files stored on a disk to occupy contiguous storage locations, a technique called *defragmentation*.

Defragmenting a disk minimizes head travel, which reduces the time it takes to read files from and write files to the disk.

❑ Backup Utility

A *backup utility* is a computer program used to perform backup; they create exact copies of files, databases or entire storage. These programs may later use the copies to restore the original contents in the event of data loss.

The purpose of backup is to create a duplicate copy of data to safeguard it and enable recovery in the event it is lost, corrupted or infected by malware.

3.7 OPEN SOURCE CONCEPTS

Software are mainly categorized into the following categories based on their licenses:

- Open Source Software
- Freeware
- Shareware
- Proprietary Software

❑ Open Source Software

The term *open source* refers to something that can be modified and shared because its design is publicly accessible.

Open source software (OSS) is software with source code that anyone can use, inspect, modify, enhance and redistribute.

Source code is the part of software that programmers can improve that software by adding features to it or fixing parts that don't always work correctly.

Linux, PHP, MySQL, Java, and Python, etc., are few examples of Open Source Software.

❑ Freeware

Freeware is any copyrighted software that may be freely downloaded, installed, used and shared. Such programs are available for use at no cost to general end users. Freeware differs from free software, as the latter allows a user to modify source code for republishing or integration with other software.

Generally, freeware is a concise and limited version of a larger and paid software program. Vendors publish freeware to provide a limited but free version of software to prospective buyers prior to purchase. Additionally, large independent software vendors publish freeware to enhance brand buzz and market reputation.

❑ Shareware

Shareware is a copyrighted software that is distributed free, for specified period of time, on a trial basis with the intention that the user may buy it later. When the trial period ends, the software must be purchased or uninstalled.

Some shareware come with a built-in expiration date such as after 30 days, the user can no longer get access to the software.

❑ Proprietary Software

Proprietary means something owned by a specific company or an individual.

Therefore, proprietary software is a software that is either owned by a company or an individual. It is a commercial software that can be bought, leased or licensed from its vendor/developer.

The restrictions or conditions imposed by the vendor/developer on the use of proprietary software are elaborated within the software's end-user license agreement (EULA), terms of service agreement (TOS) or other related use agreements. The user/organization must accept the agreement prior to installing or using the software. The software developer/vendor can take legal action against the end-user/organization for violating the EULA or TOS.

3.8 APPLICATION SOFTWARE

Application software is a term which is used for software created for a specific purpose. It is generally a program or collection of programs used by end users. It can be called an application or simply an app.

An application software can be of two types – *general purpose* and *customized.*

Office tools come under the category of general purpose application software where as *domain specific tools* come under the category of customized application software.

3.8.1 Office Tools

Office tools represent that category of application software that is developed for the common users for their day-to-day applications and uses. The users may use them in the manner they want.

Some of the commonly used office tools are *word processor software*, *presentation tool/software*, *spreadsheet software* and *database management system*.

These office tools are described below, in brief.

- **Word Processor**

An application of computers to create, edit, and print documents, is known as *word processing*. Of all computer applications, word processing is the most common application. To perform word processing, you need a computer, a special program called a word processor, and a printer.

A word processor enables you to create a document, store it electronically on a disk, display it on a screen, modify it by entering commands and characters from the keyboard, and print it on a printer.

The great advantage of word processing over using a typewriter is that you can make changes without retyping the entire document. If you make a typing mistake, you simply back up the cursor and correct your mistake. If you want to delete a paragraph, you simply remove it, without leaving a trace. It is equally easy to insert a word, sentence, or paragraph in the middle of a document. Word processors also make it easy to move sections of text from one place to another within a document, or between documents. When you have made all the changes you want, you can send the file to a printer to get a hardcopy.

The most commonly used word processor program is *Microsoft Word*

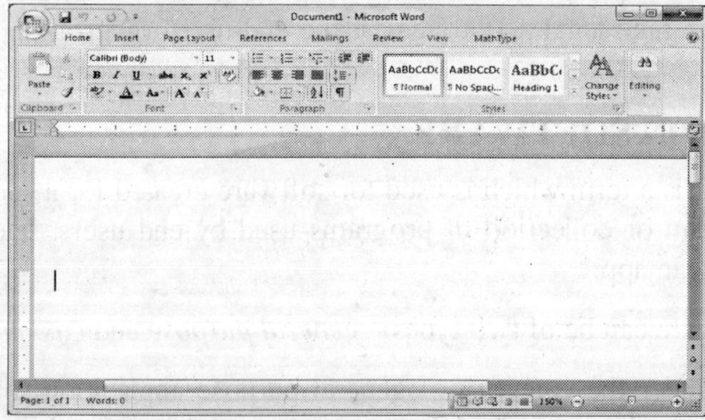

Figure 3.6: Microsoft Word Window

❑ Presentation Software/Tool

Presentation is the process of showing and explaining the content of a topic to an audience. The basic element of a presentation is a slide that can include text as well as graphics (pictures). *Presentation tool* is a program used to display information, normally in the form of a slide show.

A presentation tool typically includes following three major functions:

- ❑ An editor that allows text to be inserted and formatted,
- ❑ A method for inserting and manipulating graphic images, and
- ❑ A slide-show system to display the content.

The most commonly used presentation tool is *Microsoft PowerPoint*.

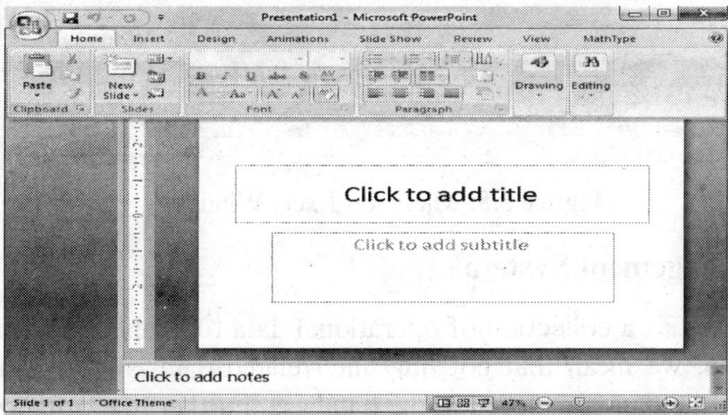

Figure 3.7: Microsoft PowerPoint Window

❑ Spreadsheet Software

A *worksheet* is a table of values arranged in rows and columns. A *cell* in a worksheet can be thought of as a box for holding a data value. A single cell is usually referenced by its column and row. Its physical size can usually be tailored for its content by dragging its height or width at box intersections (or for entire columns or rows by dragging the column or rows headers).

Each cell can have a predefined relationship to the other cells. If you change value of one cell, therefore, you may need to change values of other cells as well.

A *spreadsheet software* is a computer application that simulates a paper worksheet. It displays multiple cells that together make up a grid consisting of rows and columns, each cell containing either alphanumeric text or numeric values. A spreadsheet cell may alternatively contain a formula that defines how the contents of that cell is to be calculated from the contents of any other cell (or combination of cells) each time any cell is updated.

Spreadsheets are frequently used for financial information because of their ability to re-calculate the entire sheet automatically after a change to a single cell is made.

The most commonly used spreadsheet software is *Microsoft Excel*.

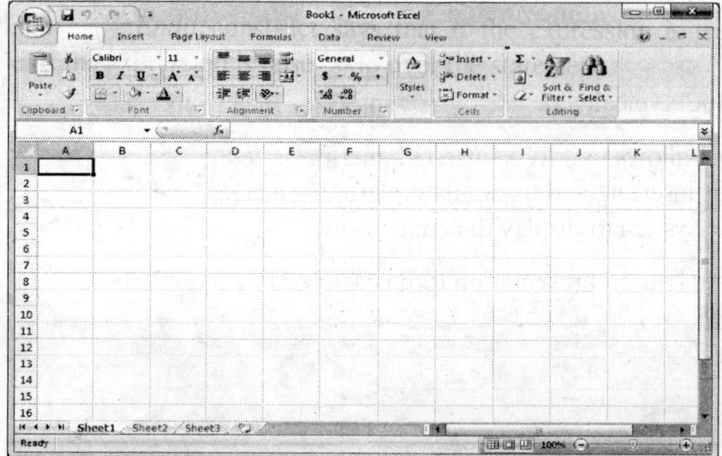

Figure 3.8: Microsoft Excel Window

❑ Database Management System

A *database* is defined as a collection of operational data to support multiple applications. By operational data, we mean that not only interrelated data is stored, also all possible relationship among the data are stored in the database. Further, the organization of data is independent of the programs and vice a versa, *i.e.*, organization of data can be changed without affecting the programs and programs can be modified without effecting the organization of data. Data in a database is structured in such a way so as to support future applications.

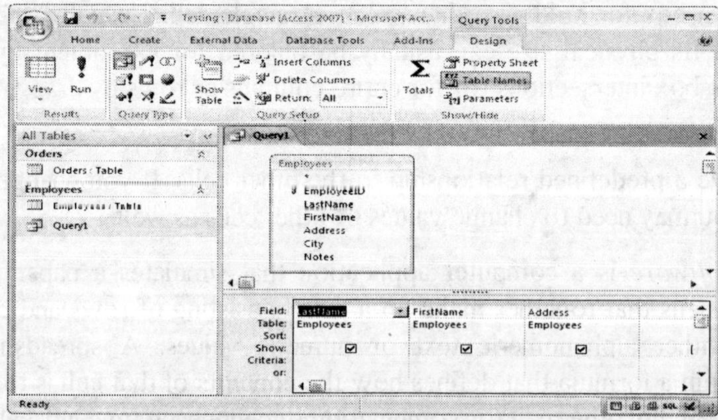

Figure 3.9: Microsoft Access Window

Database Management System (DBMS), is a computer-based record keeping system that contains information about an enterprise. The information maintained may be necessary to support day to day operations or in the decision making processes involved in the management of an enterprise. A common and controlled approach is used in adding new data to the database, modifying the existing data in the database, removing existing data from the database, querying the database to answer users enquiries and generating reports of different kinds as desired by the management. .

Some of the more popular examples of DBMS software include *Microsoft Access*, *Oracle*, *MySQL*, *Microsoft SQL Server* and DB2.

3.8.2 Domain Specific Software/Tools

Domain specific software/tools represent that category of application software that is developed as per the user's requirement. Such type of software is customer specific. It is made keeping in mind the individual needs of the user. Such software cannot be installed and used by any other user/customer since the requirements may differ.

Some of the commonly used domain specific tools are *school management system*, *inventory management system*, *payroll system*, *financial accounting*, *hotel management*, *reservation system* and *weather forecasting system.*

These domain specific tools are described below, in brief.

- **School Management System**

School management system is a software used for managing school's day-to-day operations. It maintains all the records related to students, teachers, staff, and other resources of the school.

It aims at providing a better interaction between teachers, students and parents. User can access the relevant information within few mouse clicks.

- **Inventory Management System**

Inventory management system is a software used for tracking inventory levels, orders, sales and deliveries. The main aim of using this software is to avoid product overstock and running out of stock situations.

- **Payroll System**

A payroll system is a software that is used by organizations to manage the financial aspects of the salary of its employees. This system oversees areas related to salaries, allowances, deductions, and net pay, as well as generating pay slips.

- **Financial Accounting System**

Financial accounting system is a software that records and processes accounting transactions within functional modules such as accounts payable, accounts receivable, general ledger, payroll, and trial balance.

- **Hotel Management System**

Hotel management system is software used to automate operations related to the various tasks of hotel management. These tasks include hotel administration, recording information of customers, maintaining accounts, billing the customers, marketing and advertising, housekeeping, front office/desk, food and beverage management, catering, etc.

The advance bookings of rooms can also be made through this software. Customers can have a look at the hotel and the rooms before making bookings. At any point of time the room availability, tariff for each type of room and even booking status can be checked.

- **Reservation System**

A reservation system is a software that is used to book (reserve)

- seats in air flights
- seats in trains
- movies tickets in a cinema hall
- tables in a restaurant

Input to the reservation system is a user request for booking. The processing of the request involves checking if bookings are possible, and if so making the bookings. The outputs are booking confirmations/rejections.

The reservation system can also be used to track status of bookings, reschedule bookings, as well as cancel bookings.

- **Weather Forecasting system**

Weather forecasting is a prediction of what the weather will be like in an hour, tomorrow, or next week. Weather forecasting involves a combination of computer models, observations, and a knowledge of trends and patterns. By using these methods, reasonable accurate forecasts can be made up to seven days in advance.

Weather Forecasting system is a software that makes it possible to forecast the weather for days and even for a week in advance. The detailed weather reports can also be generated.

EXERCISE

1. What is software? What are its broad categories?
2. Hardware is of no use without software and software cannot be used without hardware.' Explain.
3. Differentiate between system software and application software.
4. How is utility software different from application software?
5. Explain the layered architecture of a computer system.
6. What is an operating system?
7. What is the need of an operating system?
8. What are various types of operating system? Explain each one in brief.
9. What is the various function performed by an operating system?
10. How is a hard real-time OS different from soft real-time OS?
11. Enumerate commonly used operating systems.
12. What is the purpose of a language processor?
13. Differentiate between an interpreter and a compiler.
14. Explain any two utilities.
15. What is anti virus? What are the essential components of a good anti virus?
16. What is the use of file management tools?
17. How is the working of disk cleanup different from disk defragmenter?
18. Name the tool that used to reduce the size of a large seined file.
19. What is backup? What is its purpose?
20. What do you mean my open source software?
21. What is a proprietary software?
22. Differentiate between proprietary software and freeware.
23. Name the types of software where there is no end-user license agreement or terms of service agreement.
24. How are freeware and free software different?
25. What is the difference between an open source software and a freeware. Write two examples of each.
26. Name various office tools, and describe the use of each in brief.
27. What is word processing? Discuss the purpose of word processing software.
28. What is a database? Discuss the purpose of database management system.
29. What is the difference between office tools and domain specific tools?
30. Describe, in brief, the following domain specific tools:
    (*a*) School management system
    (*b*) Reservation system
    (*c*) Weather forecasting system
    (*d*) Inventory management system

❑ ❑ ❑

Chapter 4

Problem Solving and Program Planning

Learning Objectives

After reading this chapter, students will be able to

- explain the importance of problem solving
- explain the importance of program planning and design
- explain the various program design tools
- design solutions of typical problems

4.1 INTRODUCTION

Suppose you are asked by your mathematics teacher to solve an arithmetic problem and you are not familiar with the steps involved in solving that problem. In such a situation, you will not be able to solve the problem. The same principle applies to writing the program. A programmer cannot write instructions for a computer unless the programmer knows how to solve the problem manually.

Let us imagine that you know the steps to be followed for solving the given problem but while solving the problem, you forget to apply some of the steps or you apply some of the steps in wrong sequence. Obviously, you will get a wrong answer. Similarly, while writing a program, if the programmer leaves out some of the instructions or writes the instructions in wrong sequence, the computer will give a wrong answer.

Thus, to write an effective and efficient program, it is necessary that the programmer must write each and every instruction in the proper sequence. However, the sequence of instructions, *referred to as logic*, of a program can be very complex. Therefore, in order to ensure that the program instructions are appropriate for the given problem and are in the correct sequence, program must be planned before they are written.

In this chapter, we will learn about the various tools that can be used to plan the program. Further, the use of each of these tools will be demonstrated by considering number of problems with whom you are already familiar.

4.2 PROBLEM SOLVING

As mentioned earlier, you will not be able to solve a problem if you don't know the steps involved in solving that problem. The same principle applies to writing a program. A programmer cannot write instructions to be given to the computer unless the programmer knows how to solve the problem manually.

Therefore, it is very important that before attempting to write a program, the programmers must solve the problem manually. While solving a problem, the programmer will be able to learn about the various steps to be performed and the sequence in which these steps are to be performed.

To demonstrate how the programmer should proceed, let us consider a familiar example of finding the roots of a quadratic equation of type

$$ax^2 + bx + c = 0 \qquad \text{provided } a \neq 0.$$

The roots of such an equation are given by the formula:

$$root_{1,2}=\frac{-b\pm\sqrt{b^2-4ac}}{2a}$$ where $b^2 - 4ac$ is known as the discriminant.

Depending on the sign of the discriminant, there are three are mutually exclusive possibilities for the roots:

Case 1: If $b^2 - 4ac < 0$, then the root are imaginary, and we can compute real part and imaginary part separately as

$$\text{real part} = -\frac{b}{2a} \quad \text{and} \quad \text{imaginary part} = \frac{\sqrt{-(b^2-4ac)}}{2a}$$

Once we know the real and imaginary part of the root, we can determine the actual roots as (real part $\pm$ *i* imaginary part).

Case 2: If $b^2 - 4ac = 0$, then the roots are real and equal, and are computed as

$$\text{each root} = -\frac{b}{2a}$$

Case 3: If $b^2 - 4ac > 0$, then the roots are real and distinct and are computed as

$$\text{root1} = \frac{-b-\sqrt{b^2-4ac}}{2a} \quad \text{and} \quad \text{root2} = \frac{-b+\sqrt{b^2-4ac}}{2a}$$

Therefore, we will proceed as

For a given set of values of *a*, *b* and *c*, compute expression $b^2 - 4ac$. Now compare the computed value of $b^2 - 4ac$ with zero. If it is less than zero, compute the roots as shown in case 1; if it is equal to zero, compute the roots as shown in case 2; and if it is greater than zero, compute the roots as shown in case 3.

In this book, for each problem considered, we will first see how to solve it.

4.3 PROGRAM PLANNING AND DESIGN

Planning is very important in every walk of life. Even for our routine kind of things, we have to plan. Such a plan of doing things is also as *process*. For example, we have to plan our monthly budget otherwise things can go astray and we may not enough money left in our pocket towards the end of the month.

Planning should not be in the mind only (*adhoc process*), you must write it down, *i.e.*, you must document it (*defined process*). The results of *adhoc process* are not guaranteed where as the results of *defined process* are guaranteed and predictable.

Likewise, if you know the steps to be followed for solving a given problem but you have not documented them, you may forget to apply some of the steps or you may apply some of the steps in wrong sequence. Obviously, you will get a wrong answer. Similarly, while writing a program, if the programmer leaves out some of the instructions or writes the instructions in wrong sequence, the computer will give a wrong answer.

The various tools collectively referred to as *program design tools*, that helps in planning the program are *algorithm*, *flowchart* and *pseudocode*.

In the subsequent section, we will discuss about these tools, and demonstrate their use through illustrative examples.

4.4 ALGORITHMS

An *algorithm* is defined as a finite sequence of instructions defining the solution of a particular problem, where each instruction is numbered.

However, in order to qualify as an algorithm, every sequence of instructions must satisfy the following criteria:

- ***Input***: There are zero or more values which are externally supplied.
- ***Output***: At least one value is produced.
- ***Definiteness***: Each step must be clear and unambiguous, *i.e.*, having one and only one meaning).
- ***Finiteness***: If we trace the steps of an algorithm, then for all cases, the algorithm must terminate after a finite number of steps.
- ***Effectiveness***: Each step must be sufficiently basic that it can in principle be carried out by a person using only paper and pencil. In addition, not only each step is definite, it must also be feasible.

Example 4.1:

Formulate an algorithm to display the nature of roots of a quadratic equation of type

$ax^2 + bx + c = 0$ provided $a \neq 0$.

Solution: Roots of the quadratic equation are given by the formula:

$$x_{1,2} = \frac{-b \pm \sqrt{b^2 - 4ac}}{2a}$$

where the expression $b^2 - 4ac$ is known as the discriminant.

Depending on the sign of discriminant, there are three possibilities for roots:

1. If $b^2 - 4ac < 0$, then the root are imaginary.
2. If $b^2 - 4ac = 0$, then the roots are real and equal.
3. If $b^2 - 4ac > 0$, then the roots are real and distinct.

The complete algorithm will look like

Algorithm 4.1

Step 1: Input values of *a, b* and *c*

Step 2: Compute $b^2 - 4ac$ and denote its value by variable *disc*

Step 3: Is *disc* < 0? If yes then goto step 7 else goto step 4

Step 4: Is *disc* > 0? If yes then goto step 9 else goto step 5

Step 5: Output "roots are real and equal"

Step 6: Goto step 10

Step 7: Output "roots are imaginary"

Step 8: Goto step 10

Step 9: Output "roots are real and distinct"

Step 10: Stop

4.5 FLOWCHARTS

A flowchart is a pictorial representation of an algorithm. A flowchart uses different shapes to denote different types of instructions. The actual instructions are written within the shapes using clear and concise statements. These shapes are connected by directed lines to indicate the sequence in which instructions are to be executed.

Normally, an algorithm is first represented in the form of a flowchart and then the flowchart is expressed in some programming language to prepare a program. The main advantage of this approach in program writing is that while drawing a flowchart, one is not concerned with the details of the syntax of the programming language. Moreover, since a flowchart shows the sequence of instructions in a pictorial form, any error in logic can be detected more easily that in the case of a program. Once the flowchart is ready, the programmer can forget about the logic and can concentrate only on coding the instructions in each shape in terms of the syntax of the programming language. This will ensure an error-free program.

A flowchart, therefore, is a picture of the logic to be implemented by the program. It is simply a tool assisting the programmer to lay out, in a visual, two-dimensional format, ideas on how to organize a sequence of steps necessary to solve a problem by computer. It is basically the plan to be followed when the program is written. It acts like a road map for a programmer and guides him/her how to go from the starting point to the final point while writing a program.

Experienced programmers most often skip the flowchart while writing the program. However, for a beginner, it is recommended that flowchart must be drawn first in order to reduce the number of errors and omissions in the programs. Moreover, it is a good practice to have a flowchart because flowchart is very helpful during the testing of a program as well as while incorporating further modifications in the program.

Flowchart Symbols

As mentioned, flowchart uses boxes of different shapes to denote different types of instructions. The communication of the program logic through flowcharts is made easier through the use of symbols that have standardized meanings. For example, a diamond always means a decision. Only few symbols are needed to represent the necessary instructions in a flowchart. These symbols are standardized by American National Standards Institute (ANSI). Table 4.1 shows various symbols used in flowcharts along with their name and brief description.

Oval Symbol – This symbol is used to indicate the beginning (START) and ending (STOP) in the program logic flow. It is the first and the last symbol in the program logic.

Parallelogram Symbol – This symbol is used to denote the input to the program or output from the program. If there is a program instruction to input data from any input device, that may include keyboard, disk, tape, etc., that step will be indicated in the flowchart with this symbol. Similarly, if there is an instruction to output data to any output device, that may include terminal screen, printer, disk, tape, etc., that step will be indicated in the flowchart with this symbol.

Table 4.1: Various flowchart symbols and their brief description

Symbol	Name	Purpose
	Oval	*Terminal* - to mark the beginning and end of the program logic flow.
	Parallelogram	*Input/Output* - to denote the input to the program or output from the program.
	Rectangle	*Processing* - to denote the arithmetic operations and movement of data.
	Diamond	*Decision* - to denote a point where decision has to be made to branch to one of the alternatives.
	Small circle	*Connector* - To provide a logical link between segments of a flowchart.
→ ↓	Directed lines	*Flow Lines* - To indicate the sequence in which instructions are to be executed.

Rectangle Symbol – This symbol is used to denote the arithmetic and data movement instructions. Thus, all arithmetic instructions such as addition, subtraction, multiplication and division are shown by this symbol. The other instructions such as moving data from one location in memory to other locations are also shown using this symbol. When more that one arithmetic and data movement instructions are to be executed consecutively, they can be placed in the same symbol and they are assumed to be executed in the order of their appearance.

Diamond Symbol – This symbol is used to denote a point where decision has to be made to branch to one of the alternatives.

It is important to note that the criteria for making the decision should be indicated clearly within the decision box. Moreover, the expression upon which each of the possible exit paths will be executed should be identified and all the possible paths should be accounted for. During execution, the appropriate path is followed depending upon the result of the decision.

Small Circle Symbol – This symbol is used to provide a logical link between segments of a flowchart. If a flowchart is very long, the flow lines start criss-crossing at many places that cause confusion and thus reduce understandability of the flowchart. Moreover, there are instances when a flowchart becomes too long to fit in a single page and the use of flow lines becomes impossible.

Thus, whenever a flowchart becomes complex enough that the number and direction of flow lines is confusing or it spreads over more than one page, it is useful to utilize the connector symbol as a substitute for flow lines. This symbol represents an entry from, or an exit to another part of the flowchart. A connector symbol is represented by a small circle and a letter or a digit is placed within the small circle to indicate the link. A pair of identically labeled connector symbols is commonly used to indicate a continued flow when the use of flow line is confusing. Therefore, two connectors with identical label serve the same function as a long flow line. That is, they show an exit to another section of the flowchart, or they indicate an entry from another section of the flowchart.

Now the question arises – *How is it possible to determine if a connector is used as an entry or an exit point*?

It is very simple – if an arrow enters into a connector, it is an exit point and the program control is transferred to an identically labeled connector that does have an outlet; if an arrow leaves a connector, it is an entry point and the control is received from an identically labeled connector. It may be noted that connectors do not represent any operation and their use in a flowchart is only for the sake of convenience and clarity.

Directed Lines – These lines are used to indicate the sequence in which instructions are to be executed. The normal sequence is from top to bottom and left to right. The crossing of these lines should be avoided whenever possible.

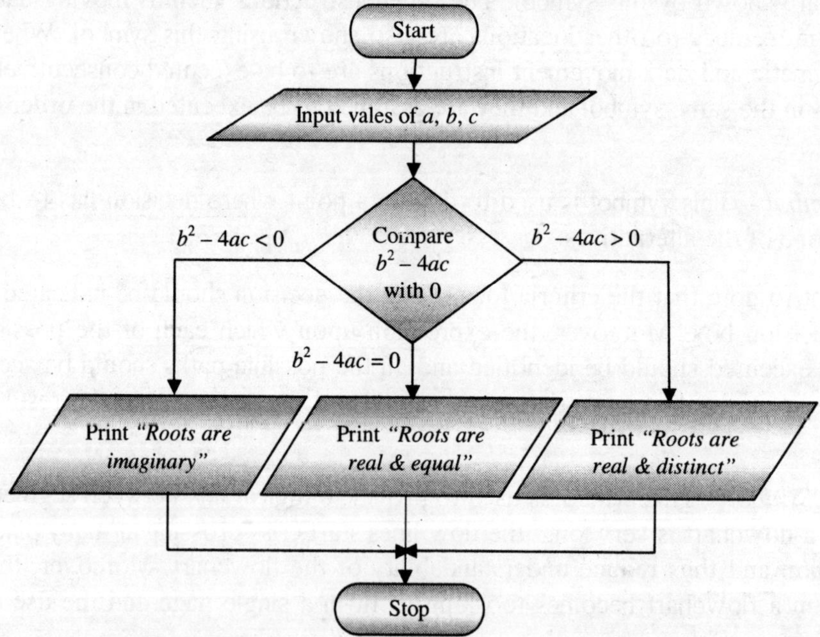

Figure 4.1: Flowchart to find the nature of roots of a quadratic equation

4.6 PSEUDOCODE

Pseudocode is another design tool that can be used for planning the program. The word "pseudo" means imitation or false and the word "code" refers to the instruction written in a programming language. Pseudocode, therefore, is an imitation of actual computer instruction. Pseudo instructions are phrases written in English like statements. Instead of using symbols to describe the logic of the program, as in flowcharts, pseudocode uses a structure that resembles computer instructions. Because, it emphasizes the design of the program, pseudocode is also called *Program Design Language* (PDL).

Pseudocode is made up of the following basic logic structures that have proved to be sufficient for writing any computer program:

1. Sequence
2. Selection (*If . . . then . . . Endif, If . . . then . . . Else . . .Endif*)
3. Iteration (*For . . . Endfor, While . . . Endwhile, Do . . . While*)

Sequence logic is used for performing instructions one after another in sequence. Thus, for sequence logic, pseudocode instructions are written in the sequence in which they are to be executed. The flow of logic is from top to bottom.

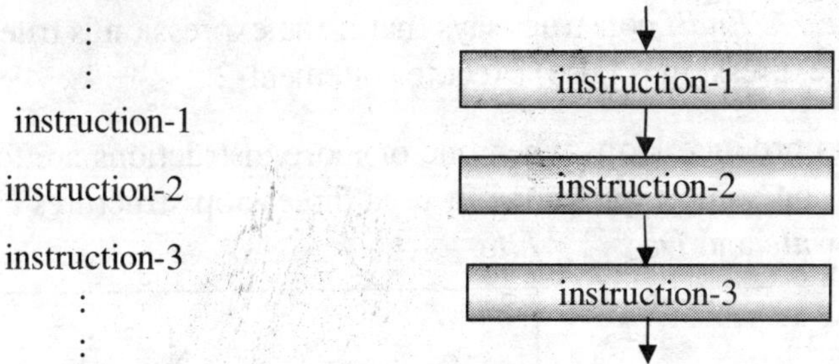

Figure 4.2: Pseudocode and flowchart for sequence structure

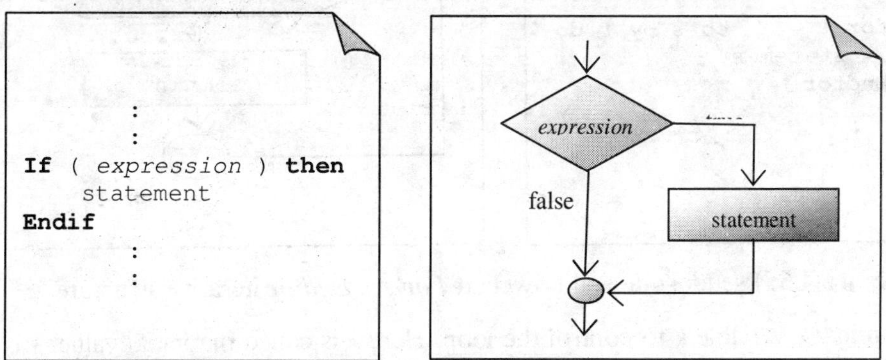

Figure 4.3: Pseudocode and flowchart for *If . . . then . . . Endif* selection structure

Selection logic, also known as decision logic, is used for making decision. It is used for selecting a proper path out of the alternative paths in the program logic. Decision logic is depicted as either *If . . . then . . . Endif* or an *If . . . then . . . Else . . . Endif* structure.

The *If . . . then . . . Endif* construct says that if the expression is true, then execute statement else (if the expression is false) skip over the statement.

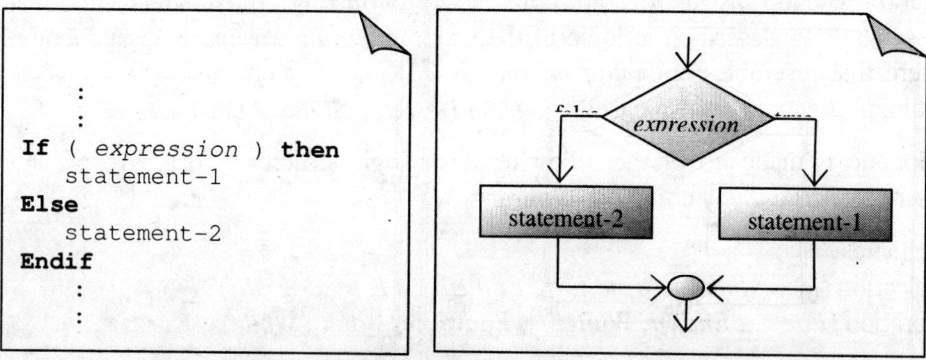

Figure 4.4: Pseudocode and flowchart for *If . . . then . . . Else . . . Endif* selection structure

The *If . . . then . . . Else . . . Endif* construct says that if the expression is true then execute statement-1, else (if the expression is false) execute statement-2.

Iterative logic is used to produce loops when one or more instructions are to be executed several times depending on some expressions. It uses three loop structures called *For . . . Endfor, While . . . Endwhile* and *Do . . . While.*

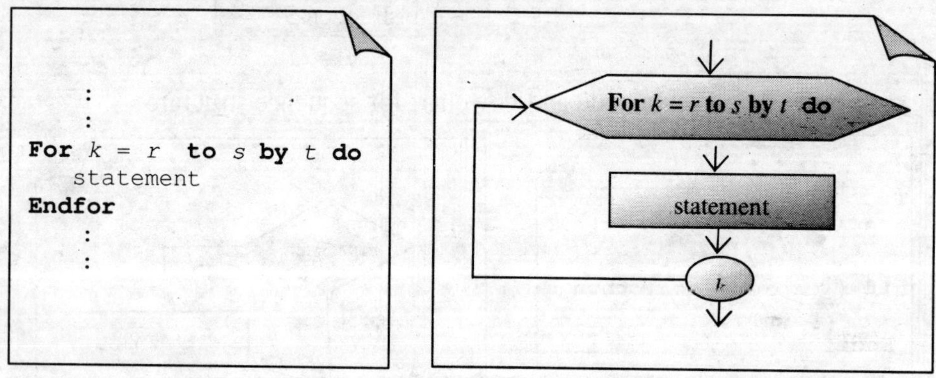

Figure 4.5: Pseudocode and flowchart *For . . . Endfor* iterative structure

It uses an index variable *k* to control the loop. Here *r* is called the initial value, *s* is called the final value and *t* is called the step size, which may be positive (increment) or negative (decrement).

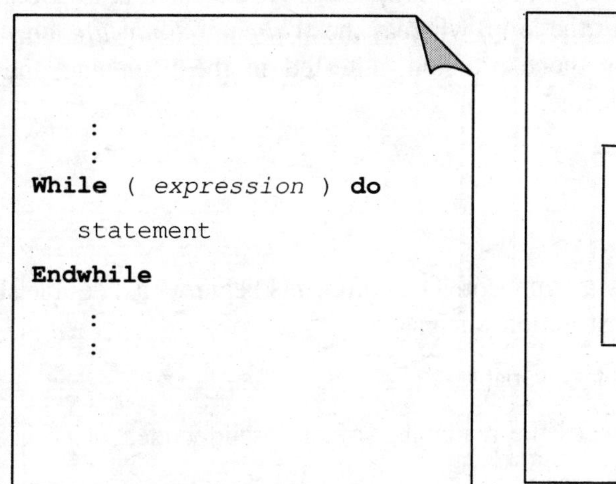

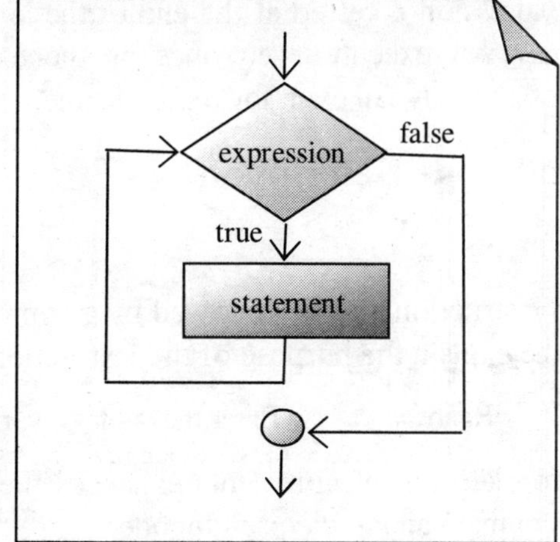

Figure 4.6: Pseudocode and flowchart for *While . . . Endwhile* iterative structure

The *For . . . Endfor* loop is used when the number of iterations is known. On the other side, *While . . . Endwhile* and *Do . . . While* loops are used when the number of iterations is not known. Both *While . . . Endwhile* and *Do . . . While* continues to execute as long as the expression is true.

The only difference between them is *Do . . . While* loop is always executed at least once as the expression is tested at the end of the loop, whereas the *While . . . Endwhile* loop may or may not execute even once as the expression is tested in the beginning and the expression may fail even for the first time.

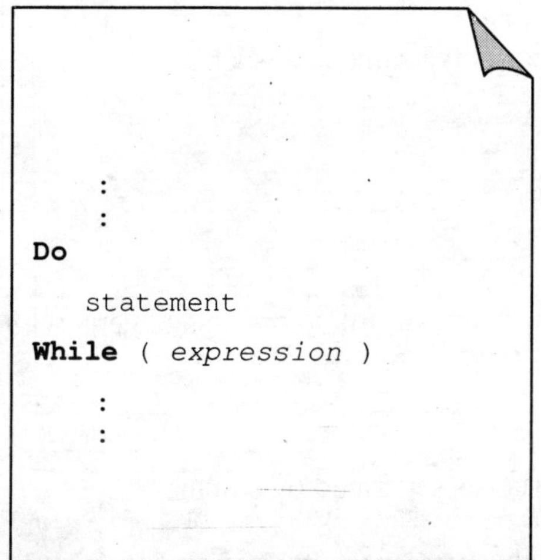

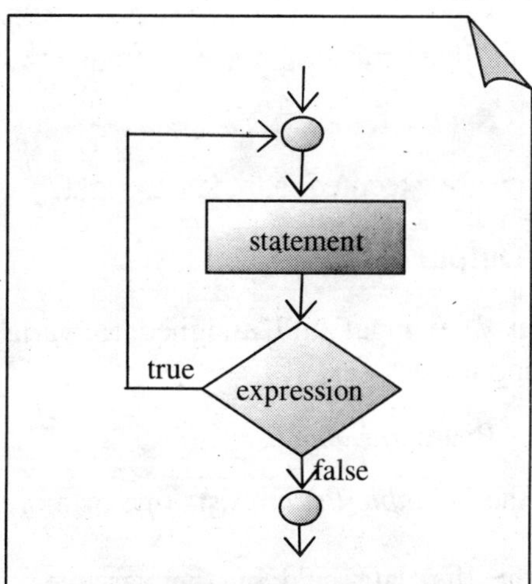

Figure 4.7: Pseudocode and flowchart for *Do . . . While* iterative structure

The only difference between them is *Do . . . While* loop is always executed at least once as the expression is tested at the end of the loop, whereas the *While . . . Endwhile* loop may or may not execute even once as the expression is tested in the beginning and the expression may fail even for the first time.

Pseudocode Description

Comments

Each instruction may be followed by a comment. The comments begin with a double slash, and the explain the purpose of the instruction, such as

Read: *n* // Enter the value of variable *n*

Appropriate use of comments enhances the readability of the pseudocode, which in turn helps in maintaining the pseudocode.

Variable Names

For variable names, we will use italicized lowercase letters such as *max*, *loc*, etc., whereas for defined constants, if any, we will use uppercase letters.

Assignment Statement

The assignment statement will use the notation as

Set $max = a_i$

to assign the value of a_i to *max*. The right hand side of the assignment statement can have a *value, a variable* or *an expression.*

However, if several assignment statements appear in the same line, such as

Set $k = 1$, $loc = 1$, $max = a_i$

then they are executed from left to right.

Input/Output

Data may be input and assigned to variables by means of a *read* statement with the following format

Read: *Variable list*

where the *Variable list* consists one or more variables separated by comma.

Similarly, the data held by the variables and the messages, if any, enclosed in double quotes can be output by means of a *write* statement with the following format

Print: *message* and/or *Variable list*

where the *message* and the variables in the *Variable list* are separated by comma.

Execution of Instructions

The instructions in the pseudocode are usually executed one after the other as they appear in the pseudocode. However, there may be instances when some instructions are skipped or some instructions may be repeated as a result of certain expressions.

Completion of the Algorithm

The pseudocode is completed with the execution of the last instruction. However, the pseudocode can be terminated at any intermediate state using the *exit* instruction.

Pseudocode to display the nature of roots of a quadratic equation of the type

$ax^2 + bx + c = 0$ provided $a \neq 0$.

Pseudocode 4.1

```
Begin
   Read: a, b, c
   Set disc = b^2 - 4ac
   If ( disc < 0 ) then
      Print: "roots are imaginary"
   Else
      If ( disc > 0 ) then
         Print: "roots are real and distinct"
      Else
         Print: "roots are real and equal"
      Endif
   Endif
End.
```

If you look at the algorithm, flowchart and pseudocode for program design to find the nature of the roots of the quadratic equation, you will find that the logic in flowchart is easy to understand whereas the pseudocode is much closer to the actual program.

In this chapter, we will consider flowchart and pseudocode to express the design of the program.

4.7 ILLUSTRATIVE EXAMPLES

Example 4.2:

Draw flowchart and write pseudocode to find the largest of three numbers, say *a*, *b*, *c*.

Solution: We first compare *a* with *b*. If *a* is greater than *b* then we compare *a* with *c*. If *a* is greater than *c*, then *a* is taken as the largest number otherwise we take c as the largest number.

However, if *a* is not greater than *b*, we compare *b* with *c*. If *b* is greater than *c* then *b* is taken as the largest number otherwise we take *c* as the largest number.

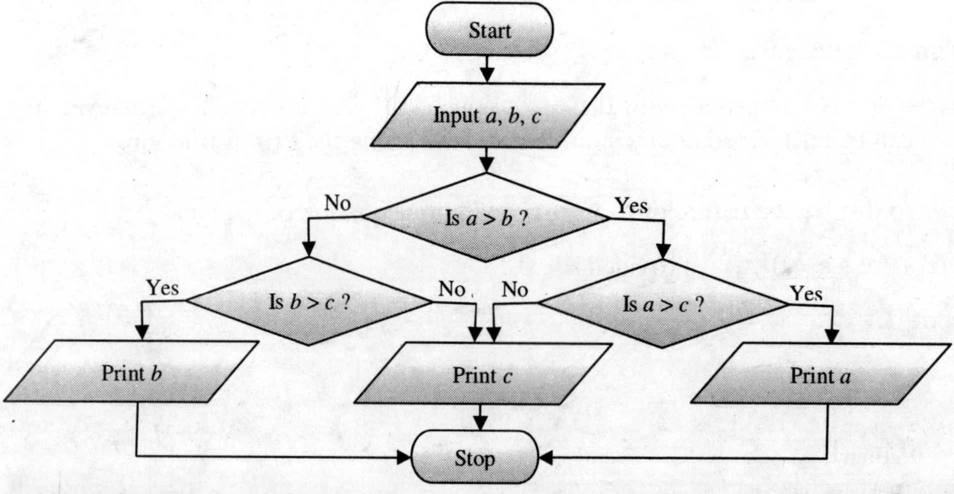

Pseudocode 4.2

```
Begin
    Read: a, b, c
    If ( a > b ) then
        If ( a > c ) then
            Print: a
        Else
            Print: c
        Endif
    Else
        If ( b > c ) then
            Print: b
        Else
            Print: c
        Endif
    Endif
End.
```

Figure 4.8: Flowchart & pseudocode to find largest of three numbers

Example 4.3:

Draw flowchart and write pseudocode to find the largest of four numbers, say *a*, *b*, *c*, *d*.

Solution: For four or more numbers, the solution of Example 4.2 will become very cumbersome. Therefore, we will follow an alternate approach.

We take first number as the largest number and store it in a variable, say *max*. Then, we compare the second number with the *max*, and if second number is greater than max, then second number is taken as the largest by storing it in *max*. .

Same process is repeated for remaining numbers, and the final value of *max* given the largest number among given four numbers.

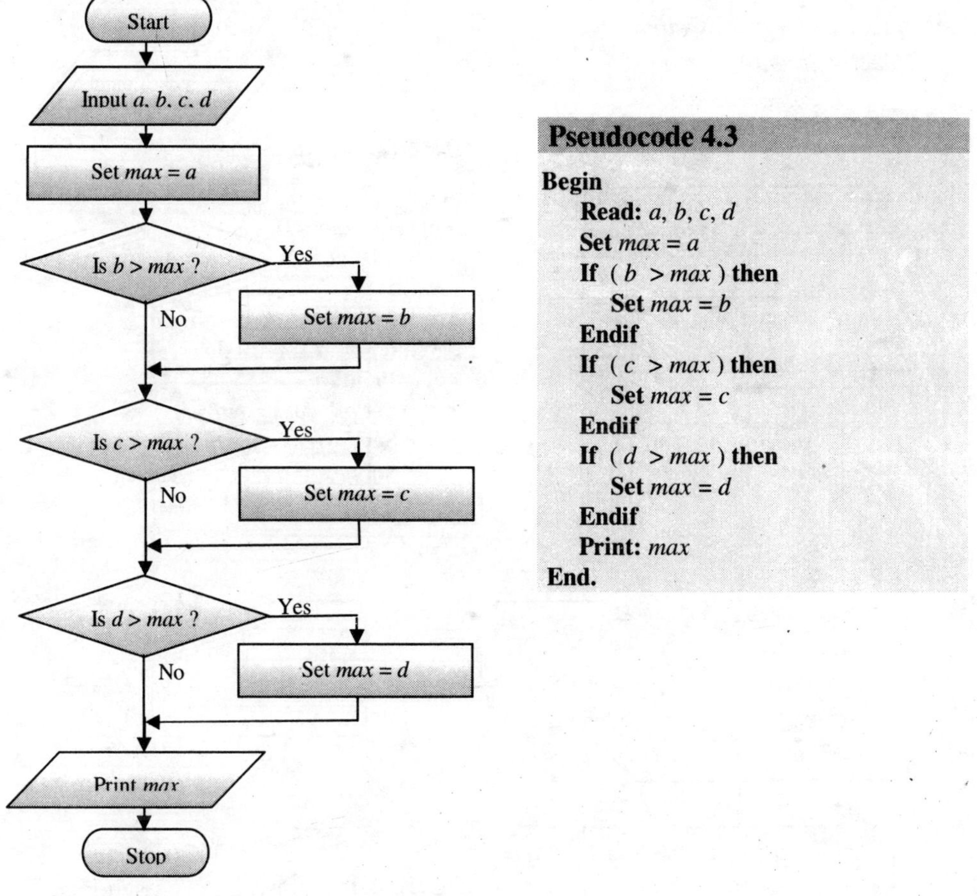

Pseudocode 4.3

```
Begin
    Read: a, b, c, d
    Set max = a
    If ( b > max ) then
        Set max = b
    Endif
    If ( c > max ) then
        Set max = c
    Endif
    If ( d > max ) then
        Set max = d
    Endif
    Print: max
End.
```

Figure 4.9: Flowchart & pseudocode to find largest of four numbers

Example 4.4:

Fibonacci sequence is given below:

0 1 1 2 3 5 8 13 21 . . .

Draw a flowchart and write pseudocode to generate the above sequence up to the term less than or equal to 100.

Solution: Observe that, leaving first two terms, each term is obtained as the sum of the immediately preceding two terms.

If we use variable *previous* for previous term, *current* for current term, *next* for next term, and setting *previous* and *current* to values 0 and 1 respectively, i.e., first two terms of the sequence, then the entire sequence can be generated by using the recurrence relation

next = *previous* + *current*
replace *previous* by *current*
replace *current* by *next*

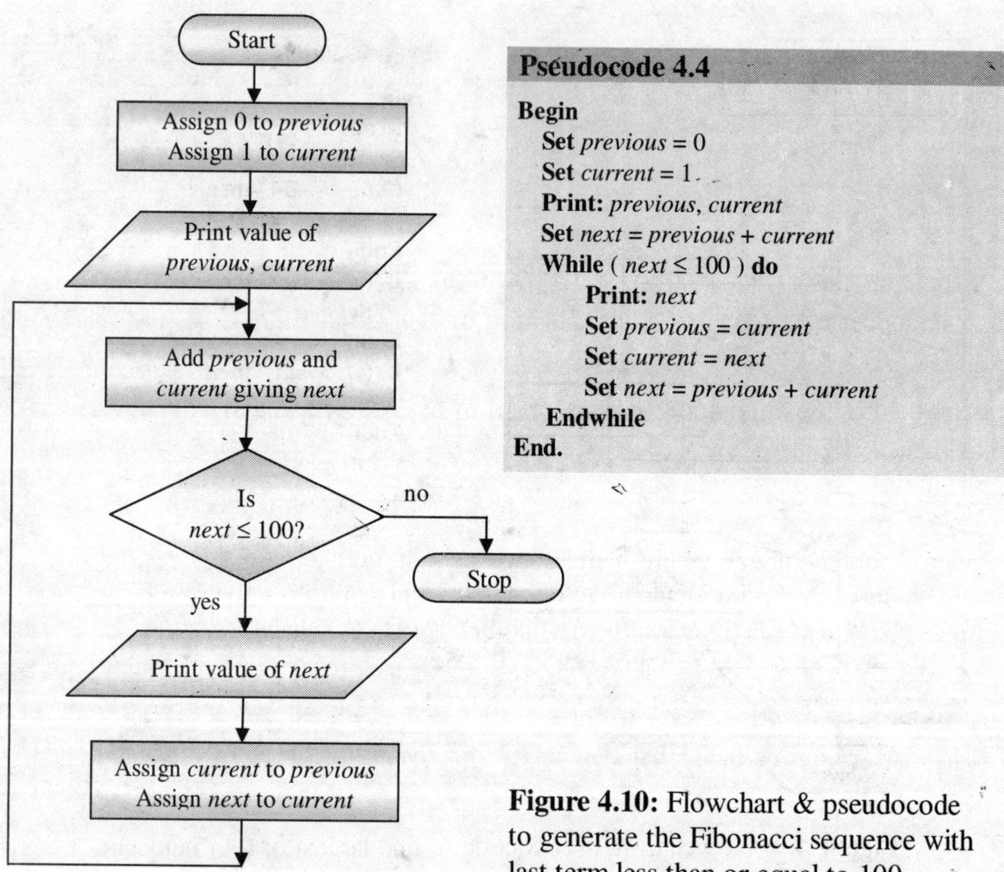

Pseudocode 4.4

```
Begin
  Set previous = 0
  Set current = 1
  Print: previous, current
  Set next = previous + current
  While ( next ≤ 100 ) do
      Print: next
      Set previous = current
      Set current = next
      Set next = previous + current
  Endwhile
End.
```

Figure 4.10: Flowchart & pseudocode to generate the Fibonacci sequence with last term less than or equal to 100

Example 4.5:

Draw a flowchart and write pseudocode to print first *n* terms of the Fibonacci sequence. For example, if input value for *n* is 8, the output should be

0 1 1 2 3 5 8 13

Solution:

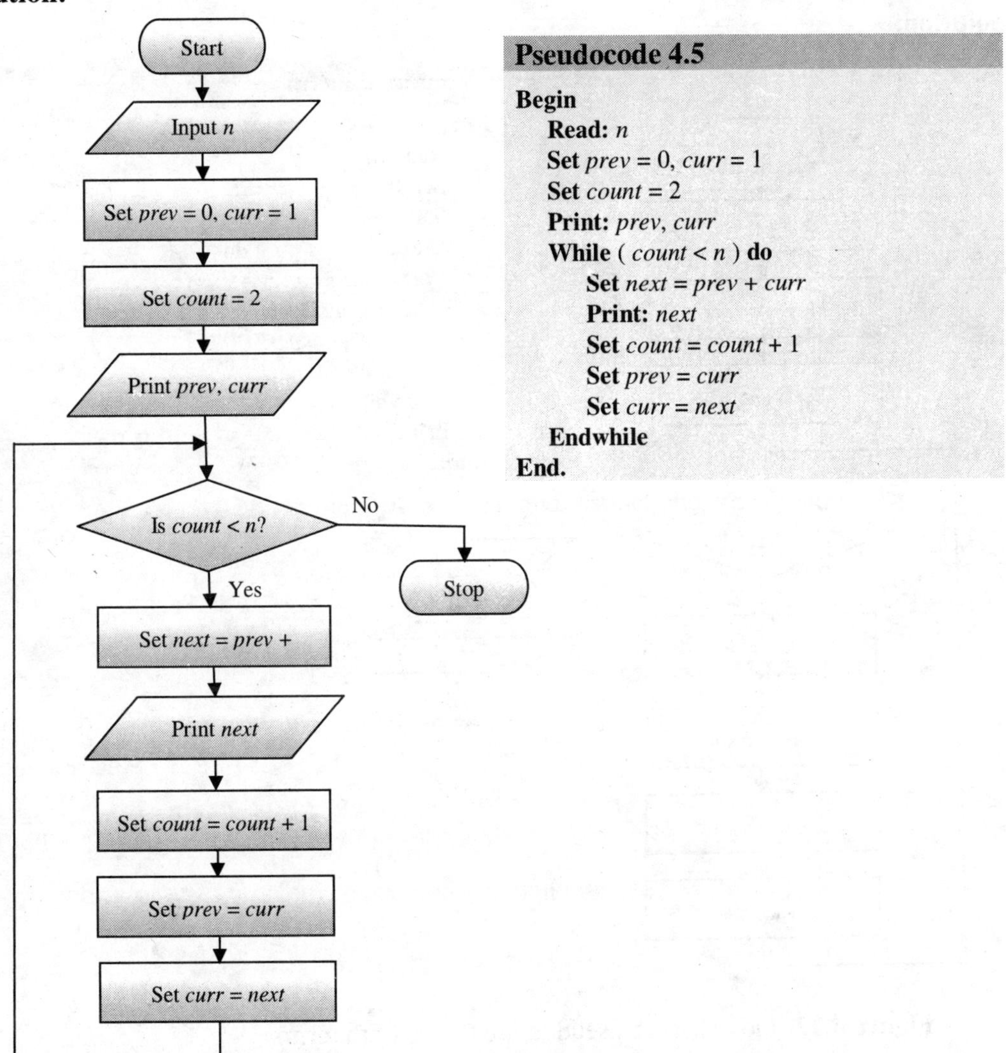

Pseudocode 4.5

```
Begin
    Read: n
    Set prev = 0, curr = 1
    Set count = 2
    Print: prev, curr
    While ( count < n ) do
        Set next = prev + curr
        Print: next
        Set count = count + 1
        Set prev = curr
        Set curr = next
    Endwhile
End.
```

Figure 4.11: Flowchart & pseudocode to print first *n* terms of the Fibonacci sequence

Example 4.6:

Draw a flowchart and write pseudocode to print *n*th term of the Fibonacci sequence. For example, if input value for *n* is 8, the output should be

13

Solution:

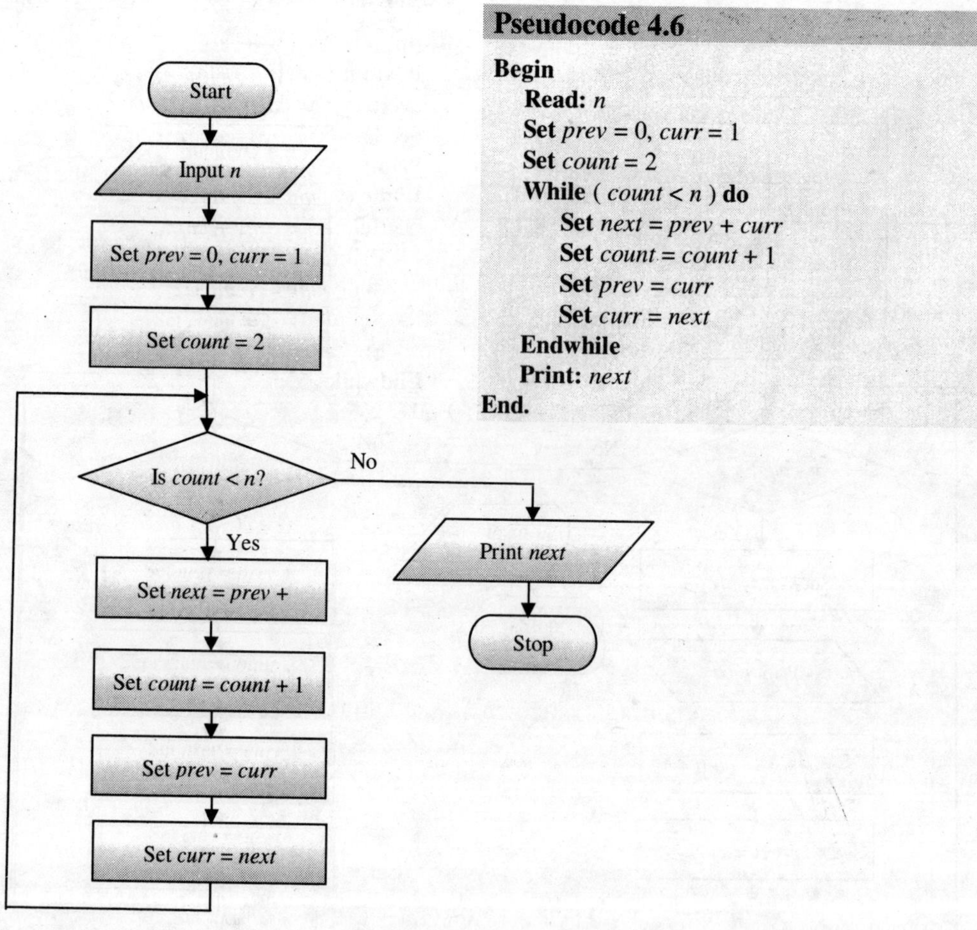

Pseudocode 4.6

```
Begin
   Read: n
   Set prev = 0, curr = 1
   Set count = 2
   While ( count < n ) do
      Set next = prev + curr
      Set count = count + 1
      Set prev = curr
      Set curr = next
   Endwhile
   Print: next
End.
```

Figure 4.12: Flowchart & pseudocode to print *n*th term of the Fibonacci sequence

Example 4.7:

Program to find whether the given natural number n is a prime number or not.

Solution: A natural number is said to be prime if it divisible by 1 and itself only, *i.e.*, it cannot be factorized. In addition, to this definition, an even number except 2 is not a prime number. Therefore, our test criteria becomes

1. If n is greater than 2 and is even then n is not a prime number.
2. If test at step 1 fails, then we try to divide number n by factors $k = 3, 5, 7, \ldots \sqrt{n}$. Therefore, if n is divisible by any value of k, number n is not a prime number.
3. If test at step 2 also fails, then n is a prime number.

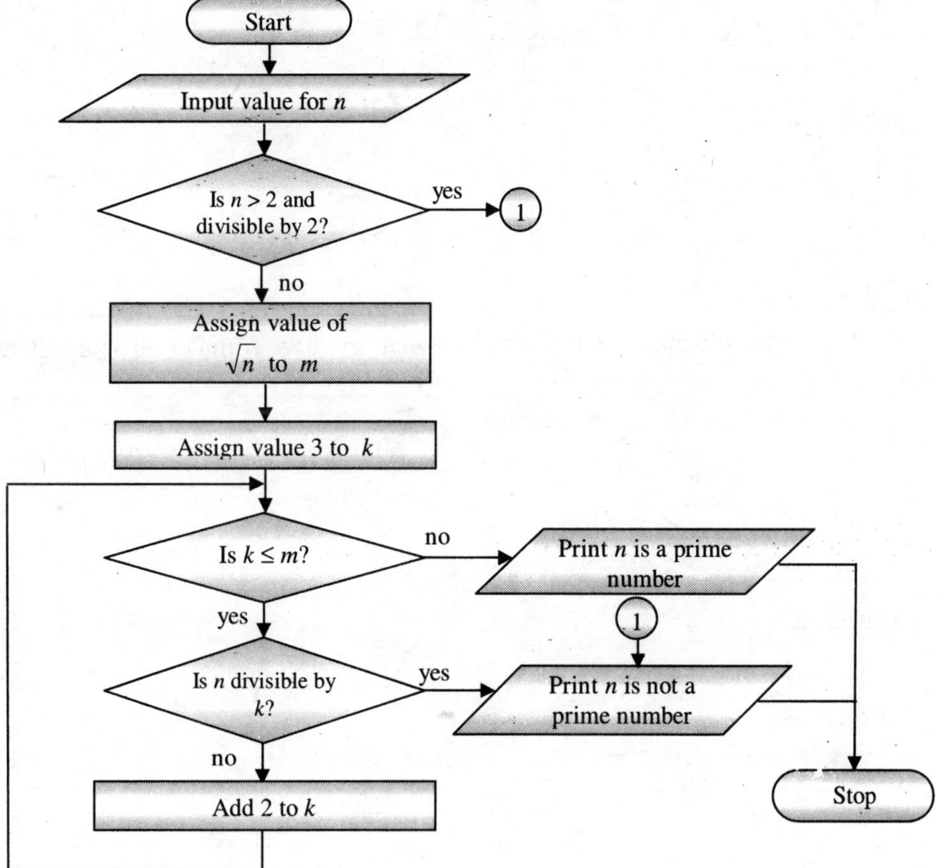

Figure 4.13: Flowchart to check whether number n is prime or not

Following is the pseudocode to find whether the given positive number *n* is a prime number or not.

Pseudocode 4.7

```
Begin
  Read: n
  If ( n > 2 and n mod 2 == 0 ) then
      Print: n, " is not a prime number"
      Exit
  Else
     Set m = √n
     For k = 3 to m by 2 do
         If ( n mod k == 0 ) then
             Print: n, " is not a prime number"
             Exit
         Endif
     Endfor
     Print: n, " is a prime number"
  Endif
End.
```

Example 4.8:

To find highest common factor (HCF)/, also known as greatest common divisor (GCD), of two natural numbers *m* and *n*.

Solution:

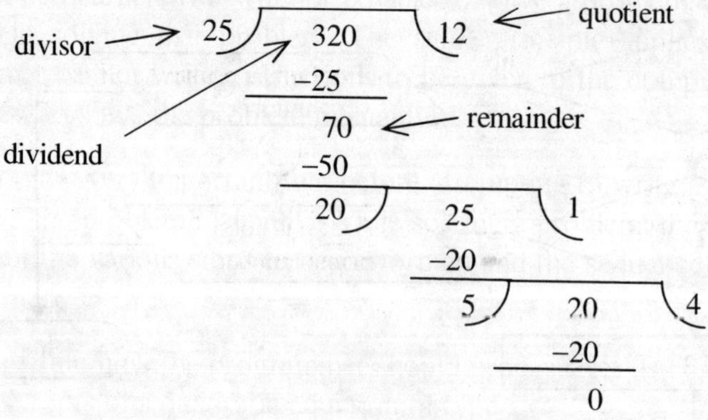

Figure 4.14: Illustration of computational procedure for HCF/GCD

Figure 4.14 demonstrates the long/continued division method to find the HCF/GCD of two natural numbers. You must have observed that in successive divisions, the divisor of the previous division becomes dividend, remainder of becomes divisor, and division is again carried out. This process is carried out till the reminder becomes zero, and the current divisor is taken as HCF/GCD of the given natural numbers.

This process can be implemented by using the following steps

1. Perform division.
2. If remainder is zero, then stop and take the divisor as HCF/GCD.
3. Replace dividend by divisor.
4. Replace divisor by remainder.
5. Repeat from step 1.

Start

Input m, n

Divide m by n and let the remainder be r

Is $r = 0$?

yes

Print "HCF/GCD = ", n

Stop

no

Replace m by n and n by r

Pseudocode 4.8

```
Begin
    Read: m, n
    Set r = m mod n
    While ( r ≠ 0 ) do
        Set m = n
        Set n = r
        Set r = m mod n
    Endwhile
    Print: "HCF/GCD = ", n
End.
```

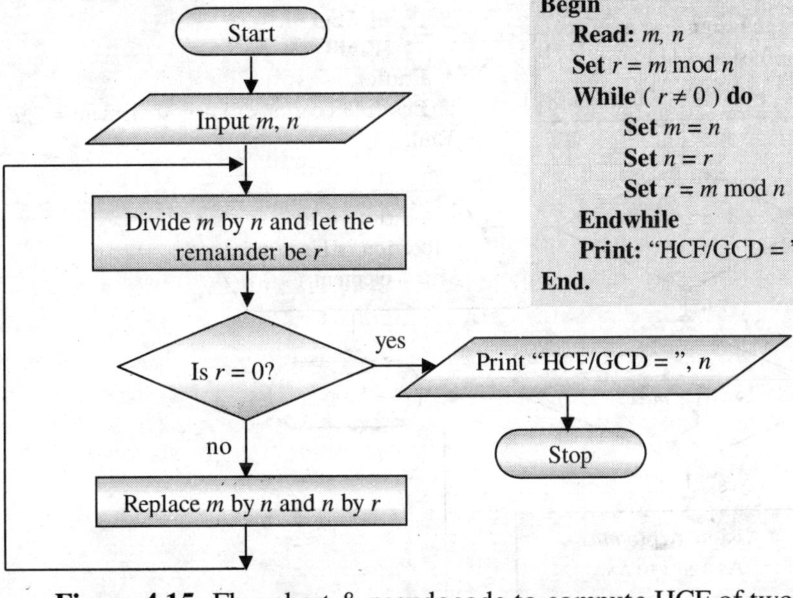

Figure 4.15: Flowchart & pseudocode to compute HCF of two numbers

Example 4.9:

Suppose a is a list of n real numbers, and we want to find the location, say *loc*, of the largest element of the list.

Solution: *This problem can be solved as follows*: We begin with *loc* = 1, and *max* = *a*[1]. We then compare *max* with each successive element *a*[*k*] of the list. If *a*[*k*] is greater than *max*, we then update *loc* and *max* as *loc* = *k* and *max* = *a*[*k*], respectively. The final value of *loc* gives the location of the largest element of the list.

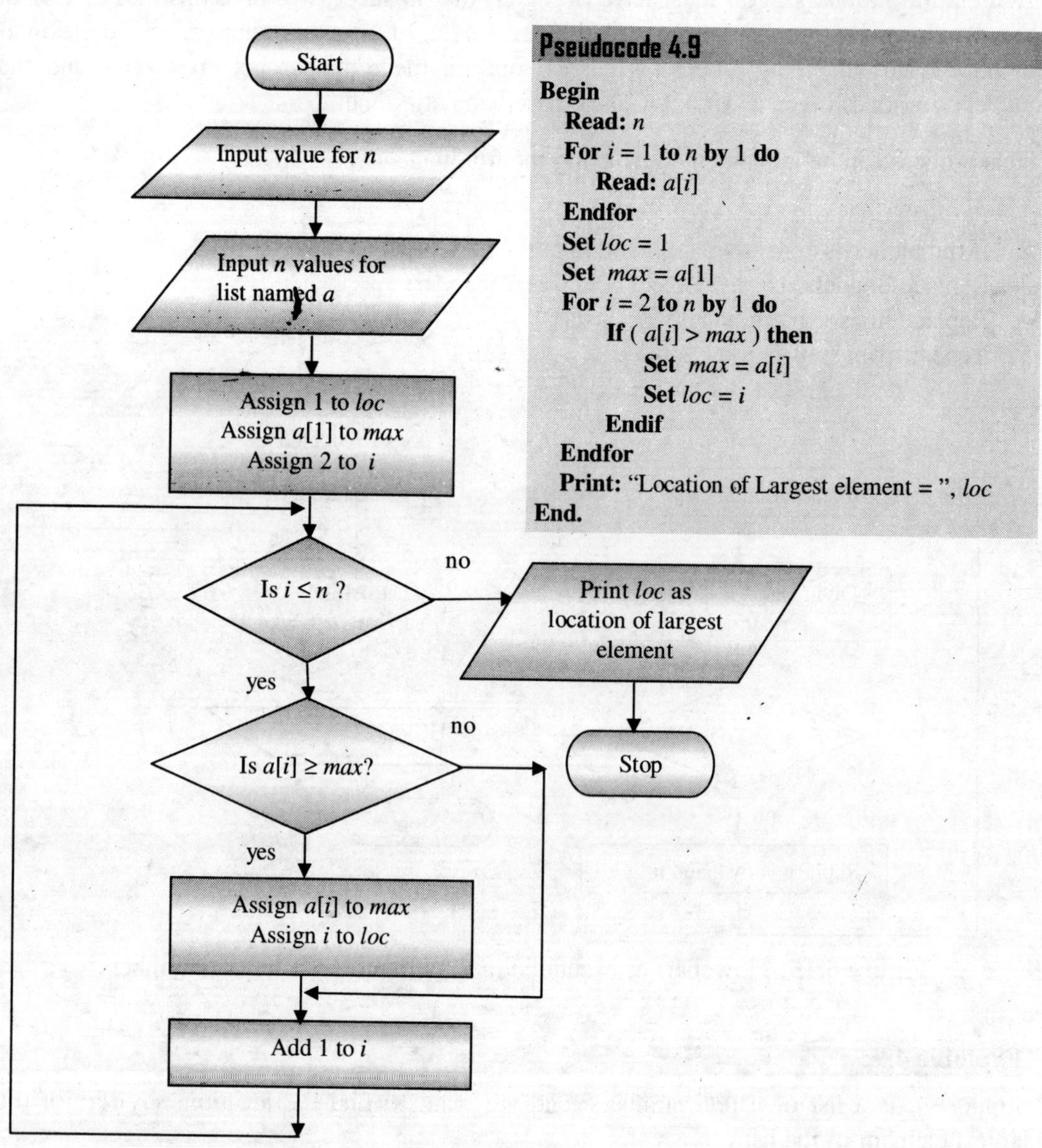

Pseudocode 4.9

```
Begin
  Read: n
  For i = 1 to n by 1 do
     Read: a[i]
  Endfor
  Set loc = 1
  Set max = a[1]
  For i = 2 to n by 1 do
       If ( a[i] > max ) then
           Set max = a[i]
           Set loc = i
       Endif
  Endfor
  Print: "Location of Largest element = ", loc
End.
```

Figure 4.16: Flowchart to find the location of the largest element from a list of numbers

Example 4.10:

Income tax for individuals is computed on slab rates as follows:

Income	Tax Payable
Upto Rs. 1,00,000/-	Nil
From Rs. 1,00,001/- to Rs. 2,00,000/-	10% of the excess over Rs. 1,00,000/-
From Rs. 2,00,001/- to Rs. 3,00,000/-	20% of the excess over Rs. 2,00,000/-
Above Rs. 3,00,000/-	30% of the excess over Rs. 3,00,000/-

Draw a flowchart and write a pseudocode that reads the income and prints the income tax due.

Solution: Note the following:

- If the income is upto Rs. 1,00,000/- only, then the tax is *nil.*
- If the income is in the range of Rs. 1,00,001/- to Rs. 2,00,000/-, then the tax is 10% of the amount in excess of Rs. 1,00,000/-.
- If the income is in the range of Rs. 2,00,001/- to Rs. 3,00,000/-, then the tax is 10% of Rs. 1,00,000/- (Rs. 10,000/-) for a slab of Rs. 1,00,001 to Rs. 2,00,000/- plus 20% of the amount in excess of Rs. 2,00,000/-.
- If the income is more than Rs. 3,00,000/-, then the tax is 10% of Rs. 1,00,000/- (Rs. 10,000/-) for a slab of Rs. 1,00,001 to Rs. 2,00,000/- plus 20% of Rs. 1,00,000/- (Rs. 20,000/-) for a slab of Rs. 2,00,001 to Rs. 3,00,000/- plus 30% of the amount in excess of Rs. 3,00,000/-.

Let us have hands on by computing the tax if the given income is

(*a*) Rs. 2,50,000/-
(*b*) Rs. 1,75,000/-
(*c*) Rs. 3,20,000/-

(*a*) *Tax Computations for income of Rs. 2,50,000/-*

For first Rs. 1,00,000/- Tax is Nil
For next Rs. 1,00,000/- Tax is 10,000/- (@ 10%)
For next Rs. 50,000/- Tax is 10,000/- (@ 20%)

Total Tax due Rs. 20,000/-

(*b*) *Tax Computations for income of Rs. 1,75,000/-*

For first Rs.1,00,000/- Tax is Nil
For next Rs. 75,000/- Tax is 7,500/- (@ 10%)

Total Tax due Rs. 7,500/-

(*c*) *Tax Computations for income of Rs. 3,20,000/-*

For first Rs. 1,00,000/-	Tax is Nil
For next Rs. 1,00,000/-	Tax is 10,000/- (@ 10%)
For next Rs. 1,00,000/-	Tax is 20,000/- (@ 20%)
For next Rs. 20,000/-	Tax is 6,000/- (@ 30%)
Total Tax due	Rs. 36,000/-

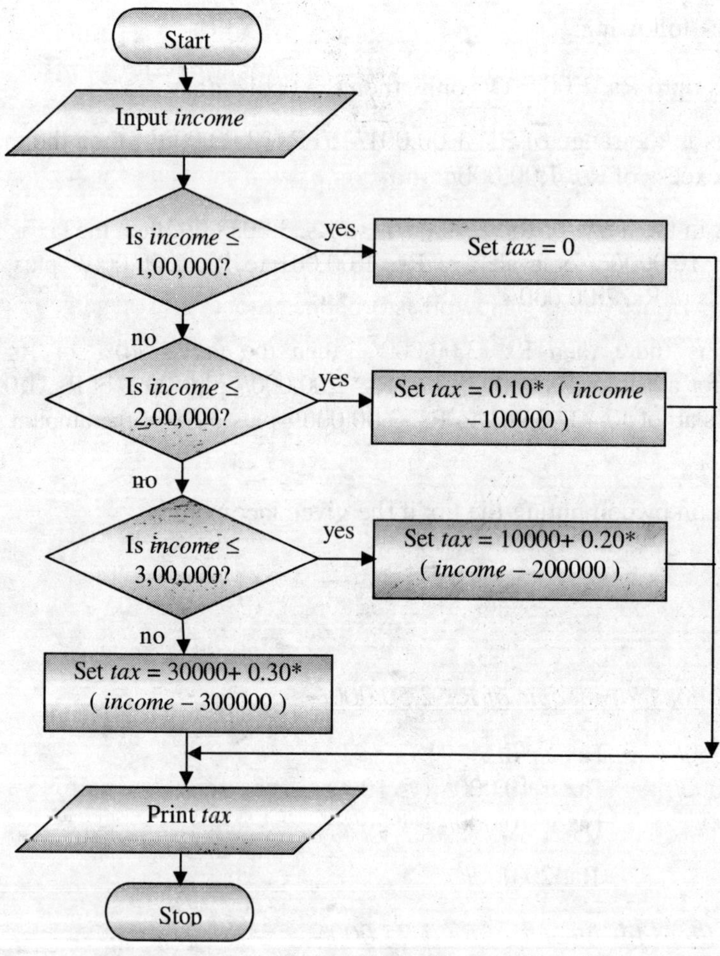

Figure 4.17: Flowchart to compute tax

Pseudocode 4.10

Begin
  Read: *income*
  If (*income* < 100000) **then**
    Set *tax* = 0
  Else if (*income* < 200000) **then**
    Set *tax* = 0.01 × (*income* − 100000)
  Else if (*income* < 300000) **then**
    Set *tax* = 10000 + 0.02 × (*income* − 200000)
  Else
    Set *tax* = 30000 + 0.03 × (*income* − 300000)
  Endif
  Print: *tax*
End.

Example 4.11:

Given measure of three line segments as a, b, and c. Draw a flowchart and also write pseudocode to check whether the line segments can be used to make a triangle.

Solution: By the Triangle Inequality, in order for three line segments to make a triangle, the sum of the lengths of any two line segments must exceed the length of the third line segment.

Pseudocode 4.11

Begin
  Read: *a*, *b*, *c*
  If ($a + b > c$) **then**
    If ($b + c > a$) **then**
      If ($c + a > b$) **then**
        Print: "Yes"
      Else
        Print: "No"
      Endif
    Else
      Print: "No"
    Endif
  Else
    Print: "No"
  Endif
End.

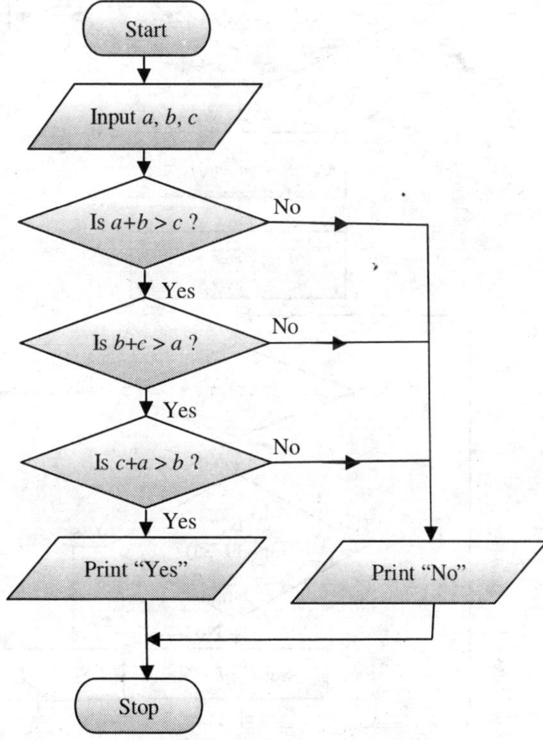

Figure 10.18: Flowchart & pseudocode to check whether a triangle can be formed from given three line segments

Example 4.12:

Draw a flowchart to print first *n* prime numbers.

Solution:

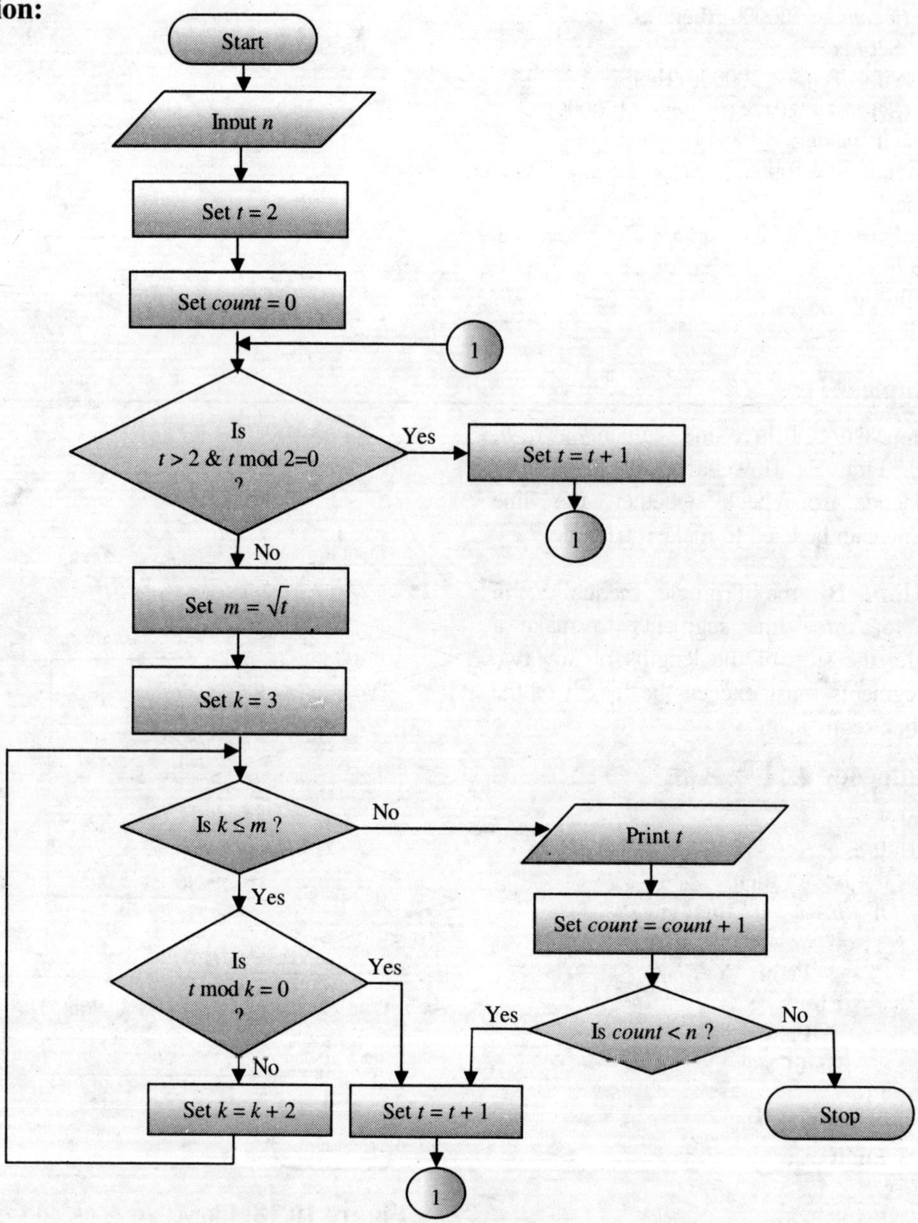

Start

Input n

Set $t = 2$

Set *count* = 0

1

Is $t > 2$ & t mod 2=0 ?

Yes

Set $t = t + 1$

1

No

Set $m = \sqrt{t}$

Set $k = 3$

Is $k \leq m$?

No

Print t

Set *count* = *count* + 1

Yes

Is t mod $k = 0$?

Yes

Yes

Is *count* < n ?

No

No

Set $k = k + 2$

Set $t = t + 1$

Stop

1

Figure 4.19: Flowchart to print first *n* prime numbers

Example 4.13:

Draw a flowchart to print *n*th prime number.

Solution:

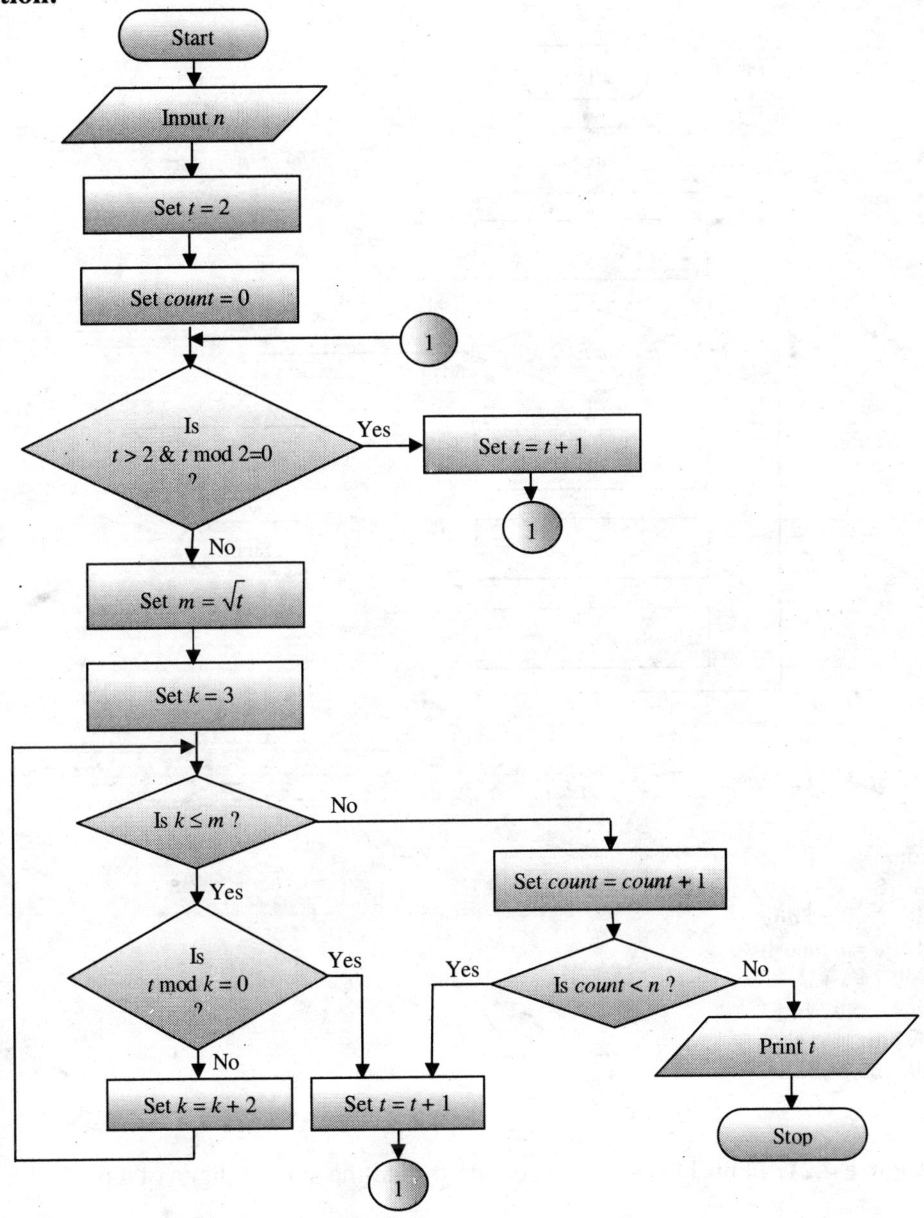

Figure 4.20: Flowchart to print *n*th prime number

Example 4.14:

Draw a flowchart and write pseudocode to find the sum of digits of a number *n*.

Solution:

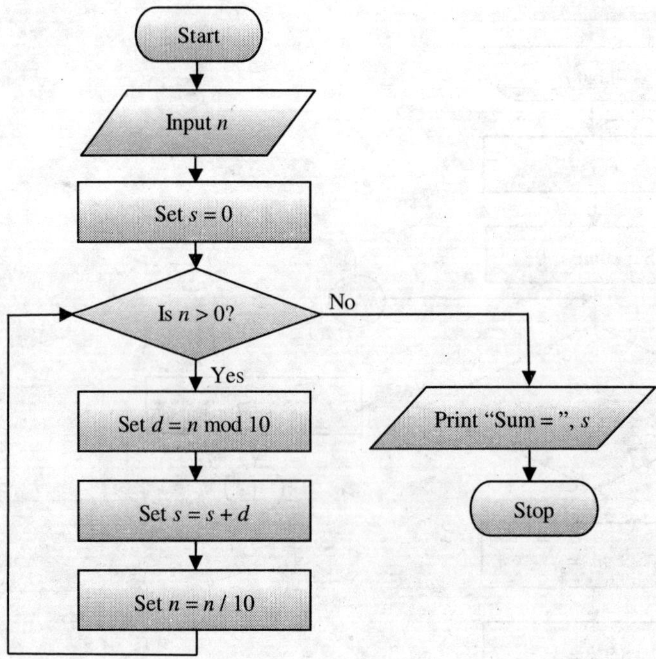

Pseudocode 4.12

```
Begin
   Read: n
   Set s = 0
   While ( n > 0 ) do
       Set d = n mod 10
       Set s = s + d
       Set n = n / 10
   Endwhile
   Print: "Sum = ", s
End.
```

Figure 4.21: Flowchart and pseudocode to find the sum of digits of a number

Example 4.15:

Draw a flowchart and write pseudocode to find the largest digit of a number *n*.

Solution:

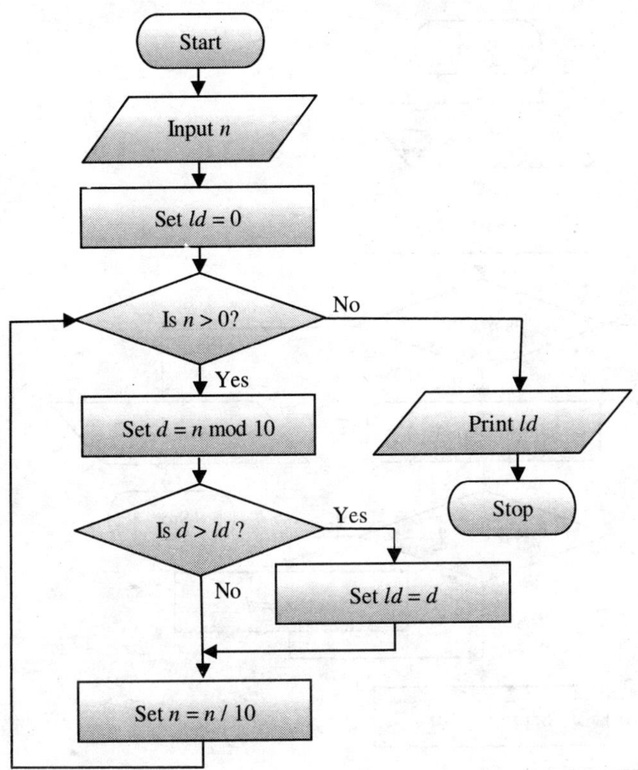

Pseudocode 4.13

```
Begin
   Read: n
   Set ld = 0
   While ( n > 0 ) do
      Set d = n mod 10
      If ( d > ld ) then
         Set ld = d
      Endif
   Endwhile
   Print: "Largest digit = ", ld
End.
```

Figure 4.22: Flowchart and pseudocode to find the largest digit of a number

Example 4.16:

Draw a flowchart and write pseudocode to find the largest digit of a number *n*.

Solution:

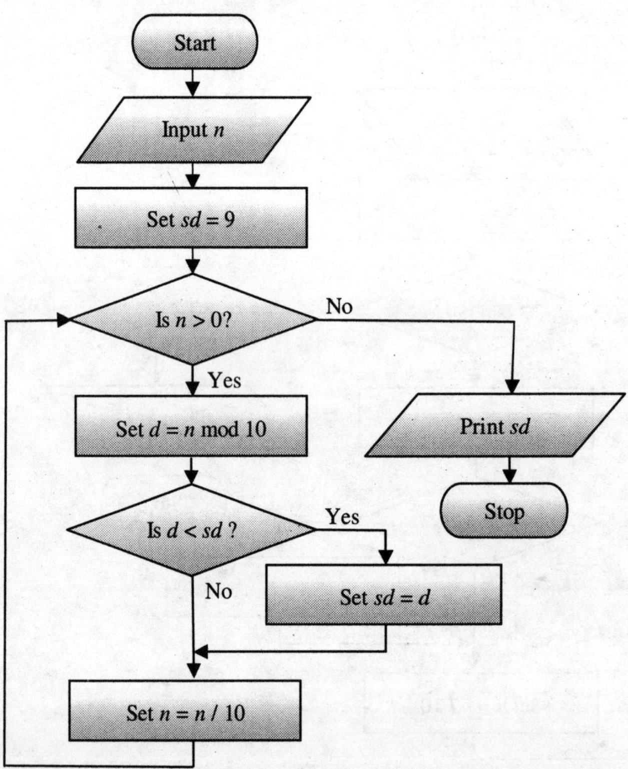

Pseudocode 4.14

```
Begin
   Read: n
   Set sd = 9
   While ( n > 0 ) do
      Set d = n mod 10
      If ( d < sd ) then
         Set sd = d
      Endif
   Endwhile
   Print: "Smallest digit = ", sd
End.
```

Figure 4.23: Flowchart and pseudocode to find the smallest digit of a number

Example 4.17:

Draw a flowchart and write pseudocode to check whether the given number n is palindrome or not.

Solution:

A number is called palindrome if it reads same from both the ends. For example, the number 1991 is a palindrome, whereas the number 1932 is not.

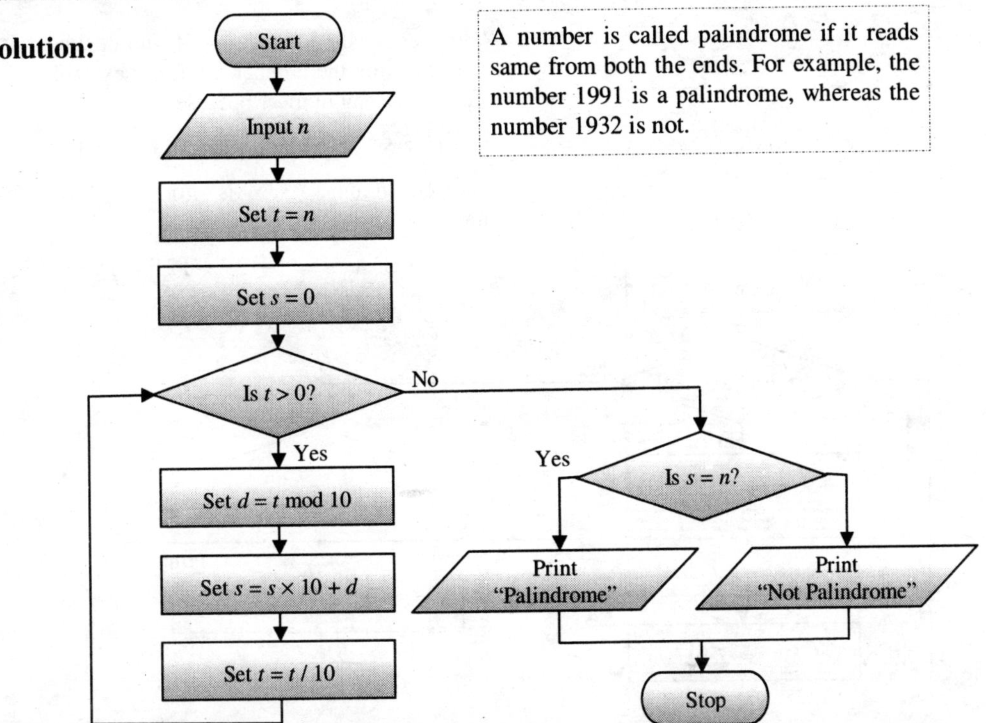

Pseudocode 4.15

Begin
    Read: n
    Set $t = n,\ s = 0$
    While $(t > 0)$ **do**
        Set $d = t \bmod 10$
        Set $s = s \times 10 + d$
        Set $t = t / 10$
    Endwhile
    If $(s = n)$ **then**
        Print: "Palindrome"
    Else
        Print: "Not a Palindrome"
    Endif
End.

Figure 4.24: Flowchart & pseudocode to check whether the given number n is palindrome or not

Example 4.18:

Draw a flowchart and write pseudocode to check whether the given number n is Armstrong number or not.

Solution:

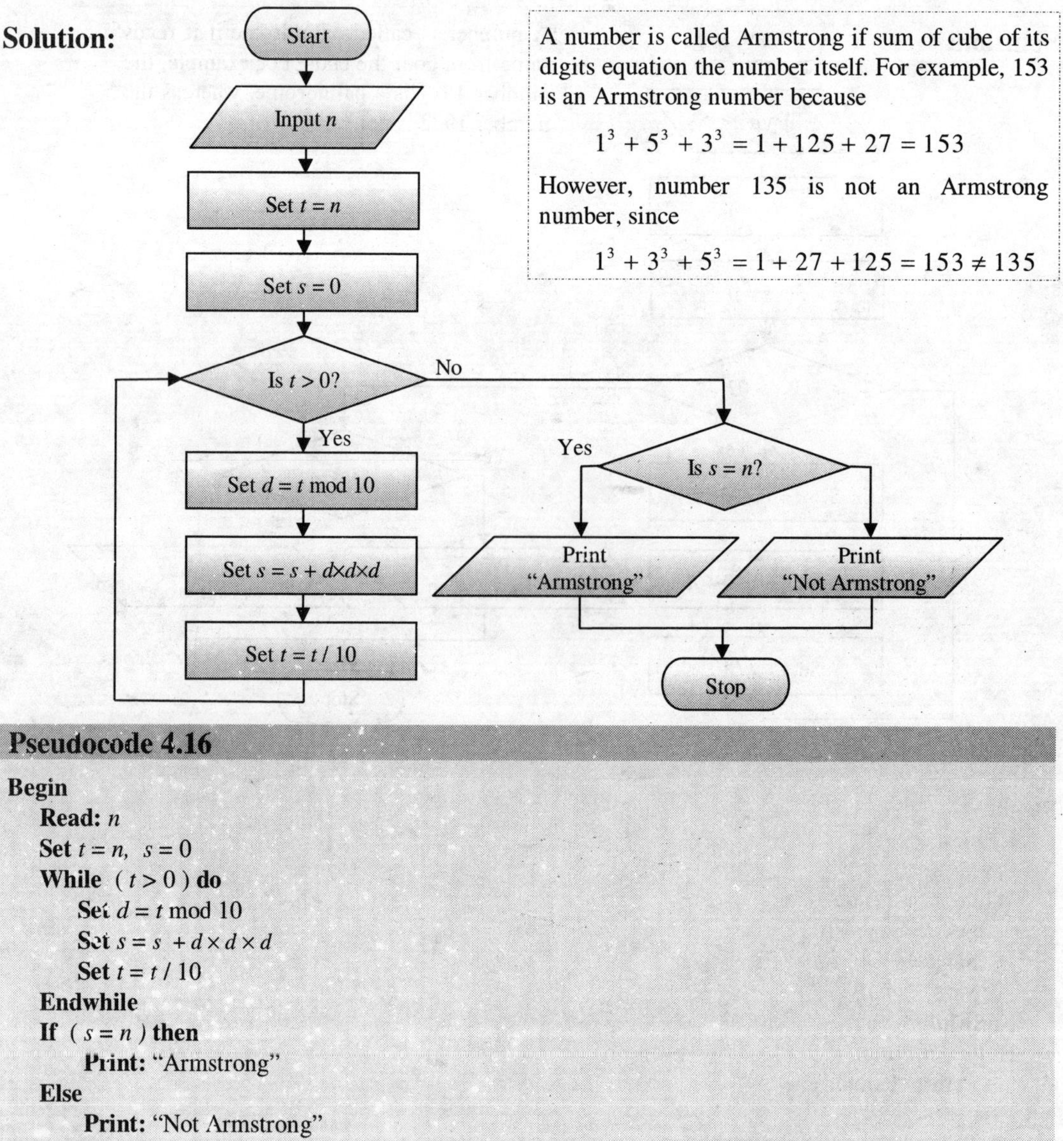

A number is called Armstrong if sum of cube of its digits equation the number itself. For example, 153 is an Armstrong number because

$$1^3 + 5^3 + 3^3 = 1 + 125 + 27 = 153$$

However, number 135 is not an Armstrong number, since

$$1^3 + 3^3 + 5^3 = 1 + 27 + 125 = 153 \neq 135$$

Pseudocode 4.16

```
Begin
   Read: n
   Set t = n,  s = 0
   While ( t > 0 ) do
       Set d = t mod 10
       Set s = s + d × d × d
       Set t = t / 10
   Endwhile
   If ( s = n ) then
       Print: "Armstrong"
   Else
       Print: "Not Armstrong"
   Endif
End.
```

Figure 4.25: Flowchart and pseudocode to check whether the given number n is Armstrong number or not

Example 4.19:

A notion of *well-ordered* number is introduced here. Any number whose digits from left to right are in increasing order (with no digit repeated) is called a *well-ordered* number. For example, number 138 is called *well-ordered* because the digits in the number (1, 3, 8) increase from left to right, *i.e.*, 1 < 3 < 8. On the other hand, the number 365 is not *well-ordered* because 6 is larger than 5.

Draw a flowchart and also write pseudocode to check whether the given number *n* is *well-ordered* not.

Solution:

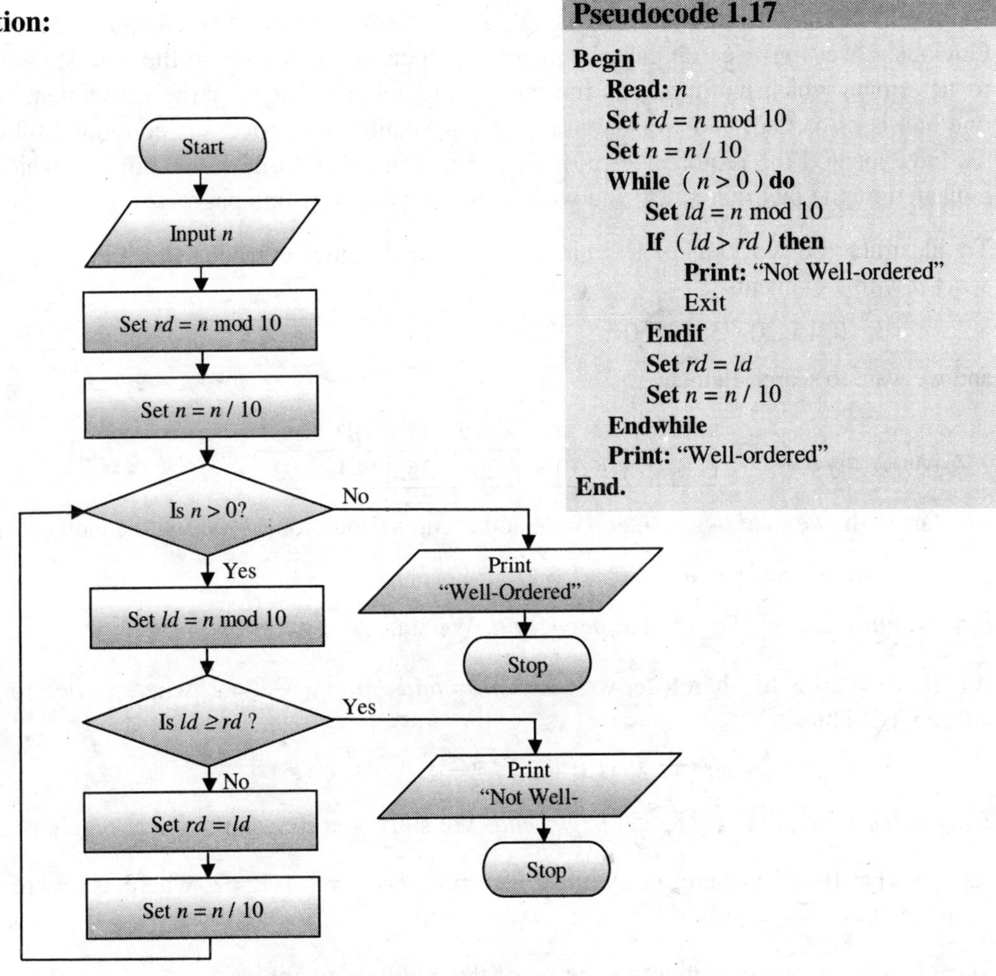

Pseudocode 1.17

```
Begin
    Read: n
    Set rd = n mod 10
    Set n = n / 10
    While ( n > 0 ) do
        Set ld = n mod 10
        If ( ld > rd ) then
            Print: "Not Well-ordered"
            Exit
        Endif
        Set rd = ld
        Set n = n / 10
    Endwhile
    Print: "Well-ordered"
End.
```

Figure 4.26: Flowchart and pseudocode to check whether the given number *n* is well-ordered or not

Example 4.20:

Write a pseudocode to search a given element in a list, named *a* having *n* elements, which is maintained in ascending order.

Solution: Searching is a process of finding the location of given element in the list. The search is said to be successful if the given element is found, *i.e.*, the element does exist in the list; otherwise unsuccessful.

As the list is sorted, the best searching algorithm, called *binary search,* is used to find the location of the given element. We do use this approach in our daily life. For example, suppose we want to find the meaning of the term *modem* in a computer dictionary. Obviously, we don't search page by page. We open the dictionary in the middle (roughly) to determine which half contains the term being sought. Then for the subsequent search one half is discarded, and we search in the other half. This process is continued till either we have located the required term or that term is missing from the dictionary, which will indicated by the fact that at the end we will be left with only one page.

To illustrate the working of the binary search technique, consider the following sorted array *a* with 7 elements

3, 10, 15, 20, 35, 40, 60

and we want to search element 15.

	a[0]	*a*[1]	*a*[2]	*a*[3]	*a*[4]	*a*[5]	*a*[6]
Given Array *a*	3	10	15	20	35	40	60

To start with, we take $beg = 0$, $end = 6$, and compute location of the middle element as

$$mid = (beg + end) / 2 = (0 + 6) / 2 = 3$$

Since $a[mid]$, *i.e.*, $a[3] \neq 15$, and $beg < end$. We start next iteration.

As $a[mid] = 20 > 15$, therefore, we take $end = mid - 1 = 3 - 1 = 2$, where as *beg* remains unchanged. Thus

$$mid = (beg + end) / 2 = (0 + 2) / 2 = 1$$

Since $a[mid]$, *i.e.*, $a[1] \neq 15$, and $beg < end$. We start next iteration.

As $a[mid] = 10 < 15$, therefore, we take $beg = mid + 1 = 1 + 1 = 2$, where as *end* remains unchanged.

Since $beg = end$, again compute location of the middle element as

$$mid = (beg + end) / 2 = (2 + 2) / 2 = 2$$

Since $a[mid]$, *i.e.*, $a[2] = 15$, the search terminates on success.

In case, the value of variable *beg* becomes greater than variable *end*, it indicates that search is unsuccessful.

Pseudocode 4.18

```
Begin
   Read: n
   For i = 0 to (n–1) by 1 do          // input elements of sorted list
       Read: a[i]
   Endfor
   Read: item
   Set beg = 0
   Set end = n–1
   Set mid = ( beg + end ) / 2
   While ( ( beg ≤ end ) and ( a[mid] ≠ item ) ) do
        If ( item < a[mid] ) then
             Set end = mid-1
        Else
             Set beg = mid+1
        Endif
        Set mid = ( beg + end ) / 2
   Endwhile
   If ( beg > end ) then
        Print: "Search unsuccessful"
   Else
        Print: item, " found at location ", mid
   Endif
End.
```

Example 4.21:

Write a pseudocode to sort a list, named *a* having *n* elements, in ascending order.

Solution: Sorting is the process of arranging the elements in some logical order. This logical order may be ascending or descending in case of numeric values or dictionary order in case of alphanumeric values. We do, almost, use this process daily in our routine activities. For example, we do arrange our class notes in order of date so we can refer them quickly later on. Like this there are many situations, which you can enumerate.

Bubble sort is one of most popular technique for this purpose. It requires $(n-1)$ pass to sort an array. In each pass, every element $a[i]$ is compared with $a[i+1]$, for $i = 0$ to $(n-k)$, where k is the pass number and if they are out of order, *i.e.*, if $a[i] > a[i+1]$, they are swapped (interchanged).

This will cause the largest element to move or bubble up. Thus, after the end of first pass the largest element in the array will be placed in *n*th position, and on each successive pass, the next largest element is placed at position (n–1), (n–2), ..., 2, respectively. For more clarity, carefully examine the following steps.

Pass 1.

Step 1. If $a[0] > a[1]$ then swap $a[0]$ and $a[1]$.
Step 2. If $a[1] > a[2]$ then swap $a[1]$ and $a[2]$.
:
Step n–1. If $a[n-2] > a[n-1]$ then swap $a[n-2]$ and $a[n-1]$.

Pass 2.

Step 1. If $a[0] > a[1]$ then swap $a[0]$ and $a[1]$.
Step 2. If $a[1] > a[2]$ then swap $a[1]$ and $a[2]$.
:
Step n–2. If $a[n-3] > a[n-2]$ then swap $a[n-3]$ and $a[n-2]$.

:

Pass *k*.

Step 1. If $a[0] > a[1]$ then swap $a[0]$ and $a[1]$.
Step 2. If $a[1] > a[2]$ then swap $a[1]$ and $a[2]$.
:
Step n–k. If $a[n-k+1] > a[n-k]$ then swap $a[n-k+1]$ and $a[n-k]$.

:

Pass *n*–1.

Step 1. If $a[0] > a[1]$ then swap $a[0]$ and $a[1]$.

Note that, the output of a given pass becomes the input for the next pass.

To illustrate the working of bubble sort method, consider the sorting of the following array in ascending order.

12 40 3 2 15

Note that, the output of a given pass becomes the input for the next pass.
Given array can be shown as

$a[0]$	$a[1]$	$a[2]$	$a[3]$	$a[4]$
12	40	3	2	15

Pass-1:

$a[0]$	$a[1]$	$a[2]$	$a[3]$	$a[4]$
(12)	(40)	3	2	15

(*a*) Compare *a*[0] and *a*[1]. Since *a*[0] < *a*[1] (12 < 40), no action is taken.

a[0]	*a*[1]	*a*[2]	*a*[3]	*a*[4]
12	(40)	(3)	2	15

(*b*) Compare *a*[1] and *a*[2]. Since *a*[1] > *a*[2] (40 > 3), swap these elements.

a[0]	*a*[1]	*a*[2]	*a*[3]	*a*[4]
12	3	(40)	(2)	15

(*c*) Compare *a*[2] and *a*[3]. Since *a*[2] > *a*[3] (40 > 2), swap these elements.

a[0]	*a*[1]	*a*[2]	*a*[3]	*a*[4]
12	3	2	(40)	(15)

(*d*) Compare *a*[3] and *a*[4]. Since *a*[3] > *a*[4] (40 > 15), swap these elements.

a[0]	*a*[1]	*a*[2]	*a*[3]	*a*[4]
12	3	2	15	40

Thus, after first pass, the largest element, 40, has moved to its final position. However, the rest of the numbers, which may have changed their positions, are yet to be sorted. The shaded part shows the elements that have been sorted.

For the remaining passes, only comparisons and swaps, if required, are shown.

Pass-2:

a[0]	*a*[1]	*a*[2]	*a*[3]	*a*[4]	Action
(12)	(3)	2	15	40	Swap
3	(12)	(2)	15	40	Swap
3	2	(12)	(15)	40	No swap
3	2	12	15	40	

After second pass, the second largest element, 15, has moved to its final position.

Pass-3:

a[0]	*a*[1]	*a*[2]	*a*[3]	*a*[4]	Action
(3)	(2)	12	15	40	Swap
2	(3)	(12)	15	40	No swap
2	3	12	15	40	

After third pass, the third largest element, 12, has moved to its final position.

Pass-4:

a[0]	*a*[1]	*a*[2]	*a*[3]	*a*[4]	Action
(2)	(3)	12	15	40	No swap
2	3	12	15	40	

After fourth pass, the fourth largest element, 3, has moved to its final position. Thus, the array is completely sorted in 4 passes.

Pseudocode 4.19

```
Begin
   Read: n
   For i = 0 to (n–1) by 1 do
      Read: a[i]
   Endfor
   For k = 1 to (n–1) by 1 do
      For j = 0 to (n–k–1) by 1 do
         If a[j] > a[j+1] then
            Set temp = a[j]            // variable temp is used to facilitate
            Set a[j] = a[j+1]          // interchange of values
            Set a[j+1] = temp
         Endif
      Endfor
   Endfor
   For i = 0 to (n–1) by 1 do
      Print: a[i]
   Endfor
End.
```

EXERCISE

1. Why is it advisable to plan the program before writing it?
2. What is an algorithm? What are the essential characteristics for a sequence of instructions to qualify as an algorithm?
3. What is a flowchart? What are the various symbols used in flowcharts?
4. What is a pseudocode? Why is it so called?
5. Among algorithm, flowchart and pseudocode, which makes the logic of the underlying program clearer and easily understandable?
6. Given a chance to plan a program, will you prefer to choose algorithm, flowchart or a pseudocode? Give reasons for your choice.
7. Draw a flowchart to find largest of the five numbers *a*, *b*, *c*, *d*, and *e*.
8. Write a pseudocode to display first 20 prime numbers.
9. Write a pseudocode to find the sum of first 100 odd numbers.
10. Suppose an amount *p* is deposited in a commercial bank, which pays compound interest at the rate of *r*% annually, for *n* years. Write a pseudocode that prints the amount in account after each year.
11. Write a pseudocode to find LCM and HCF of two natural number *m* and *n*.
12. Write a pseudocode to find factorial of a natural number *n*.
13. Write a program to print first *n* pairs of twin prime numbers. Note that two consecutive prime numbers are said to twin prime numbers if they differ by 2.
14. The monthly telephone bill is to be computed as follows:

    Minimum Rs. 200 for upto 100 calls
    plus Rs. 0.60 per call for next 50 calls
    plus Rs. 0.50 per call for next 50 calls
    plus Rs. 0.40 per call for any call beyond 200 calls.

    The input contains name of the customer and number of calls made and the desired output is the name and telephone bill to be paid by the customer. Draw a flowchart for logical steps needed to accomplish the above task.
15. State pollution control board has the following classification policy:

Pollution Index	Classification
< 30	Pleasant
30 – 60	Unpleasant
> 60	Hazardous

Draw a flowchart that accepts the pollution index and prints the appropriate classification.

16. A department store places an order with a company for *n* pieces of miners, *m* pieces of toasters, and *p* number of fans. The cost of items are as follows:

Item Description	Price per Unit (in Rupees)
Miners	1,500
Toaster	200
Fan	450

The discount allowed for various items are 5% for miners, 15% for fan, and 10% for toaster. The company charge 10% as sales tax on all items on net value after deducting the discount. Write pseudocode that reads *m*, *n*, and *p* and computes the amount to be paid by the store.

❑ ❑ ❑

Chapter 5

Overview of C Language

Learning Objectives

After reading this chapter, students will be able to explain

- history and evolution of C language
- why C language is called middle level language
- key characteristics of C language
- potential areas where C language is predominantly used
- general structure of C program
- steps required in building a C program
- usage of various C Compilers

5.1 INTRODUCTION

Invented and first implemented by Dennis Ritchie, a system programmer at Bell Laboratories, on a DEC PDP-11 computer system running the UNIX operating system. Later on, the UNIX operating system was rewritten almost entirely in C language. The development of C language was the result of the development process that started with an older language known as Basic Combined Programming Language (BCPL), developed by Martin Richards. The BCPL language influenced a language called B language, developed by Ken Thompson, which lead to the development of C language in the 1970s. It was a mere coincidence that the letters B and C are in alphabetic order.

For many years the de facto standard for C language was the one supplied with the UNIX operating system and described in book entitled "*The C Programming Language*" by Brain Kernighan and Dennis Ritchie (Prentice-Hall, 1978). The C language was formally standardized in December 1989, when the American National Standards Institute (ANSI) standard for C was adopted.

The creation of C language was considered many to have marked the beginning of the modern age of programming languages. It was designed, developed, and implemented by the working programmers, reflecting the way they approached the job of programming. Its features were honed, tested, thought about, and rethought by the people who actually used the language. The result was a language that programmers liked to use. Indeed, the C language quickly attracted many followers who had a near-religious zeal for it. As such it found wide and rapid acceptance in the programmer community.

In short, the C language is a language designed by and for programmers.

5.2 ANATOMY OF COMPUTER LANGUAGES

To see how C language compares with other programming languages, let us have a look on the programming languages in general. The programming language can be divided into two broad categories, depending on their level of interaction with the underlying hardware of the computer:

- Low-level Languages
- High-level Languages

5.2.1 Low-level Languages

In this category, we have machine language and assembly language. These languages permit the efficient use of the computer.

But the problems with these languages are:

- These languages are hardware dependent, *i.e.*, programs written using these languages is not portable, i.e., cannot be used on other computers.
- Programming using these languages is not an easy job. One must have thorough knowledge of the architecture of the computer.

5.2.2 High-level Languages

In this category, we have FORTRAN, BASIC, PASCAL, COBOL, PL/1, etc. These languages are designed for better programming efficiency, *i.e.*, faster program development. These languages have following advantages:

- The syntax for writing program instructions is very much like English statements. This enables the readers to learn high-level languages (HLLs) quickly. In addition, the programs written in HLLs can be easily understood, which facilitates its maintenance.
- The programs written in HLLs are not hardware dependent. This means that program written for one machine can be transferred to another machine with minimal changes or none at all.

The C language stands between these two categories. That is why it is often called *middle-level* language, since it was designed to have best of both the worlds, *i.e.*, a good programming efficiency as well as good machine efficiency.

- To achieve programming efficiency, the C language has all the elements as of any other modern high-level language.
- To achieve machine efficiency, the C language has requisite features to access any hardware component of the system, to operate at register level, and to interface with high-speed assembly language routines.

5.3 CHARACTERISTICS OF C LANGUAGE

The C language was and will remain as one of the popular programming languages. Some of the key characteristics that add to its popularity are:

- It is a general purpose programming language, and therefore, can be used to solve vide variety of problems.
- It is supports structuring programming, and therefore, programs developed in it can easily be understood.

- It is free form, *i.e.*, no rigid format for writing programs. Any instruction can start from anywhere and end anywhere. In addition, a single instruction can span (can be written in) many lines.
- It is case sensitive. It distinguishes between lowercase (small) and uppercase (capital) alphabets.
- It was the first language to provide rich set of operators.
- It allows you, through pointers, to access any storage location and the devices connected to your computer through your program.
- It allows you to manipulate internal processor registers, and thus it is very useful for low-level programming.
- It is portable, that means any program written in it can be used on any computer without or with little modification(s).
- It allows you to develop your own library of functions that can be linked to your any program like standard library functions.

5.4 APPLICATION AREAS OF C LANGUAGE

The strength of C language makes it a natural choice for

- Systems programming that include writing software for language translators, device drivers, editors, linkers, loaders, etc.
- Network software to implement different communication protocols.
- Graphics programming that include writing software for graphical user interfaces (GUIs), scientific visualisation, and presentation graphics, etc.
- Embedded systems where C routines are interfaced high speed assembly language routines and the resulting code is stored in ROM chip which is a part of the embedded system.

5.5 GENERAL STRUCTURE OF A C PROGRAM

The usual order of statements written in a C program is as shown in Figure 5.1.

Section 1 is optional. If present it contains the description about the program. This description usually contains the information about the task being accomplished by the program. In addition, it can also contain the name of the author (programmer), the date on which it was written, the date on which it was last modified, etc.

Section 2 contains the preprocessor directives. The frequently used preprocessor directives are *include* and *define*. These directives tell the preprocessor how to prepare the program for compilation. The *include* directive tells which header files are to be included in the program and the *define* directive is usually used to associate an identifier with a literal (constant) that is to be used at many places in the program.

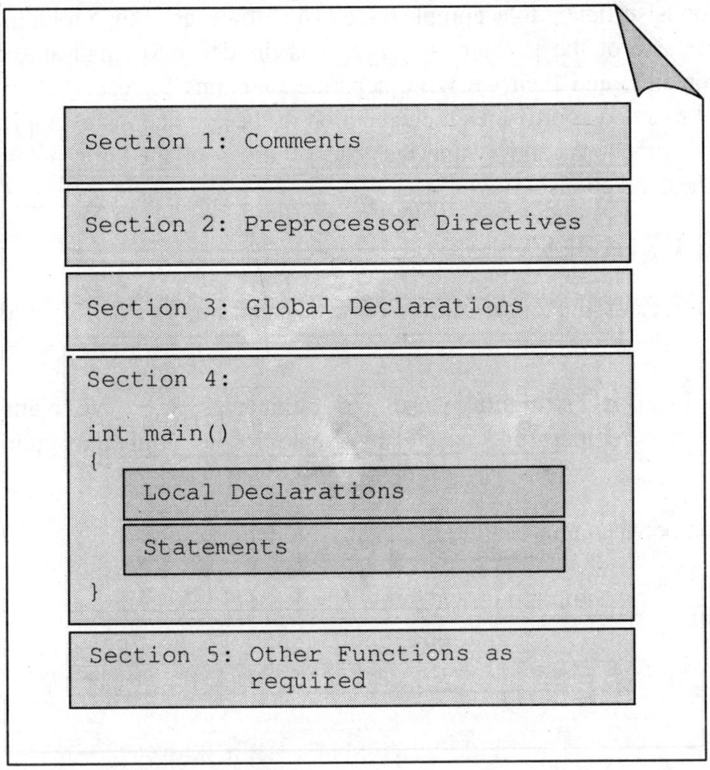

Figure 5.1: General Structure of a C Program

Section 3 is optional. If present, it contains the global declarations. These declarations usually include the declaration of the data items (variables) which are to be shared between many functions in the program. In addition, these declarations can also include the decorations of functions (prototypes), except the *main()* function, to be used in the program.

Section 4 contains the *main()* function. The execution of the program always begins with the execution of the *main()* function. The *main()* function can call any number of other functions, and those called function can further call other functions. The first section in the *main()* function, as well as other functions, contains local declarations. These declarations are local in the sense that they pertain to the requirements of that function only. The second section in the *main()* function, as well as in other functions, contains the statements that defines the actions to be performed by the function.

Section 5 is also optional. If present, it contains the other functions.

If the problem to be solved is simple and small in size, then only the *main()* function is sufficient to accomplish the task. However, if the problem is complex and the size of the problem is large, it is divided into small and independent subproblems, and then we write separate functions for each subproblem. The *main()* function coordinates the execution of these functions by appropriate calls to these functions, and synthesizes the solutions of the subproblems obtained from these functions.

5.6 SAMPLE C PROGRAM

In order to have a feel of the organization of a C program, let us consider the simple example C program, given overleaf.

Problem considered is very straightforward and familiar to you. We want to write a program that converts temperature in Celsius scale to its equivalent temperature in Fahrenheit scale.

We know the relation between temperature in Celsius and Fahrenheit is:

$$\frac{C}{100} = \frac{F-32}{180} \qquad \text{Simplifying, we get} \quad F = 1.8 \times C + 32$$

Listing 5.1

```
/*
* Program to convert temperature from Centigrade scale
* to Fahrenheit scale
*/
#include <stdio.h>
int main(void)
{
  float fahrenheit, centigrade;
  printf( "\nEnter temperature in Celsius scale: ");
  scanf( "%f", &centigrade );
  fahrenheit = 1.8 * centigrade + 32;
  printf( "\nEquivalent temperature in Fahrenheit scale");
  printf( " = %.2f\n",fahrenheit);
  return 0;
}
```

Here the line numbers are added for ready reference.

Test Run

```
Enter temperature in Celsius scale: 30
Equivalent temperature in Fahrenheit scale = 86.00
```

Dissection of the Program

If you are familiar with other programming languages, this program may look strange to you. One reason for this strangeness is that the entire program is written in lowercase letters. In most other languages, usually uppercase letters are used, though they permit the use of lowercase letters. So you have to become accustomed to lowercase as quickly as possible. Also, it is important to remember that C language is case sensitive, *i.e.*, it differentiates between lowercase and uppercase letters. Lowercase letters are characteristic of the C language.

A C program is written in a free format. By free format, we mean that an instruction can start anywhere in a line and can end anywhere. Even an instruction can span many lines. Spacing is of no consequence in C language, it is used to enhance the readability of the program.

Lines 1-4 demonstrate the style used in C language to add comments in a program. This is done by starting the comments with two characters '/*' and ending with the characters '*/'. Between these pair of characters, called *delimiters*, any characters may be included in either uppercase or lowercase.

In other words, a comment appears as follows:

```
/*  You type here what you want   */
```

In addition to this style, comments can also be added after the instruction on the same line as shown below:

```
#include<stdio.h>     /* include stdio.h file */
```

Comments may not be essential in a simple program, but in complex programs they are lifesaver. For any program, no matter how well it is written, the day will come when we have to make amendments to incorporate the changing conditions. The chances are quite high that the original author of the program may have left the organization. Even the original author may not remember the logic of a program that he wrote several months or years ago.

In order to reduce the burden on the person, who will make amendments to the program, ample comments should be included at the time when the program is being written. Too often we postpone the task of adding comments until the program is finally Okayed, but this practice is not very useful.

Some programmers feel that C language is such a concise and cryptic language that every line of code should be accompanied by a comment. But too many comments actually reduce the readability of the program. Still, it is better to have too many comments than few.

Line 5 demonstrates the way pre-processor directives are used. These directives instruct the compiler process the source code in a specific way. In this case, *include* directive, also called *file inclusion* directive, and instructs the compiler to include the specified file at this point. In this case, the specified file is a header file (a file with extension *.h*) that is part of the C compiler.

The other often-used pre-processor directive is *#define* whose syntax is

```
#define MAX 100
```

This directive, called *macro expansion* directive, tells the compiler to replace every occurrence of MAX with value 100 during pre-processing. There are many other directives that we will discuss later.

Line 6 specifies a function named *main*. This is a special name that is recognized by the system. It points to the precise place in the program where execution begins. Every C program must have a *main* function. We cannot have more than one main function in a program.

Every C function has a return type associated with it. Where return type is one of the data types that determine the type of the value returned by the function. If a function is not supposed to return any value, its return type is specified as *void*. Since main function is the function from where execution begins, it will usually be declared with type *int*. A pair of parentheses follows the word main. The matter, if any, contained in these parentheses specifies the formal arguments of the function. If there are no arguments, we write *void*.

The *main()* Function

The *main()* function is a part of every C program. The C language permits following forms of *main()* function:

- `main()`
- `main(void)`
- `void main()`
- `int main()`
- `void main(void)`
- `int main(void)`

The empty pair of parenthesis indicates that the *main()* function takes no arguments. This may be explicitly indicated by using the keyword *void* inside the parenthesis. We may also specify the keyword *void* or *int* before the word main. When the keyword *void* is used, it indicates that the function *main()* does not return any value to the operating system. When the keyword *int* is used, it indicates that the function *main()* will return an integer value to the operating system. Value 0 is returned to the operating system to indicate that the program terminated on completion of its intended task whereas the value 1 is used to indicate that the program terminated prematurely (could not complete its intended task).

Line 7 contains character '{', called left brace or left curly bracket. There is also matching right brace '}' in line 14, which appears at the end of the main function. These pair of matching braces encloses the body of the function.

Line 8 declares two variables, *fahrenheit* and *centigrade* of type *float,* which can represent and store two real numbers (float) in computer memory. Variable *centigrade* is used to hold the value, representing temperature in Celsius scale, entered by the user during program execution. Variable *fahrenheit* is to used to hold the computed value, representing temperature in Fahrenheit scale, equivalent to given temperature in Celsius scale. Note that the names of the variables used are self-explanatory. It is always recommended to use meaningful names. This will help to increase the readability of the program.

Line 9 uses library function *printf()* that displays "*Enter temperature in Celsius scale:* " on the computer screen. We call these kinds of messages as *user prompts* as they guide the user to enter the desired input. In this case, the value to be entered is temperature in Celsius scale.

You must have observed that the entire sequence of characters enclosed in double quotes is not printed. Then, *what is the role of characters '\n' in the beginning*? These two characters together represent the *new line* character. Although *new line* character is a combination of two characters, *i.e.*, '\' and 'n', they are translated by the C compiler into a single character. The *new line* character instructs the compiler to advance to the next line before printing subsequent information.

Line 10 uses another library function *scanf()* that accepts the user input and stores in variable *centigrade* (in fact, in a memory location that is reserved for the *centigrade*). The first argument is a *format string* that is enclosed in double quotes and tells the system how the entered values are to be interpreted. Following the format string, there will be a list of one or more variables; each variable prefixed with character '&', called *address of operator.*

Line 11 is an assignment statement that computes the temperature in Fahrenheit scale equivalent to given temperature in Celsius scale, and assigns to variable *fahrenheit, i.e.*, stores in variable *fahrenheit.*

Lines 12-13 uses library function *printf()* that outputs the stored value in variable *fahrenheit* along with the message "*Equivalent Temperature in fahrenheit* = ". The use of these kinds of messages is not mandatory, but is very useful as they make the output easy to interpret.

Line 14 uses *return* statement, which on execution terminates the execution of the program and return the control back to the operating system. In addition, it also returns value 0 to the operating system indicating that the program terminated on success. In case of failure, value 1 is returned. This retuned value can be used by the operating system for deciding further line of action.

Line 15 marks the end of the *main* function as well as end of the program as this is the only function in the program.

- If there is more than one function in a file, each will have its own body enclosed in pair of braces.
- Variables can only be declared in the beginning of a block before any executable statement.

5.7 PROGRAM DEVELOPMENT LIFE CYCLE

Program development life cycle (PDLC) is a systematic way of developing quality programs (and hence software). It provides an organized plan for breaking down the task of program development into manageable chunks, each of which must be successfully completed before moving on to the next phase. The program development process is divided into following phases:

- Defining the problem
- Designing the program
- Building the program
- Testing the program
- Documenting the program
- Deploying and maintaining the program

5.7.1 Defining the Problem

The first step in developing a program is to define the problem. In major software projects, this is a job for system analyst, who provides the results of their work to programmers in the form of a *program specification.* The program specification precisely defines the input data, the processing that should take place, the format of the output reports and the user interface. Depending on the size of the job, the program development might be handled by an individual or a team.

5.7.2 Designing the Program

An architect doesn't design a home just by going to the site with a bunch of boards and bricks. After determining the needs of the house's owner, the next step in designing a house is an architectural drawing – a plan drawn up on the paper that can be discussed and reviewed until everything is right. Likewise, programmers create program designs. Like an architect's drawing, the program design specifies the components that make the program work.

Program design begins by focusing on the main goal that the program is trying to achieve and then breaking the program into manageable components, each of which contributes to this goal. This approach of program design is called *top-down program design* or *modular programming*. The first step involves identifying the *main routine* (*main()* function), which is the program's major activity. From there, programmers try to break down the various components of the main routine into smaller units called *modules*, until each module is highly focused. Experience shows that this is the best way to ensure program quality. If an error appears in a program designed this way, it is relatively easy to identify the module that must be causing the error.

For each module, the programmer draws a conceptual plan using an appropriate program design tool to visualize how the module will do its assigned job.

The various familiar program design tools are:

- **Structure Chart** – A *structure chart*, also called *hierarchy chart*, show the top-down design of a program. Each box in the chart indicates a task that the program must accomplish. The top module, called the *main module* or *control module*, oversees the transfer of control to other modules.

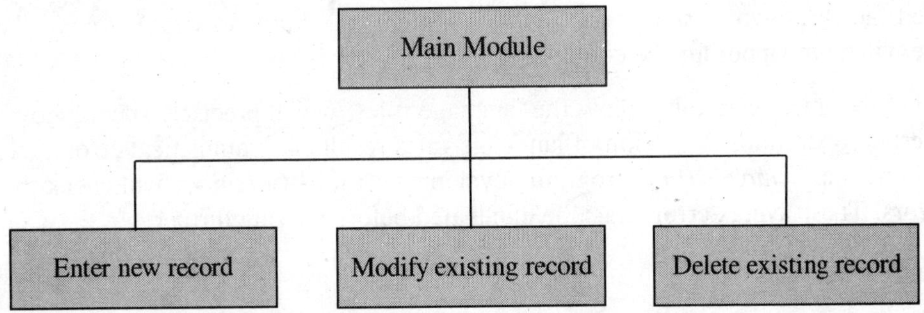

Figure 5.2: Structure Chart for a Data Entry Program

- **Algorithm** – An *algorithm* is a step-by-step description of how to arrive at a solution. Algorithms are not restricted to computers. In fact, we use them every day.

- **Flowchart** – A *flowchart* is a diagram that shows the logic of the program. Programmers create flowcharts either by hand using a flowchart template or on the computer. Each flowcharting symbol has a meaning. For example, parallelogram indicates an input or output, rectangle indicates a process, and diamond indicates a condition.

- **Pseudocode** – A *pseudocode* is another tool to describe the way to arrive at a solution. In some sense, it is considered as a form of an algorithm. The only difference is that instead of expressing the action to be carried in form of steps, they are expressed in program language like constructs.

We have already discussed in detail about various program design tools such as *algorithms*, *flowcharts* and *pseudocodes*, in *Chapter 4*. The use of these tools was also demonstrated by taking familiar illustrative examples.

5.7.3 Building the Program

Once the design of the program is ready, the next step is to convert the program design into a computer program. During this conversion each of the steps of the program design is coded as one or more C language instructions. Here also it is recommended that one should write the program first on a piece of paper before keying in the computer.

Creating and Editing Programs

Once the program is ready on paper, we key in computer memory using a *text editor*. A text editor helps us to enter the character data into computer memory, allows editing (changing) the data in computer memory, and save the data from memory in a disk file on secondary memory with extension "*.c*".

This stored file is known as *source file*, and its contents are known as *source code*. This source file will be the input for the compiler.

The programmer must carefully follow the language rules, which precisely specify how to express certain operations. Violation of language rules results in grammatical errors, more precisely known as *syntax errors*. Program development tool - *Compiler*, will check these syntax errors. These syntax errors must be eliminated before moving further.

Compiling Programs

The source code in the source file, stored on the disk, must to be translated into machine language. This job is done by the *compiler*. The C compiler actually is a combination of two separate programs – the *preprocessor* and the *translator*.

The *preprocessor* reads the source code and prepares it for translation. While reading the source code, it scans the code for preprocessor directives and processes them accordingly. For example, when it encounters the *include* directive, it substitutes that directive with the contents of the specified header file (such as *stdio.h*), and when it encounters the *define* directive, it substitutes the identifier with the specified literal (constant). The output from the preprocessor is an intermediate file, known as *translation unit*.

The translator reads the translation unit instruction-by-instruction and checks them for their grammatical accuracy. If there is a syntax error in it, it flags an error message – called *diagnostic message* on the screen. These diagnostics messages help the programmer to identify the cause of the syntax error and the place where it is present.

Therefore, if there is even a single syntax error, the translation process, known as *compilation*, is terminated. In that case, open the source file using the text editor, and make the necessary corrections and repeat the compilation.

However, if there are no syntax errors in the translation unit, the translator rereads the instruction from the beginning, translates them into machine language, and writes them onto a disk file. The translated version of the source code is known as *object code*, and is stored in the disk file with extension "*.obj".

Linking Programs

Once the source code is translated into object code, though it is in machine language, still it is not in executable form. The reason being is that it may be referring to other functions which are not included in the object code. These referred functions can be library functions (pre-written functions supplied with the compiler in the form of libraries) or user-defined functions stored in other source files and which are compiled separately. All these functions also need to be included in the object code to get a final machine code which is in the executable form, known as *executable code*. This task is performed by the *linker*.

A *linker* is a development tool that extracts the referred library functions from the system libraries, reads the object codes of the user-defined functions from the object files and integrates them with the current object code to produce the final executable code, which is stored in disk file with extension "*.exe". This executable code is the final form of the program that is ready for execution.

Executing Programs

Once the program is linked, it is ready for execution. To execute a program we give an operating system command, such as *run*, to load the program into computer memory and execute it. Getting the program into memory is the function of an operating system program known as *loader*. The loader locates the executable program in the secondary storage, reads it and brings into the computer memory. Once the program is loaded, the operating system transfers the control to the program and the program begins its execution.

The complete process of *designing*, *creating*, *compiling*, *linking* and *executing* the program, referred to as building the program, is depicted in Figure 5.3.

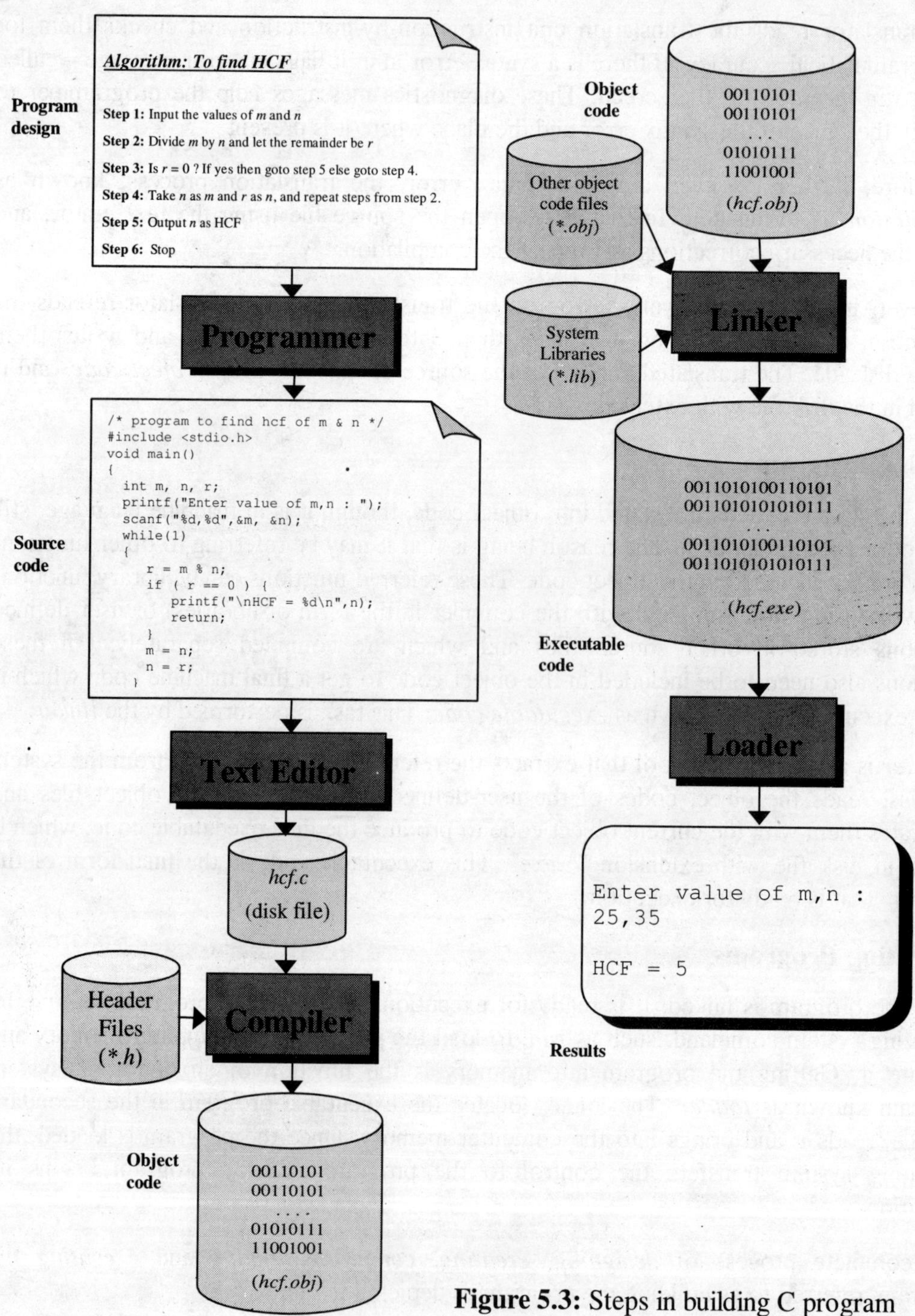

Figure 5.3: Steps in building C program

5.7.4 Testing the Program

Even when the program is executing, the output of the program may not be correct. This will be because of logical errors in the program. A *logical error* is a mistake that the programmer made while designing the solution to the problem. For example, a programmer tells the computer to calculate the net pay by adding deductions to the gross salary instead of subtracting. A program development tool, such as compiler, cannot detect these errors. Therefore, the programmer must find and correct logical errors by carefully examining the program output for a set of data for which results are already known. Such type of data is known as *test data*.

Syntax errors and logical errors collectively are known as *bugs*. The process of identifying and eliminating these errors is known as *debugging*.

5.7.5 Documenting the Program

After testing, the program development is almost complete. The *structure charts*, *algorithms*, *pseudocodes*, and *flowcharts* developed during the design phase become documentation for others who are associated with the program. In addition, more documentation needs to be done as the programs are being coded such as list of variable names and definitions, description of files that the program need to work with, and format of output that the program produces. All of this documentation needs to be saved and placed together for future reference.

This phase ends by writing a manual that provides an overview of the program's functionality, tutorials for the beginner, in-depth explanations of major program features, reference documentation of all program commands and a thorough description of the error messages generated by the program. This manual is given to the user when the program is installed.

5.7.6 Deploying and Maintaining the Program

In the final phase, the program is deployed (installed) at the user's site. Here also, the program is kept under watch till the user gives green signal to it. Users may discover errors that were not caught in the testing phase, no matter how exhaustively the program was tested.

Even after the development project is complete, it needs to be maintained and evaluated regularly. In program maintenance, the programming team fixes program errors that users discover during its day-to-day use. In periodic evaluations, the team asks whether the program is fulfilling its objectives. This evaluation may lead to modifications to update the program or to add more features for the user. It may even lead to a decision to abandon the current system and develop a new one, and so the program development life cycle begins afresh.

5.8 USING VARIOUS C COMPILERS

5.8.1 Using C Compiler on Windows Platform

If you are using Window based platform, then Turbo C/C++ Compiler is the user's preferred choice.

Turbo C/C++ Compiler provides an Integrated Development Environment (IDE)., where the necessary operations for program development are available in a unified screen display with menus and windows. It provides an ideal environment for learning C language.

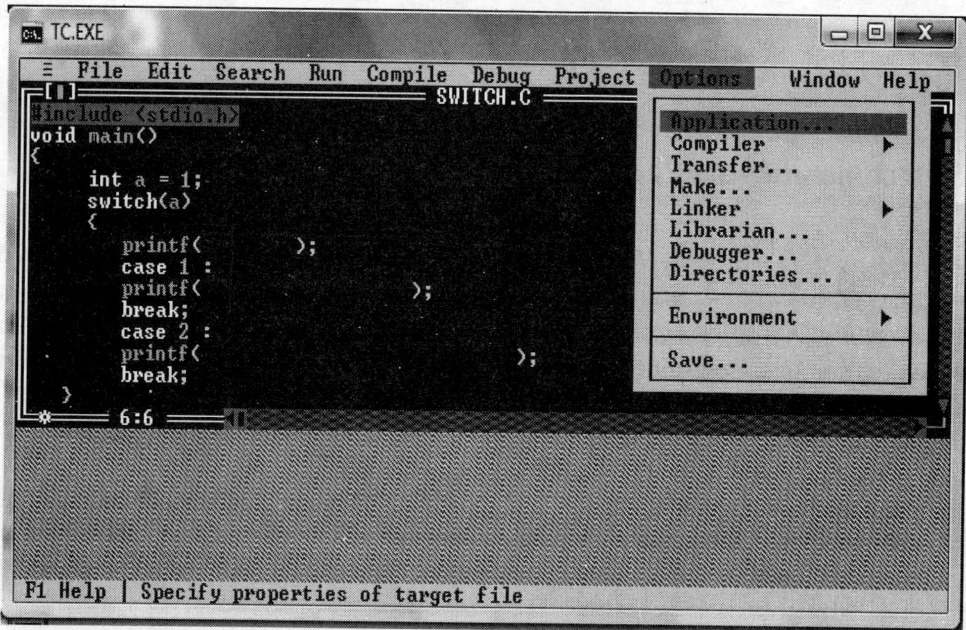

Figure 5.2: IDE of Turbo C++, which can be used create C programs as well as C++ programs

5.8.2 Using C Compiler on Unix Platform

To compile a C program, type the command as

```
cc myprog.c
```

The program will be compiled and if there is no syntax error, it subsequently will be linked with system libraries and the executable code is stored in file *a.out*.

To run the program, enter the command as

```
./a.out
```

However, if you want to save the executable file on the user specified file, type the command as

```
cc -o myprog myprog.c
```

Now to run the program, enter the command as

```
./myprog
```

5.8.3 Using C Compiler on Linux Platform

To compile a C program, type the command as

```
gcc myprog.c
```

The program will be compiled and if there is no syntax error, it subsequently will be linked with system libraries and the executable code is stored in file *a.out*.

To run the program, enter the command as

```
./a.out
```

However, if you want to save the executable file on the user specified file, type the command as

```
gcc -o myprog myprog.c
```

Now to run the program, enter the command as

```
./myprog
```

5.9 SOME KEY POINTS TO REMEMBER

List of some key points about which every C programmer must be aware:

- The C language is a free form language, *i.e.*, any instructions can start from anywhere and end anywhere. Even a single instruction can span many lines.
- Pre-processor directive can be used anywhere in the C program but the recommended place is in the beginning of the source file.
- Each instructions end with character semicolon ';'.
- The C language is a case sensitive, *i.e.*, it will treat identifiers abc, Abc, aBc, ABC, abC, etc. as different identifiers.
- The C program is usually written in lower case. Uppercase letters are usually used for symbolic names and predefined names.
- Comments can be placed anywhere.
- Execution of program always begins with first executable statement in *main* function.
- Variable can only be declared in the beginning of the function, *i.e.*, prior to any executable statement.

- Entire calculations involving real numbers are done in double precision mode, *i.e.*, with 12 decimal digits precision.
- A C program can contain any number of functions. It basically depends on the size and complexity of the problem under consideration.

EXERCISE

1. Name the predecessor of the C language.
2. Name the person who developed C language.
3. When and where the C language was developed?
4. Why C language is called middle-level language?
5. List the application areas of C language.
6. Describe the general structure of a C program.
7. What is PDLC? Describe various phases of PDLC.
8. Describe the following - *text editor*, *compiler*, *linker*, *loader*.
9. What symbol or character is used to terminate every C statement?

❑ ❑ ❑

Chapter 6

Built-in Data Types

Learning Objectives

After reading this chapter, students will be able to

- explain the concept of character set
- explain what does tokens, identifiers and keywords mean
- explain the rules for naming an identifier
- explain the concept of data types and various data types supported by C language
- explain the built-in data types
- explain about literals, constants, symbolic constants and variables
- describe the declaration and initialization of variables
- explain the various type modifiers
- explain the concept of storage class and its types

6.1 INTRODUCTION

A program must be able to store its input somewhere so that it can work with the data and process it into a form that is meaningful to the user. All the data processed by a program is stored either as a *variable* or as a *constant*. Each variable in C language has some characteristics associated with it, called its *storage class*.

The ability to divide the data into different types is one of the most important features of the modern programming languages. It enables us to work with relatively complex data objects instead of elementary data objects that a computer can understand and manipulate.

This chapter attempts to describe these semantic units of the C language.

6.2 CHARACTER SET

In a most basic sense, a C program is a sequence of characters. When these characters are submitted to the compiler, they are interpreted in various contexts as characters, identifiers, constants, and statements. The characters used in a C source program belong to the American Standard Code for Information Interchange (ASCII pronounced as *ass-kee*) set.

The characters in C language are grouped into the following categories:

- Letters
- Digits
- Special characters
- White space characters

Table 6.1: Character set of C Language

Letters	Digits	
Uppercase : A–Z Lowercase : a–z	All decimal digit : 0–9	
	Special Characters	
, comma	. period	: colon
; semicolon	~ tilde	! exclamation mark
# hash/number sign	% percentage sign	^ caret
& ampersand	* asterisk	– hyphen/minus sign
+ plus sign	= equal sign	| vertical bar
′ single quote	″ double quote	/ slash
\ backslash	_ underscore	$ dollar sign

[left bracket	] right bracket	(left parenthesis
) right parenthesis	{ left brace	} right brace
< left angle bracket or less than sign	> right angle bracket or greater than sign	? question mark
		@ at the rate of sign
White Space Characters		
Blank space	Horizontal Tab	Carriage return
Formfeed	Newline	

All C compilers ignore white space characters. These characters are basically used to enhance the readability and understandability of a C program.

6.3 TOKENS

A *token* is a smallest entity that have a meaning in itself. A C program is a sequence of tokens.

Tokens in C language can be classified into following categories:

- Keywords
- Identifiers
- Literals
- Punctuators
- Operators

6.3.1 Keywords

Every word in C is either classified as a *keyword* or an *identifier*.

Keywords are basically those words that have predefined and fixed meaning and these meanings cannot be changed. These keywords serve as basic building blocks for forming program instructions (statements). All keywords are written in lowercase. There incorrect usage results in a syntax error.

For example, the following statement

```
float const pie = 2.1412;
```

consist of six tokens: 'float', 'const', 'pie', '=', '2.1412', and ';'.

The list of keywords of C language, as per American National Standard Institute (ANSI) standard, is given in Table 6.2.

Table 6.2: Keywords in C

asm	default	for	short	union
auto	do	goto	signed	unsigned
break	double	if	sizeof	void
case	else	int	static	volatile
char	enum	long	struct	while
Const	extern	register	switch	
continue	float	return	typedef	

6.3.2 Identifiers

An identifier is basically a name in a program. Identifiers can be used to denote variables, arrays and functions. These user-defined names consist of sequence of characters, where each character can be a letter, a digit or an underscore '_', and cannot start with a digit. Both uppercase and lowercase letters are permitted, however, lowercase are commonly used. The underscore is usually used to link the two or more words to create meaning full names.

Since C language is case sensitive (it distinguishes between lowercase and uppercase), therefore, the identifiers *price* and *Price* will be treated as two different identifiers.

RULES FOR IDENTIFIERS

1. The first character must be an alphabet or an underscore.
2. Must consist of letters, digits or underscore only.
3. Cannot use a keyword.
4. Cannot contain a white space.

Examples of valid identifiers:

myFile	roll_no	date_of_birth	_chk
file10	N1TO10	area	AbCdE

Examples of invalid identifiers:

my-File	contains character other than letter, digit and underscore
pin.code	contains character other than letter, digit and underscore
12file	starts with a digit

6.3.3 Literals

A *literal* (often referred to as constants) refer to fixed value that do not change during the execution of a program. The C language supports several types of literals as illustrated in Figure 6.1.

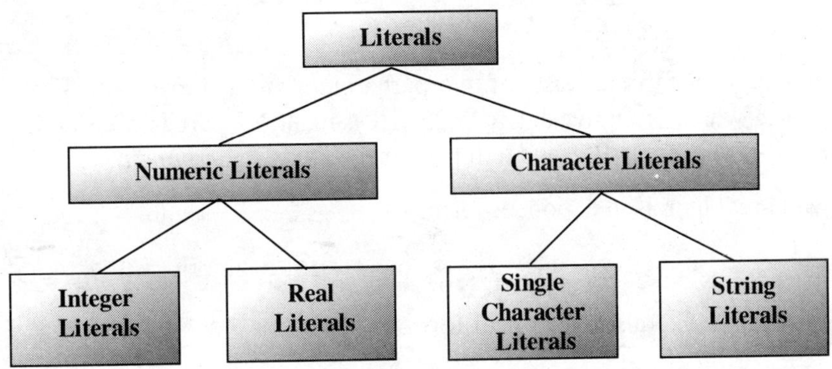

Figure 6.1: Types of Literals

Integer Literal

An *integer literal* refers to a sequence of digits. Such a sequence without a leading sign is assumed as positive integer literal.

Following are valid integer literals of type *int*:

```
    123         +123          0        32765
    3445        7523      -2000        0300
```

Following are invalid integer literals of type *int* because of the reasons as given:

```
    .123      (Decimal point not allowed)
   3,452      (Comma not allowed)
   45234      (Value larger than permissible range)
```

An integer literal by default is treated as an integer value of type *int*, and the compiler reserves 2-bytes of memory for its storage.

Real Literals

A *real literal* are numbers having fractional parts. The real literals can be specified in two forms – *fractional form* (*fixed-point form*) and *exponent form* (*scientific notation*).

A real literal in fractional form consists of signed or unsigned digits including a decimal point.

Examples of valid real literals in fractional form:

```
   -125.50        +100.5        1.       .454
```

Examples of valid real literals in fractional form:

```
        155     (Decimal point missing)
  12,500.25     (Comma not allowed)
```

A real literal in exponent form consists of two parts: *mantissa* and *exponent*. For example, in literal 5.25E+2 (which is equivalent to 5.25×10^2), mantissa part is 5.25 and exponent part is +2. Here E+2 represent 10^2, and letter *E* (or *e*) stands for *exponent*.

Examples of valid real literals in exponent form:

```
   1.25E12      .0001E+2      5.E-3      100.00E0      5.5E+10
```

Examples of invalid real literals in exponent form:

```
   +145.80E     (No digit specified for exponent)
   12.35E5.5    (Exponent cannot be a fraction)
   12,75E-5     (Comma allowed)
```

Single Character Literals

A character literal consists of a single character enclosed in single quotes (') such as 'A'. Internally, each character is represented by an integral value that represents the ASCII code of the character. For example, character 'A' will be represented by integral value 65, character 'B' by 66, etc.

Table 6.2: Common Escape Sequences

Escape Sequence	Represents	Effect
\n	Newline	the subsequent output starts from new line.
\t	Tab	moves over to the next eight-space-wide field.
\b	Backspace	moves the cursor one space left.
\r	carriage return	carriage return.
\f	formfeed	advances to the top of the next page on printer.
\a	beep	produces one audio tone of the speaker
\'	single quote	insert character ' in the output
\"	double quote	insert character " in the output
\\	backslash	insert character \ in the output
\0	null	terminates a string

An escape sequence actually represents a single character.

The C language allows certain characters that cannot be entered/typed directly from the keyboard such as *backspace*, *tab*, *carriage return*, *newline,* etc. These characters are represented by a sequence that begin with character \ (back slash), and are known as *escape sequences.*

String (multi-character) Literals

A string literal is a sequence of characters enclosed in double quotes. The characters can be from any character in the character set.

Valid examples of string literals are:

```
"hello"     "Well done . . ."     "123.24"     "X"     "10+5"
```

Note that single character literal such as 'A' is not equivalent to single character string literal as "A".

Escape sequences can also appear in a string literal. For example printing string

```
"\"String literals are double-quoted.\""
```

will give the following result

```
"String literals are double-quoted."
```

6.3.4 Punctuators

Punctuators are also called separators. Various punctuators used in C++ are described in following table.

Table 6.3: List of punctuators and their description

Punctuators	Description
Brackets [ ]	Used to enclose array subscripts.
Parentheses ( )	Used to enclose arguments in function declaration as well as function definition, parameters in function calls and expressions.
Braces { }	Used to enclose the block of statements. Also used to enclose list of elements while initializing arrays.
Comma ,	Used to separate arguments in function definition, and parameters in function call.
Semicolon ;	Used to terminate a statement.
Equal to sign =	Used to initialize a variable and as an assignment operator.
Pound sing #	Used for preprocessor directives.

6.3.5 Operators

Operators are the verbs of C++ language that let the user perform computations on values. You can think of operators as verbs and of operands as the subjects and object of those verbs. C++ language's rich set of operators is one of its distinguished features.

These operators can be enumerated in following categories:

- Arithmetic Operators (+, -, *, /, %)
- Relational Operators (<, <=, >, >=, ==, !=)
- Logical Operators (!, &&, ||)
- Bit-wise Operators (~, >>, <<, &, |)
- Special Operators
  - Increment & Decrement Operators (++ - -)
  - The *sizeof* Operator
  - The *addressof* Operator (&)
  - Indirection Operator (*)
  - Ternary/Conditional Operator (? :)
  - Comma Operator (,)

6.4 CONCEPT OF DATA TYPE

A *data type* is a classification of the type of data that a variable can hold in a computer program. Data types are an important factor in all computer programming languages, including When programmers create computer applications, data types must be referenced and used correctly, to ensure the proper result and an error-free program.

Data types in C are of two types:

- **Built-in Data Types**
  - Built-in data types are the most basic data types in C.
  - The term built-in means that they are pre-defined in C and can be used directly in a program.
  - *char, int, float* and *double* are the most common built-in data types.
  - Apart from these, we also have *void* data type.
- **Derived Data Types**
  - Also called user-defined data types, are those which are first declared and defined by the user before use.
  - They are composed of built-in data types.
  - *Array, structure, union, class, pointers,* etc. are most common derived data types

In this chapter, we will discuss about built-in data types only.

6.5 BUILT-IN DATA TYPES

The various kinds of built-in data types supported by C under this category are summarized in Table 6.2 along with description and their memory requirements.

Table 6.2: Built-in data types and their memory requirements

Name	Description	Bytes
Integer *int*	integer numbers	2
Real/Floating-point *float* *double*	Single precision floating-point numbers Double precision floating-point numbers	4 8
Character *char*	A Single Character	1

6.5.1 The *int* Data Type

The *int* data type is used for integers. Integers are numbers with no decimal point. For example: 124, –75, 1200, 0, etc.

An integer number consists of a sequence of digits preceded by an optional sign, plus (+) or minus (–). A decimal point and comma is not allowed in an integer value.

The integer data type consists of a subset of integers. An integer value is an exact representation of the corresponding integer. Table 6.3 shows the different types of integer numbers, their memory requirements, and the range of values for each type.

Table 6.3: Type of Integer Numbers

Type	Bytes	Range
short int or int	2	–32768 to +32767
long int	4	–2147483648 to +2147483647
unsigned short int or unsigned int	2	0 to 65535
unsigned long int	4	0 to 4294967295

An integer value consists of a sequence of digits preceded by an optional sign, plus (+) or minus (–). A decimal point and comma is not allowed in an integer value.

The following are valid integer values of type *int*:

```
123     +123     0      32765
3445    7523     -2000  -3578
```

The following are invalid integer values of type *int* because of the reasons as given:

```
  .123    (Decimal point not allowed)
 3,452    (Comma not allowed)
 45234    (Value larger than permissible range)
```

6.5.2 The *float* and *double* Data Types

The *float* data type is used for numbers that have a decimal point which are commonly called floating-point numbers. For example: 75.50, 12.45, –95.6, 100.25, etc.

The *double* data type is also used for floating-point numbers. The only difference between *float* and *double* data types is that the range and precision of the *double* data type is greater than that of *float* data type.

In other words, *double* data type is used for large floating-point numbers, the ones that do not fit in the scope of the *float* data type.

The real/floating-point data type consists of a subset of the real numbers. A real value is an approximation of the desired real number correct to certain decimal positions. A real value of type *float* is accurate to six decimal positions, a real value of type of *double* is accurate to twelve decimal positions, and a real value of type of *long double* is even accurate to more than twelve decimal positions.

Table 6.4 shows the different types of real numbers, their memory requirements, and the range of values for each type.

Table 6.4: Type of Real Numbers

Type	Bytes	Range
float	4	3.4×10^{-38} to $3.4\times10^{+38}$
double	8	1.7×10^{-308} to $1.7\times10^{+308}$

Real values are numbers having fractional parts. The real values can be specified in two forms – *fractional form* (*fixed-point form*) and *exponent form* (*scientific notation*). A real value in fractional form consists of signed or unsigned digits including a decimal point.

The rule for writing a real value in fractional form is:

> *"A real value in fractional form can have zero or more digit before a decimal point followed by zero or more digits after the decimal point. It may have either + or – sign preceding it. A value without sign is assumed to be positive."*

Examples of valid real values in fractional form:

```
-123.345      +125.50.456      1234.
```

Examples of valid real values in fractional form:

```
      15      (Decimal point missing)
12,34.23      (Comma not allowed)
```

A real value in exponent form consists of two parts: *mantissa* and *exponent*. For example, in value 2.5E–1 (which is equivalent to 2.5×10^{-1}), mantissa part is 2.5 and exponent part is –1. Here E–1 represents 10^{-1}, and letter *E* (or *e*) stands for *exponent*.

The rule for writing a real value in exponent form is given below:

> *"A real value in exponent form has two parts – mantissa and en exponent. The mantissa can either be an integer value or a real value in fractional form. The mantissa is followed by a letter E (or e) and the exponent. The exponent must be an integer value."*

Examples of valid real values in exponent form:

```
+1.25E12     .0001E+2     1.E-2     100.00E0      5E+10
```

Examples of invalid real values in exponent form:

```
+145.80E      (No digit specified for exponent)
12.35E5.5     (Exponent cannot be a fraction)
12,235E-5     (No comma allowed)
```

6.5.3 The *char* Data Type

The *char* data type is used for characters. It can be used for any valid character in C and not just alphabets.

Here is a special thing about *char* data type: characters are stored in memory using their ASCII codes which are numeric, *i.e.*, integers. Thus, *char* data type is basically the same as the *int* data type.

6.5.4 The *void* Data Type

The word *void* means empty. So *void* data type has no value.

It is useful in many situations. One such situation that it is used as return type for functions that do not return a value.

6.6 LITERALS/CONSTANTS

A constant (also known as simply literal or literal constant) refers to fixed values that do not change during the execution of a program.

Integer Constants

An integer constant refers to a sequence of digits. Such a sequence without a leading sign is assumed as positive integer constant.

Following are valid integer constants of type *int*:

```
123          +123          0          32765          3445
```

An integer constant by default is treated as an integer value of type *int*, and the compiler reserves 2-bytes of memory for its storage.

However, we can suffix letter 'L' with the integer value to denote that integer value is of type *long*, and for this value compiler reserves 4-bytes of memory for its storage.

The following are valid integer constants of type *long*:

```
120L          +122L          0L          -2000L          -112L
```

Real Constants

Real constants are numbers having fractional parts. The real constants can be specified in two forms – *fractional form* (*fixed-point form*) and *exponent form* (*scientific notation*).

Real constant in fractional form consists of signed/unsigned digits including a decimal point.

Examples of valid real constants in fractional form:

```
-125.50     +100.5     1.     .454
```

A real constant in exponent form consists of two parts: *mantissa* and *exponent*. For example, in constant 5.25E+2 (which is equivalent to 5.25×10^2), mantissa part is 5.25 and exponent part is +2. Here E+2 represent 10^2, and letter *E* (or *e*) stands for *exponent*.

Examples of valid real constants in exponent form:

```
1.25E12     .0001E+2     5.E-3     100.00E0     5.5E+10
```

Single Character Constants

A character constant consists of a single character enclosed in single quotes (') such as 'A'.

String Constants

A string constant is a sequence of characters enclosed in double quotes. The characters can be from any character in the character set.

Valid examples of string constants are:

```
"hello"      "Well done . . ."     "123.24"      "X"        "10+5"
```

Note that single character constant such as 'A' is not equivalent to single character string constant as "A".

Escape sequences can also appear in a string constant. For example printing string

```
"\"String constants are double-quoted.\""
```

will give the following result

```
"String constants are double-quoted."
```

6.7 SYMBOLIC CONSTANTS

A symbolic constant is a name that substitutes a literal constant. As an example, assume that we are computing the area of circle with given radius using the following statement:

```
area = 3.14159 * radius * radius;
```

In the above statement, numeric constant 3.14159 represents the value of the mathematical constant π, and can be replaced by symbolic constant named *PI*. The task is accomplished as follows:

```
#define PI 3.14159
area = PI * radius * radius;
```

In the above statements, *#define* pre-processor directive associates the name PI with the numeric constant 3.14159. Note that no semicolon is used after the *#define* preprocessor directive, and also to other directives as well.

During the compiling, the preprocessor will replace each occurrence of name PI with numeric constant 3.14159.

The use of symbolic constant has following advantages:

- The use of symbolic constants enhances the readability of the program, as the appropriately chosen names pronounce much as their counter parts in the real world (actual use).

- Suppose the same numeric constant is used at many places in the program, and you want to change its value, you can do it in following ways:
  - At every place, change the value manually in the program, which is cumbersome and time consuming. Also there may be chances that at some place values may be left unchanged.
  - Use symbolic constant, *i.e.*, associate a name with the constant, and then at each place of the value use symbolic constant. Now, if you want to change the value of the constant, you have to do only at one place. During compilation, every occurrence of the symbolic constant will be replaced with the new value.

6.8 VARIABLES

A variable provides us with named storage that we can write to, retrieve, and manipulate throughout the course of the program. In other words, variables are memory locations in the computer's memory that holds data. Contents of a variable may vary — hence the name *variable*. Variables hold different kind of data and the same variable might hold different values during the execution of a program.

Further, each variable in C language is associated with a specific type, which determines the size and layout its associated memory, the range of values that can be stored within that memory, and the set of operations that can be applied to it.

Unlike a constant, a variable is *addressable* and its address can be accessed using *addressof* (&) operator.

There are two values associated with a variable:

1. Its data value that is stored at some memory address. This sometimes referred to as variable's *rvalue* (pronounced as "are-value"). We may think *rvalue* as meaning *read value*. Both a literal constant and a variable can serve as *rvalue*.
2. Its address value that is its address in memory within which its data value is stored. This sometimes referred to as variable's *lvalue* (pronounced as "ell-value"). We may think *lvalue* as meaning *location value*. Only a variable can serve as *lvalue*.

Consider the following statement

```
y = y + 3.5;
```

Here variable *y* appears on both sides of an assignment operator. The right-hand instance is read. Its associated data value is fetched from its address in memory. The left-hand instance is written. The result of the addition operation is stored at its location value and its previous value is overwritten. Therefore, variable *y* on the left-hand side serves as *lvalue* and on the right-hand side it serves as *rvalue*.

6.8.1 Declaring Variables

In C language, each variable in a program must be declared and defined. Declaration is used to name a variable while definition is used to create (allocate memory) a variable. The definition of variable assumes that the declaration of the variable has been done or is being done at the same time.

When we create variables, the declaration gives them a symbolic name and the definition reserves memory for them. Once variables are defined, they are used to hold the data that are required by the program for its operation.

To create a variable, we first specify the data type and then its name. If two or more variables of same data type are to be created, their names are separated using comma. The syntax for declaring and defining a variable is

```
type v1, v2, . . ., vn;
```

where *v1*, *v2*, ..., *vn* are the names of the variables separated by comma.

A variable's type can be any of the fundamental data types or user-defined data types. The one exception is the *void* type, *i.e.*, a variable cannot be of type *void*.

Following are some examples of variable declarations and definition:

```
int count, m, n;
float value, sum;
char ch;
double deviation;
```

First statement declares variables *count*, *m* and *n* of type *int*. Compiler reserves 2-bytes for each of these variables.

Second statement declares variable *value* and *sum* of type *float*. Compiler reserves 4-bytes for each of these variables.

Third statement declares variable *ch* of type *char*. Compiler reserves 1-bytes for it.

Fourth statement declares variable *deviation* of type *double*. Compiler reserves 8-bytes for it.

6.8.2 Initializing Variables

It is important to note that during the declaration and definition, a variable is normally not initialized. However, in C language, it is possible to give an initial value to a variable during its declaration and definition. To do that, a variable is followed by character '=' and then the value to be given to the variable. Consider the following statement

```
int sum = 0;
```

It declares variable *sum* of type *int*, reserves 2-bytes of memory for it, and places integer value 0 in those 2-bytes, *i.e.*, initializes variable *sum* to a value 0.

As declarations and definitions of variables of same type can be combined in one statement, likewise initialization of variables of same type can also be done. The following statement illustrates this:

```
int sum = 0, count = 0;
```

6.8.3 The *const* Access Modifier

When the *const* access modifier is used along with the variable, it allows the value to be assigned once and that too using initialization. Afterwards, the value of this variable cannot be modified, *i.e.*, variable behaves as a constant. Consider the following declaration statement

```
const float pie = 3.1428;
```

It stores real constant in a variable *pie* (π – a useful constant in mathematics).

Any further assignment to this variable *pie* is not permitted, *i.e.*, any assignment statement of type

```
pie = value/variable/expression/function-call;
```

will result in a syntax error as the compiler will not allow to do that.

6.8.4 The Type Modifiers

The *type* modifiers changes the meaning of the fundamental data type with which they are used. The type modifiers supported by the C language are *unsigned*, *signed*, *short*, and *long*.

6.8.4.1 The *signed* Type Modifier

The *signed* type modifier can only be used with *int* and *char* fundamental data types. Even if the signed modifier is omitted, it is assumed by default. When a variable is of signed type, implicitly or explicitly, it can hold negative as well as positive values

In the following cases, variable *x* can hold any value in the range –32768 to +32767, and variable *y* can take any value in the range –128 to +127.

```
signed int x;            signed char y;
int x;                   char y;
```

6.8.4.2 The *unsigned* Type Modifiers

The *unsigned* type modifier can also be used only with *int* and *char* fundamental data types. When it is used, a variable can hold only positive values.

In following cases, variable *x* can hold any value in the range 0 to 65535, and variable *y* can take any value in the range 0 to 255.

```
unsigned int x;          unsigned char y;
```

6.8.4.3 The *short* Type Modifier

The *short* type modifier can be used only with *int* fundamental data type. With *short* type modifier, the base type can be omitted, and it is assumed to be *int*. When it is used, a variable use memory as half of the memory as that of base type *int*, and can hold only smaller values. However, in the implementations of C language such as Turbo C, *int* and *short int* are synonymous, *i.e.*, both use 16-bits (2 bytes).

Both of the following statements serve the same purpose, and variable *x* can hold values in the range –32768 to 32767.

```
short int x;      OR       short x;
```

6.8.4.4 The *long* Type Modifier

The *long* type modifier can be used with *int*, *float*, and *double* fundamental data types. With *long* type modifier, the base type can be omitted, and it is assumed to be *int*. When it is used, a variable use memory as double of the memory as that of base type, and can hold large values.

Both of the following statements serve the same purpose.

```
long int x;      OR      long x;
```

Following statements also serve the same purpose.

```
long float x;    OR      double x;
```

Table 6.5 sums up the fundamental data types, their possible combinations with type modifiers, memory requirements for each and the range of values on Turbo C/C++ compiler.

Table 6.5: Possible combinations of type modifiers and fundamental data types

Type	Memory Requirement	Range
unsigned char	1 byte	0 to 255
char	1 byte	–128 to 127
unsigned int	2 bytes	0 to 65,535
int	2 bytes	–32,768 to 32,767
short int	2 bytes	–32,768 to 32,767
long int	4 bytes	–2,147,483,648 to 2,147,483,647
long	4 bytes	–2,147,483,648 to 2,147,483,647
unsigned long	4 bytes	0 to 4,294,967,295
float	4 bytes	3.4×10^{-38} to $3.4\times10^{+38}$
long float	8 bytes	1.7×10^{-308} to $1.7\times10^{+308}$
double	8 bytes	1.7×10^{-308} to $1.7\times10^{+308}$
long double	10 bytes	3.4×10^{-4932} to $1.1\times10^{+4932}$

6.9 STORAGE CLASSES

Every variable in C language possesses a characteristic called its *storage class.* The storage class defines two main characteristics of the variable, apart from the place of storage and the initial value. These are

- Lifetime
- Visibility or scope

Lifetime — *Lifetime* of a variable is the length of time it retains a particular value.

Visibility — *Visibility* or *scope* of a variable refers to those parts of a program that will be able to recognize it.

At first instance, a question arises: *why are storage classes necessary*? The answer is that by using variables with the appropriate lifetime and visibility, we can write programs that use memory more efficiently, run faster, and are less prone to programming errors. The correct use of storage class is especially important in large programs.

The storage class precedes the variable's declaration and tells the compiler regarding *where the variable should be stored, what should be its initial value, what will be its scope*, and for *how much time it will be available for use*.

The C language supports following four storage classes:

- auto
- static
- register
- extern

If the storage class in the variable declaration is omitted, it is assumed of type *auto*, *i.e.*, storage class is *auto* by default. Let us examine these storage classes one by one.

For example, consider the following declaration statement

```
static unsigned int x;
```

It tells the compiler that the storage class for variable *x* is static, which signifies the following things:

- Variable *x* will be stored in computer main memory.
- Since variable *x* is not initialized, it will automatically be initialized with value is zero.
- Variable *x* will be visible to the block in which it is declared.
- The variable *x*, if declared in a function other than *main()* function, will retain its value during different function calls.

We will learn more about storage classes in *Chapter 11*.

EXERCISE

1. What are various data types supported by C language? Give memory requirement of each. Also give at least two examples of each data type.
2. List various types of operators available in C language and also give their precedence, if any.
3. Suppose *x*, *y*, and *z* have been declared variables of type *float*, write a C segment which changes the values of *x*, *y*, and *z* so that *x* has *y*'s value, *y* has *z*'s value, and *z* has *x*'s value.
4. What is an integer? Which of the following are invalid 2-byte integers, and why?

```
   123      -435     +4567    32767
-32768    +32768    -40000    4.50
```

5. What is a variable? What are the rules for naming a variable? Which of the following are invalid variable names and why?

```
roll-no    12_items   temperature
height     float      Interest_Paid     SUM
```

6. What is another name for floating point numbers?
7. What is a character constant? What is the maximum number of character that a variable of type *char* can hold?

❑ ❑ ❑

Chapter 7

Operators and Expressions

Learning Objectives

After reading this chapter, students will be able to explain

- various operators and their usage
- concept of precedence and associativity among operators
- various type of expressions and their evaluation
- type conversion in assignment and expressions
- assignment statement and its forms
- library functions

7.1 INTRODUCTION

Operators are the verbs of a language that let the user perform computations on values. You can think of operators as verbs and of operands as the subjects and object of those verbs. C language's rich set of operators is one of its distinguished features.

An *expression* is a formula consisting of one or more operands and zero or more operators linked together to compute a value. The computed values are to be stored in a variable for future use. This is done using an assignment statement.

In a computer program, variety of computations is to be performed as per requirements of the problem in hand. Yet there are some routine type computations that may be part of almost every program. Therefore as a convenience, every modern programming language provides a support for these routine type computations in the form of library functions.

This chapter attempts to describe these semantic units of the C language.

7.2 OPERATORS

As mentioned earlier, operators are the verbs of a language that let the user perform computations on values. You can think of operators as verbs and of operands as the subjects and object of those verbs.

The C language's rich set of operators is one of its distinguished features. These operators can be enumerated in following categories:

- Arithmetic Operators
- Relational Operators
- Logical Operators
- Bitwise Operators
- Special Operators
  - Increment & Decrement Operators
  - The *sizeof* Operator
  - The *addressof* Operator
  - Indirection Operator
  - Conditional Operator
  - Comma Operator

7.2.1 Precedence and Associativity of Operators

Precedence is used to determine the order in which different operators are evaluated in an expression.

Associativity is used to determine the order in which different operators with same precedence are evaluated in an expression.

Precedence is applied before associativity to determine the order in which expressions are evaluated. Associativity is applied later, if necessary.

Precedence

The concept of precedence is well defined in the subject of mathematics. You must be aware of rule BODMAS – Brackets, Of, Division, Multiplication, Addition, and Subtraction. In algebra, division and multiplication is performed before addition and subtraction.

The following is a simple example of precedence:

```
5 + 3 * 4
```

This expression consists of one addition and one multiplication operator. As you know from the knowledge of algebra, multiplication has higher precedence than addition, and this multiplication is performed before addition.

Therefore, the expression will be evaluated as

```
( 5 + ( 3 * 4 ) ) → ( 5 + 12 ) → 17
```

giving value 17 as the value of the entire expression.

Associativity

Associativity is applied when more then one operator of same precedence is used in an expression. Associativity can be *left-to-right* or *right-to-left*. Left-to-right associativity evaluates the expression by starting on the left and moving to the right whereas the right-to-left associativity evaluates the expression by starting on the right and moving to the left.

The following is a simple example of associativity:

```
2 + 5 + 7
```

This expression consists of two addition operators. Here the associativity determines how the sub expressions are grouped together. Since the addition operator has left-to-right associativity, the expression will be grouped as

```
( ( 2 + 5 ) + 7 ) → ( 7 + 7 ) → 14
```

giving value 14 as the value of the entire expression.

We will learn more about precedence and associativity as we proceed with the discussion on various operators. *Appendix A* summarizes the precedence and associativity of all the operators supported by C language.

7.2.2 Arithmetic Operators

Different arithmetic operators supported by C language are listed in Table 7.1. All of the operators may be used as binary operators, which appear between their operands. The plus (+) and minus (–) may also be used as unary, and precede their operand.

Table 7.1: Arithmetic Operators

Symbol Used	Operation Performed
+	Addition
–	Subtraction
*	Multiplication
/	Division
%	Modulus

1. Modulus (%) operators, that give remainder, work only on operands of type *int*, *long int*.
2. There is no operator for exponentiation operation in C language.

Integer Arithmetic

When both the operands are integers, the operations will be called *integer arithmetic* and will always yield an integer value. Consider the following statements

```
int x = 13, b = 5;
```

then we have the following results:

```
x - y = 8
x + y = 18
x * y = 65
x / y = 2 (decimal part truncated)
x % y = 3 (remainder of division)
```

In the integer division, if both the operands are of same sign, the result of the division is truncated towards 0. If one of them is negative, the direction of truncation is implementation dependent. On Turbo C/C++ compilers, it is towards 0.

Therefore,

`3/4, -3/-4, -3/4` and `3/-4`

all yields value 0 on Turbo C/C++ compiler.

Similarly in modulus operation, the sign of the result is always the sign of the first operand. Therefore,

```
-13/5 = -3        -13/-5 = -3        13/-5 = 3
```

Real Arithmetic

When both the operands are real numbers, the operations will be called *real arithmetic* and will always yield a real value. The real operand may be in *fractional form* or *exponent form*. Since real numbers (floating-point values) are rounded to permissible number of significant digits, result of arithmetic operations is an approximate value of correct result.

That is

```
 6.0 /  7.0  =  0.857143
-1.0 /  3.0  = -0.333333
 3.0 / -2.0  = -1.500000
```

The modulus operation cannot be used with real operands.

Mixed-mode Arithmetic

When one of the operands is real and the other is integer, the operations will be called *mixed-mode arithmetic* and will always yield a real value. The integer operand is converted into real operand and then real arithmetic is performed, resulting in a real value.

That is

```
 6 / 7.0  →    6.0 / 7.0  =  0.857143
-1.0 / 3  →   -1.0 / 3.0  =  -0.333333
```

Note that

```
15 / 10.0 = 1.5
15.0 / 10 = 1.5
```

where as

```
15 / 10 = 1
```

7.2.3 Relational Operators

These operators are used to compare the values of the operands that must be compatible, in order to facilitate decision-making. If the comparison succeeds, they return a value 1 (equivalent to Boolean value *true*) and if comparison fails then returns value 0 (equivalent to Boolean value *false*).

Table 7.2: Relational Operators

Symbol Used	Operation Performed
<	Less than
<=	Less than or equal to
>	Greater than
>=	Greater than or equal to
==	Equal to
!=	Not equal to

The C language supports all six relational operators. These relational operators are listed in Table 7.2, along with their descriptions.

Note that in C language, the non-zero value is treated as equivalent to Boolean true and zero value as equivalent to Boolean false. Further note that, there is no support for Boolean data as such in C language in old versions of C language. The new version of C language, known as C99 standard, supports the Boolean type.

Table 7.3 lists some example relational expressions and the result of their evaluation.

Table 7.3: Relational Expressions

Relation Expressions	Result of operation
`20 > 10`	1
`15 != 12`	1
`15 == 13`	0
`20 >= 35`	0
`10 <= 19`	1
`13 > 20`	0

Expressions such as

```
100 >= 59      15 < 25
```

are known as relational expressions.

However, if the relational expression is of following type

```
a + b == x + y
```

then firstly arithmetic expressions on both the sides of the relational operators are evaluated then the comparison is performed, *i.e.*, arithmetic operators have a higher precedence that relational operators.

7.2.4 Logical Operators

These operators are used to form compound conditions by joining two or more simple conditions formed using relational operators. Different logical operators supported by C language are listed in Table 7.4.

Table 7.4: Logical Operators

Symbol Used	Operation Performed
!	Logical NOT
&&	Logical AND
||	Logical OR

NOT Operator

The NOT operator (!) is a unary operator. It inverts the value, *i.e.*, it changes a *true* value to *false* and false value to *true*.

Table 7.5: Rules for Logical Operators

NOT Operation

x	*!x*
false	true
true	false

AND Operation

x	*y*	*x&&y*
false	false	false
false	true	false
true	false	false
true	true	true

OR Operation

x	*y*	*x* || *y*
false	false	false
false	true	true
true	false	true
true	true	true

AND Operator

The AND operator (&&) is a binary operator. Four distinct combinations of values of its operands are possible. The result is *true* only when both the operands are *true*, in all other cases, the result is *false*.

OR Operator

The OR operator (||) is also a binary operator. Four distinct combinations of values of its operands are possible. The result is *false* only when both the operands are *false*, in all other cases, the result is *true*.

Evaluating Logical Expressions

There are two methods to evaluate a logical expression. In the first method, the expression must be completely evaluated before the result is determined. This means that AND expression must be completely evaluated even when the first operand is *false* and it is therefore known that result will be *false*. Likewise, an OR expression must be completely evaluated even when first operand is *true* and it is therefore known that result will be *true*.

In the second method, also known as *short-circuit evaluation*, the expression need not be evaluated completely. As soon as it is known that what the final result will be, the rest of the expression is not evaluated. Therefore, in evaluating the AND expression, if the first operand is *false*, the second operand is not evaluated since it is apparent that the result will be *false*. Likewise, in evaluating the OR expression, if the first operand is *true*, the second operand is not evaluated since it is apparent that the result will be *true*.

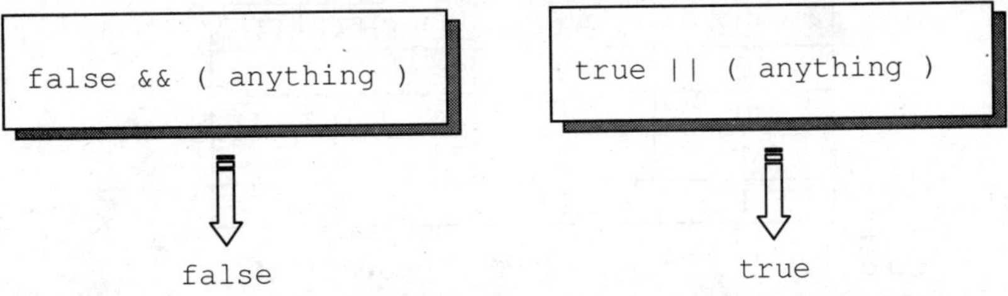

Figure 7.1: Short-circuit evaluation of AND/OR Operation

7.2.5 Bitwise Operators

These operators operate at bit-level, and allow us to manipulate the individual bits. Specifically, these operators find their use in low-level programming.

Different bit-wise operators supported by C language are listed in Table 7.6.

Table 7.6: Bitwise Operators

Symbol Used	Operation Performed
>>	Shift-right
<<	Shift-left
~	1's Complement
&	Bitwise AND
^	Bitwise Exclusive OR
|	Bitwise Inclusive OR

To illustrate working of bitwise operators, consider the following declarations statement

```
int a = 20, b = 94, c, d;
```

The value of *a* will be internally stored as 0000000000010100, and of *b* as 0000000001011110, *i.e.*, as two byte binary numbers.

7.2.5.1 Logical Bitwise Operators

The logical operators look at data to be manipulated as individual bits. Following four operators are used to manipulate the bits: bitwise AND (&), bitwise inclusive OR (|), bitwise exclusive OR (^), and one's complement (~). The first three are binary operators while the fourth one is unary operator.

7.2.5.1.1 Bitwise AND Operator

The bitwise AND operator (&) is a binary operator, and it performs the bitwise AND operation on the corresponding bits of the operands. The rules for bitwise AND operation are given in Table 7.7.

Table 7.7: Bitwise AND Operator

bit1	bit2	bit1 & bit2
0	0	0
0	1	0
1	0	0
1	1	1

```
Operand 1        ----    0000000000010100
Operand 2        ----    0001000010001110
Bitwise AND      ----    0000000000000100
```

This can be accomplished using the statement of type

```
c = a & b;
```

Using the value of *a* and *b*, as per type declaration statement, find out the value of *c*.

7.2.5.1.2 Bitwise Exclusive OR Operator

The bitwise exclusive OR operator (^) is a binary operator, and it performs the bitwise exclusive OR operation on the corresponding bits of the operands. The rules for bitwise exclusive OR operation are given in Table 7.8.

Table 7.8: Bitwise Exclusive OR Operator

bit1	bit2	bit1 ^ bit2
0	0	0
0	1	1
1	0	1
1	1	0

```
Operand 1                   ----    0000000000010100
Operand 2                   ----    0001000010001110
Bitwise Exclusive OR        ----    0001000010011010
```

This can be accomplished using the statement of type

```
c = a ^ b;
```

Using the value of *a* and *b*, as per type declaration statement, find out the value of *c*.

7.2.5.1.3 Bitwise Inclusive OR Operator

The bitwise inclusive OR operator (|) is a binary operator, and it performs the bitwise inclusive OR operation on the corresponding bits of the operands. The rules for bitwise inclusive OR operation are given in Table 7.9.

Table 7.9: Bitwise Inclusive OR Operator

bit1	bit2	bit1 | bit2
0	0	0
0	1	1
1	0	1
1	1	1

```
Operand 1                   ----    0000000000010100
Operand 2                   ----    0001000010001110
Bitwise Inclusive OR        ----    0001000010011110
```

This can be accomplished using the statement of type

```
c = a | b;
```

Using the value of *a* and *b*, as per type declaration statement, find out the value of *c*.

7.2.5.1.4 One's Complement Operator

One's complement operator is a unary operator. The One's complement is obtained by just inverting the individual bits.

That is, if the value of a is 0000000000010100, then its one's complement will be 1111111111101011

This can be achieved by using ~ operator as shown in the following statement

```
c = ~a;
```

7.2.5.2 Shift Operators

The shift operators move bits of the operand to the left or right. When applied to unsigned numbers, these operators are independent of the underlying implementation (hardware and software). When applied on signed numbers, however, the implementation is left to the software engineer who designs the system.

It is often known for which hardware and software platform the compiler is written. Therefore, the C standard leaves the implementation details up to the compiler writer (there is no standard), the code that shifts signed negative numbers may not be portable to other platforms.

7.2.5.2.1 Bitwise Shift-Right Operator

The shift-right operator is a binary operator where the value of the second operand specifies the by how many bit positions the value of the first operand is to be right shifted. The rightmost bit is discarded, whereas the 0 or 1 (depending on whether the operand is positive number or negative number) is inserted in the leftmost bit position.

Consider the following statement

```
c = a >> 1;
```

This statement causes the value of *a* (0000000000010100) shifted to right by one bit and 0 bit is added to the left, and finally the resultant value is assigned to variable *c*.

So the value of *c* will be 0000000000001010, *i.e.*, decimal 10. The right shift by 1 bit is equivalent to division by a factor of 2.

However, if the original left most bit is 1 (*i.e.*, the value is negative), then bit 1 is added to the left for every shift.

The signed numbers are stored in two's complement form. In two's complement form, the leftmost bit is used for sign. The sign bit is 0 for positive and 1 for negative numbers. For 2-byte integers, remaining 15 bits hold the magnitude of the number, whereas for 4-byte integers (*i.e.*, long integers) remaining 31-bits contain the magnitude of the number. But for unsigned integers, all the bits are used to hold the magnitude as all the numbers are positive and therefore no bit is used for sign to distinguish positive integers from negative integers.

7.2.5.2.2 Bitwise Shift-Left Operator

Like shift-right operator, shift-left operator is also a binary operator where the value of the second operand specifies the by how many bit positions the value of the first operand is to be left shifted. The leftmost bit is discarded, whereas 0 bit is inserted in the rightmost bit position.

Consider the following statement

```
c = a << 1;
```

This statement causes the value of *a* (0000000000010100) shifted to left by one bit and 0 bit is added to the right, and finally the resultant value is assigned to variable *c*.
So the value of *c* will be 0000000000101000, *i.e.*, decimal 40. The left shift by 1 bit is equivalent to multiplication by a factor of 2.

7.2.6 Special Operators

These operators were not supported by earlier high-level languages, and were incorporated for the first time in C. Most of the later high-level languages are influenced by C and almost all such languages, for example C, JAVA, etc., support these kind of operators. Let us discuss each of them briefly, and their utility you will be able to appreciate in the subsequent sections and chapters.

7.2.6.1 Increment & Decrement Operators

The C language supports two very useful operators – increment operator (++) and decrement operator (--). These operators can be used with all basic data types. The increment operator adds 1 to the operand, while decrement operator subtracts 1 from the operand.

Both operators are unary operators and can be used in the prefix as well as postfix notation as shown below:

```
++k;        or      k++;
--k;        or      k--;
```

Here, `++k` (as well as `k++`) is equivalent to `k = k + 1` or `k += 1`, and `--k` (as well as `k--`) is equivalent to `k = k - 1` or `k -= 1`.

These operators are most frequently used in *while* and *for* loops as control variables.

While `++k` or `k++` means the same thing when they form statements independently, they behave differently when they are used as part of other expressions.

Consider the following statements

```
int y, k = 5;
y = ++k;
```

In this case, first the value of *k* is incremented and then assigned to *y*, and hence y and k will have same value as 6. Thus, the above statements are equivalent to following statements

```
int y, k = 5;
++k;
y = k;
```

However, if we write the above statements as

```
int y, k = 5;
y = k++;
```

then first the current value of *k* (value 5) is assigned to y and then the value of k is incremented, and hence *y* will have value 5 while and *k* will have value as 6.
Thus, the above statements are equivalent to following statements

```
int y, k = 5;                   int y, k = 5;
y = k;            or            y = k;
++k;                            k++;
```

Similar is the case, when these operators are used in accessing elements of an array.

Therefore, the statement

```
a[i++] = 5;
```

is equivalent to

```
a[i] = 5;
i = i + 1;
```

These operators can also be used in complex expressions, such as

```
k = m++ - j / 10;
```

where exiting value of *m* is used in evaluating expression, and afterwards *m* is incremented.

Rules for Increment & Decrement Operators

1. These operators are unary operators and require variable as operand.
2. These operators mean the same thing, irrespective whether they are used in prefix or postfix notation, when they form statements independently.
3. When these operators are used in prefix notation in an expression, then first value of the variable is changed accordingly and the new value is used in evaluating the expression.
4. When these operators are used in postfix notation in an expression, then first existing value of variable is used in evaluating expression and then value is changed accordingly.
5. The precedence and associativity of these operators is same as that of unary plus and unary minus.

7.2.6.2 The *sizeof* Operator

The *sizeof* operator returns the size, in bytes, of the given operand. The syntax of *sizeof* operator is

```
sizeof( exp )
```

where *exp* represents a data type (built-in or user-defined), a literal/constant or a variable. For example

```
sizeof( float )
```

returns value 4.

Table 7.10: Use of *sizeof* Operator

sizeof Operator used as	Returns	Justification
`sizeof(12)`	2	Integer constant by default belong to data type *int*, and size for *int* is 2.
`sizeof('a')`	1	Size of Character constant is 1.
`sizeof(int)`	2	Size of data type *int* is 2.
`sizeof(125.25)`	8	Real constant by default belong to data type *double*.
`sizeof(125UL)`	4	Size of data type *unsigned long int* is 4.
`sizeof(125.25F)`	4	Real constant is of data type *float*, and size for *float* is 4.
`double x;` `sizeof(x);`	8	Variable *x* is of type *double*, and size for *double* is 8.

7.2.6.3 The *addressof* Operator

Character '&' when prefixed with a variable returns the address of the memory locations, hence its name *addressof* operator. It is used in the *scanf()* function and to initialize the pointers. The use of *addressof* (&) operator is demonstrated in Table 7.11.

7.2.6.4 Indirection Operator

Character '*' when prefixed with a pointer variable returns the value stored in a memory location whose address is held in pointer variable. That is, value is accessed through pointer variable indirectly, hence its name indirection operator. Consider following statements

```
int y = 10, x;
int *py;
py = &y;
x = *py;
```

The expression *"*py"* returns the values at address which held in pointer variable *py*, *i.e.*, value of variable y which is 10, and that get assigned to variable *x*.

Table 7.11: Use of *addressof* (&) Operators

addressof (&) Operator used as	Task Performed

`int y = 10;`
`int *py;`
`Py = &y;`
	First statement declares and defines variable *y* of type *int*. It also initializes it with value 10.
	Second statement declares and defines a pointer variable *py* that can hold an address of a memory location reserved for storing value of type *int*.
	Third statement assigns the address of variable y to pointer variable *py*.

`int x, y;` `scanf("%d %d", &x, &y);`	First statement declares and defines two variable *x* and *y* of type *int*. Second statement takes two integer values as input from the keyboard and stores those values at addresses of variable *x* and *y*, respectively.

7.2.6.5 Conditional/Ternary Operator

Consider the following segment, written in pseudocode

```
if ( a > b ) then
   set big = a
else
   set big = b
endif
```

This segments assigns the maximum of the values of *a* and *b* to *big*. As it is clear that the value assigned to variable *big* will depend on the outcome of the test condition "*a* > *b*". Such expressions are known as *conditional expressions*, and can be written using conditional operator. The syntax of using ternary operator is

```
expl ? exp2 : exp3;
```

where *exp1*, *exp2*, *exp3* are expressions.

The expression *exp1* is evaluated first. If it is non-zero (true), then the expression *exp2* is evaluated, and that is the value of the conditional expression; otherwise expression *exp3* is evaluated, and that is the value of the conditional expression. Note that only one of the expression *exp2* and *exp3* is evaluated.

Thus, the above pseudocode segment using conditional operator can be written as

```
big = ( a > b ) ? a : b;
```

Parentheses are not necessary around the first expression of the conditional expression since the precedence of '?:' is very low, just above assignment operator. However, the use of parentheses is recommended as they make the condition part easier to see.

7.2.6.6 Comma Operator

A comma operator is used to combine several related expressions. The group of expressions separated by comma ',' are evaluated left-to-right and the result of the right-most expression becomes the value of the total comma separated expression.

For example, the statement

```
a = ( b = 10, b+1 );
```

first assigns the value 10 to *b*, and then adds 1 to *b* and finally the resultant value, *i.e.*, 11 is assigned to *a*. In the above expression, the use of parenthesis is mandatory because the comma operator has a lower precedence than the assignment operator. In fact comma operator has the lowest precedence among all the operators.

Comma operator can be used in *for loop* to separate expressions, as shown below:

```
for ( i = 0, j = n; i < j; i++, j-- )
{
    // some code
}
```

In the above *for loop*, first variable *i* is initialized to 0 and then variable *j* is initialized to *n*, and this happens only once. Then for every subsequent iteration, first variable *i* is incremented and then variable *j* is decremented before testing the terminating condition which states that the loop will execute till the value of *i* is less than *j*.

Comma operator can also be used in *while loop* to separate expressions such as

```
while ( ch = cin.get(), ch != '\r' )
{
    // some code
}
```

In the above *while loop*, the first expression accepts a character input from the user and assigns the same character to *char* variable *ch*, then variable *ch* is tested against carriage return. If the character input is not the carriage return, the loop continues to execute for next iteration.

Following is another example of use of the comma operator to swap the values of two integer variables *x* and *y*:

```
temp = x, x = y, y = temp;
```

Variable *temp* is used as a temporary variable just to facilitate swapping of values.

7.3 EXPRESSIONS

An *expression* is a formula consisting of one or more operands and zero or more operators linked together to compute a value. An operand may be a function reference, a variable, an array element or a constant. In the expression

```
a + b
```

plus character '+' is an operator and *a* and *b* are operands.

There are four types of expressions in C. These are

1. Arithmetic expressions
2. Relational expressions
3. Logical expressions
4. Conditional expressions

Each type of expression takes certain types of operands and uses a specific set of operators. Evaluation of every expression produces a value of specific type. Expressions are not statements, but may be components of statements.

For example, consider the line

```
x = 2.0/3.0 + a * b;
```

The entire line is a statement, but the portion after the equal sign is an expression.

7.3.1 Arithmetic Expressions

An arithmetic expression is made up of operands and arithmetic operators. It produces a value that is of type *int*, *float* or *double*. When an expression involve only integral operands, it is known as *pure integer expression*, when it involves only real operands it is known as a *pure real expression*, and when it involves both integral and real operands it is known as a *mixed mode expression*.

Following are some mathematical expressions and their corresponding C expressions. For simplicity, we have considered only those expressions that don't involve the use of any mathematical or trigonometric functions.

Table 7.12: Some Sample Arithmetic Expressions

Mathematical/Algebraic Expressions	The C Arithmetic Expressions
$\frac{a+b}{2}$	`(a+b)/2`
$a+\frac{b}{c}+d$	`a+b/c+d`
$\frac{ab}{c-d^2}+d$	`(a*b)/(c-d*d)+d`
$1+\frac{a}{b+\frac{1}{c}}$	`1+a/(b+1/c)`
$\frac{\frac{a}{c+b}-e}{d}$	`a/((c+b)/d)-e`
ax^2+bx+c	`a*x*x+b*x+c`
$ut+\frac{1}{2}at^2$	`u*t+0.5*a*t*t`
$m\left(a\times h+\frac{v^2}{2}\right)$	`m*(a*h+(v*v)/2)`

While converting mathematical/algebraic expressions into C arithmetic expressions, parentheses can be used to control associativity and the order in which operators are evaluated. If parentheses are present in an expression, then the expression within the parentheses is evaluated first and within the parentheses the implicit precedence is observed. If there is nesting of parentheses (parentheses inside parentheses), then the inner most parentheses are evaluated first.

7.3.1.1 Evaluation of Arithmetic Expressions

As you know expressions are evaluated by performing one operation at a time, and same is the case when expressions are evaluated by a computer. The order of evaluation of individual operations is governed by the precedence and associativity of operators. However, when individual operations are performed, the following cases can happen:

- When both of the operands are of type integer (*short*, *int*, *long*), the integer arithmetic will be performed and the results of the operation will an integer value. For example, 5/2 will yield 2 not 2.5 as the fractional part is ignored.
- When both of the operands are of type real (*float*, *double*), the real arithmetic will be performed and the results of the operation will a real value. For example, 5.0/2.0 will yield 2.5.
- However, when one operand is of type integer and the second one is of type real, the mixed mode arithmetic will be performed. In this case, first integer operand will be converted into real operand, and then real arithmetic will be performed and the results of the operation will a real value. For example, 5/2.0 or 5.0/2 will yield 2.5, because in the first case first value 5 will be converted to 5.0 and then division will be performed while in the second case value 2 will be converted to 2.0 and then the division will be performed.

To illustrate the way arithmetic expression are evaluated, consider the following expression

```
5 * 4 / ( 1 + 5 * 2 / 3 + 6 ) + 8 * ( 7 / 4 )
```

This expression is evaluated as depicted below:

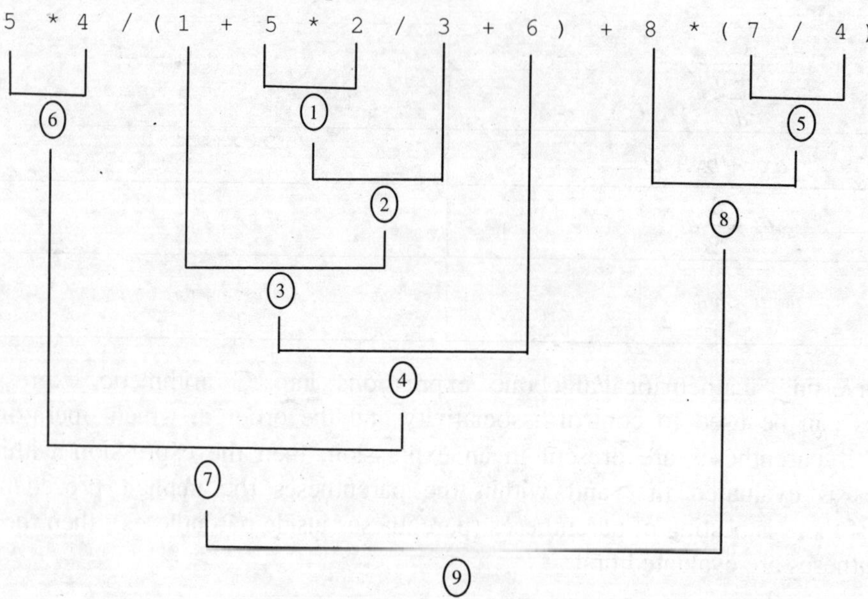

7.3.1.2 Type Conversion

When values of different types are mixed in an expression, then they are converted to the same type before performing the particular operation. This process of converting values for one type to another type is known as *type conversion*.

The C language facilitates type conversion in following two forms:

- Implicit type conversion
- Explicit type conversion

7.3.1.2.1 Implicit Type Conversion

An implicit type conversion is automatically performed by the compiler without programmer's intervention. This is done when expression is in mixed mode, so as not to lose the information. For implicit type conversion, the C language follows certain rules that are introduced next.

Conversion Rank

Before we discuss how conversions are handled, we will discuss the concept of conversion rank. We can assign a rank to integral and real types. The operand of larger size is given a higher rank than that of a smaller size.

Figure 7.5 shows the ranks that will be used for conversions. The *long double* has a higher rank than a *long int* while the *short* has a higher rank than a *char*.

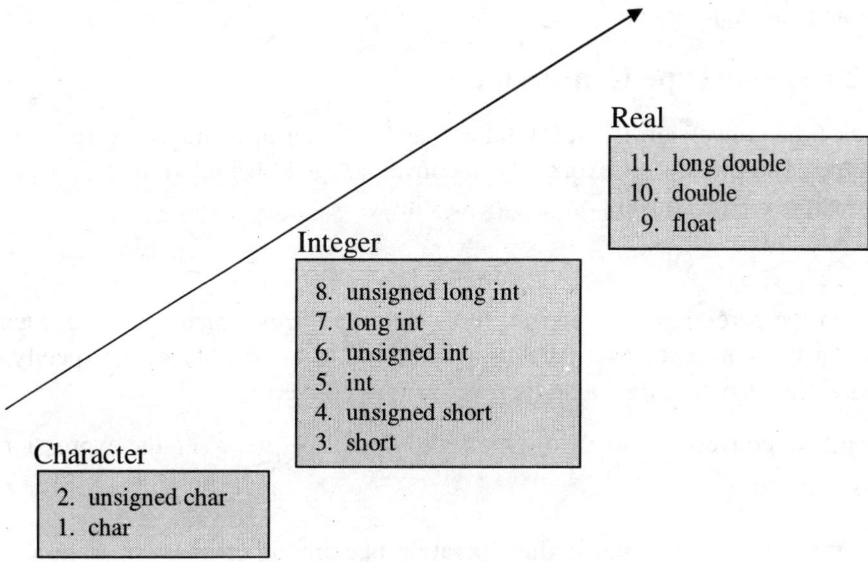

Figure 7.5: Conversion Rank

Conversion in Evaluation of Expressions

When an operation is to be performed on operands of different ranks, then operand of lower rank is converted to type so as to match the operand of higher rank. Once this conversion of the ranks is done, the operation is performed and the result of the operation will of type having higher rank.

For example, suppose variables *x* and *y* are of type *float* and variables `i` and `j` are of type *integer*, in expression:

```
x / i + y * j
```

While evaluating expression "*x/i*", integer operand *i* will be converted to *float* type and then operand *x* will be divided by *i*, and the result of the expression will be a value of type *float*.

Conversions in Assignment Statements

A simple assignment statement involves an assignment operator (=) and two operands. The operand on the left hand side of assignment operator is a variable while the operand on the right side can be a literal/constant, variable or a value after evaluation of an expression.

Depending on the difference of the rank of the operands, the C system tries to either *promote* or *demote* the right operand so as to make its rank match the left operand (variable). *Promotion* occurs if the right operand has lower rank; *demotion* occurs if the right operand has higher rank.

7.3.1.2.2 Explicit Type Conversion

An explicit type conversion is user-defined that forces an operand or expression to be of specific type. The process of explicit type conversion is also known as *type casting*. The syntax for explicit type conversion or type casting is

```
(type)operand        OR        (type)expression
```

Here *type* in the parentheses is referred to as *cast operator*, which has a precedence of 2. As shown in the syntax, to cast data from one type to another type, we specify the new type in parentheses before the value that we want to convert.

For example, to convert variable *x* of type *int* to *float* type, we write the expression as

```
(float)x
```

It is important to note here that in this operation like any other unary operation, the value stored in *x* is still of type *int*, but the value of the expression is promoted to type *float*.

One use of the cast operator is to ensure that the result of a divide operation on integer operands results in a real number.

For example, if we want to calculate the average, which may contain fraction as well, without a cast operator, the result will be an integer number because of integer division.

To force the real result, we can write the statement to compute average as

```
average = (float)total / n;
```

In this statement, there is explicit conversion of *total* to *float*, and then implicit conversion of *n* to *float*. Now real division will take place and the result will be a real number, as desired, which will be assigned to *average*.

7.3.2 Relational Expressions

Relational expressions compare the values of two operands. A relational expression is used to test a condition in order to decide whether an action should be taken or not. In relational expression, an arithmetic value should not be compared with a string value. Result of a relational expression is either zero or non-zero. Here, non-zero value is equivalent to a boolean *true* and zero to a boolean *false*.

Table 7.14: Sample Relational Expressions

Relation Expression	Description
`x % 2 == 0`	Used to test whether the operand *x* is an even number or not. The relational expression results in value 1 if *x* is even otherwise results in value 0.
`a != b`	Used to test whether the operands *a* is not the same as *b*. The relational expression results in value 1 if *a* is different from *b* otherwise results in value 0.
`a + b == x + y`	Used to test whether value of expression "*a+b*" is equal to the value of expression "*x+y*" or not.
`x >= 35`	Used to test whether the operand *x* is greater than or equal to 35. The relational expression results in value 1 if *x* is greater than or equal to 35 otherwise results in value 0.

Relational expressions with arithmetic operands may have one operand of *int* type and one of *float* type. In this case, the *int* operand is converted to *float* type before the relational expression is evaluated.

7.3.3 Logical Expressions

A logical expression also produces a zero or non-zero value. A logical expression is used to form a complex test condition in order to take a decision. For example, an assurance company has framed an assurance policy that states like

> "*Assure a person if he is married or his/her age is more than 30 years*"

Suppose marital status of a person is denoted by value '0' if unmarried and '1' if married. Let us further suppose that we use character variable *status* to store this value, and integer variable *age* is used to store age of the person.

Then, these two conditions separately can be written as

> **Condition 1** : status = '1'
>
> **Condition 2** : age ≥ 30

So according to the company's policy, the person is eligible for assurance, if at least one of the two conditions is satisfied.

In pseudo-language, the above decision criteria can written as

```
if ( ( status = '1' ) or ( age ≥ 30 ) ) then
    Insure the person
else
    Person not eligible for insurance
endif
```

The above test condition for Assurance Company can be written as

```
status == '1'  ||  age >= 30
```

Table 7.15: Sample Logical Expressions

Logical Expression	Description
`( x > 2 ) && ( x % 2 == 0 )`	Used to form a test condition to check whether the operand *x* is greater than 2 and x is even (divisible by 2). The result of this test condition will be 1 only if both the conditions hold true simultaneously.
`age >= 40 || sex == 'F'`	Used to form a test condition to check whether the operand *age* is greater than or equal to 40 or sex is 'F' (for female). The result of this test condition will be 1 only if either or both the conditions hold true.
`! ( x > 5 ) && ( y == 0 )`	Used to form a test condition to check whether the operand *x* is not greater than 5 and *y* is equal to 0. The result of this test condition will be 1 only if both the conditions hold true simultaneously.

7.3.4 Conditional Expressions

Note that the conditional expression is indeed an expression, and can be used wherever any other expression can be. A conditional expression looks like

```
exp1 ? exp2 : exp3
```

where *exp1* is a simple or compound condition; *exp2* and *exp3* are any other kind of expressions. The final value of this conditional expression depends on the outcome of condition represented by *exp1*. If condition *exp1* evaluates zero (true), then value of the condition expressional will be as represented by *exp2* otherwise as represented by *exp3*. Since, the final value of condition expression depends on the outcome of condition, hence its name.

For example, in the following condition expression

```
big  = a > b ? a : b;
```

it will assume value of *a* if *a* > *b* else as of *b*, and this value of conditional expression is then assigned to variable *big*.

Note that the use of parentheses are not necessary around the first expression of the conditional expression since the precedence of '?:' is very low, just above assignment operator. However, the use of parentheses is recommended as they make the condition part of the expression easier to see.

The above statement using parentheses can be written as

```
big  = ( a > b ) ? a : b;
```

Table 7.16: Sample Conditional Expressions

Logical Expression	Description
`(a%2==0)?1:0`	The conditional expression takes value 1 if *a* is divisible by 2 otherwise it takes value 0.
`(a>b)?((a>c)?a:c):((b>c)?b:c)`	The conditional expression takes largest of the three number (*a*, *b* and *c*) as its value.
`(x>y)? x--: y++`	Decrement *x* if *x* is greater than *y* else increment *y*.

7.4 ASSIGNMENT STATEMENTS

As we know that an expression is a formula consisting of one or more operands and zero or more operators linked together to compute a value. These computed values are to be stored in a variable for future use. This is done by using an *assignment statement*. The C language supports variety of assignment statements. These are

- Simple assignment statement
- Multiple assignment statement
- Shorthand assignment statement

7.4.1 Simple Assignment Statement

The syntax of simple assignment statement is

```
var = exp;
```

where *var* is a variable or array element reference; *exp* is any expression; and '=' is an *assignment operator*.

The unique feature about C is that it treats assignment operator in a way it treats other operators. For example, the following statement

```
printf( "\nValue of c = %d\n", c = a + b );
```

will be valid.

This statement first assigns the sum of variables *a* and *b* of type *int* to variable *c*, also of type *int*, and then the value of variable *c* is printed. The type of the variable or array element and the type of the expression must be compatible.

The following are valid assignment statements:

(Given *a, b, c, y, x, disc* are *float* variables)

(*a*) `a = 5.0;`
(*b*) `y = 4.0 * x + 7.5;`
(*c*) `disc = b * b – 4.0 * a * c;`
(*d*) `x = y;`

The following are invalid assignment statements with the reasons indicated:

(Given *a, b, c, y* are real variables)

(*a*) `b + c = a;` (*b + c* is not a valid variable)
(*b*) `abs(a) = x;` (abs(*a*) is not a valid variable)
(*c*) `y = 'R';` (*y* is not a character variable)

7.4.2 Multiple Assignment Statement

If the same value is to be assigned to different variable of same type, the usual way is to use different assignment statement for each variable. However, C language permits us to assign the same value to more than one variable using multiple assignment statement. The syntax of a multiple assignment statement is

```
v1 = v2 = v3 = exp;
```

where *v1*, *v2*, and *v3* are variables of same type; and *exp* is a literal, variable or expression.

The order of assigning the value is from right-to-left. For example, the following statement assigns value 0 to variables *a*, *b*, *c*, and *d*.

```
a = b = c = d = 0;
```

7.4.3 Shorthand Assignment Statement

Consider the following assignment statements

```
a = a + 5;
a = a / j;
```

Its purpose is to increase the value of *a* by factor of 5, *i.e.*, add value 5 to the current value of variable *a* and assign the new value to *a* itself.

Similarly, in the second assignment statement, the value of *a* is divided by *j*, and the result is again stored in *a*.

Such types of assignment statements are known as *self replacement* statements as the value of one of the variables of the assignment statement is being replaced with a new value.

The same task can also be accomplished using following statements

```
a += 5;
a /= j;
```

The '+=' and '/=' (in general "op=" operator) are called *shorthand assignment operators*, and the entire statements is known as arithmetic assignment statements.

Table 7.17: Use of shorthand assignment operators

Assignment statement with simple assignment operator	Assignment statement with shorthand assignment operator
`k = k + m;`	`k += m;`
`k = k - m;`	`k -= m;`
`k = k * m;`	`k *= m;`
`k = k / ( n + 1 );`	`k /= ( n + 1 );`
`k = k % b;`	`k %= b;`

Only arithmetic and bitwise operators can be combined with the assignment operator.

7.5 LIBRARY FUNCTIONS

Quite often it is necessary to evaluate several mathematical functions that are used quite frequently, such as square root, logarithms, exponentials, etc. They are written and incorporated into the C language. Rather than each user writes these subprograms, C compiler provides these built-in library functions as a convenience.

The programmer has to include *math.h* header file in his program unit. In addition to these functions, there are many other library functions that perform specialized functions, and are defined in different header files. For example, library functions that manipulate strings are defined in *string.h*.

Arguments to certain library functions are limited by the definition of the function. For example, the logarithm of a negative number is mathematically undefined. Similarly, the square root of a negative number is mathematically undefined, and therefore not permitted.

The following table describes some popular and frequently used mathematical functions. The user must include header file *math.h* in the program in order to use these functions.

Table 7.18: Some Commonly Used Mathematical Functions

Function	Description
`pow(x,y)`	Returns *x* raised to power *y*, *i.e.*, x^y .
`pow10(p)`	Returns the value 10^p .
`exp(x)`	Returns *e* to the *xth* power, *i.e.*, e^x .
`log(x)`	Returns the value of *ln*(*x*).
`log10(x)`	Returns the value of *log10*(*x*).
`sqrt(x)`	Returns the value of $\sqrt{x}$.
`sin(x)`	Returns the value sine of *x*, where the angle *x* is in radians.
`ceil(x)`	Returns the smallest integer greater than or equal to *x*.
`floor(x)`	Returns largest integer less than or equal to *x*.
`ploy(x,n, coeffs[])`	Returns the value of the polynomial in *x*, of degree *n*, with coefficients *coeffs*[0], *coeffs*[1], . . ., *coeffs*[*n*].

Turbo C/C++'s IDE provides very good features, and I personally feel every C/C++ programmer must be familiar with it. These features are in the form of on-line help. To know about any library function in detail, just type the name of the function, position the cursor on the name and press *Ctrl+F1*, you will the entire details. Even the Turbo C++ compiler goes one step further by providing examples that illustrate the use of the functions.

EXERCISE

1. List various types of operators available in C language and also give their precedence, if any.
2. Suppose *x*, *y*, and *z* have been declared variables of type *float*, write a C segment which changes the values of *x*, *y*, and *z* so that *x* has *y*'s value, *y* has *z*'s value, and *z* has *x*'s value.
3. In order to store the result of the computation, which statement must be used?
4. What are various forms of assignment statement in C?

5. Which of the following statements are not valid and why?

   (*a*) `float = area * pie * 0.05;` (*b*) `c = 5 / 9 ( f - 32 );`
   (*c*) `pie * r * r = area;` (*d*) `si = p * r * t / 100;`
   (*e*) `area = 3.141 * r ** 2;`

6. Find the value of each of the following expressions.

   (*a*) 3 – 5 * 2.5 (*b*) 10 / (2 * 3)
   (*c*) 22 % 3 * 12 / 3 (*d*) (3 / 7) / (6 / 5)

7. What is the role played by parentheses in expressions?

8. What is the effect of dividing an integer value by a real value? What is this effect called?

9. How would you use the *cast operator* to convert expression `(7*12/10)` to double type?

10. Write C expressions equivalent to the following algebraic expressions:

   (*a*) $a - \frac{a}{a^{-x}} + b$ (*b*) $1 + \frac{1}{a + \frac{1}{a}} + b$ (*c*) $x + \frac{y^{-z}}{k} - \sqrt{x}$

   (*d*) $x^3 - \frac{y^7}{-z} + e^x$ (*e*) $\left(\frac{1-x}{1+x}\right) / \left(\frac{1+y}{1-y}\right)$ (*f*) $\frac{1}{r} = \frac{1}{r_1} + \frac{1}{r_2}$

   (*g*) $\sqrt{\left(x^2 + y^2 + z^2\right)^3}$ (*h*) $\frac{-b - \sqrt{b^2 - 4ac}}{2a}$

❑ ❑ ❑

Chapter 8

Standard Input/Output

Learning Objectives

After reading this chapter, students will be able to explain the

- standard Input/Output facility provided by C I/O subsystem
- working of character I/O functions
- working of string I/O functions
- working of formatted I/O functions
- various features to format the output

8.1 INTRODUCTION

In almost every computer program, the users have to input some data that will be stored in computer's memory, and then subsequently processed. This input data may be from a keyboard, a disk file, or from another computer via a communication channel. The intermediate and final results of the computations are also stored in computer's memory. And finally, there is need to output the results of the computations so that user can use them in their day-to-day work. The output can be displayed on the computer screen, stored on a disk, or transmitted via a communication channel to other computer.

In microcomputers (PCs), the common input device is the keyboard and the output device is a computer screen, sometimes called the *monitor*. This subsystem comprising keyboard and monitor is referred to as a *console*.

The various forms of input and output, abbreviated as I/O, obviously are very different. It would have been easier if all these forms of I/O can be handled in a unified manner as they are handled in other high level languages, such as in Pascal and FORTRAN. But one of the objectives of Dennis Ritchie, developer of C, was to have C language as compact as possible. Therefore, he deliberately omitted I/O statements that generate extra overhead. Instead, every C compiler provides several I/O functions that can be linked with any C program. Though, these I/O functions are not part of C's formal definition, they have become a standard feature of C language.

This chapter describes the various I/O functions that perform the input from a standard input device and output to a standard output device. To use entire range of I/O functions, we need to include header file named *stdio.h* in all our programs.

8.2 STANDARD INPUT/OUTPUT

When a C program begins execution, it has access to the following pre-defined files:

- The first one, known as the *standard input* (*stdin*), is the file from which input is received. This file is usually a keyboard, but it can also be redirected to obtain input from a disk file or other device.
- The second one, known as *standard output* (*stdout*), is the file to which output is directed. The file is usually a computer screen, but it can be redirected to a disk file or to another device.
- The third one, known as *standard error* (*stderr*), is the file used to keep error messages separate from program's output. For example, if output is going to a disk file, the standard error file can be a computer screen, so that the user sees error messages immediately.

8.3 STANDARD I/O FUNCTIONS

There are many library functions available for standard I/O. These functions are divided into two categories:

- unformatted
- formatted

The only difference between these functions is that the formatted functions permit the input from a standard input device or output sent to a standard output device to be formatted as per requirements. For example, if different values are to be displayed, how much field width i.e. how many columns on screen, is to be used, and how much space between two values is to be given. If a value to be displayed is of real type, then how many decimal places to output.

8.3.1 Unformatted I/O Functions

In the unformatted I/O category, we have functions for performing input/output of one character at a time, known as *character I/O functions* and functions that perform input/output of one string at a time, known as *string I/O functions*. These functions are described in the next sections.

8.3.1.1 Character I/O Functions

For character input, the functions is *getchar()* that is available in all versions of C language. In addition, Turbo C provides two more versions of character input functions in the form of *getche()*, and *getch()*. For character output, the function available is *putchar()*.

***getchar() function*:** This function returns a character that has been recently typed. The typed character is echoed to the computer screen. After typing the appropriate character, the user is required to press *Enter* key.

***putchar() function*:** This function output a character constant or a character variable to the standard output device.

Following character input functions are only supported by Turbo C/C++ Compilers

***getche() function*:** Like *getchar()* function, this function also returns a character that has been recently typed. The typed character is also echoed to the computer screen. But the user is not required to press *Enter* key after typing a character. The advantage of this function over *getchar()* function is that as soon as the user types a character, the character is immediately accepted. In reduces the user's action to single key.

getch() function: This function too returns a character that has been recently typed. But, neither the user is required to press *Enter* key after entering the character nor the typed character is echoed to the computer screen. This function has advantages over the other functions in the applications where the user wants to hide the input.

This input is usually the password used for system security. A *password* is a secret word or a code set by the programmer in case of software or assigned by a system administrator of a multi-user system or a computer network to the individual users. Whenever they want to use that particular software or want to work on that particular system, they have to enter their password. If their password is valid, they will be permitted to use the software or system.

Following program illustrates the working of all these functions. In this program, to display user prompt, *printf()* function, which will be described in the later sections, is used.

Listing 8.1

```
/* Program to illustrate working of character I/O functions   */
#include <stdio.h>
int main(void)
{
   char ch;
   printf( "\nEnter any character: " );
   ch = getchar();
   printf( "\nCharacter you typed is " );
   putchar(ch);

   printf( "\nEnter any other character: " );
   ch = getche();
   printf( "\nCharacter you typed is " );
   putchar(ch);

   printf( "\nEnter any other character: " );
   ch = getch();
   printf( "\nCharacter you typed is " );
   putchar(ch);
   return 0;
}
```

Test Run

```
Enter any character: A
Character you typed is A
Enter any other character: x
Character you typed is x
Enter any other character:
Character you typed is H
```

8.3.1.2 String I/O Functions

For string input, the function is *gets()* is used, and for string output, the function is *puts()* is used.

gets() function: This function accepts a string from the standard input device. The length of the string is limited by the declaration of the string variable. The input string may consist of multiple words. Typing Enter key completes the input.

puts() function: This function outputs a string constant or a string variable to the standard output device. The following program illustrates the working of these string I/O functions.

Listing 8.2

```
/* Program to illustrate working of string I/O functions  */

#include <stdio.h>

void main()
{
    char str[31];
    printf( "\nEnter string of length <= 30: " );
    gets( str );
    printf( "\nString you typed is " );
    puts( str );
}
```

Test Run

```
Enter string of length <= 30: string input
String you typed is string input
```

8.3.2 Formatted I/O Functions

In the formatted I/O category, we have *scanf()* function for input and *printf()* function for output. The working of these functions is described in this section.

8.3.2.1 The *scanf()* Function

This function allows us to input data in a fixed format. Its syntax is

```
scanf( "format string", list of addresses of variables );
```

where the *format string* contains the format specifiers that begin with character '%' and are, usually, separated by space or comma.

It returns the number of items read from the keyboard.

Table 8.1 lists various format specifiers used with *scanf()* function. The list of addresses of variables are used so that *scanf()* function can place the data received from a standard input device. The address of a variable is obtained by using address operator, character '&' and pronounced as *addressof* operator.

Table 8.1: List of Format Specifiers

Format Specifier	Used For
`%d`	signed decimal integer
`%ld`	signed long decimal integer
`%u`	unsigned decimal integer
`%f`	single precision floating real number
`%lf`	double precision floating real number
`%e`	floating point (exponential notation)
`%x`	unsigned hexadecimal integer
`%o`	unsigned octal integer
`%c`	single character
`%s`	single-word string
`%[^\n]s`	multi-word string

On execution, the input data must be supplied strictly according to the specified format string otherwise results can be very strange. This strange behavior is illustrated next.

Consider the following segment:

```
int a;
float b;
char c;
 :
scanf( "%d,%f,%c", &a, &b, &c );
 :
```

Suppose that the input data is 20 for *a*, 50.25 for *b*, and character 'A' for *c*.

The data must be entered or typed in the following format

```
20,50.25,A
```

In case, if your enter the data as

```
20 50.25 A
```

results can be very surprising.

8.3.2.1.1 Limitation of *scanf()* Function

Consider the following statement

```
scanf( "%d", &intVariable );
```

If we input the value as

```
75.50
```

the *scanf()* function will accept 75 only.

Similarly, in the following statement

```
scanf( "%f", &floatVariable );
```

If we input the value as

```
25
```

the *scanf()* function will store this value as 25.0 i.e. integer value is converted to a real value.

However, in the following statement

```
scanf( "%d,%f", &intVariable, &floatVariable );
```

If we input the above values as

```
75.50,25
```

the *scanf()* function will store a value 75 in *intVariable* but the value of the *floatVariable* will be unpredictable.

8.3.2.2 The *printf()* Function

The *printf()* function allows to output the data in a fixed format. Its general form looks like

```
printf( "format string", list of variables );
```

where the *format string* contains the format specifiers, the sequences that begin with character '\' (back slash), known as *escape sequences*, and the text to be output along with the output data.

It returns the number of characters displayed in the output.

All the format specifiers used with *scanf()* function are valid for *printf()* function. Another format specifier "%p" is used to print the value of a pointer variable in hexadecimal notation. Table 8.2 lists common *escape sequences*.

Table 8.2: Common Escape Sequences

Escape Sequence	Represents	Effect
\n	newline	has the effect of both a carriage return and linefeed, *i.e.*, the subsequent output starts from new line.
\t	tab	moves over to the next eight-space-wide field.
\b	backspace	moves the cursor one space left.
\r	carriage return	carriage return.
\f	formfeed	advances to the top of the next page on printer.
\a	beep	produces one audio tone of the speaker
\'	single quote	insert character ' in the output
\"	double quote	insert character " in the output
\\	Backslash	insert character \ in the output

Consider the following segment:

```
int a = 15;
float b = 23.75;
char c = 'V';
      :
printf( "%d,%f,%c", a, b, c );
      :
```

The output of the above segment will look like

```
15,23.75,V
```

But if the segment is written like

```
int a = 15;
float b = 23.75;
char c = 'V';
      :
printf( "%d%f%c", a, b, c );
      :
```

The output of the above segment will look like

```
1523.75V
```

Needless to say, the output in this form is very difficult to understand.

The above segment can also be written as

```
int a = 15;
float b = 23.75;
char c = 'V';
    :
printf("\nValue of a=%d\nValue of b=%f\nValue of c=%c", a, b, c );
    :
```

The output of the above segment will look like

```
Value of a=15
Value of a=23.75
Value of a=V
```

You must have noticed that, in the later case the output is self-explanatory and is the preferred way for the output.

Let us see how the *printf()* function interprets the format string.

We will consider the following example of *printf()* function

```
printf( "\nValue of a = %d\nValue of b = %f\n", a, b );
```

Let us further assume that $a = 15$, and $b = 23.46$.

The *printf()* function examines the format string from left to right. It keeps on sending the characters to the standard output device until it encounters either character '%' or character '\'. The moment it encounters character %, it picks up the corresponding variable and outputs its value in the specified format. Similarly, the moment the character '\' is encountered, it indicates the presence of escape sequence, the action taken will depend on the next character.

In our example, the first character is '\', and the next character is *n*, so the action of '\n' is to insert *newline* character so that subsequent output can continue from the next line. So the string

```
Value of a =
```

is send to the standard output device, and then character % is encountered following by character *d*, so it picks up the variable *a* and print its value. The output up to this stage appears as

```
Value of a = 15
```

As the scanning of the format string continues, it finds another *newline* character, and the subsequent output is sent to the next line up to % character. Up to this the output appears as

```
Value of a = 15
Value of b =
```

Now it picks up the second variable and outputs its value, and after outputting the value of variable *b*, it finds another *newline* character that causes the subsequent output to be sent to the next line. The final output appears as

```
Value of a = 15
Value of b = 23.46
```

8.3.2.2.1 More About *printf()* Function

As you must have observed in the output of the above program that the *printf()* function outputs six decimal digits for a real value, because in the format specifier we have not specified any additional information. In general, to have a control over the output, we can pass additional information to the *printf()* function.

With this additional information, the format specifier for a real value takes the form

```
%w.df
```

where *w* is the total width or space used for outputting a real value including decimal point and the number of decimal digits; and *d* is the number of decimal digits to be outputted.

This field width is the minimum width to be used. If the real value is small, the output value is right justified in the field and if the value can not be accommodated in the specified field width, then the field width is assumed to be large enough to accommodate the output value.

Similarly for a integer value, it takes the form

```
%wd
```

For a string value, it takes the form

```
%ws
```

By default, the output value is always right justified in the field.

The output value can be left justified in the field by writing hyphen '–' after character % as shown below

```
%-5d
```

In this case, the corresponding value will appear left justified i.e. if the value is small, it will be padded with blanks on the right. To fix these ideas, let us consider an example.

Consider the following segment

```
    :
int a = 123;
float b = 123.564;
char name[20] = "Language";
    :
printf( ":%d:  :%f:  :%s:\n", a, b, name);
printf( ":%6d:  :%8.2f:  :%20s:\n", a, b, name);
printf( ":%-6d:  :%-8.2f:  :%-20s:\n", a, b, name);
    :
```

The output of this segment will appear as

```
:123:   :123.564:   :Language:
:      123:  :   123.56:  :               Language:
:123       :  :123.56    :  :Language             :
```

8.4 SUPPLEMANTARY PROBLEMS

Let us write a few example programs to use the features that we have learned so far.

Problem 8.1:

Program to find the sum of digits of a given 4-digit positive integer number.

Listing 8.3

```
/*
*  Program to find sum of digits of a 4-digit positive
*  integer number
*/
#include<stdio.h>
int main(void)
{
  int number, sum, digit1, digit2, digit3;
  int digit4, temporary;
  printf( "\nEnter 4-digit positive number: ");
  scanf( "%d", &number );
  temporary = number;
  digit1 = temporary % 10;
  temporary /= 10;
  digit2 = temporary % 10;
  temporary /= 10;
  digit3 = temporary % 10;
  temporary /= 10;
  digit4 = temporary % 10;
  sum = digit1 + digit2 + digit3 + digit4;
  printf( "\n\nSum of digits of %d = %d\n", number, sum );
  return 0;
}
```

Test Run

```
Enter 4-digit positive number: 2375

Sum of digits of 2375 = 17
```

Problem 8.2:

Program to reverses the digits of a given 4-digit positive integer number.

Listing 8.4

```
/* Program to print 4-digit positive integer number in reverse order
*/
#include<stdio.h>
int main(void)
{
  int number, sum, digit1, digit2, digit3;
  int digit4, temporary;
  printf( "\nEnter 4-digit positive number: ");
  scanf( "%d", &number );
  temporary = number;
  digit1 = temporary % 10;
  temporary /= 10;
  digit2 = temporary % 10;
  temporary /= 10;
  digit3 = temporary % 10;
  temporary /= 10;
  digit4 = temporary % 10;
  sum = digit1*1000+digit2*100+digit3*10+digit4;
  printf( "\nNumber after reversing digits of %d is %d\n",
          number, sum );
  return 0;
}
```

Test Run

```
Enter 4-digit positive number : 2375
Number after reversing the digits of 2375 is 5732
```

Problem 8.3:

Program to convert time in seconds to time in hours, minutes and seconds.

Listing 8.5

```
/*  Program to convert time in seconds to time in hours,
*   Minutes and seconds
*/
#include<stdio.h>
void main()
{
  int seconds,minutes, hours, total_seconds, temp;
  printf( "\nEnter time in seconds: " );
  scanf( "%d", &total_seconds );
  temp = total_seconds;
  hours = temp / 3600;
  temp %= 3600;
```

```
  minutes = temp / 60;
  seconds = temp % 60;
  printf( "\nTime in %d seconds = ", total_seconds);
  printf( "%d hour(s),%d minute(s) & %d secs.\n", hours,
          minutes,seconds );
}
```

Test Run

```
Enter time in seconds: 3678
Time in 3678 seconds=1 hour(s),1 minute(s) & 18 secs.
```

Problem 8.4:

Program to compute the area of a triangle whose sides are given.

Suppose that length of the sides is *a*, *b* and *c*, then area of triangle is given by formula

$$\text{Area of triangle} = \sqrt{s(s\text{-}a)(s\text{-}b)(s-c)}, \text{ where } s = \frac{a+b+c}{2}$$

Listing 8.6

```
/*  Program to find area of triangle whose sides are given   */
#include<stdio.h>
#include<math.h>
void main()
{
  float sideA, sideB, sideC, s, area;
  printf( "Enter side A: " );
  scanf( "%f", &sideA );
  printf( "Enter side B: " );
  scanf( "%f", &sideB );
  printf( "Enter side C: " );
  scanf( "%f", &sideC );
  s = ( sideA + sideB + sideC ) / 2;
  area = sqrt((double)(s*(s-sideA)*(s-sideB)*(s-sideC)));
  printf( "\nArea of triangle: %.3f\n", area );
}
```

Test Run

```
Enter side A: 3
Enter side B: 3
Enter side C: 3

Area of triangle: 3.897
```

The program is run for an equilateral triangle with each side equal to 3 units.

Problem 8.5:

On an amount of rupees, say *P*, program to compute simple interest and compound interest if the interest rate is *R*% annually and the time is *N* years.

We know that formulae to compute simple interest and compound interest are

$$\text{Simple interest } (si) = \frac{P \times R \times N}{100}$$

$$\text{Compound interest } (ci) = P\left(1 + \frac{R}{100}\right)^N - P$$

Listing 8.7

```
/*
 *   Program to compute simple interest & compound interest
 */
#include<stdio.h>
#include<math.h>
void main()
{
  float p, r, n, si, ci;
  printf( "Enter amount: " );
  scanf( "%f", &p );
  printf( "Enter rate of interest: " );
  scanf( "%f", &r );
  printf( "Enter time: " );
  scanf( "%f", &n );
  si = ( p * r * n ) / 100;
  ci = p * pow((double)1.0+r/100, (double)n ) - p;
  printf( "\nSimple Interest  : %.2f\n", si );
  printf( "\nCompound Interest: %.2f\n", ci );
}
```

Test Run

```
Enter amount: 100
Enter rate of interest: 5
Enter time: 5

Simple Interest  : 25.00
Compound Interest: 27.63
```

EXERCISE

1. How many decimal places are displayed when a number has a corresponding format specifier "%f"?
2. How does the %u format specifier compare with %d format specifier?
3. What is the difference between 'x' and "x"?
4. How does the %15s format specifier compare with %–15s format specifier?
5. How the % sign can be printed with a *printf()* function as a part of the output?
6. How the output will appear as a result of the following statement?

```
printf("\n:%20s:\n:% -20s:\n", "Test String", "Test String" );
```

7. Find the errors, if any, in the following segment of code.

```
float a, b;
printf("\nEnter value of a: ");
scanf( "%f", a );
b = a * 3;
printf("\nValue of b = %f\n", b);
```

9. Find errors, if any, in the following program. What will be the output of the C program if it is error free?

```
int i = 3, j = 2, k;
k = 2 * i + j;
i += 3;
j = i + 2 * j - k;
k += 2 * i;
printf("\ni=%d\tj=%d\tk=%d\n",i,j,k);
```

9. What will the output of the following code?

```
printf(" %d\n", printf("\nGood Bye\n"));
```

10. What will be the output of the following segment of code?

```
int m, j = 1, k = 3;
m = 2 * j + k;
j = 2 * m + j / 3;
k /= 2;
m = j + k+ m;
printf ( "\nj = %d\tk = %d\tm = %d\n", j, k, m );
```

11. What will the output of the following code?

```
int intVar = 20;
printf("\n%d,%d,%d\n", intVar == 20,intVar = 35,intVar < 50);
```

PROGRAMMING EXERCISE

1. Write a program that accepts a decimal integer and prints it in the octal form.
2. Write a program that accepts a character in uppercase and prints it as lowercase.

3. Write a program that accepts a temperature in Fahrenheit scale and prints its equivalent temperature in Centigrade scale.
4. An amount of rupees, say *P*, is deposited in a commercial bank for *N* years, which pays simple interest at the rate of *R*% annually. Write a C program that prints the amount after *N* years.
5. Write C program to find real roots of a quadratic equation of type $ax^2+bx+c = 0$.
6. Basic salary (BS) of an employee is input through the keyboard. The dearness allowance (DA) is 25% of the basic salary while the house rent allowance (HRA) is 15% of the basic salary. Provident fund (PF) is deducted at the rate of 10% of the gross salary (BS+DA+HRA). Write a program to calculate the net salary (NS).
7. A department store places an order with a company for *n* pieces of miners, *m* pieces of toasters, and *p* number of fans. The cost of items are as follows:

Item Description	Price per Unit (in Rupees)
Miners	1,500
Toaster	200
Fan	450

The discount allowed for various items are 5% for miners, 15% for fan, and 10% for toaster. The company charge 10% as sales tax on all items on net value after deducting the discount. Formulate an algorithm that reads *m*, *n*, and *p* and computes the amount to be paid by the store.

❑ ❑ ❑

Chapter 9

Decision Making and Branching

Learning Objectives

After reading this chapter, students will be able to

- explain the need for control transfer
- explain the kind of control statement available in C language
- explain the working of *if* and *if-else* statements for decision making
- explain the working of nested *if* statements
- explain the usefulness of *if - else if* ladder in multiple alternatives in decision making
- explain the working of *switch* statement
- use these decision making statements to write programs to solve problems requiring decision making

9.1 INTRODUCTION

A computer program is a set of instructions for a computer. These instructions, also known as *statements*, are executed sequentially, *i.e.*, one after the other as they appear in a program. This order of executing the statement works well for simple problems where neither any decision making process is involved nor any repetition of statements is involved. However, in practice, it is often required to change the order of execution of statements or repeat a group of statements for known number of times or until certain specified expressions are met. In such cases, the order in which these statements will be executed is to be controlled.

Changing the order of execution of the statements *i.e.* changing the flow of control, might involve one of the following situations.

- *Jumping* — transferring control from one point to another point in the same program unit.
- *Branching* — executing one group of instructions depending on the outcome of a decision.
- *Looping* — executing a group of instructions repetitively either for a given number of times or until the required expressions are met.

The C Language provides facilities for controlling the order of execution of the statements, which are referred to as *flow control statements* or simply as *control statements*. The various flow control statements are clubbed in the following categories:

1. *Decision Making Statements* — In this category, C language provides the following statements
   - *if* statement
   - *if – else* statement
   - *else if* ladder
   - *switch* statement
2. *Looping Statements* — In this category, C language provides the following statements
   - *for* statement
   - *while* statement
   - *do – while* statement
3. *Jumping Statements* — In this category, C language provides the following statements
   - *break* statement
   - *continue* statement
   - *goto* statement

This chapter describes various decision making statements, and the *break* statement. The remaining statements will be discussed in *Chapter 10*.

9.2 DECISION MAKING STATEMENTS

These statements allow the execution of selective statements based on certain decision criteria. We will see their working supported by well-designed illustrative examples.

9.2.1 The *if* Statement

The syntax of *if* statement is

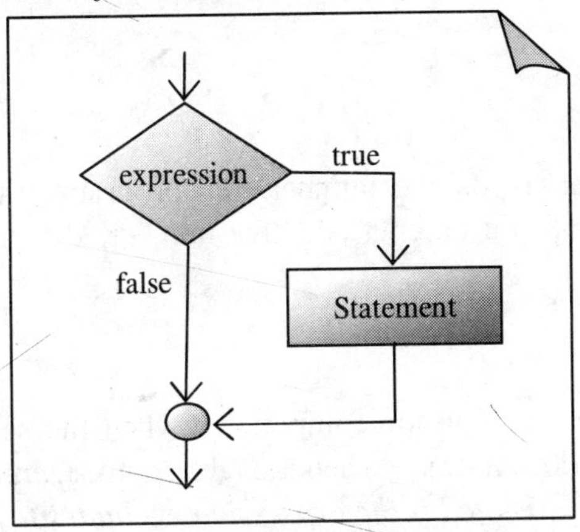

(*a*) Logic Flow Control of *if* Statement

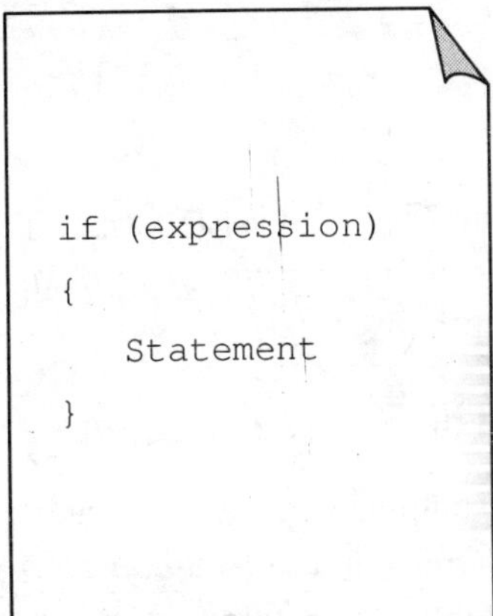

(*b*) Code of *if* Statement

Figure 9.1: Logic flow control and code of *if* statement

The *expression* may represent a relation expression, a logical expression, a numeric variable or a numeric constant. The specified expression may be a simple expression or compound expression.

The expression in C++ evaluates to a *zero* or *non-zero* value. If expression evaluates to a *non-zero* value, then the statements in the statement-block are executed; otherwise they are bypassed.

Listing 9.1

```
/* Program to find largest of three numbers using 'if' statement  */
#include <stdio.h>
int main()
{
   int a, b, c, max;
   printf( "\nEnter value for a : " );
   scanf( "%d", &a );
   printf( "\nEnter value for b : " );
   scanf( "%d", &b );
   printf( "\nEnter value for c : " );
   scanf( "%d", &c );
```

```
    max = a;
    if ( b > max )
        max = b;
    if ( c > max )
        max = c;
    printf("\nLargest number = %d\n", max);
    return 0;
}
```

Test Run

```
Enter three numbers : 10 25 22
Largest number = 25
```

You must have observed that if you enter a positive number, the program prints the message *Number entered is positive*. But, if you enter a negative number, the program prints nothing.

9.2.2 The *if – else* Statement

The *if* statement executes a single statement (simple or compound), when the specified expression evaluates to a *non-zero* value. It does nothing when it evaluates to a *zero* value. *Is there any way whereby a one statement is executed if the expression evaluates to a non-zero value and another statement if the expression evaluates to a zero value*? The answer is yes. This objective is achieved by using *if – else* statement whose syntax is

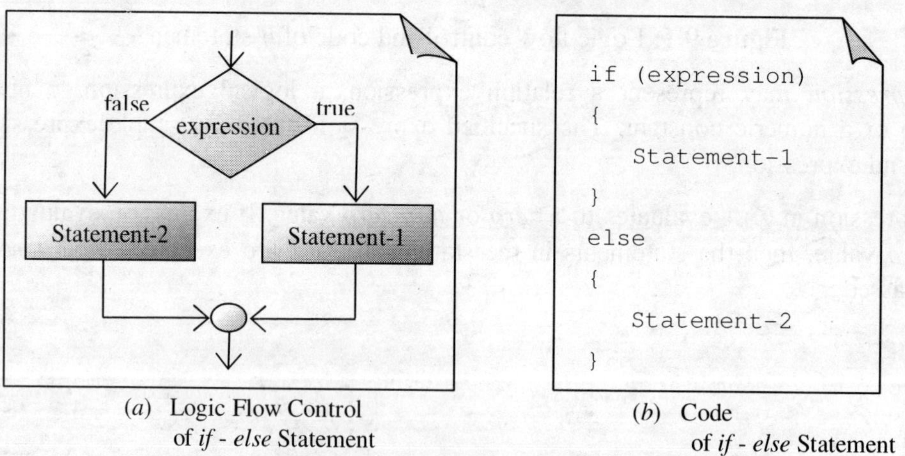

(*a*) Logic Flow Control of *if* - *else* Statement

(*b*) Code of *if* - *else* Statement

Figure 9.2: Logic flow control and code of *if-else* statement

If expression evaluates to a non-zero value, the *statement-1* is executed and *statement-2* is bypassed. However, if the expression evaluates to a zero value, the *statement-1* is bypassed and *statement-2* is executed.

Listing 9.2

```
/*
*  Program to demonstrate the use of if-else statement
*/
#include<stdio.h>
int main()
{
   int n;
   printf( "\nEnter any whole number : " );
   scanf( "%d", &n );
   if ( n % 2 == 0 )
      printf( "\nNumber entered is EVEN\n" );
   else
      printf( "\nNumber entered is ODD\n" );
   return 0;
}
```

Test Runs

First Run

```
Enter any whole number: 22
Number entered is EVEN
```

Second Run

```
Enter any number: 15
Number entered is ODD
```

You must have observed that if you enter a even number, then the program prints the message *Number entered is EVEN*. If you enter odd number, then the program prints the message *Number entered is ODD*.

Listing 9.3

```
/*
*  Program to find the largest of two numbers 'a' and 'b'
*/
#include<stdio.h>
int main()
{
    int a, b;
    printf( "\nEnter value for a : " );
    scanf( "%d", &a );
    printf( "\nEnter value for b : " );
    scanf( "%d", &b );
    if ( a > b )
       printf( "\n%d is the largest\n", a );
    else
       printf( "\n%d is the largest\n", b );
    return 0;
}
```

Test Runs

First Run

```
Enter value for a : 20
Enter value for b : 10
20 is the largest
```

Second Run

```
Enter value for a : 15
Enter value for b : 25
25 is the largest
```

9.2.3 Nested *if* and *if – else* Statements

If statements can be nested, *i.e.*, an *if* statement can be contained within another *if* statement. The inner *if* statement will be executed if expression of outer *if* statement evaluates to *non-zero* value.

Likewise, *if-else* statements can also be nested. Here, *if* statement can be nested in *if* part *or else* part. Likewise, *if - else* statement can be nested in *if* part *or else* part.

Listing 9.4

```
/*
 *  Program to create equivalent of four function ( +, -, *, / )
 *  calculator using nested if statements
 */
#include<stdio.h>
int main()
{
   int a, b;
   int result;
   float result2;
   char op;
   printf("\nEnter expression such as 5+3 : ");
   scanf("%d%c%d", &a, &op, &b );
   if ( op == '+' ) {
      result = a + b;
      printf("\n%d%c%d=%d\n",a,op,b,result);
   } else {
      if ( op == '-' ) {
         result = a - b;
         printf("\n%d%c%d=%d\n",a,op,b,result);
      } else {
         if ( op == '*' ) {
            result = a * b;
            printf("\n%d%c%d=%d\n",a,op,b,result);
         } else {
            if ( op == '/' ) {
               result2 = (float)a / b;
```

```
               printf("\n%d%c%d=%.2f\n",a,op,b,result2);
            } else {
               printf("\nWrong Operator...\n");
            }
         }
      }
   }
   printf("\n");
   return 0;
}
```

Test Run

```
Enter expression such as 5+3 : 10-3
10 - 3 = 7
```

Listing 9.5

```
/*
*  Program to find the largest of three numbers a, b, and c
*  using nested if-else statements
*/
#include<iostream.h>
int main()
{
    int a, b, c;
    printf( "\nEnter value for a : " );
    scanf( "%d", &a );
    printf( "\nEnter value for b : " );
    scanf( "%d", &b );
    printf( "\nEnter value for c : " );
    scanf( "%d", &c );
    if ( a > b ) {
        if ( a > c )
           printf("\nLargest number = %d\n", a );
        else
           printf("\nLargest number = %d\n", c );
    } else {
        if ( b > c )
           printf("\nLargest number = %d\n", b );
        else
           printf("\nLargest number = %d\n", a );
    }
    return 0;
}
```

Test Run

```
Enter three numbers : 12 25 13
Largest number = 25
```

Listing 9.6

```
/* Program to print the name of the day of week when we are given the
 * day of week as number (0 for Sunday, 1 for Monday, ..., 6 for
 * Saturday) using nested if-else statements (Example deep nesting)
*/
#include <stdio.h>
int main()
{
    int day;
    printf("\nEnter day of week as number ( 0 - 6 ) : ");
    scanf("%d", &day);
    if ( day == 0 )
       printf("\nDay of week is Sunday");
    else
       if ( day == 1 )
          printf("\nDay of week is Monday");
       else
          if ( day == 2 )
            printf("\nDay of week is Tuesday");
          else
             if ( day == 3 )
                printf("\nDay of week is Wednesday");
             else
                if ( day == 4 )
                   printf("\nDay of week is Thursday");
                else
                   if ( day == 5 )
                      printf("\nDay of week is Friday");
                   else
                      if ( day == 6 )
                         printf("\nDay of week is Saturday");
                      else
                         printf("\n Wrong input");
    printf("\n");
    return 0;
}
```

Test Run

First Run

```
Enter day week as number ( 0 - 6 ) : 2
Day of week is Tuesday
```

9.2.4 The *if - else if* Ladder

Consider the listing 9.7, which demonstrates how *if-else* statements are nested. As the resulting indentation gets deep and deep, the program becomes more and more difficult to read. There is another way to write and think about this situation.

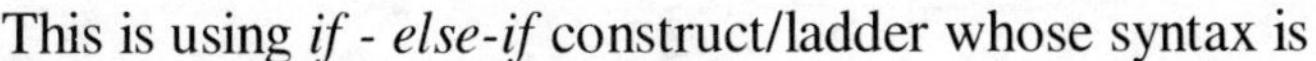

This is using *if - else-if* construct/ladder whose syntax is

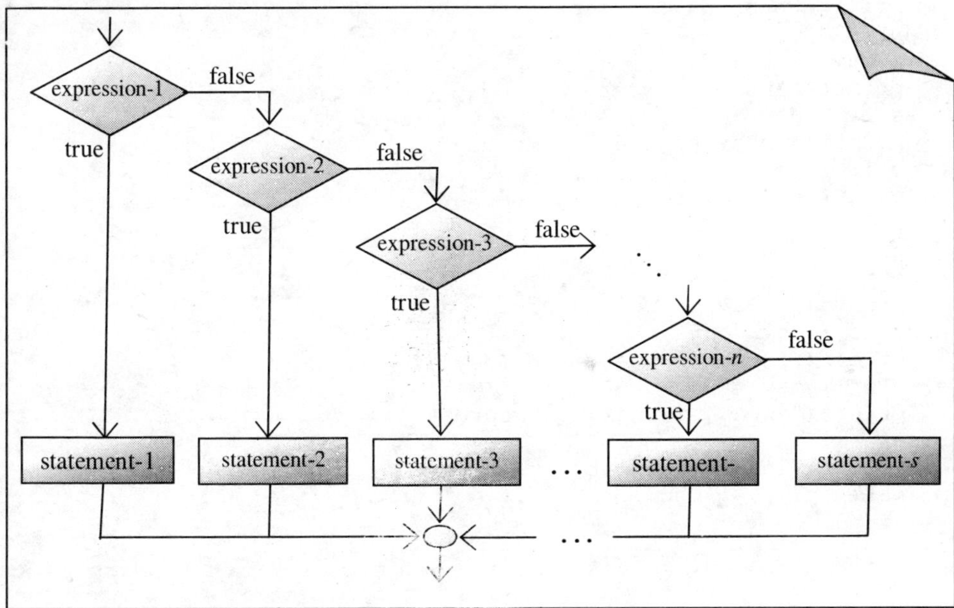

Figure 9.3: Logic Flow Control of *if - else if* Ladder

The expressions are evaluated in order, and if any expression is true then the statement block associated with it is executed, and this terminates the whole chain. The last *else* part handles *none of the above* or default case where none of the specified expressions are satisfied.

This sequence of *if* statements is the most general way of writing a multi-way decision. The program listing 9.7 can be rewritten using *if - else if* construct/ladder as shown in program listing 9.7.

```
if ( expression-1 )
   statement-1
else if ( expression-2 )
   statement-2
else if ( expression-3 )
   statement-3
      :
      :
else if ( expression-n )
   statement-n
else
   statement-s
```

Figure 9.4: Code of *if - else if* Ladder

Listing 9.7

```
/* Program to print the name of the day of week when we are given the
 * day of week as number (0 for Sunday, 1 for Monday, ..., 6 for
 * Saturday) using if - else if ladder.
 */
#include <stdio.h>
int main()
```

```
{
    int day;
    printf("\nEnter day of week as number ( 0 - 6 ) : ");
    scanf("%d", &day);
    if ( day == 0 )
       printf("\nDay of week is Sunday");
    else if ( day == 1 )
       printf("\nDay of week is Monday");
    else if ( day == 2 )
       printf("\nDay of week is Tuesday");
    else if ( day == 3 )
       printf("\nDay of week is Wednesday");
    else if ( day == 4 )
       printf("\nDay of week is Thursday");
    else if ( day == 5 )
       printf("\nDay of week is Friday");
    else if ( day == 6 )
       printf("\nDay of week is Saturday");
    else
       printf("\n Wrong input");
    printf("\n");
    return 0;
}
```

Example 9.1:

The commission on sales by a salesman is calculated as per following policy:

Amount of Sale (in Rs.)	Commission Rate
0 – 5000	Nil
5001 – 10000	5 %
10001 – 15000	7.5 %
15001 – 20000	9 %
> 20000	10 %

Write a program that accepts sales made by a salesman and displays the commission.

Listing 9.8

```
/* Program to compute the commission as per the stated policy  */
#include <stdio.h>
int main()
{
    float sales, comm;
    printf("\nEnter sales made by the salesman (in Rs.) : ");
    scanf("%f", &sales);
    if ( sales <= 5000 )
       comm = 0;
    else if ( sales <= 10000 )
       comm = ( sales - 5000 ) * 0.05;
```

```
    else if ( sales <= 15000 )
        comm = 250 + ( sales - 10000 ) * 0.075;
    else if ( sales <= 20000 )
        comm = 675 + ( sales - 15000 ) * 0.09;
    else
        comm = 1125 + ( sales - 20000 ) * 0.1;

    printf("\nThe computed commission = Rs. %.f", comm);
    return 0;
}
```

Test Runs

First Run

```
Enter sales made by the salesman (in Rs.) : 4500
The computed commission = 0
```

Second Run

```
Enter sales made by the salesman (in Rs.): 17500
The computed commission = Rs. 900
```

9.2.5 The *switch* Statement

The *switch* statement provides an alternative to *else if* construct. The *switch* statement has more flexibility and a clearer format than *else if* construct. The syntax of *switch* statement is shown in Figure 9.5.

If *expression* takes any value from *val-1*, *val-2*, *val-3*, ..., *val-n*, the control is transferred to that appropriate case. In each case, the statements are executed and then the *break* statement transfers the control out of *switch* statement.

```
switch ( expression )
{
    case val-1 :
                    statement-1
                    break;
    case val-2 :
                    statement-2
                    break;
    case val-3 :
                    statement-3
                    break;
          :
    case val-n :
               statement-n
               break;
    default    :
               statement-d
}
```

Figure 9.5: Code of *switch* Statement

If no *break* statement is used following a case, except the last one in the absence of *default* keyword, the control will fall through to the next case. If the value of the *expression* does not match any of the case values, control goes to the *default* keyword, which is usually at the end of the *switch* statement. The use of the *default* keyword can be of a great convenience. If there is no *default* keyword, the whole *switch* statement simply terminates when there is no match.

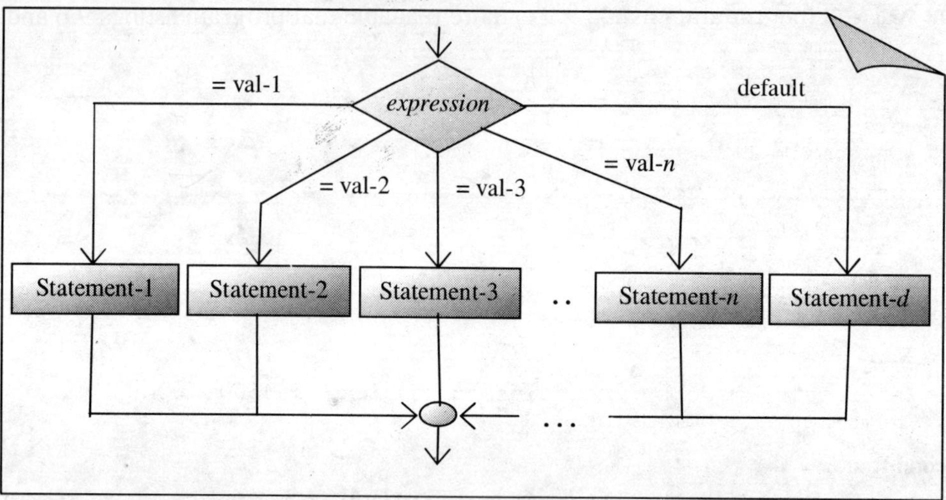

Figure 9.6: Logic Flow Control of *switch* Statement

Listing 9.9

```
/*  Program to demonstrate the use of switch statement  */
#include<stdio.h>
int main()
{
   int day;
   printf( "\nEnter day of week as number: " );
   scanf( "%d", &day );
   switch ( day )
   {
     case 0  : printf("\nDay of week is Sunday" );
               break;
     case 1  : printf("\nDay of week is Monday" );
               break;
     case 2  : printf("\nDay of week is Tuesday" );
               break;
     case 3  : printf("\nDay of week is Wednesday" );
               break;
     case 4  : printf("\nDay of week is Thursday" );
               break;
     case 5  : printf("\nDay of week is Friday" );
               break;
     case 6  : printf("\nDay of week is Saturday" );
               break;
     default : printf("\nWrong input" );
   }
   printf( "\n" );
   return 0;
}
```

You will find that program listing 9.9 is more readable that program listings 9.6 and 9.7.

Listing 9.10

```
/* Program to create equivalent of four function ( +, -, *, / )
 * calculator using switch statement
 */
#include<stdio.h>
int main()
{
    float a, b, result;
    char op;
    printf("\nEnter expression such as 5+3 : ");
    scanf("%d%c%d", &a, &op, &b );
    switch ( op )
    {
        case '+' : result = a + b;
                   break;
        case '-' : result = a - b;
                   break;
        case '*' : result = a * b;
                   break;
        case '/' : result = a / b;
                   break;
        default :  printf("\nWrong input\n");
                   return 0;
    }
    printf("\n%.2f%c%.2f = %.2f\n", a, op, b, result);
    return 0;
}
```

However, if you want that a same statement is to executed for more than one value of the *expression*, then we have to code these *cases* one after the other, and then the specified statement as shown below:

```
switch ( expression )
{
     :
   case val-4 :
   case val-5 :
   case val-6 :
                statement-block
                break;
     :
}
```

The *statement-block* will be executed whenever the value of the *expression* is *val-4*, *val-5*, or *val-6*.

9.2.5.1 More About *switch* Statement

Following are some important points about switch statement.

1. The *expression* of switch statement must be of type integer or character type.
2. The *default* case need not be used as the last case. It can be placed at any place.
3. The case values must be integer constants or character constants. These values can also be constant expressions as these are evaluated at compilation time. For example, if expression 5 + 7 appears as case value, it will be evaluated to value 12 at compilation. Similarly, if expression 5 < 7 appears as the case value, it will evaluate to 1 by compiler at compilation time.
4. The case statements can only be used within the scope of switch statement otherwise the compiler will display en error message similar to *"Case outside of switch statement in function ..."*.
5. The case values need not be in any specific order.

9.3 SUPPLEMENTARY PROBLEMS

Let us write a few more C programs to use the features that we have learned in this chapter.

Problem 9.1:

Program to find roots of a quadratic equation of type $ax^2 + bx + c = 0$ provided $a \neq 0$.

Solution: The roots of the quadratic equation are given by the formula:

$$x_{1,2} = \frac{-b \pm \sqrt{b^2 - 4ac}}{2a},$$ where expression $b^2 - 4ac$ is known as the discriminant.

Depending on the sign of the discriminant, there are three possibilities for the roots:

1. If $b^2 - 4ac < 0$, then the root are imaginary, and we can compute real part and imaginary part separately as

$$\text{real part} = -\frac{b}{2a} \qquad \text{imaginary part} = \frac{\sqrt{-(b^2 - 4ac)}}{2a}$$

2. If $b^2 - 4ac = 0$, then the roots are real and equal, and root is simply computed as

$$\text{root} = -\frac{b}{2a}$$

3. If $b^2 - 4ac > 0$, then the roots are real and distinct and are computed as

$$\text{root one} = \frac{-b - \sqrt{b^2 - 4ac}}{2a} \qquad \text{root two} = \frac{-b + \sqrt{b^2 - 4ac}}{2a}$$

The complete program will look like as shown below:

Listing 9.11

```
/*  Program to find the roots of an quadratic equation of type
*   of  type a*x^2+b*x+c = 0, where a is not equal to zero
*/

#include<stdio.h>
#include<math.h>

int main()
{
   float a, b, c, disc, root1, root2, twoA;
   float realPart, imagPart;
   printf( "\nEnter values of a,b,c: " );
   scanf( "%f,%f,%f", &a, &b, &c);
   if ( a == 0 ) {
      printf( "\nIt is not an quadratic equation\n" );
      return 0;
   }
   disc = b * b - 4.0 * a * c;
   twoA = a + a;
   if ( disc < 0 ) {
      realPart = - b / twoA;
      imagPart = sqrt((double)-disc) / twoA;
      printf( "\nRoots are imaginary" );
      printf( "\nReal part = %.3f", realPart );
      printf( "\nImaginary part = %.3f\n", imagPart );
   } else if ( disc == 0 ) {
      root1 = - b / twoA;
      printf( "\nRoots are real and equal" );
      printf( "\nEach root = %.3f\n", root1 );
   } else {
      root1 = (-b-sqrt((double)disc ))/twoA;
      root2 = (-b+sqrt((double)disc ))/twoA;
      printf( "\nRoots are real and distinct" );
      printf( "\nRoot 1 = %.3f", root1 );
      printf( "\nRoot 2 = %.3f\n", root2 );
   }
   return 0;
}
```

Test Run

```
Enter values of a,b,c: 2,3,5

Roots are imaginary

Real part = -0.750
Imaginary part = 1.392
```

Problem 9.2:

Write a program to determine whether the given year is a leap year.

Under the current (Gregorian) calendar, a year is said to be a leap year if it is divisible by 400 or by 4 but not by 100

Listing 9.12

```
/* Program to determine whether the given year is a leap year  */
#include<stdio.h>
int main()
{
   int year;
   printf("\nEnter any year : ");
   scanf("%d",&year);
   if ((year % 400==0)||((year % 4==0) )&&(year % 100!=0))
      printf("\nYear %d is a leap year.\n", year);
   else
      printf("\nYear %d is not a leap year.\n", year);
   return 0;
}
```

Test Runs

First Run

```
Enter any year : 2000
Year 2000 is a leap year.
```

Second Run

```
Enter any year : 2008
Year 2000 is a leap year.
```

Third Run

```
Enter any year : 2006
Year 2000 is not a leap year.
```

Problem 9.3:

Income tax for individuals is computed on slab rates as follows:

Income	Tax Payable
Upto Rs. 1,00,000/-	Nil
From Rs. 1,00,001/- to Rs. 2,00,000/-	10% of the excess over Rs. 1,00,000/-
From Rs. 2,00,001/- to Rs. 3,00,000/-	20% of the excess over Rs. 2,00,000/-
Above Rs. 3,00,000/-	30% of the excess over Rs. 3,00,000/-

Write a program that reads the income and prints the income tax due.

Listing 9.13

```
/*  Program to compute income tax for given gross income  */
#include<stdio.h>
void main()
{
   float income, tax;
   printf( "\nEnter gross income (in Rs.): " );
   scanf( "%f", &income );
   if ( income <= 100000.0 )
      tax = 0;
   else if ( income <= 200000.0 )
      tax = ( income - 100000.0 ) * 0.1;
   else if ( income <= 300000.0 )
      tax = 10000 + ( income - 200000.0 ) * 0.2;
   else
      tax = 30000 + ( income - 300000.0 ) * 0.3;
   printf( "\nTax due = Rs. %.2f\n", tax );
}
```

Test Run

```
Enter gross income : 250000
Tax due = Rs. 20000.00
```

Problem 9.4:

Given roll number, name and marks in four subjects. Write a program to print the roll number, name and grade, where grade is computed as follows:

Percentage of Marks	Grade
percentage $\geq$ 90	A
90 > percentage $\geq$ 75	B
75 > percentage $\geq$ 60	C
60 > percentage $\geq$ 50	D
percentage < 50	F

Listing 9.14

```
/*  Program to compute grade of student  */
#include<stdio.h>
int main()
{
   int   rollno, i;
   char  name[21], grade;
   float marks[4], total, percent;
   printf("\nEnter name (max 20 characters) : ");
   fgets(name, 21, stdin);
   printf("Enter rollno number : ");
   scanf("%d", &rollno);
```

```
    printf("\nEnter marks in FOUR subjects\n");
    for (i = 0; i < 4; i++ )
       scanf("%f", &marks[i]);
    total = 0;
    for ( i = 0; i < 4; i++ )
       total += marks[i];
    percent = total/4;
    if ( percent >= 90 )
       grade = 'A';
    else if ( percent >= 75 )
       grade = 'B';
    else if ( percent >= 60 )
       grade = 'C';
    else if ( percent >= 50 )
       grade = 'D';
    else
       grade = 'F';
     printf("\nParticulars of Student\n\n");
     printf("\nRoll number : %d", rollno);
     printf("\nName        : %s", name);
     printf("\nGrade       : %c\n", grade);
     return 0;
}
```

Test Run

```
Enter name (max 20 characters) : Ram Murti

Enter rollno number : 1200

Enter marks in FOUR subjects

75 80 90 85

Particulars of Student

Roll number : 1200
Name        : Ram Murti
Grade       : B
```

EXERCISE

1. If the *if* statement do not have associated *else*, then what happens if the condition evaluates to zero value?
2. What is the advantage of *switch* statement over *else-if* construct?
3. What does nesting mean?
4. Is any thing wrong with the following program?

```
void main()
{
     char ch;
     if ( ( ch = cin.get() ) == 'a' )
          printf("\nYou typed character a\n");
}
```

5. Where the *break* statement is used, and what is its function?
6. Rewrite the following code fragment using the *switch* statement:

```
char code;
code = getchar();
if ( code == 'A' )
   printf("\nAccountant\n");
else if ( code == 'C' || code == 'G' )
   printf("\nGrade IV\n");
else if ( code == 'F' )
   printf("\nFinancial Advisor\n");
else
   printf("\nIncorrect code\n");
```

7. Rewrite the following code fragment using the *if-else* statements:

```
int month;
scanf("%d", &month);
switch ( month )
{
  case 1 :
  case 3 :
  case 5 :
  case 7 :
  case 8 :
  case 10:
  case 12: printf("\nIt is a month having 31 days\n");
           break;
  case 4 :
  case 6 :
  case 9 :
  case 11: printf("\nIt is a month having 30 days\n");
           break;
  case 2:  printf("\nIt is a month having 28/29 days\n");
  default: printf("\nIncorrect month\n");
}
```

8. Rewrite the following code segments using the *switch* statement:

```
if ( ch == 'N' )
   north++;
if ( ch == 'S' )
   south++;
if ( ch == 'E' )
   east++;
if ( ch == 'W' )
   west++;
else
   unknown++;
```

```
if (ch == 'O')
   Outstanding++;
else if (ch == 'E')
   Excellent++;
else if (ch == 'G')
   Good++ ;
else if (ch == 'P')
   Poor++;
else
   Unknown++ ;
```

9. Write any two point of difference in operation in *switch* and *if- else*.
10. What is the effect of the absence of *break* statement in *switch* statement.

PROGRAMMING EXERCISE

1. Given three numbers, determine whether they can form sides of a triangle.
2. Given three points $A(x_1, y_1)$, $B(x_2, y_2)$ and $C(x_3, y_3)$, determine whether they are collinear, i.e., lie on the same line.

3. Write a program to determine whether the number is divisible by 2, without performing the division by 2.
4. Given three numbers, determine whether they can form sides of an isosceles triangle.
5. The monthly telephone bill is to be computed as follows:

   Minimum Rs. 200 for upto 100 calls
   plus Rs. 0.60 per call for next 50 calls
   plus Rs. 0.50 per call for next 50 calls
   plus Rs. 0.40 per call for any call beyond 200 calls.

   Write a program to compute monthly bill for given number of calls.
6. A department store places an order with a company for *n* pieces of miners, *m* pieces of toasters, and *p* number of fans. Cost of each item is as follows:

Miners	: Rs. 1,500 per piece
Toaster	: Rs. 200 per piece
Fan	: Rs. 450 per piece

   The discount allowed for various items are 5% for miners, 15% for fan, and 10% for toaster. The company charge 10% as sales tax on all items on net value after deducting the discount. Write a program that reads *m*, *n*, and *p* and computes the amount to be paid by the store.
7. Suppose the postal rates for mailing letters are as follows:

   Rs. 0.50 per 10 grams for the first 50 grams,
   Rs. 0.40 per 10 grams for the next 100 grams,
   Rs. 0.25 per 10 grams for the next 250 grams, and
   Rs. 25 per kilogram for letters weighing more than 400 grams.

   Write a program that prompts for weight of a letter and prints the postage to be paid.

❑ ❑ ❑

Chapter 10

Decision Making and Looping

Learning Objectives

After reading this chapter, students will be able to

- explain the working of *while* statement
- explain the working of *for* statement
- explain the working of *do-while* statement
- explain the nesting of looping statements
- explain the working of *break*, *continue* and *goto* statements
- explain the usefulness of *else if* ladder in multiple alternatives in decision making
- use these statements to write programs to solve problems requiring iteration

10.1 INTRODUCTION

As discussed in the last chapter, a computer program is a set of instructions for a computer that are executed sequentially, *i.e.*, one after the other as they appear in a program.

However, following situations may arise:

- There may be situations when we need to alter this sequence by choosing a particular set of statements (*selection*) among two or more alternatives, based on certain criteria (*i.e.*, when certain conditions are satisfied/not satisfied) is met.
- There may also be situations when we need to repeat (*iteration*) certain group of statements over either fixed number of times or till certain criteria (*i.e.*, when certain conditions are satisfied/not satisfied) is met.
- There may also be situations when we need to transfer the control from one part of the program to another part (*jumping*) in order to skip certain instructions or go back to repeat certain instructions either depending on the satisfaction of certain condition (*conditional transfer*) or without the involvement of any condition (*unconditional transfer*).

This means, we may need to control the execution of the instructions.

In the previous chapter, we had discussed the control statements that allow us to perform the action of selection. This chapter focuses on the control statements that allow us to perform the action of iteration. In addition, the statements that allow us to perform the action of transfer of control within the program conditionally or unconditionally are also discussed.

10.2 THE *while* STATEMENT

The *while* statement is suited for problems where it is not known in advance that how many times a statement or a statement-block will be executed.

Te logic flow and the syntax of the while statement is shown in Figure 10.1. Here *expression* can be a constant, a variable or an expression. The *statement* is executed repeatedly till the *exp* evaluates to a *non-zero* value. Whenever *exp* evaluates to a *zero* value, the execution of *while* statement will terminate and control will pass to a statement immediately following it.

Though in C language there are certain exceptions, but in general, the following points must be kept in mind while using the *while* statement:

- There must be a statement prior to *while* statement that initializes the *exp*.
- In the statement-block, there must be a statement that modifies the expression.

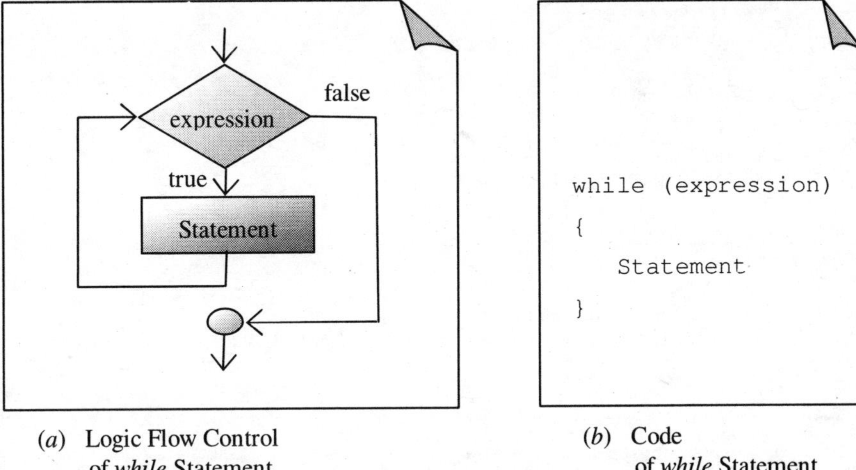

(*a*) Logic Flow Control of *while* Statement

(*b*) Code of *while* Statement

Figure 10.1: Logic flow control and code of *while* statement

To illustrate the use of *while* statement, let us develop some programs.

Listing 10.1

```
/* Program to find sum of first 100 positive integer numbers */
#include <stdio.h>
int main()
{
    int sum = 0, number;
    number = 1;
    while ( number <= 100 )
    {
        sum += number;
        number++;
    }
    printf( "Sum of first 100 positive " );
    printf( "integer numbers = %d\n", sum );
    return 0;
}
```

Test Run

```
Sum of first 100 positive integer numbers = 5050
```

Listing 10.2

```
/* Program to find sum of even and odd numbers from
*  first 100 positive integer numbers   */
#include<stdio.h>
int main()
```

```
{
   int sumOdd = 0, sumEven = 0, number;
   number = 1;
   while ( number <= 100 )
   {
      if ( ( number % 2 ) == 0 )
         sumEven += number;
      else
         sumOdd += number;
      number++;
   }
   printf( "Sum of even numbers = %d\n", sumEven );
   printf( "Sum of odd numbers  = %d\n", sumOdd );
   return 0;
}
```

Test Run

```
Sum of even numbers = 2550
Sum of odd numbers  = 2500
```

Listing 10.3

```
/* Program to find sum of digits of a positive
   integer number    */
#include<stdio.h>
int main()
{
   int sum = 0, digit;
   long number, temp;
   printf( "Enter any positive integer number: " );
   scanf( "%ld", &number );
   temp = number;
   while ( temp > 0 )
   {
      digit = temp % 10;
      temp /= 10;
      sum += digit;
   }
   printf( "\nSum of digits of %ld = %d\n", number, sum );
   return 0;
}
```

Test Run

```
Enter any positive integer number : 3265
Sum of digits of 3265 = 16
```

Listing 10.4

```
/*
* Program to count number of characters, vowels & words
* in a paragraph
*/

int main()
{
   int vowelCount=0,characterCount=0,wordCount=0;
   char ch;

   printf( "Type in the paragraph and terminate");
   printf( "\nby ENTER key\n\n" );

   while ( ( ch = getche() ) != '\r' )
   {
      characterCount++;
      if ( ( ch == ' ' ) || ( ch == '\t' ) )
         wordCount++;
      if ( (ch=='a')||(ch=='A')||(ch=='e')||
           (ch=='E')||(ch=='i')||(ch=='I')||
           (ch=='o')||(ch=='O')||(ch=='u')||
           (ch == 'U') )
         vowelCount++;
   }

   wordCount++;

   printf( "\nCharacter count = %d", characterCount);
   printf( "\nVowel count = %d", vowelCount);
   printf( "\nWord count = %d\n", wordCount);
   return 0;
}
```

Test Run

```
Type the paragraph and terminate by ENTER key

i enjoy programming in c++ like anything ↵

Character count = 40
Vowel count = 11
Word count = 7
```

10.3 THE *for* STATEMENT

The *for* statement is suited for problems where the number of times a statement or statement-block will be executed is known in advance.

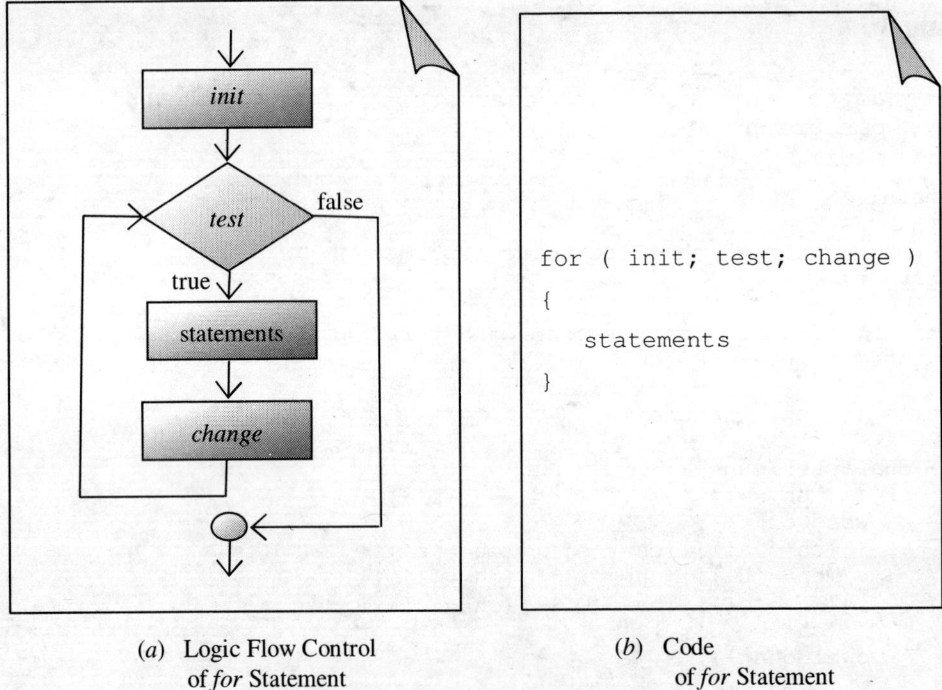

(*a*) Logic Flow Control of *for* Statement

(*b*) Code of *for* Statement

Figure 10.2: Logic flow control and code of *for* statement

where *init* is an expression to initialize the counter, the *test* is an expression to see when to stop iterating, and *change* is an expression to change the counter for each pass of the loop. The *init* and *change* parts can have more than one statement separated by a comma.

To demonstrate the use of *for* statement, let us develop some program making using of *for* statement.

Listing 10.5

```
/*
*  Program to find sum of first 100 positive numbers using for loop
*/
#include<stdio.h>
int main(void)
{
   int i, sum = 0;
   for ( i = 1; i <= 100; i++ ) {
     sum = sum + i;
   }
   printf( "\nSum of first 100 positive\n" );
   printf( "integer numbers = %d\n", sum );
   return 0;
}
```

Listing 10.6

```
/* Program to find sum of even and odd numbers from first 100
  Positive numbers using 'for' loop    */
#include<stdio.h>
int main()
{
   int sumOdd = 0, sumEven = 0, number;
   for ( number = 0; number <= 100; number++ ) {
      if ( ( number % 2 ) == 0 )
         sumEven += number;
      else
         sumOdd += number;
   }
   printf( "\nSum of even numbers = %d\n", sumEven );
   printf( "Sum of odd numbers  = %d\n", sumOdd );
   return 0;
}
```

Listing 10.7

```
/*  Program to compute average of 'n' real numbers    */
#include<stdio.h>
int main()
{
   int i, n;
   float number, sum = 0, average;
   printf( "Enter value of n: " );
   scanf( "%d", &n );
   for ( i = 1; i <= n; i++ ) {
      printf( "Enter real number %d: ", i );
      scanf ( "%f", &number );
      sum += number;
   }
   average = sum / n;
   printf( "\nAverage of numbers = %.2f\n", average );
   return 0;
}
```

Test Run

```
Enter value of n: 8

Enter real number 1: 2.5
Enter real number 2: 12.0
Enter real number 3: 10.25
Enter real number 4: 8.75
Enter real number 5: 11.0
Enter real number 6: 20.25
Enter real number 7: -7.75
Enter real number 8: 9.0

Average of numbers = 8.25
```

10.4 THE *do –while* STATEMENT

The *do-while* statement, like *while* statement, is also suited for problems where it is not known in advance that how many times a statement will be executed.

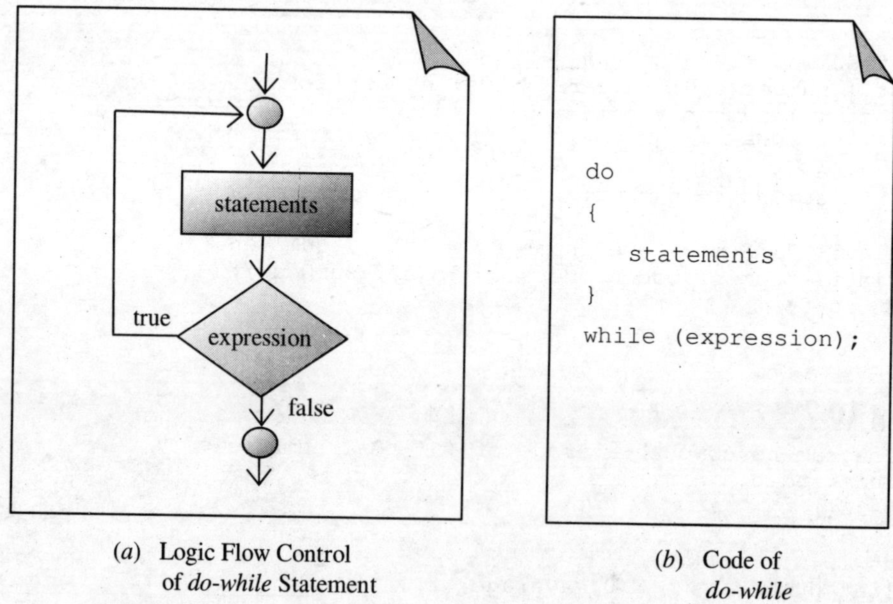

(*a*) Logic Flow Control of *do-while* Statement

(*b*) Code of *do-while*

Figure 10.3: Logic flow control and code of *do-while* statement

where *expression* is a constant, a variable or an expression. The *statement-block* is executed repeatedly till the *exp* evaluates to a *non-zero* value.

To demonstrate the use of *do – while* statement, let us develop a program to find the average of unknown real numbers.

Listing 10.8

```
/*
*  Program to compute average of unknown real numbers
*/
#include<stdio.h>
int main()
{
   int n = 0;
   char yesno;
   float number, sum = 0, average;
   do {
      printf( "\nEnter number %d: ", n+1 );
      scanf( "%f", &number );
      n++;
```

```
        sum += number;
        printf( "\nAny more number [yn]?: " );
        yesno = getchar();
    }
    while ( ( yesno == 'y' ) || ( yesno == 'Y' )  );
    average = sum / n;
    printf( "\n\nAverage of given numbers = %.2f\n", average );
    return 0;
}
```

Test Run

```
Enter number 1: 2.5
Any more number [yn]?: y
Enter number 2: 12.0
Any more number [yn]?: y
Enter number 3: 10.25
Any more number [yn]?: y
Enter number 4: 8.75
Any more number [yn]?: y
Enter number 5: 11.0
Any more number [yn]?: n
Average of given numbers = 8.90
```

10.5 NESTED *while*, *for* and *do —while* STATEMENTS

Just as *if* statements can be nested, these statements can also be nested. The inner loop is executed from the beginning for each iteration of the outer loop. The following sections of code show the nesting of looping statements within their own types.

```
for(i=0;i<m;i++)
{
    :
    for(j=0;j<n;j++)
    {
        :
    }
}
```

```
i=0;
while(i<m)
{
    :
    j=0;
    while(j<n)
    {
        :
        j++;
    }
    i++;
}
```

```
i=0;
do
{
    :
    j=0;
    do
    {
        :
        j++;
    } while(j<n);
    i++;
} while(i<m);
```

In general, it is possible to nest while and do-while statements inside *for* statement, *for* statement inside the *while* and *do-while* statements, *i.e.*, all sort of nesting combinations are permitted.

Listing 10.9

```
/* Program to print following pattern using nested for loops
         1
         2   2
         3   3   3
         4   4   4   4
         5   5   5   5   5
*/

#include <stdio.h>
int main()
{
    int i, j;
    printf("\n");
    for ( i = i; i < 5; i++ )
    {
        for ( j = 1; j <= i; j++ )
        {
            printf("%4d", i);
        }
        printf("\n");
    }
    return 0;
}
```

Listing 10.10

```
/* Program to print following pattern using nested for loops
        5   5   5   5   5
        4   4   4   4
        3   3   3
        2   2
        1
*/

#include <stdio.h>
int main()
{
    int i, j;
    printf("\n");
    for ( i = 5; i >= 1; i-- )
    {
        for ( j = 1; j <= i; j++ )
        {
            printf("%4d", i);
        }
        printf("\n");
    }
    return 0;
}
```

Listing 10.11

```
/* Program to print following pattern using nested for loops
       1
       1   2
       1   2   3
       1   2   3   4
       1   2   3   4   5
*/

#include <stdio.h>
int main()
{
    int i, j;
    printf("\n");
    for ( i = i; i < 5; i++ )
    {
        for ( j = 1; j <= i; j++ )
        {
            printf("%4d", j);
        }
        printf("\n");
    }
    return 0;
}
```

Listing 10.12

```
/* Program to print following pattern using nested for loops
        *
        *   *
        *   *   *
        *   *   *   *
        *   *   *   *   *
*/

#include <stdio.h>
int main()
{
    int i, j;
    printf("\n");
    for ( i = i; i < 5; i++ )
    {
        for ( j = 1; j <= i; j++ )
        {
            printf("    *");
        }
        printf("\n");
    }
    return 0;
}
```

Listing 10.13

```
/*
 *  Program to demonstrate the nesting of 'for' statements
 */
#include <stdio.h>
#include <ctype.h>
int main()
{
    int j, i, jj;
    for ( i = 2; i <= 10; i++ ) {
        printf ( "\n\t\t    Table of %d", i );
        printf ( "\n\t\t    ==========\n" );
        for ( j = 1; j <= 10; j++ ) {
            jj = j + 10;
            printf("\n\t%3d x %2d = %3d\t%3d x %3d = %3d",
                   i, j, i*j, i, jj, i*jj );
        }
        printf( "\n\n\tPress any key to continue...");
        getch();
    }
    return 0;
}
```

When you run this program, it will print the tables from 2 to 10, one table per screen. After printing one table, it will ask the user to press any key to continue.

Test Run

```
                Table of 2
                ==========

    2 x  1 =   2  2 x  11 =  22
    2 x  2 =   4  2 x  12 =  24
    2 x  3 =   6  2 x  13 =  26
    2 x  4 =   8  2 x  14 =  28
    2 x  5 =  10  2 x  15 =  30
    2 x  6 =  12  2 x  16 =  32
    2 x  7 =  14  2 x  17 =  34
    2 x  8 =  16  2 x  18 =  36
    2 x  9 =  18  2 x  19 =  38
    2 x 10 -  20  2 x  20 -  40

  Press any key to continue...
```

10.6 JUMPING STATEMENTS

These statements transfer the control from one part of the program to another part. In this section, we will see their working.

10.6.1 The *break* Statement

The *break* statement is always used inside the body of the *switch* statement, and looping statements.

```
switch ( expression )
{
    case val-1 : statement-1
                 break;
    case val-2 : statement-2
                 break;
    case val-3 : statement-3
                 break;
       :
       :
    case val-n : statement-n
                 break;
    default    :
                statement-d
}
```

Figure 10.4: Action of *break* statement in *switch* statement

In *switch* statement, it is used as the last statement of every case except the last one. When executed, it transfers the control out of *switch* statement and the execution of the program continues from the statement following *switch* statement.

In *for*, *while* and *do-while* statements, it is always used in conjunction with *if* statement. Note that it is never used with *if* statement if it is not part of the body of the looping statement. When executed, it transfers the control out of looping statement and the execution of the program continues from the statement following looping statement.

```
for(i=0;i<m;i++)        i=0;                   i=0;
{                       while(i<m)             do
  :                     {                      {
  if (expression)         :                      :
     break;               if (expression)        if (expression)
  :                          break;                 break;
}                         :                      :
                        }                      } while(i<m);
```

Figure 10.5: Action of *break* statement in *for, while* and *do-while* statements

In simple terms, we can say that the *break* when executed terminates the execution of the loop.

Consider the following code segment

```
  :
i = 0;
while ( i <= 100 )
{
    . . . . . .
    scanf("%d", &k);
    if ( k == 0 )
        break;
    m = i / k;
     . . . . . .
}
  :
```

The execution of the *while* loop will be terminated as soon as the user enters value 0 for variable *k* as input or the value of variable *i* exceeds 100, which ever happens earlier.

10.6.2 The *continue* Statement

The *continue* statement is always used inside the body of the looping statements. In looping statements, sometimes a situation may arise where we want that from a given statement onward, the rest of the statement up to the last statement of the loop are to be bypassed. This task is accomplished by using *continue* statement.

The *continue* statement transfers the control to the beginning of the next iteration of the loop thus bypassing the statements which are not yet executed. Note that the *continue* statement is always used in conjunction with the *if* statement.

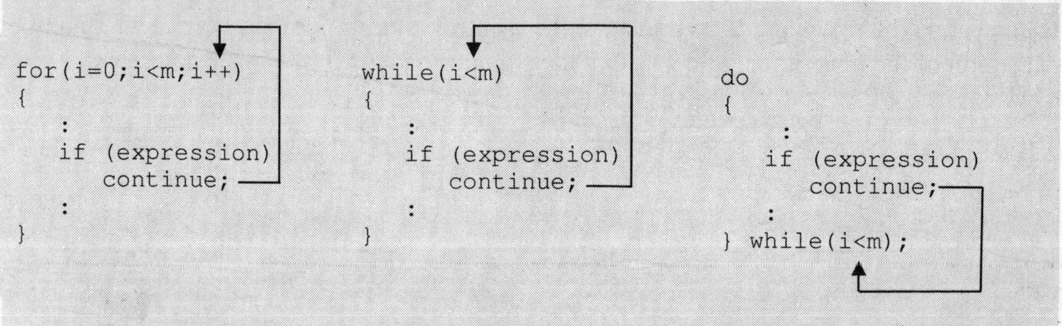

Figure 10.6: Action of *continue* statement in *for, while* and *do-while* statements

In simple terms, we can say that the continue statement when executed terminates the current iteration of the loop.

Consider the following segment

```
  :
i = 0;
while ( i <= 100 )
{
    . . . . . .
    if ( i % 10 == 0 )
       continue;
    . . . . . .
}
  :
```

The use of *continue* statement in conjunction with *if* statement skips the rest of the statements of the *while* loop for values of *i* divisible by 10.

10.7 SUPPLEMENTARY PROBLEMS

Let us write a few more C programs to use the features that we have learned in this chapter.

Problem 10.1:

Program to find whether the given positive number *n* is a prime number or composite.

I hope you know that a positive integer number is said to be prime if it divisible by 1 and itself only, *i.e.*, it cannot be factorized. In addition, to this definition, an even number except 2, is not a prime number.

Therefore, our test criteria becomes

1. If *n* is greater than 2 and is even then *n* is not a prime number.
2. If test at step 1 fails, then we try to divide number *n* by factors $k = 3, 5, 7, \ldots \sqrt{n}$. Therefore, if *n* is divisible by any value of *k*, number *n* is not a prime number.
3. If test at step 2 also fails, then *n* is a prime number.

The following program implements this criterion.

Listing 10.14

```
/* Program to find whether given positive number 'n' is prime  */
#include<stdio.h>
#include<math.h>
int main()
{
   int n, k, m;
   printf( "\nEnter a positive integer number: " );
   scanf("%d", &n);
   if ( ( n > 2 ) && ( ( n % 2 ) == 0 ) ) {
      printf( "\n%d is not a prime number.\n", n );
   } else {
```

```
      m = sqrt( n );
      for ( k = 3; k <= m; k += 2 ) {
         if ( ( n % k ) == 0 )
            break;
      }
      if ( k > m )
         printf( "\n%d is a prime number.\n", n );
      else
         printf( "\n%d is not a prime number.\n", n );
   }
   return 0;
}
```

Test Runs

First Run

```
Enter a positive integer number: 43

43 is a prime number.
```

Second Run

```
Enter a positive integer number: 92

92 is not a prime number.
```

Problem 10.2:

Program to find the *n*th prime number.

We know that first prime number is 2, second prime number is 3, fourth prime number is 5, and so on.

Therefore, we start with number 2 and generate the subsequent numbers. On each number we apply primality test, if is passes the test, we count it. After every count, we see do we have reached the desired prime number, if yes we print that number and stop.

The following program implements this criterion.

Listing 10.15

```
/*  Program to find the nth prime number    */
#include<stdio.h>
#include<math.h>
int main()
{
  int n, k, m, count=0, num = 2;
  printf("Program to find nth prime number\n\n");
  printf("Enter positive value for n: ");
  scanf("%d", &n);
  while ( 1 )
  {
```

```
    if ( ( num > 2 ) && ( ( num %2 ) == 0 ) ) {
      num++;         /* move to next number, it is even   */
      continue;
    } else {
        m = (int) sqrt ( (double) n );
        for ( k = 3; k <= m; k+= 2 ) {
            if ( ( num % k ) == 0 ) {
              num++;                 /* move to next number,      */
              break;                 /* as it is divisible by k */
            }
        }
        if ( k > m ) {
          count++;                    /*  increase the count       */
          if ( count == n ) {         /* is it desired number      */
          {
             printf("\n%dth prime number = %d\n", n, num);
             return;
          }
          num++;                      /*  move to next number      */
        }
    }
  }
  return 0;
}
```

Test Run

```
Program to find nth prime number
Enter positive value for n: 10
10th prime number = 29
```

Problem 10.3:

Program to check whether the given positive integer number is an Armstrong number.

Note that a positive integer number is an Armstrong number if the sum of cubes of its digits equals the number itself. For example, number 153 is an Armstrong number as

$$1^3 + 5^3 + 3^3 = 1 + 125 + 27 = 153$$

Listing 10.16

```
/* Program to check whether the given positive integer
   number is an Armstrong number
*/
#include<stdio.h>
int main()
{
  int intNumber, intTempNumber, intSum = 0, digit;
  printf( "Enter positive integer number : " );
```

```
    scanf("%d", &intNumber);
    intTempNumber = intNumber;  /* create copy */
    while ( intTempNumber > 0 ) {
       digit = intTempNumber % 10;
       intTempNumber /= 10;
       intSum += digit * digit * digit;
    }
    if ( intSum == intNumber )
       printf("\n%d is an Armstrong Number\n", intNumber);
    else
       printf( "\n%d is not an Armstrong Number\n", intNumber);
    return 0;
}
```

Test Runs

First Run

```
Enter positive integer number: 153
153 is an Armstrong number
```

Second Run

```
Enter positive integer number: 120
120 is not an Armstrong number
```

Problem 10.4:

A Fibbonacci sequence is defined as follows: the first and second terms in the sequence are 0 and 1. Subsequent terms are found by adding the preceding two terms in the sequence. Write a program to generate the first *n* terms of the sequence.

Listing 10.17

```
/*  Program to generate the first 'n' terms of Fibonacci sequence  */
#include<stdio.h>
int main()
{
    int previous = 0, current = 1, next, n, count;
    printf( "\nEnter value for n (>2) : " );
    scanf( "%d", &n );
    printf( "%d  %d", previous, current );
    count = 2;
    while ( count < n )
    {
         next = previous + current;
         printf( "%d  ", next );
         count++;
         previous = current;
         current = next;
```

```
    }
    printf( "\n" );
    return 0;
}
```

Test Run

```
Enter value for n : 10
0  1  1  2  3  5  8  13  21  34
```

Problem 10.5:

Write a program to generate all the prime numbers between *m* and *n*, where value of *m* and *n* is supplied by the user.

Listing 10.18

```
/*
* Program to generate all prime numbers between 1 and n, where
* value for n is supplied by the user
*/
#include<stdio.h>
int main()
{
    int i, m, n, k, flag;
    printf( "\nEnter value for m,n : " );
    scanf( "%d,%d", &m, &n );
    for ( i = m+1; i < n; i++ )
    {
        if ( ( i > 2 ) && ( ( i % 2 ) == 0 ) )
            continue;
        else
        {
            flag = 1;
            m = (int) sqrt ( (double) i );
            for ( k = 3; k <= m; k += 2 )
            {
                if ( ( n % k ) == 0 )
                {
                    flag = 0;
                    break;
                }
            }
            if ( flag == 1 )
                printf( "%d   ", i );
        }
    }
    printf( "\n" );
    return 0;
}
```

Test Runs

First Run

```
Enter value for n : 0
Incorrect value for n, re-run the program with correct value for n
```

Second Run

```
Enter value for n : 10
2 3 5 7 9
```

Problem 10.6:

Write a program to print a pyramid of numbers with *n* rows. An example pyramid with 5 rows is shown below:

```
                1
            2   3   2
        3   4   5   4   3
    4   5   6   7   6   5   4
5   6   7   8   9   8   7   6   5
```

Listing 10.19

```
/*  Program to print pyramid of numbers with 'n' rows    */
#include<stdio.h>
int main()
{
   int i, j, k, n;
   printf("\nEnter number of rows for the pyramid (n) : ");
   scanf("%d",&n);
   printf("\n");
   for ( i = 1; i <= n; i++ )
   {
      for ( j = 1; j <= n-i; j++ )
         printf("    ");
      k = i;
      for ( j = 1; j <= i; j++ )
         printf("%4d", k++);
      k = k-2;
      for ( j = 1; j < i; j++ )
         printf("%4d", k--);
      printf("\n\n");
   }
  return 0;
}
```

Test Run

```
Enter number of rows for the pyramid : 5

                1
            2   3   2
        3   4   5   4   3
    4   5   6   7   6   5   4
5   6   7   8   9   8   7   6   5
```

Problem 10.7:

Write a program to find greatest common divisor (GCD), of two positive integer *m* and *n*.

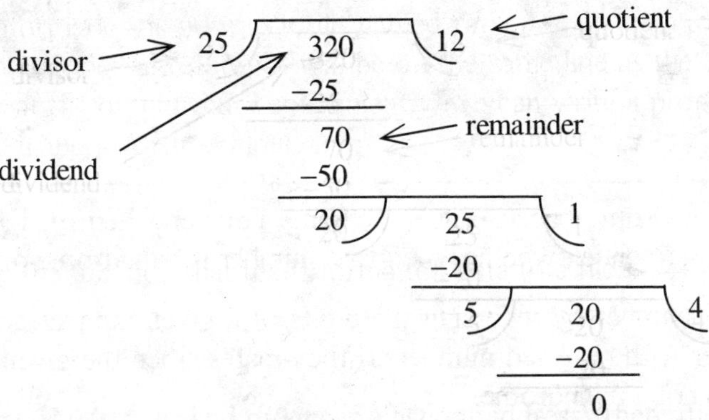

Figure 10.5: Illustration of computational procedure for GCD

From above figure, you must have observed that in successive divisions, the divisor of the previous division becomes dividend, remainder of becomes divisor, and the division is again carried out. This process is carried out till the reminder becomes zero, and the current divisor is taken as GCD of the given integer numbers.

This process can be implemented by using the following steps

1. Perform division.
2. If remainder is zero, then stop and take the divisor as HCF.
3. Replace dividend by divisor.
4. Replace divisor by remainder.
5. Repeat from step 1.

Listing 10.20

```
/*  Program to compute GCD of two positive Integer numbers  */
#include<stdio.h>
int main()
{
```

```
    int m, n, r = 1;
    printf( "\nEnter value for m,n : " );
    scanf( "%d,%d",&m, &n );
    while ( r != 0 )
    {
       r = n % m;
       n = m;
       m = r;
    }
    printf( "\nGCD = %d\n", n );
    return 0;
}
```

Test Run

```
Enter value for m,n : 35,155
GCD = 5
```

Problem 10.8:

The number 1991 is a palindrome because it is the same number when read forward or backward. Write a program to check whether the given number is palindrome or not.

Here, we first find a new number by reversing the digits of a given number and then we compare the given number with reversed number. If they match, then the given number is palindrome otherwise it is not a palindrome.

Listing 10.21

```
/* Program to check whether given number is palindrome or not   */
#include<stdio.h>
int main()
{
   int sum = 0, digit;
   int number, temp;
   printf( "\nEnter any positive integer number: " );
   scanf( "%d", &number );
   temp = number;
   while ( temp > 0 ) {
      digit = temp % 10;
      temp /= 10;
      sum = sum * 10 + digit;
   }
   if ( number == sum )
      printf( "\n%d is a palindrome number.\n", number );
   else
      printf( "\n%d is not a palindrome number.\n", number );
   return 0;
}
```

Test Runs

First Run

```
Enter any positive integer number: 1991
1991 is a palindrome number.
```

Second Run

```
Enter any positive integer number: 1234
1234 is not a palindrome number.
```

EXERCISE

1. What happens if the expression of a *while* statement is initially false?
2. What is the difference between *while* and *do - while* statements?
3. When is the *do - while* statement preferred over *while* statement?
4. Can there be multiple increment expressions in increment part of the *for* statement?
5. When is the *while* statement preferred over a *for* statement?
6. Where the *break* statement is used, and what is its function?
7. What is the action of *continue* statement?
8. Differentiate between the working of *break* and *continue* statement.

PROGRAMMING EXERCISE

1. Two prime are said to be twin prime numbers if they differ by 2, such as 11 and 13, 17 and 19, etc. Write a program to print first *n* pairs of twin prime numbers.
2. Write programs to generate following patterns:

```
*                                          *   *   *   *   *
*   *                                      *   *   *   *
*   *   *                                  *   *   *
*   *   *   *                              *   *
*   *   *   *   *                          *

*                                          *   *   *   *   *
*   *                                      *   *   *   *
*   *   *                                  *   *   *
*   *   *   *                              *   *
*   *   *   *   *                          *
*   *   *   *                              *   *
*   *   *                                  *   *   *
*   *                                      *   *   *   *
*                                          *   *   *   *   *
```

```
*                               *         *   *   *   *   *   *   *   *   *
*   *                       *   *         *   *   *   *       *   *   *   *
*   *   *               *   *   *         *   *   *               *   *   *
*   *   *   *       *   *   *   *         *   *                       *   *
*   *   *   *   *   *   *   *   *         *                               *
*   *   *   *       *   *   *   *         *   *                       *   *
*   *   *               *   *   *         *   *   *               *   *   *
*   *                       *   *         *   *   *   *       *   *   *   *
*                               *         *   *   *   *   *   *   *   *   *
```

3. Write programs to generate following patterns:

```
1                         5   5   5   5   5
2   2                     4   4   4   4
3   3   3                 3   3   3
4   4   4   4             2   2
5   5   5   5   5         1

1                         5   5   5   5   5
2   2                     4   4   4   4
3   3   3                 3   3   3
4   4   4   4             2   2
5   5   5   5   5         1
4   4   4   4             2   2
3   3   3                 3   3   3
2   2                     4   4   4   4
1                         5   5   5   5   5
```

4. A factorial chart from 1 to 5 looks like the following:

   1! = 1
   2! = 1×2
   3! = 1×2×3
   4! = 1×2×3×4
   5! = 1×2×3×4×5

   Write a program that will generate a factorial chart from 1 to *n* for any ≤ 9.

5. Write a program to print all prime numbers between *m* and *n*. The value for *m* and *n* will be supplied by the user.

6. Suppose an amount (say *amount*) is deposited in a commercial bank, which pays compound interest at the rate of *r*% annually, for *n* years. Write a program that prints the amount in account after each year.

7. A sample inverted pyramid of numbers with 5 rows is shown:

```
5  6  7  8  9  8  7  6  5
   4  5  6  7  6  5  4
      3  4  5  4  3
         2  3  2
            1
```

Write a program to print a inverted pyramid of numbers with n rows, where the value of *n* will be supplied by the user at execution time.

8. A positive integer number IJK is said to be *well-ordered* if I < J < K. For example, number 138 is called *well-ordered* because the digits in the number increase from left to right, *i.e.*, 1 < 3 < 8. Number 365 is not *well-ordered* because 6 is larger than 5. Write a program that displays all possible three digit *well-ordered* numbers.

9. The numbers in the triangles below reveal a pattern for a *number triangle*.

```
1
2   6
3   7   10
4   8   11   13
5   9   12   14   15
```

Discover this pattern and write a program to generate *number triangles* for any size (number of rows) *n* between 1 and 9.

10. The square arrangement of whole numbers

```
1   2   3   4
2   3   4   1
3   4   1   2
4   1   2   3
```

is called a 4×4 LATIN SQUARE because each whole numbers 1, 2, 3, and 4 appear once and only once in each row and column. There are many ways to arrange numbers and still make a LATIN SQUARE. Of all the 4×4 LATIN SQUARES, the one above has a simple pattern. We call it a SIMPLE 4×4 LATIN SQUARE. Write a program that will generate a similar SIMPLE *n*×*n* LATIN SQUARE for any whole number, say *n,* between 2 and 9.

11. You know that an even number is a number which is divisible by 2. However there is another approach that can be used to check whether the given number is even or not. The approach is by inspecting the unit digit - *if the unit digit is 0, 2, 4, 6, or 8, the number is even.* So you are required to write a program to check whether the given number is even or not without performing the division by 2.

❑ ❑ ❑

Chapter 11

User-Defined Functions

Learning Objectives

After reading this chapter, students will be able to

- explain the concept of top-down design and its advantages
- use structure charts to depict the top-down design of their software solution
- explain the concept of local data and global data
- explain the way functions are declared, defined, and accessed
- explain the different ways in which arguments can be passed to a functions
- explain the use of *return* statement
- explain the concept of recursion, and will be able to write recursive functions
- explain and use command-line arguments
- explain the concept of storage classes and their usage

11.1 INTRODUCTION

The programs we have discussed so far were very simple and straightforward. They could solve problems that can be understood without much effort. As we move to larger and larger and more complex problems and hence programs, you will discover that it is not possible to understand all aspects of such problems and hence programs without some how reducing them to more elementary parts.

The best way to handle large and complex problems is to split the problem into small problems, called *subproblems* that can be handled easily. This we are used to do in our day-to-day working. Once all these sub problems are solved separately, solutions of these subproblems can be synthesized to generate the solution of the given complex problem.

Like wise, if program to be developed is very large and complex, it is always recommended to break into two or more functions (modules) that can be developed separately, tested separately and then integrated.

The planning for large and complex program starts with understanding the problem as a whole; then breaking it into smaller, simpler and understandable parts. We will call each of these parts of a program a *module* and the process of subdividing a problem into manageable parts *top-down design*.

The principles of top-down design and structured programming dictate that a program should be divided into main module and its related modules. Each module further be divided into submodules and this process should be continued until each submodule performs some specialized task and cannot be further subdivided. This process is known as *factoring*.

In top-down design, a program is divided into a main module and its related modules. Each module, in turn, is divided into submodules until the resulting modules are small enough, specialized and cannot be further subdivided.

Top-down design is usually done using a visual representation of the modules, known as *structure chart*. The structure chart shows the relation between each module and its submodules. The main module represents the entire set of code to solve the problem.

Moving down and left, we then read Module 1. One the same level with Module 1 are Module 2 and Module 3. The main module consists of three submodules. At this point, however, we are dealing only with Module 1. We now note that Module 1 is further subdivided into three modules, Module 1*a*, Module 1*b* and Module 1*c*.

The Main Module is known as the *calling* module because it has submodules. Each of its submodules is known as *called* module. Since Module 1, Module 2 and Module 3 also have submodules, they are also called calling modules; they are both *called* and *calling* modules.

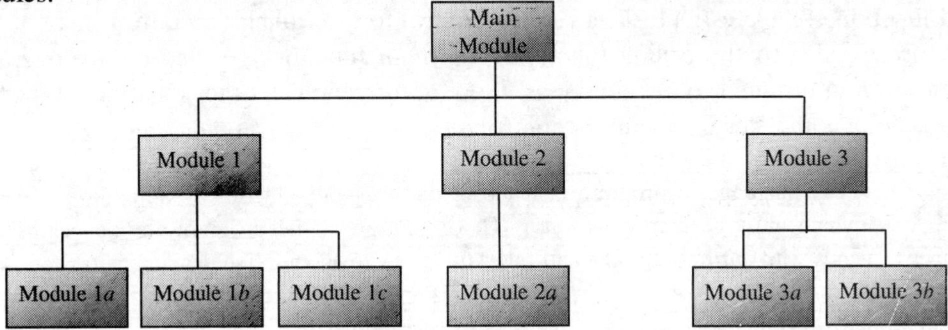

Figure 11.1: Structure Chart

Communication between modules in a structure chart is allowed only through a calling module. If Module 1 needs to send data to Module 2, the data must be passed through the calling module, Main Module. No communication can take place directly between modules that do not have a calling relationship.

The technique used to pass data to a module is known as *argument passing*. The arguments are contained in a list that is a definition of the data passed to the module by the caller. The list serves as the formal declaration of the data types and names.

11.2 FUNCTIONS IN C LANGUAGE

In C language, the idea of top-down design is done using functions. A C program is made of one or more functions, one and only one of which must be named as *main*. The execution of the program always begins and ends with *main*, but it can call other functions to accomplish designated tasks.

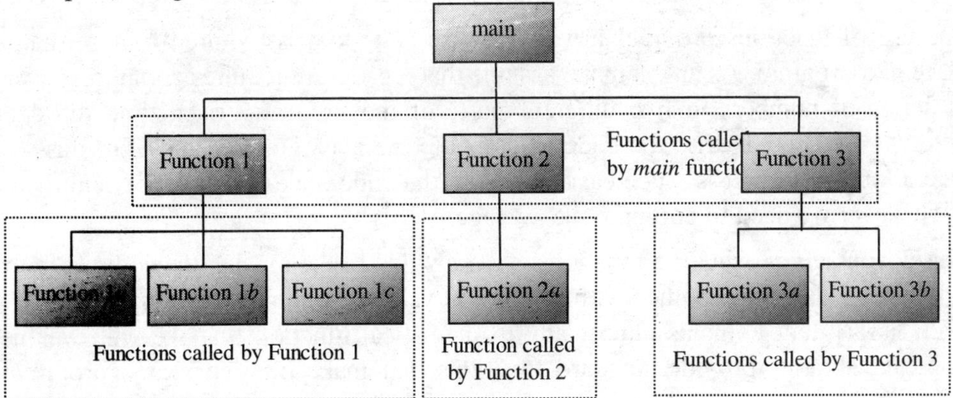

Figure 11.2: Structure Chart for a C Program

A function in C (including *main*) is an independent module that will be called to do a designated task. A *called function* receives control from a *calling function*. When the called function completes its task, it returns control to the calling function. It may or may not return a value to the calling function. The *main* function is called by the operating system; *main* in turn calls other functions, those in turn can call other functions. When the *main* function completes it execution, control returns to the operating system.

In C language, a program is made of one or more functions, one and only one of which must be named as *main*. The execution of the program always begins and ends with *main*, but it can call other functions to accomplish designated tasks.

We had already discussed some library functions in *Chapter 4*. These library functions are actually subprograms, which are written and incorporated into the C compiler because they are used in many situations. Rather than each user writes these subprograms, the C compilers provide these library functions as a convenience. Obviously, the C library cannot contain all the functions used in all application areas. However, it is possible for users to write their own functions whenever such a need arises.

In this chapter, we will study the way functions in C language are declared, defined and accessed, arguments are passed, data types of arguments is specified, the concept of recursion, and building your own library of user-defined functions.

11.3 ADVANTAGES OF USING FUNCTIONS

Several advantages are associated with the use of functions. Some of the major advantages are

1. The use of functions allows managing large and complex problems by factoring them into small, simple and manageable parts.
2. The use of functions provides a way to reuse code that is required n more than one place in a program. As an example, assume that a program requires computing average of series of numbers in five different parts of the program. Each time the data is different. We could write the code to compute the average five times, but this would take a lot of effort. It is much easier to write the code once as a function and then call it whenever we need to compute the average.
3. This advantage of using the functions is closely tied to the reusing the code. Like many language, C language comes with a rich and valuable library. For example, there is a math library that contains almost any mathematical function that we will ever need. These C libraries provide standard functions that make our work as a programmer much easier. We can also create our personal libraries that make developing new systems much easier.

4. The use of functions can protect data. This is done using the concept of *local data.* Local data consist of data described in a function. This data is available only to the function and only while the function is executing. When the function is not executing, the data is not accessible. Data in one function, then, cannot be seen or changed by another function.

11.4 CONCEPT OF LOCAL DATA & GLOBAL DATA

The formal arguments and variables declared in the body of a function are unknown outside the function. The factor that determines which function recognizes a variable and which don't is called the *visibility* of variable. A local variable will be visible to the function in which it is declared, but not to others.

A local variable used in this way in a function is known as *automatic* variable, because it is automatically created when a function is called and destroyed when the function returns except variable having *static* storage class. The length or duration of time a variable lasts is called its *lifetime.*

In contrast to a local variable, a global variable is visible to more functions, and is declared outside all functions. The usual place of declaration of a global variable is in the beginning of the program file, *i.e.*, before all function definitions. In this case, it will be visible to all functions and exists till the program terminates. If the variable is not declared before all the functions, then it will be visible to only those functions following its declaration i.e. global in the restricted sense.

11.5 DECLARING AND DEFINING FUNCTIONS

Like every other data item in C, function also need to declared and defined. The syntax for function declaration and definition is illustrated in Figure 11.3 and Figure 11.4, respectively.

```
returnType functionName(formal argument list);
```

Figure 11.3: Syntax for function declaration

The function declaration, which needs to be done before the function call, gives the whole picture of the function that needs to be defined later. The declaration mentions the name of the function, the return type, and the type and order of formal arguments. In other words, the declaration uses only the header of the function definition ended in a semicolon.

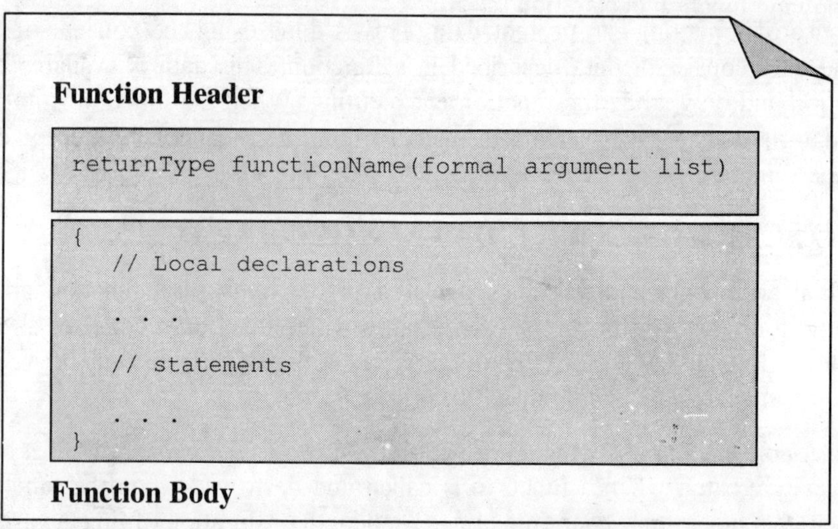

Figure 11.4: Syntax for function definition

The function definition, which is traditionally coded after the function that makes the call, contains the code needed to complete the task.

11.5.1 Declaring a Function

Function declaration consists only of a function header; it contains no code. Function header consists of three parts: *the return type*, *the function name*, and *the formal argument list*. A semicolon follows the function header.

If the function has no arguments, then write *void* in the parentheses. If the function has two or more arguments, each is separated by comma.

It is not mandatory (essential) to include the names of the arguments in the argument list. The purpose of the argument list is to tell the compiler *the number*, *data type* and *order of arguments*. However, readability and understandability are improved if the names of arguments are used. One point to note, however, is that the names of arguments do not need to be the same in the function declaration and the function definition. On the other hand, if the data types do not match, the compiler will flag an error. The compiler checks the data types of the arguments in the function call to ensure that they are same or at least compatible.

A function declaration statement is also known as *prototype* of the function or as *function prototype*.

The following function declaration

```
int larget(int a, int b, int c);
```

tells the compiler that the return type of the function is *int*, name of the function is *largest*, and it has three argument, all of type *int*. The names of argument are not significant.

The following function declaration

```
int larget(int, int, int);
```

is equally good and serves the purpose as earlier declaration

11.5.2 Defining a Function

Function definition consists two parts; *function header* and *function body*.

Function Header

Function header consists of three parts: *the return type*, *the function name*, and *the formal argument list*. A semicolon is not used at the end of function header. With the implementation of new standard of C (new standard is C99), the return type is mandatory. In the earlier implementations, if the return type was omitted in the function header, it was taken as *int*, by default. When nothing is to be returned, the return type *void* is used in the function header.

The formal argument list declares the variable that will receive the data from the calling function and may also contain variable that can be used to send the data back to the calling function.

Function Body

The function body contains the local declarations and the statements that define the task to be accomplished by the function. The body starts with local declarations that specify the variables needed by the function. After the local declarations, the function statements, followed by the *return* statement, are written.

If the return type of function is *void*, it can be written without *return* statement.

It is recommended that the default statements should be explicitly written for clarity. Therefore, even for a function with *void* as its return type, the return statement must be written.

SOME RULES FOR DEFINING FUNCTIONS

Following are some points to remember while defining functions in C:

- The first statement of the function must be the function defining statement specifying the return type, name and formal arguments.
- If the type of the function is omitted, then it is assumed of type integer (*int*). But it is recommended that the return type must be explicitly specified.
- Rules for naming a function are same as for variable names.
- The formal arguments should neither be constants or expressions.
- If a formal argument is an array name, it must be declared as an array in a type declaration statement before the body of the function starts and its maximum size must be equal to the actual size in the calling function.

As an example, let consider a task where we are concerned to find the largest of three integer numbers.

Listing 11.1

```
/*
*    Function that returns largest of three integer numbers (Ver 1)
*/
int largest(int x, int y, int z)
{
   if ( ( x > y ) && ( x > z ) )
      return x;
   else if ( y > z )
      return y;
   else
      return z;
}
```

The logic of the above function can also be written as shown below.

Listing 11.2

```
/*
*    Function that returns largest of three integer numbers (Ver 2)
*/
int largest(int x, int y, int z)
{
   int big;
   big = x;
   if ( y > big ) big  = y;
   if ( z > big ) big  = z;
   return big;
}
```

11.6 INVOKING/CALLING/ACCESSING A FUNCTION

Like library functions, the user-defined functions are accessed from a function simply by its name, including the actual arguments, if any, enclosed within parentheses. However, parentheses must follow the function name even if there is no actual argument to be passed to the function. The actual arguments, if any, must correspond in *number*, *type*, and *order* with formal arguments. The actual arguments can be constants, variable names, subscripted variables, or expressions.

When the name of the function is encountered, the control is transferred to the called function. The formal arguments are replaced by the actual arguments and the execution of the function is carried out. When the *return* statement is executed or last statement has finished its execution, the control is transferred back to the calling function.

The *largest()* function will be accessed/invoked/called using a statement of type

```
big = largest(a, b, c);
```

11.7 THE *return* STATEMENT

The syntax of *return* statement is

```
return;          or      return (exp);
```

where *exp* can be a constant, variable or expression. Use of parentheses around *exp* is optional. The first form is used with functions defined with return type as *void*.

The *return* statement serves two purposes:

- Execution of *return* statement immediately transfers control from the function back to the calling function.
- Whatever is following the *return* statement is returned as a value to the calling function.

In the functions described in Listing 11.2, the statement

```
return big;
```

return the value of variable *big*.

The *return* statement need not be at the end of the function. It can be used any where in the function. As soon as it is executed, the control will return to the calling function. A function can contain any number of *return* statements.

Consider the following function:

Listing 11.3

```
/* Function that returns value 1 if number is even else return 0  */

int oddOrEven( int number )
{
   if ( number % 2 == 0)
      return 1;
   else
      return 0;
}
```

This function returns value 1 if the *number* is not divisible by 2, *i.e.*, *number* is odd; otherwise it returns value 0. So here, different *return* statement will be executed depending on whether the *number* is odd or even.

There is key limitation of *return* statement — it can return only one value. If you want your function to return two or more values to the calling function, you need another mechanism.

11.8 PASSING ARGUMENTS TO A FUNCTION

The mechanism used to pass data to a function is via argument list, where individual arguments are called *actual arguments*. These arguments are enclosed in parentheses after the function name. The actual arguments must correspond in *number*, *type*, and *order* with formal arguments specified in the function definition. The actual arguments can be *constants*, *variables*, *array names*, or *expressions*.

There are two approaches to passing arguments to a function:

- Call by value
- Call by reference

Let us describe these one by one.

11.8.1 Call by Value

In this approach, the actual arguments are used in the function call. The actual argument can be a variable, a constant, or an expression. The values of the actual arguments are passed to the function. When control is transferred to the called function, the values of the actual arguments are substituted to the corresponding formal arguments and the body of the function is executed. If the called function is supposed to return a value, it is returned via *return* statement.

The following points must be noted about passing arguments using call by value mechanism:

1. The actual arguments can be constants, variables, or expressions.
2. When the control is transferred from the calling function to the called function, the memory for formal arguments and local variables is allocated, values of the actual arguments are substituted in the corresponding formal arguments, and the statements in the function body are executed.
3. As soon as the called function finishes its execution, the memory allocated for it is de-allocated, *i.e.*, the values of formal arguments and local variable are destroyed, and finally the control is transferred back to the calling function.
4. Any change made to the formal arguments will have no effect on actual arguments, since the function will only be using the local copy of the arguments.

Following function definition illustrates the mechanism of passing arguments by value.

```
void swap( int a, int b )
{
    int temp;
    temp = a;
    a = b;
    b = temp;
}
```

The above function will be accessed as

```
swap(x,y);
```

where *x* and *y* are actual arguments in the calling function.

Listing 11.4

```
/* Program to illustrate the passing of arguments by value. It calls a
 *  function swap() that interchanges values of arguments.
 */
#include <stdio.h>
void swap(int a, int b);     /* declaration of function */
int main()
{
    int x, y;
    printf("\nEnter value for x : ");
    scanf("%d", &x);
    printf("\nEnter value for y : ");
    scanf("%d", &y);
    printf("\nBefore calling swap function\n");
    printf("\nValue of x = %d, Value of y = %d\n", x, y);
    swap(x,y);  /* function call    */
    printf("\nAfter returning from swap function\n");
    printf("\nValue of x = %d, Value of y = %d\n", x, y);
```

```
    return 0;
}
void swap( int a, int b )
{
    int temp;
    temp   = a;
    a = b;
    b = temp;
}
```

Test Run

```
Enter value for x : 10
Enter value for y : 12
Before calling swap function
Value of x = 10, Value of y = 12
After returning from swap function
Value of x = 10, Value of y = 12
```

You must have observed that any change made to the formal arguments have not effect on the actual arguments.

11.8.2 Call by Reference

In this approach, the addresses of the actual arguments are used in the function call. In this way the addresses of the actual arguments are passed to the function. When control is transferred to the called function, the addresses of the actual arguments are substituted to corresponding formal arguments and the body of the function is executed. The formal arguments are declared as pointers to *types* that match the data types of the actual arguments. This approach is of practical importance while passing arrays and structures among function, and also for passing back more than one value to the calling functions.

If the called function is supposed to return a value, it is returned via *return* statement. Additional values can be returned to the calling function via formal arguments which will be of pointer type.

Following points must be noted about passing arguments using call by reference mechanism:

1. The actual arguments can only be variables.
2. When the control is transferred from the calling function to the called function, the memory for formal arguments and local variables is allocated, addresses of the actual arguments are substituted in the corresponding formal arguments, and the statements in the function body are executed.

3. As soon as the called function finishes its execution, the memory allocated for it is de-allocated, *i.e.*, the values of formal arguments and local variable are destroyed, and finally the control is transferred back to the calling function.
4. Any change made to the formal arguments will have immediate effect on actual arguments, since function will be working on actual arguments through pointers.

Following function illustrates mechanism of passing arguments by reference (address).

```
void swap( int *a, int *b )
{
   int temp;
   temp   = *a;
   *a = *b;
   *b = temp;
}
```

The above function will be accessed as

```
swap(&x,&y);
```

where *x* and *y* are actual arguments in the calling function.

Listing 11.5

```
/* Program to illustrate the passing of arguments by reference. It
 *  calls a function swap() that interchanges values of arguments.
 */
#include <stdio.h>
void swap(int *a, int *b);     /* declaration of function */
int main()
{
   int x, y;
   printf("\nEnter value for x : ");
   scanf("%d", &x);
   printf("\nEnter value for y : ");
   scanf("%d", &y);
   printf("\nBefore calling swap function\n");
   printf("\nValue of x = %d, Value of y = %d\n", x, y);
   swap(&x,&y);   /* function call    */
   printf("\nAfter returning from swap function\n");
   printf("\nValue of x = %d, Value of y = %d\n", x, y);
   return 0;
}
void swap( int *a, int *b )
{
   int temp;
   temp   = *a;
   *a = *b;
   *b = temp;
}
```

Test Run

```
Enter value for x : 10
Enter value for y : 12
Before calling swap function
Value of x = 10, Value of y = 12
After returning from swap function
Value of x = 12, Value of y = 10
```

You must have observed that any change made to the formal arguments is reflected back in the actual arguments.

Next program is another example to demonstrate the passing of arguments using call by reference.

Listing 11.6

```
/* Program that calls function example() to find the average of
*  two numbers, largest & smallest of these numbers. The
*  average is retuned via return statement while largest and
*  smallest numbers are returned via formal arguments
*/
#include <stdio.h>
/* function declaration  */
float example(float x, float y, float *big, float *small);
int main()
{
   float x, y, avg, larger, smaller;
   printf("\nEnter value for x : ");
   scanf("%f", &x);
   printf("\nEnter value for y : ");
   scanf("%f", &y);
   avg = example(x,y,&larger,&smaller); /*  function call  */
   printf("\nAverage of %.2f and %.2f is %.2f\n", x, y, avg);
   printf("\nLarger number is %.2f\n", larger);
   printf("\nSmaller number is %.2f\n", smaller);
   return 0;
}
/*
   Function to compute the average of two numbers and find the
   largest and smallest of these numbers
*/
float example(float x, float y, float *big, float *small)
{
    float average;
    average = ( x + y ) / 2;
    if ( x > y )
    {
```

```
        *big = x;
        *small = y;
    }
    else
    {
        *big = y;
        *small = x;
    }
    return average;
}
```

Test Run

```
Enter value for x : 10.5
Enter value for y : 12.5
Average of 10.50 and 12.50 is 11.50
Larger number is 12.50
Smaller number is 10.50
```

11.8.3 Comparison between Call by Value and Call by Reference

Table 11.1 highlights the key points of differences regarding the prototype, definition and function call.

Table 11.2 highlights the key points of differences regarding the nature of actual arguments, nature of formal arguments and the impact of any change/modification of formal arguments on actual arguments.

Table 11.1

<table>
<tr><th>CALL BY VALUE</th><th>CALL BY REFERENCE</th></tr>
<tr><td>Function Prototype:
<code>void swap(int a, int b);</code></td><td>Function Prototype:
<code>void swap(int *a, int *b);</code></td></tr>
<tr><td>Function Definition:
<code>void swap(int a, int b)
{
   int temp;
   temp = a;
   a = b;
   b = temp;
}</code></td><td>Function Definition:
<code>void swap(int *a, int *b)
{
   int temp;
   temp = *a;
   *a = *b;
   *b = temp;
}</code></td></tr>
<tr><td>Function Call:
<code>swap(x, y);</code></td><td>Function Call:
<code>swap(&x, &y);</code></td></tr>
</table>

Table 11.2

CALL BY VALUE	CALL BY REFERENCE
Actual arguments can be constants, variables, or expressions.	Actual arguments can only be variables.
Formal arguments are ordinary variables.	Formal arguments are pointer variables.
Values of actual arguments are substituted in formal arguments.	Addresses of the actual arguments are substituted in formal arguments.
Any change made to formal arguments will have no effect on actual arguments, since the function will only be using the local copy of the arguments.	Any change made to pointer variables will have immediate effect on actual arguments, since the function will be working on actual arguments through address.

11.9 SUPPLEMENTARY PROBLEMS

To have hands on defining functions, let use consider some examples.

Problem 11.1:

An integer function to compute the factorial of a positive integer number *k*.

Listing 11.7

```
/*
*    Function to compute factorial of a +ve integer number
*/

int factorial ( int k )
{
   int product = 1, i;
   for ( i = 2; i <= k; i++ )
      product *= i;
   return product;
}
```

Problem 11.2:

Using the definition of factorial function of Example 11.1, let us write a complete program to compute the Binomial coefficient ^nc_r defined as

$$^nc_r = \frac{n!}{r!(n-r)!}$$

Listing 11.8

```
/*  Program to compute Binomial coefficient (Version 1)  */
#include <stdio.h>
int factorial ( int k );  /*  function prototype  */
int main()
{
    int ncr, n, r;
    printf( "\nEnter value of n: " );
    scanf( "%d", &n );
    printf( "\nEnter value of r: " );
    scanf( "%d", &r );
    ncr = factorial(n)/(factorial(r)*factorial(n-r));
    printf( "\nValue of ncr = %d\n" , ncr);
    return 0;
}
```

This program calls the factorial function thrice with argument *n*, *r*, (*n*–*r*) respectively, and then using these values computes the binomial coefficient.

Problem 11.3:

A function to find highest common factor (HCF), also known as greatest common divisor (GCD), of two positive integers *m* and *n*.

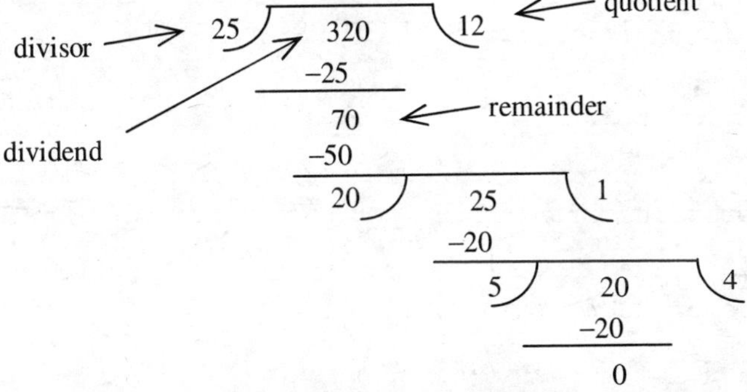

Figure 11.5: Illustration of computational procedure for HCF

From Figure 11.5, you must have observed that in successive divisions, the divisor of the previous division becomes dividend, remainder of becomes divisor, and division is again carried out. This process is carried out till the reminder becomes zero, and the current divisor is taken as HCF of the given integer numbers.

This process can be implemented by using the following steps

1. Perform division.
2. If remainder is zero, then stop and take the divisor as HCF.
3. Replace dividend by divisor.
4. Replace divisor by remainder.
5. Repeat from step 1.

Listing 11.9

```
/*  Function to compute HCF of two +ve integer numbers     */
int computeHCF ( int m, int n )
{
   int k = 1;
   while ( k != 0 )
   {
      k = n % m;
      n = m;
      m = k;
   }
   return n;
}
```

Problem 11.4:

Using the definition of function to compute HCF of Example 11.3, let us write a complete program to compute the HCF of two given integers.

Listing 11.10

```
/* Program to compute HCF of two given integers (m and n)   */
#include <stdio.h>
int computeHCF( int, int );    /*  function declaration   */
int main()
{
    int m, n, r;
    printf( "\nEnter value of m: " );
    scanf( "%d", &m );
    printf( "\nEnter value of n: " );
    scanf( "%d", &n );
    r = computeHCF(m,n);
    printf( "\nValue of HCF = %d\n" , r);
    return 0;
}
```

Test Run

```
Enter value of m: 125
Enter value of n: 35
Value of HCF = 5
```

11.10 RECURSIVE FUNCTIONS

Recursion is an important concept in computer science and is convenient for a variety of problems that would be difficult to solve using *iterative* constructs such as *for, while* and *do* loops. Recursive functions can be directly implemented in C language.

11.10.1 Factorial Function

The factorial of a positive number n, written as $n!$, is the product of the positive integers from 1 to n:

$$n! = 1.2.3. \ldots (n-2).(n-1).n \qquad \text{where as } 0! = 1$$

Thus, definition of the iterative version of the factorial function can be written as

$$n! = \begin{cases} 1 & \text{if } n = 0 \\ \prod_{i=1}^{n} i & \text{if } n > 0 \end{cases}$$

From above definition, we have

$$\begin{aligned} 0! &= 1 \\ 1! &= 1 \\ 2! &= 1.2 = 2 \\ 3! &= 1.2.3 = 6 \\ 4! &= 1.2.3.4 = 24 \\ 5! &= 1.2.3.4.5 = 120 \end{aligned} \qquad \text{and so on.}$$

Observe that

$$4! = 4.3! = 4.6 = 24 \quad \text{and} \quad 5! = 5.4! = 5.24 = 120$$

And this is true for every positive integer n; that is

$$n! = n.(n-1)!$$

Thus the factorial function can be defined as

$$n! = \begin{cases} 1 & \text{if } n = 0 \\ n(n-1)! & \text{if } n > 0 \end{cases}$$

This definition of $n!$ is recursive, since it refers to itself when it uses $(n-1)!$.

Listing 11.11

```
/*
*   Recursive function to compute factorial of a number
*/
int factorial( int n )
{
  if ( n == 0 )
     return 1;
  else
     return ( n * factorial( n - 1 ) );
}
```

Listing 11.12

```
/*
*  Program to print the factorials of first 'n' natural numbers
*/

#include <stdio.h>

int factorial( int n );          /*  function prototype    */

int main()
{
   int i, n;
   printf( "\nEnter value of n: " );
   scanf( "%d", &n );
   for ( i = 1; i <= n; i++ )
   {
       printf( "\n%d! = %d", i, factorial(i) );
   }
   return 0;
}
int factorial( int n )
{
  if ( n == 0 )
     return 1;
  else
     return ( n * factorial( n - 1 ) );
}
```

Test Run

```
Enter value of n: 6

1! = 1
2! = 2
3! = 6
4! = 24
5! = 120
6! = 720
```

11.10.2 Fibonacci Numbers

A very important sequence, *Fibonacci sequence,* usually denoted by $F_0, F_1, \ldots, F_n$, is as follows:

0, 1, 1, 2, 3, 5, 8, 13, . . .

That is, $F_0 = 0$ and $F_1 = 1$ and subsequent terms are sum of the two preceding terms.

For example, the next term in the above sequence is

8 + 13 = 21

A formal definition for Fibonacci number F_n is:

$$fib(n) = \begin{cases} n & \text{if } n \le 1 \\ fib(n-1) + fib(n-2) & \text{if } n > 1 \end{cases}$$

Notice that the recursive definition of the Fibonacci numbers differs from the recursive definitions of the factorial function and positive exponential power function in the sense that it refers to itself twice.

Listing 11.13

```
/*  Recursive function to compute Fibonacci number 'n'    */
int fibNumber( int n )
{
  if ( n <= 1 )
      return n;
  else
      return ( fibNumber(n-1) + fibNumber(n-2) );
}
```

Listing 11.14

```
/* Program to print first 'm' terms of Fibonacci sequence  */
#include <stdio.h>
int fibNumber( int n );          /*  function prototype    */
int main()
{
    int i, m;
    printf( "\nEnter value of m: " );
    scanf( "%d", &m );
    for ( i = 0; i < m; i++ )
    {
         printf( "%d ", fibNumber(i) );
    }
    return 0;
}
int fibNumber( int n )
{
  if ( n <= 1 )
      return n;
  else
      return ( fibNumber(n-1) + fibNumber(n-2) );
}
```

Test Run

```
Enter value of m: 8
0  1  1  2  3  5  8  13
```

11.10.3 Ackermann Function

The *Ackermann* function is defined recursively, for all non-negative values of m and n, as follows:

$$A(m,n) = \begin{cases} n+1 & \text{if } m = 0 \\ A(m-1,1) & \text{if } m \neq 0 \text{ but } n = 0 \\ A(m-1, A(m,n-1)) & \text{if } m \neq 0 \text{ and } n \neq 0 \end{cases}$$

Listing 11.15

```
/*
* Program to demonstrate the implementation of Ackermann function
*/
#include <stdio.h>
int Ackermann( int m, int n );      /*  function prototype   */
int main()
{
    int i, m, n;
    printf( "\nEnter value of m : " );
    scanf( "%d", &m );
    printf( "\nEnter value of n : " );
    scanf( "%d", &n );
    printf( "\nA(%d,%d) = %d\n", m,n, Ackermann(m,n) );
    return 0;
}
int Ackermann( int m, int n )
{
  if ( m == 0 )
     return (n+1);
  else if ( ( m != 0 ) && ( n == 0 ) )
     return (Ackermann(m-1,1));
  else
     return (Ackermann(m-1, Ackermann(m,n-1)));
}
```

Test Run

```
Enter value of m : 1
Enter value of n : 3
A(1,3) = 5
```

11.10.4 Positive Exponential Power Function

Like factorial function, similar iterative and recursive definitions exist for computing the positive exponential power of a number.

Its iterative version is

$$x^n = \begin{cases} 1 & \text{if } n = 0 \\ \prod_{i=1}^{n} x & \text{if } n > 0 \end{cases}$$

where as its recursive version is

$$x^n = \begin{cases} 1 & \text{if } n = 0 \\ x.x^{n-1} & \text{if } n = 0 \end{cases}$$

The implementation of computing the positive exponential power of a number is left as an exercise for the readers.

11.10.5 Greatest Common Divisor

Computation of greatest common divisor (*GCD*) or highest common factor (*HCF*) of two natural numbers *m* and *n* is demonstrated in Figure 11.5, which is reproduced here.

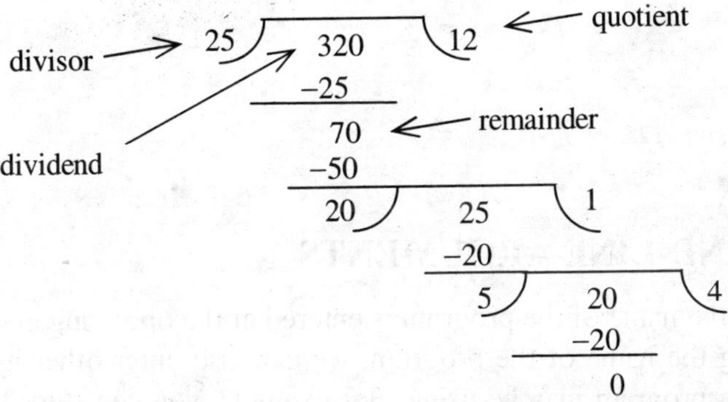

Figure 11.6: Illustration of computational procedure for *GCD*

You must have observed that in successive divisions, the divisor of the previous division becomes dividend, remainder of becomes divisor, and division is again carried out. This process is carried out till the reminder becomes zero, and the current divisor is taken as *GCD* of the given integer numbers.

The G*CD* function can be formally defined in the recursive manner as

$$\gcd(m,n) = \begin{cases} n & \text{if } m \ \% \ n = 0 \\ \gcd(n, m\%n) & \text{if } m \ \% \ n \neq 0 \end{cases}$$

Listing 11.16

```
/*  Program to compute GCD of two given natural numbers m and n  */
#include <stdio.h>
int gcd( int, int );   /*  function declaration   */
int main()
{
   int m, n;
   printf( "\nEnter value of m: " );
   scanf( "%d", &m );
   printf( "\nEnter value of n: " );
   scanf( "%d", &n );
   printf( "\nValue of GCD(%d,%d) = %d\n", m, n, gcd(m,n) );
   return 0;
}
int gcd( int m, int n )
{
   if ( m % n == 0 )
      return n;
   else
      return gcd(n, m % n);
}
```

Test Run

```
Enter value of m: 35
Enter value of n: 125
Value of GCD(35,125) = 5
```

11.11 COMMAND-LINE ARGUMENTS

To run a program, the name of the program is entered at the operating system's prompt. In addition to entering the name of the program, we can also enter other items, such as the name of the file the program may be using. For example, you can start Turbo C's IDE in the following ways:

1. By just typing TC at DOS prompt as

   ```
   C:\TC>TC↵
   ```

   In this case, the opening screen will appear, and you can load any file into the environment by using *File* option.

2. By typing TC and the name of the program file, to work on, as

   ```
   C:\TC>TC test↵
   ```

   In this case, if program file *test.c* already exists, it will be loaded into the environment, and the editing session will start. If program file *test.c* does not exist, then the environment will start the edit session to create a new file.

In the later case, the string *test* is used as a *command-line argument — an argument that appears on the command line following the operating system prompt.* We can give multiple arguments on the command line. For example, the COPY command needs two arguments, where first argument is the name of the source file and the second argument is the name of the destination file.

The question here is — *How can these arguments be used in our program*? As you know that the execution of the program always begins with the *main()* function. Accordingly, these arguments can be accessed via arguments in the *main()* function. The C system automatically adds the capability to read these arguments to all C programs. The following program illustrates this.

Listing 11.17

```
/* Program to demonstrate the use of command line arguments
*  filename : cmdline.c
*/
# include <stdio.h>
int main ( int argc, char *argv[] )
{
   int i;
   printf( "\nCommand = %s\n", argv[0] );
   printf( "\nNumber of arguments = %d", argc-1 );
   printf( "\n\nThese are\n\n" );
   for ( i = 1; i < argc; i++ ) {
        printf( "Argument number %d = %s\n", i, argv[i] );
   }
   return 0;
}
```

Test Run

```
>cmdline first second third fourth↵
Command = C:\TC\CMDLINE.EXE
Number of arguments = 4
These are
Argument number 1 = first
Argument number 2 = second
Argument number 3 = third
Argument number 4 = fourth
```

Two arguments used in the definition of function *main()* are:

- First argument is *argc* that is of type integer and holds total number of entries on command line, including the program name.

- Second argument is **argv[]*, an array of pointers to strings which holds individual arguments. Argument *argv[0]* holds the name of the program, *argv[1]* holds first argument, *argv[2]* holds second argument and so on. These arguments can also be accessed using pointer notation as **(argv+0)*, **(argv+1)*, **(argv+2)* and so on.

If we have written a program that accepts a specified number of command-line arguments, then we must check in the program whether the correct number of arguments is passed to it or not.

For example, suppose we have written a program that emulates DOS COPY command, and is given a name KOPY. Then we can add the following segment in very beginning of the program.

```
if ( argc < 3 )
{
    printf("\nCorrect Usage:>" );
    printf("\nKOPY <sourceFile><destinationFile>\n" );
    return;
}
```

to ensure that the correct number of command-line arguments as expected by the program are specified.

Note that it is not mandatory that names of formal arguments for the main function be *argc* and *argv*, only thing you have to ensure that is — first argument is of type *int* and second argument is array of pointers of type *char*.

11.12 STORAGE CLASSES REVISITED

Every variable in C language possesses a characteristic called its *storage class.* The storage class defines two main characteristics of the variable, apart from the place of storage and the initial value. These are

- Lifetime
- Visibility or scope

Lifetime — *Lifetime* of a variable is the length of time it retains a particular value.

Visibility — *Visibility* or *scope* of a variable refers to those parts of a program that will be able to recognize it.

At first instance, a question arises: *why are storage classes necessary*? The answer is that by using variables with the appropriate lifetime and visibility, we can write programs that use memory more efficiently, run faster, and are less prone to programming errors. The correct use of storage class is especially important in large programs.

The storage class precedes the variable's declaration and tells the compiler regarding where the variable should be stored, what should be its initial value, what will be its scope, and for how much time it will be available for use.

The C language supports following four storage classes:

- auto
- static
- extern
- register

If the storage class in the variable declaration is omitted, it is assumed of type *auto*, *i.e.*, storage class is *auto* by default. Let us examine these storage classes one by one.

11.12.1 The *auto* Storage Class

The variables declared with *auto* storage class, which is the storage class by default, have following features:

- Stored in memory.
- If not initialized in the declaration statement, their initial value is unpredictable, which is often called *garbage value*.
- Local (visible) to the block in which the variable is declared. If the variable is declared within a function, then it is only visible to that function. But if the variable is declared outside the function, then it is visible to all the functions following its declaration.
- It retains its value till the control remains in the block in which the variable is declared. For example, if the variable is declared within a function, it will retain its value till the control is within that function. As the execution of the function terminates, it is cleared/destroyed.

The following examples illustrate these features.

Listing 11.18

```
/* Program to illustrate the auto storage class  */
#include <stdio.h>
int main()
{
    auto int i, j = 10;
    printf( "Value of i = %d\n", i );
    printf( "Value of j = %d\n", j );
    return 0;
}
```

This example program shows how an automatic storage class is declared, and the fact that if the variable is not initialized, it contains a garbage value.

Test Run

```
Value of i = 1250
Value of j = 10
```

Next time you run this program you may get different value of *i*. The reason is that we have not initialized variable *i* prior to outputting it, so it can be assigned any garbage value depending on the storage location set aside for it. Most of the times, for un-initialized variables, we will be getting value zero. I would suggest our readers to check this fact.

Consider the following program.

Listing 11.19

```
/*   Program to illustrate the auto storage class
*   when variable is declared outside all the blocks   */
#include<stdio.h>
int main()
{
  auto int j = 10;
  {
     {
        {
           printf( "Value of auto variable j in" );
           printf( " innermost block = %d\n", j );
        }
        printf( "Value of auto variable j in" );
        printf( " next innermost block = %d\n", j );
     }
     printf( "Value of auto variable j in" );
     printf( " outermost block = %d\n", j );
  }
  return 0;
}
```

Test Run

```
Value of auto variable j in innermost block = 10
Value of auto variable j in next innermost block = 10
Value of auto variable j in outermost block = 10
```

In this program, all the *printf()* statements output value 10, the reason being that all the *printf()* statements occur within the outermost block in which the variable *j* is declared.

Consider the following program.

Listing 11.20

```
/*   Program to illustrate the auto storage class
*   when variable is declared in different blocks   */

#include <stdio.h>

int main()
{
  auto int j = 10;
  {
```

```
        {
            auto int j = 50;
            printf( "Value of auto variable j in" );
            printf( " innermost block = %d\n", j );
        }
        printf( "Value of auto variable j in" );
        printf( " outer block = %d\n", j );
    }
    return 0;
}
```

Test Run

```
Value of auto variable j in inner block = 50
Value of auto variable j in outer block = 10
```

Note that the compiler treats these *j*s as different variables, since they are defined in different blocks, although, within the same function (main function in this case). As soon as the execution of the innermost block is complete, the variable *j* loses its value 50. And in the outer loop the variable *j* refers to value 10. And finally, when the execution of the function terminates, the variable *j* also loses its value.

11.12.2 The *static* Storage Class

The variables declared with *static* storage class have the following features:

- Stored in memory.
- If not initialized in the declaration statement, their initial value is zero.
- Local (visible) to the block in which the variable is declared. If the variable is declared within a function, then it is only visible to that function. But if the variable is declared outside the function, then it is visible to all the functions following its declaration.
- It retains its value between different function calls. That is, when for the first time a function is called, a static variable is created with initial value zero, and in subsequent calls it retains its present value.

Consider the following program.

Listing 11.21

```
/*  Program to illustrate the auto storage class
 *  when variable is declared in different blocks
 */
#include <stdio.h>
int main()
{
    int sumOfDigits(int);
    int a, b;
    a = sumOfDigits(125);
```

```
    b = sumOfDigits(125);
    printf("%d, %d", a, b);
    return 0;
}
int sumOfDigits(int n)
{
   static int sum = 0;
   while ( n > 0 )
   {
      sum = sum + n % 10;
      n = n / 10;
   }
   return sum;
}
```

Test Run

```
8, 16
```

You may be expecting answer "8, 8" since we are attempting to find the sum of digits of the same number 125.

The local variable *sum* is declared with *static* storage class. Further, lifetime of a static variable is program execution time, hence a static variable is able to retain its existing value between different calls. Therefore, on the first call, the *sum* variable is initialized to 0 and at return time has value 8. In the second call, the initial value of *sum* is 8, and further 8 (sum of digits of 125) is added thus giving value 16.

11.12.3 The *register* Storage Class

Register storage class is like *auto* in the sense that the visibility and lifetime of the variable is limited to the block in which it is declared. The difference is that the compiler, if possible, will assign a register variable to one of the processor's register instead of storing it in the memory. Value stored in register can be accessed much faster than the value stored in memory. But do remember that there is limited number of registers in a processor, and secondly not all variables can be register variables. Most of the compilers (especially Turbo C compiler) only guarantee registers storage of type *int* and pointer types.

Now the question arises, *what variables should be made register variables*? The obvious candidates are those variables on which the program spends most of its time to process them such as index variables used of *for loop*.

The variables declared with *register* storage class have the following features:

- Stored in processor registers, if a register is available. If no register is available, then variable is stored in memory, and works as if its storage class is *auto*. As soon as register becomes available, storage class of that variable is converted to register type.
- If not initialized in declaration statement, their initial value is unpredictable, *i.e.*, *garbage*.
- Local (visible) to the block in which the variable is declared. If the variable is declared within a function, then it is only visible to that function. But if the variable is declared outside the function, then it is visible to all the functions following its declaration.
- It retains its value till the control remains in the block in which the variable is declared. For example, if the variable is declared within a function, it will retain its value till the control is within that function. As the execution of the function terminates, it is cleared/destroyed.

11.12.4 The *extern* Storage Class

The scope of external variables is global. External variables are declared outside all functions, *i.e.*, in the beginning of the program file. As all the function will be defined after this variable declaration, so these variables are visible to all functions in a program file. However, if we have written our functions in separate program files, then we have to declare that variable again with *extern* storage class to tell the compiler that this variable or these variables are external variables and are defined in other source file(s).

The variables declared outside all the functions (if all functions are in single file) or declared with *extern* storage class (if you have multi-file programs) have the following features:

- Stored in memory.
- If not initialized in the declaration statement, their initial value is zero.
- Global, *i.e.*, visible to all functions.
- Retains its values till the program execution terminates.

Consider the following programs stored in separate files as shown:

Listing 11.22

```
/* file : extern1.c
 *  Program to illustrate the extern storage class.
 *  A global variable is defined here.   */
#include <stdio.h>
int commonVariable = 10;    /* definition of global variable */
int main()
{
   void sample();            /* prototype of function */
   printf("\nValue of global variable in main function=");
```

```
   printf("%d\n", commonVariable);
   sample();
   return 0;
}
```

Listing 11.23

```
/* file : extern2.cpp
*  Function that uses global variable declared in other file.
*  A global variable is defined here.
*/
#include <stdio.h>
extern int commonVariable; /* declaration of global variable */
void sample()
{
   printf("\nValue of global variable in sample function=");
   printf("%d\n", commonVariable);
}
```

Test Run

```
Value of global variable in main function = 10
Value of global variable in sample function = 10
```

Table 11.3 summarizes lifetime and visibility of various types of variables. The first three types are local; those defined within a function. Their visibility is confined to that function, and their lifetime — except for static variables — is also the same as that of the functions. These first three types of variables can also be defined within a block (a pair of braces); in this case, they will only be visible within block.

Table 11.3: Lifetime and visibility of various types of variables.

Place of Declaration	Storage class	Lifetime	Visibility
Function	auto	Function	function
function	register	function	function
function	static	program	function
file	static	program	one file
file	not specified	program	one file
file	extern	program	multi-file

The next three types are defined in the beginning of the file, *i.e.*, external to any function. In the first case, the variable is confined to a single file. The *extern* keyword cannot be used to reference it from other files. We use this storage class when we wish to hide the variables in one file.

In second case, which is most common, the variable is defined externally but is not declared in any other files. The visibility of such variables is confined to a single file. In this case the variable is visible only from the place in the file where it is defined to the end of the file. It is invisible to functions occurring before it even in the same program file.

In third case, a variable is defined in one file, but also declared in other files. In this case, its visibility will extend to the appropriate parts of all the files in which it is declared.

11.12.5 Advantages of Storage Classes

By using the appropriate storage class for a variable, the programmer can economize on memory requirements by restricting the lifetime of the variables. It will also help to maintain a modular, well-structured program by allowing access to variables only to those files and functions that need it. The number of ways in which the visibility and lifetime of variables can be restricted is an important reason for C's popularity with developers of large programs and systems.

11.13 MORE SUPPLEMENTARY PROBLEMS

Problem 11.5:

Write a function, say *int smallestDigit(int x)*, that returns the smallest digit in number *x*. Use minimum number of variables and minimum number of statements. Don't use array at all. Use this function in a program to demonstrate its use.

The procedure to find the smallest digit is as follows: We know that the largest digit is 9 and the smallest digit is 0. We start with taking 9 as the current smallest digit. In each iteration, we separate a digit and compare it with current smallest digit. If digit under consideration is less than current smallest digit, we take digit under consideration as current smallest digit. This process is repeated till all digits in a number have been examined.

Listing 11.24

```
/* Program to find smallest digit in a positive integer number  */
#include <stdio.h>
int smallestDigit(int); /* prototype    */
int main()
{
    long int number;

    printf( "\nEnter positive integer number : " );
    scanf( "%ld", &number);
    printf( "\nSmallest digit in %ld is %d\n", number,
              smallestDigit(number));
    return 0;
}
/* function that returns smallest digit in a +ve integer number  */
int smallestDigit(int k)
{
    int smallDigit = 9;
```

```
    int digit;
    while ( k > 0 ) {
       digit = k % 10;
       k /= 10;
       if ( digit < smallDigit )
          smallDigit = digit;
    }
    return smallDigit;
}
```

Test Run

```
Enter positive integer number : 23145
Smallest digit in 23145 is 1
```

Problem 11.6:

Write a program that takes a list of numbers as its command line arguments, and prints the sum of these numbers.

The procedure to be followed is as follows: The command line arguments are received by the *main()* function as string. Since the command line arguments are just numbers, therefore the string are made up of only letters 0-9 and decimal point '.'. We use here a library function *atof()* to convert a string of representing a number to numeric value. Then we add these numeric values one by one after conversion. We need to include *stdlib.h* header file in order to use *atof()* library function.

Listing 11.25

```
/*  Program to add list of numbers given as command line arguments
 *  filename : sum.c          */
# include <stdio.h>
# include <stdlib.h>
int main ( int argc, char *argv[] )
{
   int i;
   float sum = 0;
   for ( i = 1; i < argc; i++ ) {
      sum = sum + atof( argv[i] );
   }
   printf("\nSum of numbers on command line = %.2f\n", sum);
   return 0;
}
```

Test Run

```
>sum 1 2 3 4 5 6 7 8 9 10
Sum of numbers on command line = 55.00
```

EXERCISE

1. What is the difference between a user-defined function and library function?
2. When is the execution of the function terminated?
3. How many arguments can be passed to a function?
4. What are the rules regarding the relationship between formal arguments and actual arguments?
5. How is a function invoked?
6. How many times can a function be called?
7. What is wrong with the following function definition?

```
testFunction( int k )
{
    float temp = 5.25;
    temp = k / 2.0;
    return temp;
}
```

8. Find the errors, if any, in the following function definition

```
void fun( int x, int y )
{
    int z;
    /*  some statement   */
    return z;
}
```

9. Find the errors, if any, in the following function definition

```
void fun( int x, y )
{
    int z;
    /*  some statement   */
    return;
}
```

10. Find the errors, if any, in the following function definition

```
int fun1( int x, int y )
{
    int z;
    /*  some statement  */
    int fun2( int t )
    {
        return (t-2);
    }
    /*  some more statements    */
    return z;
}
```

12. What will be the output of the following program?

```
void main()
{
    float r = 5.0, c;
    float func( float t );     /* function prototype    */
    c = func( r );
```

```
        printf( "\nValue returned by function" );
        printf( "  = %d\n", c);
    }
    float func( float t )
    {
        float temp;
        temp = t * t / 2;
        return 5.0;
    }
```

13. Find the errors, if any, in the following function declarations:

    (*a*) `int diff(int x, y);`

    (*b*) `void fun(void, void);`

    (*c*) `float diff(float, float);`

    (*d*) `int test(float x, int y)`

PROGRAMMING EXERCISE

1. Write a function, say *int sumOfDigits(int number)*, that returns the sum of digits of a positive integer number.
2. Write a function, say *float absValue(float value)*, that returns the absolute value of a number of type *float*.
3. Write a function, say *int round(float x)*, that returns rounded value of *x* to nearest integer value.
4. Give recursive definition of the function to compute the greatest common divisor of the two positive integer numbers. Also show its implementation.
5. Write a function, say *int sumOfN(int n, int m)*, which computes the sum of *n* integers starting with *m*th integer, *i.e.*,

   $$m + (m + 1) + (m + 2) + . . . + (m + n - 1)$$

6. The combination function *C(n, r)* can be defined recursively as *C(n–1,r) + C(n–1,r–1)*. What is the base case? Write a recursive program to compute *C(n, r)*.
7. Write a function, say *int isPrime (int n)*, that returns 1 if number *n* is prime else return 0.
8. A number is a palindrome if it is the same number when read forward or backward. For example, numbers 1991, 1001 and 1221 palindrome numbers. Write a function, say *int isPalindrome(unsigned int k)*, that returns value 1 if the number k is palindrome else returns value 0.
9. A positive integer number IJK is said to be *well-ordered* if I < J < K. For example, number 138 is called *well-ordered* because the digits in the number (1, 3, 8) increase from left to right, *i.e.*, 1 < 3 < 8. Number 365 is not *well-ordered* because 6 is larger than 5. Write a function, say *int isWellordered(unsigned int k)*, that returns value 1 if the *k* is a *well-ordered* number else returns 0.

10. Write a function, say *int largestDigit(int x)*, that returns the largest digit in number *x*. Use minimum number of variables and minimum number of statements. Don't use array at all.
11. Write a function, say *int unitDigit(int n)*, that returns the unit digit of a number represented in argument *n*.
12. Write a function, say *int IsLeapYear(int year)*, that returns value 1 if the argument *year* represents a leap year else return value 0.

❑ ❑ ❑

Chapter 12

Arrays and Strings

Learning Objectives

After reading this chapter, students will be able to

- explain the concept of arrays
- explain the usefulness of arrays in handling class of related problems
- declare , initialize and do input/output of arrays
- explain the way arrays are passed as arguments to functions
- write efficient programs using arrays to solve variety of problems

12.1 INTRODUCTION

The variables used so for are also called *scalar* variables or *non-subscripted* variables. Each such variable represents a memory cell/location in which a single value can be stored. However, there are many situations in which it is necessary to process a collection of identical/homogeneous values. To illustrate this, consider that, for a class of 50 students, we have with us score of each student in final exam, and we are interested in having the following information:

- maximum score,
- average score of the class, and
- number of students whose score is greater than class's average score

One way of solving the above problem is

- use 50 variables, where each variable represents individual score,
- input these 50 scores,
- use about 50 *if* statements to find the maximum of these scores,
- add these 50 variables scores to find the total score of the class
- divide the total score by 50 to get the average score
- use another set of about 50 *if* statements to compare the individual scores with the average score to find the scores greater than average score and count such scores
- output the results

If at later stage, we want to process the scores of students of another class with number of students less or more than 50, the above program have to be modified as the number of variables will vary in the resulting program. This change in number of variables will affect the other parts of the program. The readers must find out themselves those parts that are affected.

Thus the above approach of processing a collection of homogeneous data is too cumbersome and not flexible enough to handle the collection of data of varying size.

The C language, like other high-level languages, provides a convenient way of processing such collections of homogeneous data. This is using *arrays* or *subscripted* variables.

In this chapter, we describe the processing of arrays and strings. Strings, which basically are array of characters with null character ('\0') as the last character, are also described.

12.2 ARRAYS

An *array* is a collection of homogeneous data elements (i.e. of same data type) described by a single name, and each individual element of an array is referenced by a *subscripted* variable, formed by affixing to the array name a *subscript* or *index* enclosed in brackets.

The term subscript has the same meaning as in the mathematical notation. If single subscript is required to refer to an element of an array, the array is known as *one-dimensional* or *linear array*, and if two subscripts are required to refer to an element of an array, the array is known as *two-dimensional* array, and so on. Analogously, the arrays whose elements are referred by two or more subscripts are called *multi-dimensional* arrays.

12.2.1 One-Dimensional Arrays

A list of items can be given a common name and the individual items can be referenced using only one subscript. Such variables are referred to a *single-subscripted* variable or a *one-dimensional* array.

In mathematics, we often deal with variables that are single-subscripted. For instance, we use the equation

$$\overline{x} = \frac{\sum_{i=1}^{n} x_i}{n}$$

to calculate the average of n values of a list named x. The subscripted variable x_i refers to the ith element of x.

In C language, single subscripted variable is referred as $x[i]$.

For illustration, let us consider a list of 10 scores. The array named *scores* can be visualized as shown in Figure 12.1.

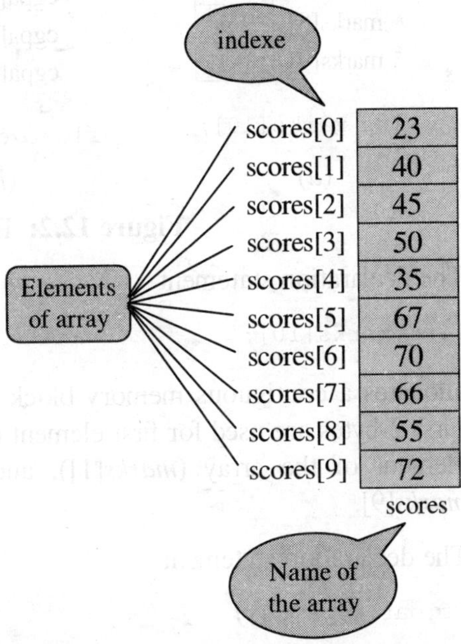

Figure 12.1: The Scores Array

12.2.1.1 Declaration and Definition

An array must be declared and defined before it can be used. Array declaration and definition tell the compiler *the name of the array*, *the type of its elements*, and *the size or number of elements in the array*. The size of the array is a constant and must have a value at compilation time.

The syntax for declaration of one-dimensional array is

```
type arrayName[arraySize];
```

Figure 12.2 shows three different array declarations, one for integers, one for floating-point numbers, and one for characters.

marks[0]	56
marks[1]	76
marks[2]	54
marks[3]	77
marks[4]	50
marks[5]	88
marks[6]	68
marks[7]	43
marks[8]	69
marks[9]	80

```
int marks[10];
```

(*a*)

cgpa[0]	5.0
cgpa[1]	4.5
cgpa[2]	7.0
cgpa[3]	8.0
cgpa[4]	6.5
cgpa[5]	7.0
cgpa[6]	5.5
cgpa[7]	6.0
cgpa[8]	8.5
cgpa[9]	9.0

```
float cgpa[10];
```

(*b*)

name[0]	A
name[1]	n
name[2]	n
name[3]	i
name[4]	
name[5]	S
name[6]	o
name[7]	o
name[8]	d
name[9]	

```
char name[10];
```

(*c*)

Figure 12.2: Declaring and defining arrays

The declaration statement

```
int marks[10];
```

allocates a contiguous memory block of 20 bytes, 2-bytes for each element of type *int*. First 2-bytes are used for first element of the array (*marks*[0]), next 2-bytes for the second element of the array (*marks*[1]), and so on. The last 2-bytes are used for element *marks*[9].

The declaration statement

```
float cgpa[10];
```

allocates a contiguous memory block of 40 bytes, 4-bytes for each element of type *float*. First 4-bytes are used for first element of the array (*cgpa*[0]), next 4-bytes for the second element of the array (*cgpa*[1]), and so on. The last 4-bytes are used for element *cgpa*[9].

The declaration statement

```
char name[10];
```

allocates a contiguous memory block of 10 bytes, 1-byte for each element of type *char*. First byte is used for first element of the array (*name*[0]), next byte for the second element of the array (*name*[1]), and so on. The last byte is used for element *name*[9].

12.2.1.2 Accessing Elements

The C language uses single *index* to access individual elements in a one-dimensional array. The index must be an integral value or an expression that evaluates to an integral value.

For example, given the *marks* array in Figure 12.2 (*a*), we would access the first element as

```
marks[0]
```

To process all the elements in *marks*, a loop similar to the following code is used:

```
for (i = 0; i < 10; i++ )
   process ( marks[i] );
```

One very interesting point that you may be keen to know is that how the C system knows where an individual element is located in memory. In *marks* one-dimensional array, there are ten elements. *How does it find just one of them*? The answer is simple – the array's name is a symbolic reference for the address to the first byte of the block of memory allocated for the array. The address of the first byte for the array is also known as *base address* of the array. Whenever we use the array's name, we actually refer to the first byte of the array. The index represents an offset from the beginning of the array to the element being referenced. With these two facts of information, the C system can calculate the address of any element in the array using the following simple formula:

```
element address = base address + ( sizeof(element) * index )
```

or simply as

```
address(marks[i]) = base address + ( sizeof(element) * i )
```

For example, assume that the base address for array *marks* is 1000. Since the elements of the array *marks* are of type *int*, the size of one element is the size of *int*, *i.e.*, 2 bytes. The address of an element at index 3 is

```
address(marks[3]) = 1000 + ( 2 * 3 ) = 1006
```

In C language, there is no built-in facility to ensure that while accessing array elements, the subscript is within the permissible range. For example, the declaration statement is *int a[10]*, and even if we attempt to access the 16th element as *a*[15], which of course is not a valid array element, in our program, the C system will not flag any error at any stage. It will just pick up a garbage value from the accessed memory location. The programmer must take care of this problem. Further, *i*th element of above array can also be accessed as *i*[*a*], in addition to normal way as *a*[*i*].

12.2.1.3 Storing Values

Declaration and definition only reserve space for the elements of the array. No values are stored in the array at this moment. To store values in the array, we must initialize the elements, read values from the keyboard, or assign values to each individual element.

12.2.1.3.1 Initialization

Just as simple variables can be initialized along with declaration and definition, the elements of the arrays can also be initialized. For each element in the array, we provide a value. The only difference is that the values must be enclosed in braces, and if there is more than one, separated by comma. The following examples provide all possible ways of initializing one-dimensional array. The following statement

```
int b[10]={12, 0, 14, -4, 7, 8, 10, 11, 9, 15};
```

initializes element *b*[0] to 12, *b*[1] to 0, *b*[2] to 14, *b*[3] to –4, *b*[4] to 7, *b*[5] to 8, *b*[6] to 10, *b*[7] to 11, *b*[8] to 9, *b*[9] to 15.

If the array is initialized like this

```
int b[] = {12, 0, 14, -4, 7};
```

Since size of the array is not specified, the compiler counts the number of elements in the initialization list and fixes that as the array size.

12.2.1.3.2 Inputting Values

The second way to fill the array with values is to read the values from the keyboard or a data file. This method of inputting values is done using a loop. The following segment shows the way data is entered into one-dimensional array.

```
for ( i = 0; i < 10; i++ )
{
    scanf( "%d", &marks[i] );
}
```

```
for ( i = 0; i <= 9; i++ )
{
    scanf( "%d", &marks[i] );
}
```

Observe the following things:

1. We start the index, *i*, at 0. Since the array has 10 elements, we must store the values from index location 0 through 9. The limit test, therefore, is set at *i* < 10 or *i* <= 9, which conveniently is the number of elements in an array.
2. Even though, we are dealing with array elements, the *address of* operator (&) is still necessary in the *scanf()* function call.

12.2.1.3.3 Assigning Values

The third way to fill the array with values is to assign the values to the individual elements using the assignment operator. Any value that is compatible can be assigned to the individual array element.

A simple assignment statement for *marks* is given below:

```
marks[3] = 45;
```

We can also assign the elements of one array to second array provided they match fully in type and size. Suppose that two arrays named *first* and *second* are compatible, and size of each array is 25, and we want to copy the elements of array *first* to *second*, the following loop will serve the purpose:

```
for ( i = 0; i < 25; i++ ) {
  second[i] = first[i];
}
```

If the values of elements of an array follow a certain pattern, we can use a loop to assign values. For example, following loop assigns a value to the element that is twice of its index:

```
for ( i = 0; i < 10; i++ ) {
  a[i] = 2 * i;
}
```

Following loop assigns value 0 to elements at even index and value 1 to elements at odd index:

```
for ( i = 0; i < 10; i++ )
{
   if ( i % 2 == 0 )
      a[i] = 0;
   else
      a[i] = 1;
}
```

One array cannot be copied to another using assignment. For instance, if *a* and *b* are two arrays that match fully in type and size, the statement "a = b;" is not acceptable.

12.2.1.4 Outputting Values

To output values of elements of an array, we use the loop as follows:

```
for ( i = 0; i < n; i++ ) {
   printf( "%d  ", a[i] );
}
printf( "\n" );
```

All the values are displayed on one line. However, if all the values cannot be displayed in one line either because of their magnitude of values or number of values, they are displayed in subsequent lines. After, the *for* loop completes, a final call to *printf()* function advances the cursor to the next line. The following *for* loop display one value per line:

```
for ( i = 0; i < n; i++ ) {
   printf( "\n%d", a[i] );
}
printf( "\n" );
```

However, if the values are more than 25, these values will scroll up. However, we can set up some of counter to control the display so that we able to view all the values.

Having understood the various aspects of the one-dimensional arrays, let us write some C functions and complete programs to demonstrate the power of one-dimensional arrays to handle complex problems.

Example 12.1:

Given an array, named *x*, of size (≤ 50) whose elements are of type *int.* Write a program that reads the actual size 'n' of the array, assigns array elements with value that is square of its index, and finally prints the elements of array such that maximum of 5 elements are printed on one line.

Listing 12.1

```
/* Program that assigns elements of the array with square of its
   index, and then prints the array such that maximum of 5 elements
   on one line
*/
#include<stdio.h>
int main()
{
   int x[50], i, n, counter = 0;
   printf("\nEnter actual size of array (<=50) : ");
   scanf("%d", &n);
   for ( i = 0; i < n; i++ )
      x[i] = i  * i;
   for ( i = 0; i < n; i++ )
   {
      printf("%d  ", x[i]);
      counter++;
      if ( counter == 5 ) {
         printf("\n");
         counter = 0;
      }
   }
   return 0;
}
```

Test Run

```
Enter actual size of array (<=50) : 18
  0    1    4    9   16
 25   36   49   64   81
100  121  144  169  196
255  256  289
```

Example 12.2:

Let us consider that for a class of *n* students, we have with us score of each student in final exam, and we are interested in generating the following information

- maximum score of the class,
- average score of the class, and
- number of students whose score is greater than class's average score

The following program accomplishes this task.

Listing 12.2

```
/* Program to find the maximum score, average score, and the
  number of students whose score is greater than class average  */
#include<stdio.h>
int main()
{
   float score[SIZE], maximumScore, averageScore, float totalScore;
   int i, n, noOfStudents = 0;
   printf("\nEnter number of students in class: ");
   scanf( "%d", &n );
   printf( "\nEnter %d scores\n\n", n );
   for ( i = 0; i < n; i++ )
      scanf( "%f", &score[i] );
   totalScore = 0;
   for ( i = 0; i < n; i++ )
      totalScore += score[i];
   averageScore = totalScore / n;
   maximumScore = score[0];
   for ( i = 1; i < n; i++ ) {
      if ( score[i] > maximumScore )
         maximumScore = score[i];
   }
   for ( i = 0; i < n; i++ ) {
      if ( score[i] > averageScore )
         noOfStudents++;
   }
   printf( "\nMaximum score of class = %.2f", maximumScore );
   printf( "\nAverage score of class = %.2f", averageScore );
   printf( "\nNo. of students with score > %.2f = %d\n",
            averageScore, noOfStudents );
   return 0;
}
```

Test Run

```
Enter number of students in class: 10

Enter 10 scores

75.25
80
65.5
59.5
72.25
35.5
55.75
69
43
85

Maximum score of class = 85.00
Average score of class = 63.58
No. of students with score > 63.58 = 6
```

Example 12.3:

Program to find the range of a set of value collected from some experiment or survey.

The *range* is defined as difference between the smallest and largest element of the given set of values. In order to find the range, first we have to find the largest and smallest element of the set. The following program accomplishes this task.

Listing 12.3

```
/* Program to find the range from a set of values   */
#include<stdio.h>
int main()
{
   float a[50], smallest, largest, range;
   int i, n;
   printf( "\nEnter size of array: " );
   scanf( "%d", &n );
   printf("Enter %d elements of the array\n",n);
   for ( i = 0; i < n; i++ )
     scanf( "%f", &a[i] );
   smallest = largest = a[0];
   for ( i = 1; i < n; i++ )
   {
      if ( a[i] > largest ) largest = a[i];
      if ( a[i] < smallest ) smallest = a[i];
   }
   range = largest - smallest;
   printf( "\nRange of set of value = %.2f\n", range );
   return 0;
}
```

Test Run

```
Enter size of array: 10
Enter 10 elements of the array
75.25
80
65.5
59.5
72.25
35.5
55.75
69
43
85
Range of set of value = 49.50
```

Example 12.4:

Program to find standard deviation (σ) for a given set of data, say X (x_0, x_1, x_2,..., x_{n-1}). Standard deviation is a valuable statistics that measures the dispersion of data, *i.e.*, how the data is dispersed (scattered) about the mean ($\bar{x}$) of data.

The formula for computing standard deviation is

$$\text{standard deviation } (\sigma) = \sqrt{\frac{\sum_{i=0}^{n-1}(x_i - \bar{x})^2}{n}}, \quad \text{where mean } (\bar{x}) = \frac{\sum_{i=0}^{n-1} x_i}{n}$$

Listing 12.4

```
/*  Program to find standard deviation for a given set of data  */
#include<stdio.h>
#include<math.h>
int main()
{
   float x[50], average, sum, stdDeviation, temp;
   int i, n;
   printf("\nProgram to compute standard deviation for" );
   printf(" a given set of data\n\n");
   printf("\nEnter number of elements in data set (n): ");
   scanf( "%d", &n );
   printf("\n\n");    /*  insert two blank lines */
   for ( i = 0; i < n; i++ ) {
      printf( "Enter data element #%d : ", i+1 );
      scanf( "%f", &x[i] );
   }
   for ( sum = 0.0, i = 0; i < n; i++ )
      sum += x[i];
   average = sum / n;
   for (sum = 0.0, i = 0; i < n; i++ ) {
```

```
        temp = x[i] - average;
        sum += temp * temp;
    }
    stdDeviation = sqrt( (double) sum / n );
    printf( "\nStandard deviation = %.3f", stdDeviation );
    printf( " (rounded to three decimal digits)\n" );
    return 0;
}
```

Test Run

```
Program to compute standard deviation for a given set of data

Enter number of elements in data set (n): 5
Enter data element #1: 1
Enter data element #2: 2
Enter data element #3: 3
Enter data element #4: 4
Enter data element #5: 5

Standard deviation = 1.414 (rounded to three decimal digits)
```

Example 12.5:

Program to sort a linear array *a* with *n* elements in ascending order. The elements of *a* are indexed from 0 to $(n-1)$.

In order to sort the above array, we will use one very important method known as Bubble sort, which is described in *Example 4.21*.

Following listing shows the implementation of bubble sort method to sort an array in ascending order.

Listing 12.5

```
/* Program to sort an array of integers in ascending order
   using Bubble sort method    */
*/
#include<stdio.h>
int main()
{
    int a[50], i, n, k, temp;
    printf( "\nEnter size of array: " );
    scanf( "%d", &n );
    printf("\nEnter %d elements of the array\n",n);
    for ( i = 0; i < n; i++ )
       scanf ( "%d", &a[i] );
    for ( k = 0;  k < n-1;  k++ ) {
       for ( i = 0; i < n-k-1; i++ ) {
           if ( a[i] > a[i+1] ) {
               temp = a[i];
               a[i] = a[i+1];
```

```
                a[i+1] = temp;
            }
        }
    }
    printf( "\nArray elements after sorting\n" );
    for ( i = 0; i < n; i++ )
        printf ( "%d  ", a[i] );
    printf( "\n" );
    return 0;
}
```

Test Run

```
Enter size of array: 10
Enter 10 elements of the array
75 80 65 59 72 35 55 69 43 85

Array elements after sorting
35  43  55  59  65  69  70  72  80  85
```

12.2.1.5 Passing One-Dimensional Array as Argument

Note that instead of passing values of all elements of an array to a function, only address of the array is passed. As you know, in C, the name of an array is a primary expression whose value is the address of the first element of the array.

```
/*  main function    */
#include <stdio.h>
void fun( int x[], int m );
void main()
{
    int a[10], n;
    /*  other local declarations */

    func(a, n); /* function call */
    /*  other statements         */
}
```

```
/*  function definition    */
void fun( int x[], int m )
{
    /*  local declarations */
    /*  other statements   */
}
```

Figure 12.3: Passing one-dimensional array as an argument to a function

Since, indexed references are simply calculated addresses, all we need to refer to any of the elements of the array is the address of the array, *i.e.*, address of the first element.

Because the name of the array is in fact its address, therefore, passing the array name allows called function to refer to the array back in the calling function.

Listing 12.6

```
/* Program to demonstrate the passing of an array as an argument  */
#include <stdio.h>
int largest( int x[], int size );   /*  function prototype */
```

```
int main(void)
{
   int a[50]={12,15,20,17,25,50,11,10,8,13};
   int i;
   printf( "Largest of the array element is %d\n", largest(a,50));
   return 0;
}
/* function that returns largest element of the array    */
int largest( const int x[], int size )
{
   int big, i;
   big = x[0];
   for ( i = 1; i < size; i++ ) {
       if ( x[i] > big )
           big = x[i];
   }
   return big;
}
```

Test Run

```
Largest of the array element is 50
```

12.2.2 Two-Dimensional Arrays

The array we have discussed for far are known as one-dimensional arrays because the data are organized linearly only in one direction (dimension). Many applications require that data be organized in more than one dimension. One common example is a matrix (a table), which is an array that consists of rows and columns.

Figure 12.4 shows a matrix (table) with 4 rows and 4 columns which is commonly used as a two-dimensional array.

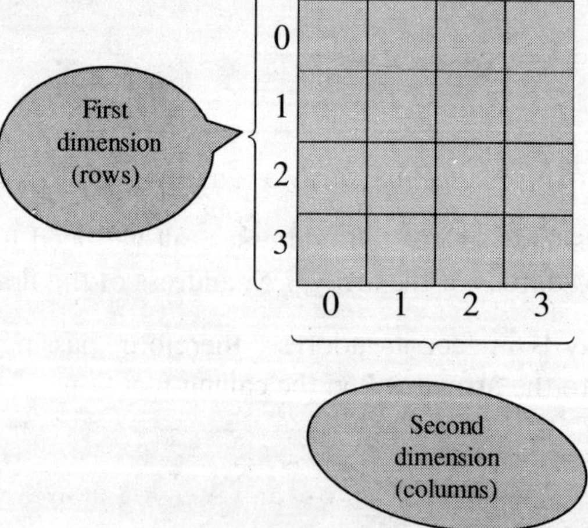

Figure 12.4: Two-dimensional array

Although two-dimensional array is exactly what is shown in Figure 12.4, C language looks at it in a different way. It looks at the two-dimensional array as am array of arrays. In other words, a two-dimensional array in C language is an array of one-dimensional arrays. This concept is shown in Figure 12.5.

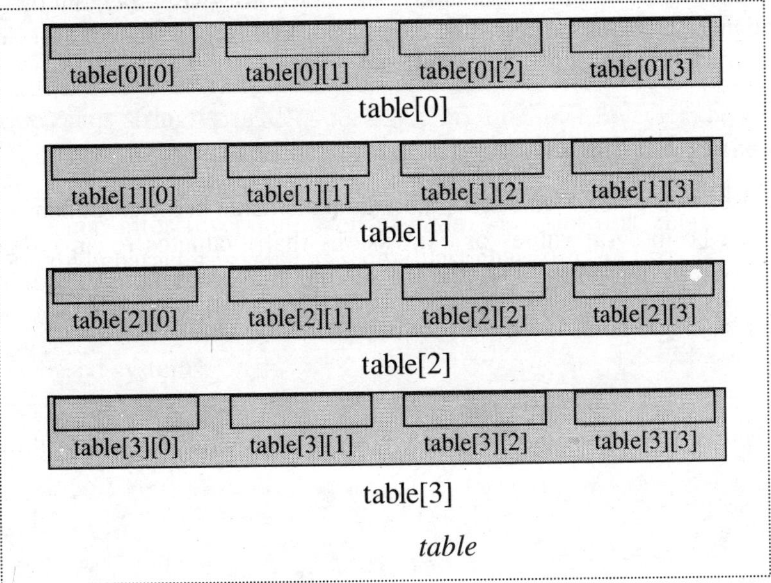

Figure 12.5: Array of arrays

12.2.2.1 Declaration and Definition

Two-dimensional arrays, like one-dimensional arrays, must be declared before being used. Declaration tells the compiler *the name of the array, the type of its elements*, and *the size of each dimension.* The syntax for declaration of two-dimensional array is

```
type arrayName[sizeOfDimension1][sizeOfDimension2];
```

By convention, the first dimension specifies the number of *rows* in the array while the second dimension specifies the number of *columns* in each row.

The declaration statement, declares the array shown in Figure 12.9

```
int table[4][4];
```

This declarations statement allocates a contiguous memory block of 32 bytes, 8-bytes for each row. First set of 8-bytes are used to store elements of first row, second set of 8-bytes are used to store elements of second row, third set of 8-bytes are used to store elements of third row and the last set of 8-bytes are used to store elements of the fourth (last) row. Within in each row, first set of 2-bytes are used to store element of the first column, next set of 2-bytes are used to store element of second column, next set of 2-bytes are used to store elements of the third column, and final set of 2-bytes are used to store element of the fourth (last) column.

Elements of two-dimensional array are stored row-wise, *i.e.*, in the allocated contiguous block of memory, first elements of first row are stored, then elements of third row, then elements of third row, and so on.

12.2.2.2 Accessing Elements

The C language uses two *indexes* to access individual elements in a two-dimensional array. These indices must be integral values or expressions that evaluates to an integral value. The first index is used to denote the row and the second index to denote the column.

Therefore, to access *j*th element of the *i*th row, we write

```
table[i][j]
```

To process all the elements row-wise of *table*, nested loops similar to the following code will be used:

```
for (i = 0; i < 4; i++ )  {
    for (j = 0; j < 4; j++ ) {
        process ( table[i][j] );
    }
}
```

12.2.2.3 Storing Values

Like one-dimensional array, the declaration and definition of two-dimensional array also only reserve space for the elements of the array. No values are stored in the array at this moment. To store values in the array, we must initialize the elements, read values from keyboard, or assign values to each individual element.

12.2.2.3.1 Initialization

One way to initialize two-dimensional arrays is as shown below:

```
int table[4][4] = { 0, 0, 0, 0, 1, 1, 1, 1, 2, 2, 2, 2, 3, 3, 3, 3 };
```

It will initialize all elements of first row with value 0, elements of second row with value 1, elements of third row with 2 and elements of fourth row with value 3.

Though, the above initialization has no problems, it highly recommended that nest braces be used to show the exact nature of the two-dimensional array.

The array *table* is better initialized as shown below:

```
int table[4][4] = { { 0, 0, 0, 0 },
                    { 1, 1, 1, 1 },
                    { 2, 2, 2, 2 },
                    { 3, 3, 3, 3 },
                  };
```

In above way of initialization, we initialize each row as a one-dimensional array of four elements enclosed in braces. The array of four rows also has its set of braces. Note that we use commas between the elements in the columns and also commas between the rows.

12.2.2.3.2 Inputting Values

The second way to fill the array with values is to read the values from the keyboard or a data file. This method of inputting values is done using nested loops. Following segment shows the way elements can be read row-wise using nested for loops:

```
for (i = 0; i < 4; i++ )  {
   for (j = 0; j < 4; j++ ) {
      scanf( "%d", &table[i][j] );
   }
}
```

In general, if the one-dimensional array is of size $m \times n$, the first loop varies from 0 to $(m-1)$ and the second loop varies from 0 to $(n-1)$.

12.2.2.3.3 Assigning Values

The third way to fill the array with values is to assign the values to the individual elements using the assignment operator. Any value that is compatible can be assigned to the individual array element. A simple assignment statement for *table* is given below:

```
table[1][2] = 40;
```

We can also assign the elements of one array to second array provided they match fully in type and size. Suppose that two arrays named *a* and *b* are compatible, and size of each array is 4×4, and we want to copy the elements of array *a* to *b*, the following loop will serve the purpose:

```
for (i = 0; i < 4; i++ )
{
    for (j = 0; j < 4; j++ )
    {
        b[i][j] = a[i][j];
    }
}
```

If the values of elements of an array follow a certain pattern, we can use nested loops to assign values. For example, if we want to initialize a 4×4 two-dimensional array to represent an identity matrix, this can be done using following nested loops as shown:

```
for (i = 0; i < 4; i++ )  {
    for (j = 0; j < 4; j++ )  {
        if ( i == j )
            a[][] = 1;
        else
            a[i][j] = 0
    }
}
```

$$\begin{pmatrix} 1 & 0 & 0 & 0 \\ 0 & 1 & 0 & 0 \\ 0 & 0 & 1 & 0 \\ 0 & 0 & 0 & 1 \end{pmatrix}$$

Figure12.6: Identity matrix

12.2.2.4 Outputting Values

To output values of elements of two-dimensional array, we use nested loops as follows:

```
for ( i = 0; i < 4; i++ ) {
    for ( j = 0; j < 4; j++ ) {
        printf( "%d", a[i][j] );
    }
    printf( "\n" );
}
```

The elements of the two-dimensional array will be output row-wise by the above segment. The first loop controls the rows while the second loop controls the columns.

Example 12.6:

Program to compute the transpose of a matrix *A* of order *m*×*n*.

We know that if we interchange the rows with columns, we get transpose of a given matrix, say B of order *n*×*m*, *i.e.*,

$$b_{ji} = a_{ij}$$

Listing 12.7

```
/*  Program to compute transpose of matrix A of size mxn   */
#include<stdio.h>
int main()
{
    int a[10][10], b[10][10];
    int n, m, i, j;
    printf( "Enter size of matrix A as m,n: " );
    scanf( "%d,%d", &m, &n);
    printf("\nEnter %d elements of matrix A row-wise\n",m*n);
    for ( i = 0 ; i < m; i++ ) {
        for ( j = 0; j < n; j++ ) {
            scanf( "%d", &a[i][j] );
        }
```

```
    }
    for ( i = 0 ; i < m ; i++ ) {
        for ( j = 0 ; j < n ; j++ ) {
            b[j][i] = a[i][j];
        }
    }
    printf( "\nTranspose is\n\n" );
    for ( i = 0 ; i < n; i++ ) {
        for ( j = 0; j < m; j++ ) {
            printf( "%5d", b[i][j] );
        }
        printf ( "\n" );
    }
    return 0;
}
```

Test Run

```
Enter size of matrix A as m,n: 3,3
Enter 9 elements of matrix A row-wise
1 2 3
4 5 6
7 8 9
Transpose is
    1    4    7
    2    5    8
    3    6    9
```

Example 12.7:

Program to add two matrices *A* and *B*, each of order *m*×*n*.

We know that if to add to matrices, we add corresponding elements to get the element of a resultant matrix, i.e.,

$$c_{ij} = a_{ij} + b_{ij}$$

Listing 12.8

```
/*  Program to add matrix A and B, each of order mxn   */
#include<stdio.h>
int main()
{
    float a[10][10], b[10][10], c[10][10];
    int n, m, i, j;
    printf( "Enter size of matrices as m,n: " );
    scanf( "%d,%d", &m, &n);
    printf( "Enter %d elements of matrix A row-wise\n", m*n );
    for ( i = 0 ; i < m; i++ ) {
        for ( j = 0; j < n; j++ ) {
            scanf( "%f", &a[i][j] );
        }
    }
```

```
    printf( "Enter %d elements of matrix B row-wise\n", m*n );
    for ( i = 0 ; i < m; i++ ) {
        for ( j = 0; j < n; j++ ) {
            scanf( "%f", &b[i][j] );
        }
    }
    for ( i = 0 ; i < m ; i++ ) {
       for ( j = 0 ; j < n ; j++ ) {
          c[i][j] = a[i][j] + b[i][j];
       }
    }
    printf( "\nSum A+B is\n\n" );
    for ( i = 0 ; i < m; i++ ) {
        for ( j = 0; j < n; j++ ) {
          printf( "%7.2f", c[i][j] );
        }
        printf ( "\n" );
    }
    return 0;
}
```

Test Run

```
Enter size of matrices as m,n: 3,3
Enter 9 elements of matrix A row-wise
1 1 1
1 1 1
1 1 1
Enter 9 elements of matrix B row-wise
2 2 2
2 2 2
2 2 2

Sum A+B is
  3.00   3.00   3.00
  3.00   3.00   3.00
  3.00   3.00   3.00
```

Example 12.8:

Program to multiply two matrices A and B. The matrix A is of order $m \times n$ matrix and the matrix B is of order $p \times q$ matrix, provided $n = p$.

As we want to multiply two matrices A and B, where the matrix A is of order $m \times n$ and the matrix B is of order $p \times q$, the product matrix, say matrix C, then will be of order $m \times p$ with entry c_{ij}, which appears in the ith row and jth column is given as:

c_{ij} = sum of the products of the entries in the ith row of matrix A with the corresponding entries in the jth column of matrix B

$$= a_{i0} \times b_{0j} + a_{i1} \times b_{1j} + a_{i2} \times b_{2j} + \ldots + a_{i(n-1)} \times b_{(n-1)j} = \sum_{k=0}^{n-1} a_{ik} b_{kj}$$

Listing 12.9

```
/*
*  Program to multiply matrix A of size mxn by matrix B of
*  size pxq. Program also checks for feasibility of product.
*/
#include<stdio.h>
int main()
{
   float a[10][10], b[10][10], c[10][10];
   int n, m, p, q, i, j, k;
   printf( "Enter size of matrix A as m,n: " );
   scanf( "%d,%d", &m, &n);
   printf( "Enter size of matrix B as p,q: " );
   scanf( "%d,%d", &p, &q);
   if ( n != p ) {
      printf( "\nMatrix Product AxB is not feasible\n" );
      return;
   }
   printf("\nEnter %d elements of matrix A row-wise\n", m*n);
   for ( i = 0 ; i < m; i++ )
   {
      for ( j = 0; j < n; j++ )
      {
         scanf( "%f", &a[i][j] );
      }
   }
   printf("\nEnter %d elements of matrix B row-wise\n", p*q);
   for ( i = 0 ; i < p; i++ )
   {
      for ( j = 0; j < q; j++ )
      {
         scanf( "%f", &b[i][j] );
      }
   }
   for ( i = 0 ; i < m ; i++ )
   {
      for ( j = 0 ; j < q ; j++ )
      {
         c[i][j] = 0;
         for ( k = 0; k < n; k++ )
         {
            c[i][j] += a[i][k] * b[k][j];
         }
      }
   }
   printf( "\nProduct AxB is\n\n" );
   for ( i = 0 ; i < m; i++ )
   {
      for ( j = 0; j < q; j++ )
      {
         printf( "%7.2f\t", c[i][j] );
```

```
        }
        printf ( "\n" );
    }
    return 0;
}
```

Test Run

```
Enter size of matrix A as m,n: 3,3
Enter size of matrix B as p,q: 3,3
Enter 9 elements of matrix A row-wise
1 1 1
1 1 1
1 1 1
Enter 9 elements of matrix B row-wise
2 2 2
2 2 2
2 2 2
Product AxB is
 6.00  6.00  6.00
 6.00  6.00  6.00
 6.00  6.00  6.00
```

12.4.5 Passing Two-Dimensional Array as Arguments

When we pass two-dimensional array to a function, we use the array name as we did with one-dimensional array. The formal argument in the argument list in the called function header must indicate the array has two dimensions. This is done by including two sets of brackets, one for each dimension. During function call, only the base address of the array is passed.

```
/*  main function    */
#include <stdio.h>
void fun(int x[][], int m, int n);
void main()
{
    int a[4][4];
    /*  other local declarations
*/

    func(a,m,n); /* function call
*/
    /*  other statements
*/
```

```
/*  function definition    */
void fun(int x[][], int m, int
n)
{
    /*  local declarations    */
    /*  other statement       */
}
```

Figure 12.7: Passing entire two-dimensional array

Listing 12.10

```
/*
*  Program to multiply matrix A of size mxn by matrix B of size
*  pxq. Program also checks for feasibility of product. This
*  program uses function to read, multiply and display matrices
*/
#include<stdio.h>
/*    function declarations    */
void readMatrix(float a[][], int m, int n);
void displayMatrix(float a[][], int m, int n);
void multiplyMatrix(float a[][],b[][],c[][],int m,int n,int q);
int main()
{
    float a[10][10], b[10][10], c[10][10];
    int n, m, p, q;
    printf( "Enter size of matrix A as m,n: " );
    scanf( "%d,%d", &m, &n);
    printf( "Enter size of matrix B as p,q: " );
    scanf( "%d,%d", &p, &q);
    if ( n != p ) {
        printf( "\nMatrix Product AxB is not feasible\n" );
        return 1;
    }
    readMatrix(a,m,n);              /* input matrix 'a'  */
    readMatrix(b,p,q);              /* input matrix 'b'  */
    multiplyMatrix(a,b,c,m,n,q); /* multiply matrix a by matrix 'b'*/
    printf( "\nProduct AxB is\n\n" );
    displayMatrix(c,m,q);             /* output matrix 'c' */
    return 0;
}
/*  function that reads a matrix 'a' of order mxn  */
void readMatrix(float a[][], int m, int n)
{
   int i, j;
   printf("\nEnter %d elements of matrix A row-wise\n", m*n );
   for ( i = 0 ; i < m; i++ ) {
      for ( j = 0; j < n; j++ ) {
         scanf( "%f", &a[i][j] );
      }
   }
}
/*  function that displays a matrix 'a' of order mxn  */
void displayMatrix(float a[][], int m, int n)
{
    int i, j;
    for ( i = 0 ; i < m; i++ ) {
       for ( j = 0; j < n; j++ ) {
           printf( "%7.3f\t", c[i][j] );
       }
       printf ( "\n" );
    }
```

```
}
/* function that multiplies matrices 'a' and 'b' and
 * stores the product in matrix 'c'  */
void multiplyMatrix(float a[][],b[][],c[][],int m,int n,int q)
{
    int i, j, k;
    float temp;
    for ( i = 0 ; i < m ; i++ ) {
        for ( j = 0 ; j < q ; j++ ) {
            c[i][j] = 0;
            for ( k = 0; k < n; k++ )
                c[i][j] = c[i][j] + a[i][k] * b[k][j];
        }
    }
}
```

12.3 CHARACTER ARRAYS AND STRINGS

Each of the arrays illustrated so far contained numeric elements. We can also have array of characters. Using array of characters, we can store string data. But do remember that as such strings are not directly supported in C language, though sometimes loosely we refer to array of characters as strings.

A string in C language is a variable length array of characters that is delimited by null character ('\0'). Generally, characters comprising a string are selected only from printable characters; however, C language does permit the use of any character except the null character. In fact, it is common to use formatting characters, such as tabs, format specifiers, etc., in strings.

Here we will discuss the various aspects related to handling of strings in C language.

The C language uses variable length, delimited strings. The null character '\0' is used as delimiting character. Though the null character '\0' looks like a sequence of two characters, '\' and '0', but in C language it is treated as single character.

12.3.1 Storing Strings

In C language, a string is stored in an array of characters. It is terminated by the null ('\0') character. Figure 12.8 shows how a string "Hello" is stored in memory. Because a string is stored in an array, the name of the array, and hence string, is a pointer to the beginning of the string.

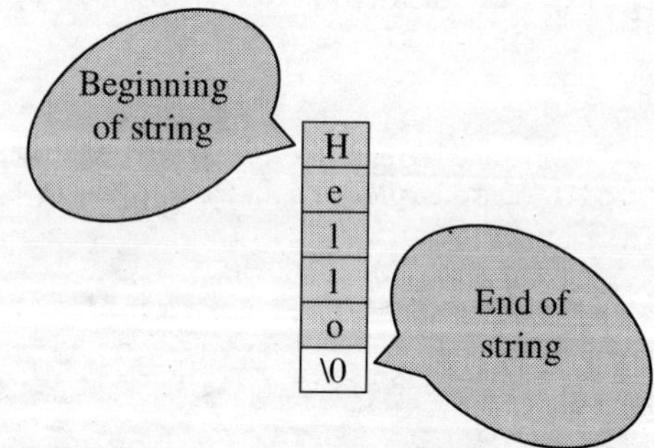

Figure 12.8: Storing a string in memory

Figure 12.9 shows the difference between the storage of a character and a one character string. The character required only one storage location (of 1-byte) whereas one character string requires two storage location (of 1-byte each); one for the character and one for the delimiter. The figure also shows how an empty string is stored. The empty string consists of null character only.

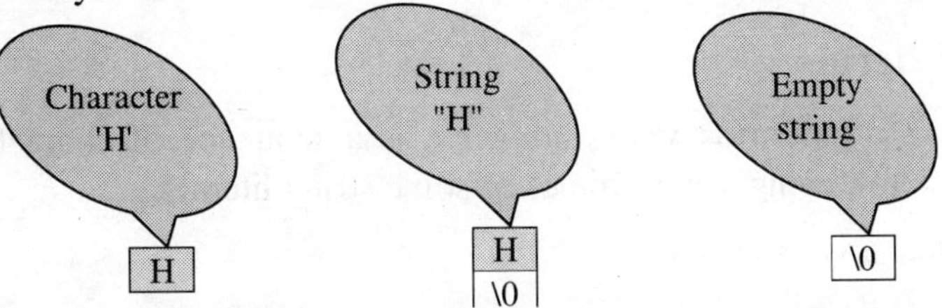

Figure 12.9: Difference in storage of characters and strings

12.3.2 Need of String Delimiter

The question – *Why actually we need a null character to terminate a string*? - may be coming in your mind. The answer to this question is that a string is not a data type; it is data structure – *an array*. Therefore, implementation of string is logical not physical. The physical structure is the array in which string is stored. Since, strings are of varying length, there is a need to identify the logical end of data within physical structure.

Let look at the need of string delimiter from another point of view. If the data is of fixed length, then we don't need string data structure to store them rather it can easily be stored in an array. When data is stored in an array, the end of the data is always indicated by the last element of the array. But, if the data is not of fixed length (*i.e.*, varying length), then we need some other way to determine the end of the data. The null character is used to mark the end of the string data.

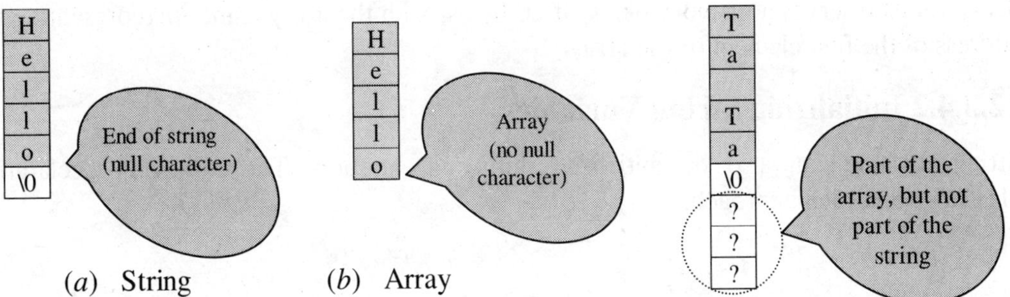

Figure 12.10: Difference between a string and an array of characters

Figure 12.11: String stored in part of array

Because strings are variable-length structures, enough space for the maximum-length string that we have to store plus one for the null character (delimiter) be reserved.

In many situations it may be possible that the entire array is not filled and we may have null character in the middle of the array. In that case, the array from the beginning to the null character is treated as string and remaining elements of the array are ignored. This means that a part of an array of characters can be treated as a string provided it ends with a null character, as shown in Figure 12.11.

12.3.3 String Literals

A *string literal*, also known as *string constant*, is a sequence of characters enclosed in double quotes. The following are examples of some string literals:

```
"Hello! you are wel come"
"Hari\'s Book"
""
"A"
```

Note that embedded spaces are significant. And if quotes, single (') or double ("), are part of the string, they must be used with the escape sequence.

12.3.4 String Variables

A string variable is actually an array of characters.

12.3.4.1 Declaring String Variables

String variables are declared as shown in the following statement

```
char str[20];
```

This statement declares string variable *str* of length 20. In fact, the maximum characters that can be stored are 19 as last character is always the null character. In fact, the above declarations reserves a memory block of 20 bytes, with the array name *str* representing the address of the first element of the array.

12.3.4.2 Initializing String Variables

String variable can also be initialized during declaration. The following declaration illustrates one such approach.

```
char mess[] = {'Y', 'o', 'u', ' ', 'a', 'r', 'e', ' ',
               'w', 'e', 'l', ' ', 'c', 'o', 'm', 'e', '\0'};
```

Here string variable *mess* is initialized as sequence of character constants. In this style it is programmer's job to specify the null character as the last character. In addition to this, as you can see, the size of the array is not specified. *Can you guess what will be the size of mess*? In fact it is the number of character constants specified, including the null character.

Since strings will be used very often, the C language provides a short and efficient approach for initializing strings.

For example, the task of above statement can also be accomplished as

```
char mess[] = "You are wel come";
```

Note that in this approach, the compiler automatically appends the null character.

12.3.5 Input/Output of Strings

A string can be read and written. The C language provides library function *gets()* and *puts()* for input and output of string data.

Listing 12.11

```
/*
*  Program to perform I/O of string data with string I/O functions
*/
#include<stdio.h>
#include<string.h>
int main()
{
   char str[30];
   printf( "\nEnter string of length <= 29" );
   printf( "\nand terminate with ENTER key\n\n" );
   gets( str );
   printf( "\nYou have entered\n\n" );
   puts( str );
   return 0;
}
```

Test Run

```
Enter string of length <= 29
and terminate with ENTER key

There is no substitute of hard work.↵

You have entered

There is no substitute of hard work.
```

12.3.6 String Manipulation Functions

Almost every C compiler provides a large number of library functions for manipulating strings. Table 12.1 lists some frequently used string functions.

Table 12.1: Frequently Used String Functions

String Function	Operation Performed
strlen	Finds length of a string.
strcat	Appends the characters of second argument at the end of first string variable.
strcpy	Copies the character of source string constant or variable to destination string variable.
strcmp	Compares two strings (comparison is case sensitive).
strrev	Reverses the string. Only supported by Turbo C.

Let us discuss some of these string functions one by one.

12.3.6.1 The *strlen()* Function

This function takes one argument that can be a string constant or a variable. It counts the number of character present in the string. Do remember that null character '\0' is not a part of the character; it is merely used to mark the end of the string, so it is not counted.

Listing 12.12

```
/*  Program to illustrate the use of strlen()function  */

#include <stdio.h>
#include <string.h>

int main()
{
   char str[30];
   int len;
   printf( "\nEnter a string of length <= 29" );
   printf( "\nand terminate with ENTER key" );
   gets (str);
   len = strlen ( str );
   printf( "Number of characters in %s = %d\n", str, len );
   return 0;
}
```

Test Run

```
Enter string of length <= 29
and terminate with ENTER key
Turbo↵
Number of characters in Turbo = 5
```

12.3.6.2 The *strcat()* Function

This function takes two arguments, of which first is a string variable and second can be a string constant or a variable. It appends the character(s) of the second arguments at the end of the first argument. There must be sufficient space available to accommodate the incoming characters from destination string, otherwise overflow occurs.

Listing 12.13

```
/*  Program to illustrate the use of strcat()function   */

#include <stdio.h>
#include <string.h>

int main()
{
   char str1[30] = "Wel", str2[30] = " Come";
   printf( "\nFirst string is %s\n", str1 );
   printf( "Second string is %s\n", str2 );
   strcat( str1, str2 );
   printf( "First string after appending\n" );
   printf( "second one: %s\n", str1 );
   return 0;
}
```

Test Run

```
First string is Wel
Second string is Come
First string after appending
second one: Wel Come
```

12.3.6.3 The *strcpy()* Function

This function takes two arguments, of which first is a string variable and second can be a string constant or a variable. It copies the character(s) of the second arguments to the first argument.

The following program illustrates its use.

Listing 12.14

```
/* Program to illustrate the use of strcpy()function */

#include <stdio.h>
#include <string.h>

int main()
{
   char str1[30] = "Wel", str2[30] = " Come";
   printf( "\nFirst string is %s\n", str1 );
   printf( "Second string is %s\n", str2 );
   strcpy( str1, str2 );
   printf( "First string after copying\n" );
   printf( "second one: %s\n", str1 );
   return 0;
}
```

Test Run

```
First string is Wel
Second string is Come
First string after copying
second one: Come
```

12.3.6.4 The *strcmp()* Function

This function takes two arguments, of which both can be string variables or constants. It compares the characters of each but one at a time and returns a value indicating the result of the comparison. For example, in the statement

```
strcmp ( str1, str2 );
```

value returned will have the following meanings:

Table 12.2: Interpretation of value returned *by strcmp()* function

Value Returned	Meaning
Less than zero	*str1* is less than *str2*, *i.e.*, *str1* comes first *str2* in dictionary order.
Zero	*str1* is identical to *str2*.
Greater than zero	*str1* is greater *str2* i.e. *str1* comes after *str2* in dictionary order.

The following program illustrates its use.

Listing 12.15

```
/*  Program to illustrate the use of strcmp()function  */
#include <stdio.h>
#include <string.h>
int main()
{
    char str1[31], str2[31];
    int value;
    printf( "Enter first  string: " );
    gets(str1);
    printf( "\nEnter second string: " );
    gets( str2 );
    value = strcmp( str1, str2 );
    if ( value > 0 )
    {
       printf("\n%s comes after %s", str1, str2);
       printf(" in dictionary order\n" );
    } else if ( value < 0 ) {
       printf("\n%s comes before %s", str1, str2);
       printf(" in dictionary order\n" );
    } else
       printf("\nBoth strings are same\n"  );
   return 0;
}
```

Test Run

```
Enter first string: software
Enter first string: hardware
hardware comes before software in dictionary order
```

12.3.6.5 The *strrev()* Function

This function takes string variable as its single argument. It reverses the string i.e. the last character becomes the first one, the second last becomes the second one, and so on. To illustrate its use, let us consider an interesting problem. A word is said to be a palindrome if it remains same after reversing, such as *radar*, *i.e.*, its first character is same as last character, second character is same as second last character, and so on.

The *strrev()* function is not supported by C compilers on Linux and Unix based systems.

Listing 12.16

```
/*  Program to illustrate the use of strrev()function   */
#include <stdio.h>
#include <string.h>
int main()
{
 char str1[31], str2[31];
 printf( "Enter any string of length <= 30: " );
 gets (str1);
 strcpy ( str2, str1 );
 strrev ( str2 );
 if ( ( strcmp ( str1, str2 ) ) == 0 )
    printf( "\n%s is a palindrome\n", str1 );
 else
    printf( "\n%s is not a palindrome\n", str1 );
 return 0;
}
```

Test Run

```
Enter any string of length <= 30: adda
adda is a palindrome
```

12.3.7 Passing Strings to a Function

A string can be passed as an argument to a function using subscripted notation for arrays. In a function definition, the formal parameter is declared as an array of characters. The following program illustrates the passing of a string to a function.

Listing 12.17

```
/*
*  Program to illustrates passing of a string to a function
*/
#include<stdio.h>
#include<string.h>

void func( char [] );    /*  function prototype  */

int main()
{
   char str1[] = "Sample string";
   func( str1 );
   return 0;
}

void func( char temp[] )
{
   printf( "String passed to it: " );
   puts( temp );
   printf( "\nand its length is: %d\n", strlen( temp ) );
}
```

Test Run

```
String passed to it: Sample string
and its length is: 13
```

12.3.8 Array of Strings

In the last section, we discussed string variables that can store one string value at a time. Suppose we want to handle list (array) of such strings, then *what is the solution*? The answer to this question can be found by using two-dimensional array of characters. In two-dimensional arrays, the first row stores the first string, the second row stores the second string, and so on.

Suppose, we want to handle a list of names of 4 persons, where the name of each person can be maximum of 30 characters long. The following will be the declaration

```
char names[4][31];
```

The following statement shows the way list of strings can be initialized.

```
char names[4][31] = { "Ram Parkash",
                      "Inder Mohan Singh Sidhu",
                      "Amanpreet",
                      "Rajan"
                    };
```

Listing 12.18

```
/* Program to illustrates the input/output of array of strings
 *  represented as two-dimensional array of characters
 */
#include <stdio.h>
#include <string.h>
int main()
{
   char names[50][31];
   int i, n;
   printf( "Enter number of strings: " );
   scanf( "%d", &n );
   for ( i = 0; i < n; ++i ) {
      printf( "Enter string number %d: ", i+1 );
      gets( names[i] );
   }
   printf( "\nList of given strings\n\n" );
   for ( i = 0; i < n; ++i )
      puts ( names[i] );
   return 0;
}
```

But this scheme of representing list of strings has one serious problem. The problem is of memory wastage. As in the above example, we assumed that the name could be up to 30 characters long, so we have declared the string length equal to 30. In fact, some names may be of few characters long while others roughly half of the declared length. So, on average, half of the allocated space is not utilized at all. Using array of pointers to strings can solve this problem of memory wastage. We will discuss this aspect in *Chapter 20*.

12.4 SUPPLEMENTARY PROBLEMS

Problem 12.1:

Write a function that takes an array of *n* integer numbers as its argument, and reverses the order of its elements without using any other array. For example, if elements of the array are

2 4 1 6 7 9 15 12

The function should rearrange the array as

12 15 9 7 6 1 4 2

Solution: To accomplish the above task, we use two index variables i and j, where index variable i is initialized with the index of the first element, and index variable j is initialized with the index of the last element. Now elements at index i and at index j are swapped. Then index variable i is incremented and index variable j is decremented, and this is continued till $i \leq j$. The function *reverseElements()* implements the above logic. Following is the complete listing for the program to accomplish above task.

Listing 12.19

```
/* Program to reverse the order of elements of the array   */
#include <stdio.h>
void reverseElements(int a[], int n);  /* function prototype */
int main()
{
    int a[100], n, i;
    printf("\nEnter even value for n as size of array : ");
    scanf("%d", &n);
    printf("Enter %d elements of array A\n", n);
    for ( i = 0; i < n; i++ )
        scanf("%d", &a[i]);
    reverseElements(a,n);         /*  call function    */
    printf("\nElements of array after reversing the order of ");
    printf(" elements of a given array\n\n");
    for ( i = 0; i < n; i++ )
        printf("%d   ", a[i]);
    return 0;
}
void reverseElements(int a[], int n)
{
   int i, j, temp;
   i = 0; j = n-1;
   while ( i <= j ) {
      temp = a[i];
      a[i] = a[j];
      a[j] = temp;
      i++;
      j--;
   }
}
```

Problem 12.2:

Write a function that takes an array of n (where n is even) integer numbers as its argument, and rearrange its elements in such a way that values of alternate locations of the array are exchanged. For example, if the elements of the array are

2 4 1 6 7 9 15 12

The function should rearrange the array as

4 2 6 1 9 7 12 15

Solution: To accomplish the above task, we use index variable *i* and vary it from 0 to (n-1) in steps of 2. In each iteration, element at index *i* and at index (i+1) are swapped. The function *rearrangeElements()* implements the above logic.

Listing 12.20

```
/*
 *  Program to rearrange the elements of array in such a way
 *  that values of alternate locations of the array are exchanged.
 */
#include <stdio.h>
void rearrangeElements(int a[],int n); /* function prototype */
int main()
{
    int a[100], n, i;
    printf("\nEnter even value for n as size of array : ");
      scanf("%d", &n);
    printf("Enter %d elements of array A\n", n);
    for ( i = 0; i < n; i++ )
       scanf("%d", &a[i]);
    rearrangeElements(a,n);    /*  call function   */
    printf("\nElements of array after swapping the alternate");
    printf(" elements of a given array\n\n");
    for ( i = 0; i < n; i++ )
       printf("%d  ", a[i]);
    return 0;
}
void rearrangeElements(int a[], int n)
{
    int i, temp;
    for ( i = 0; i < n; i += 2 ) {
       temp = a[i];
       a[i] = a[i+1];
       a[i+1] = temp;
   }
}
```

Problem 12.3:

Write a program that read a matrix of size $m \times n$, computes sum of its rows and columns and prints the output in the following format.

```
12   9  10  13  | 44
 7  11  22   5  | 45  <------  row sums
 6  25  21  15  | 67
20   8  33  16  | 77
-----------------------
 45  53  86  49 <------  column sums
```

Solution: To accomplish the above task, we create two one-dimensional arrays named *colSum* and *rowSum* to store the sum of elements of respective rows and columns. Once these sums are computed, we print the elements of the array *rowSum* as the last column after printing all elements of a given row of the given matrix. After printing all the rows of the given matrix, we print the elements of the array *colSum* as the last row.

The following program implements the details.

Listing 12.21

```
/*  Program to find row sums and column sums of the given matrix  */
#include<stdio.h>
int main()
{
    int a[10][10], rowSum[10] = {0}, colSum[10] = {0};
    int i, j, n, m;
    printf( "Enter size of matrix A as m,n: " );
    scanf( "%d,%d", &m, &n);
    for ( i = 0 ; i < m; i++ ) {
       for ( j = 0; j < n; j++ ) {
          scanf( "%d", &a[i][j] );
       }
    }
    /*   compute the sum of elements of rows    */
    for ( i = 0 ; i < m; i++ ) {
       for ( j = 0; j < n; j++ ) {
          rowSum[i] += a[i][j];
       }
    }
    /*   compute the sum of elements of columns    */
    for ( j = 0 ; j < n; j++ )
    {
       for ( i = 0; i < m; i++ ) {
          colSum[j] += a[i][j];
       }
    }
    /*   print the output    */
    for ( i = 0 ; i < m; i++ ) {
       for ( j = 0; j < n; j++ ) {
          printf("%5d", a[i][j]);
       }
       printf("   |%5d\n", rowSum[i]);
    }
    for ( j = 0; j < n; j++ )
       printf("-----");
    for ( j = 0; j < n; j++ ) {
       printf("%5d", colSum[j]);
    }
    printf("\n");
    return 0;
}
```

EXERCISE

1. What is an array?
2. Is it possible to declare and initialize an array in C simultaneously? If yes, how?
3. What are the rules for naming an array?
4. What is the subscript of the first element of the array?
5. How a real array named *data* with 100 elements will be declared? What will be the subscript of the last element?
6. Is it possible to declare more than one array in the same declaration statement?

10. Is the following array declaration is correct? If not, why?

```
int a(50);
```

11. If the declaration segment is

```
#define ROWS  100
float height[ROWS];
```

Is the following segment to enter data in array is correct?

```
for ( i = 0; i <= ROWS; i++ )
     scanf ( "%f", height[i] );
```

12. When an array is passed as an argument to a function, what is actually passed?
13. When an entire array is passed as an argument to a function, the function can alter the values of the elements of the array. We want to prevent the function from doing so, how this task can be accomplished?
14. Is any thing wrong with the following declaration? Explain.

```
int a[3][] = { { 1, 2, 3 }, { 3, 2, 1 }, { 4, 5, 2 } };
```

15. How a string is stored in C language?
16. What will be the declaration for array named *str* in which string "*C is just like sea*" is to be stored?
17. What is the difference between "A" and 'A'?
18. Consider the following declaration

```
char name[20];
```

What is the maximum length of string which can be stored correctly in name?

20. Consider the following declaration

```
char name[20];
```

Is following the correct way of assigning string "*Rajan Mehta*" to *name*?

```
name = "Rajan Mehta";
```

PROGRAMMING EXERCISE

1. Write a program that accepts an array, interchanges first element with last element, second element with second last element, and so on, and finally prints the new array.
2. Write a function, say *void transpose(float a[][], int n)*, that computes the transpose of a square matrix *A* of size $n \times n$. Note that the transpose of the matrix is to be stored in the original matrix itself not in a separate matrix.
3. Write a program to read a set of *n* integers between 1 and 10 and count the number of times each integer appears in the set. Print the integers in order of frequency, the number occurring the highest number of times first.
4. A department store chain has *m* (≤10) stores, and each store has the same *n* (≤15) departments. The weekly sales of the chain are stored in $m \times n$ array *SALES* (say). Write down the program which

   Prints the total weekly sales of each store.
   Prints the total weekly sales of each department.
   Prints the total weekly sales of the chain.
5. Write a program which inserts an element *d* in *k*th position of an array *a* of size *n*.
6. Write a program to remove duplicate elements from an array array.
7. Given a matrix *A* of order $m \times n$, write a program to find the row having the maximum number of elements which are even.
8. A square matrix *A* of size *nxn* is said to be symmetric if element $a_{ij} = a_{ji}$ for all values of *i* and *j*. Write a function, say *int isSymmetric(int a[][], int n)* that returns value 1 if the input matrix is symmetric else returns value 0.
9. Suppose you are given a sample of *n* (≤100) values between 1 and 18. Write a program that builds the frequency array and prints it in the form of a histogram.
10. Given a matrix *A* of order $m \times n$, write a program to sort the even rows in ascending order and odd rows in descending order
11. Write a program that asks the user to enter a sentence and then splits out the words in the sentence and puts them in a table.
12. Write a program that asks the user for a list of words and prints the list in reverse order.
13. Suppose you translate a number into a string of digits spelled out, one word for each digit, followed by a single space. For example, the number 407 become the digit string: "*Four Zero Seven*". If the number 407.8, then its digit string is "*Four Zero Seven Point Eight*". Write a program to accept a positive number and print out its digit string.

❑ ❑ ❑

Chapter 13

Implementation of Basic Algorithms

Learning Objectives

After reading this chapter, students will be able to

- write programs for various searching algorithms
- write programs for various sorting algorithms
- write program to find root of an equation
- write program to find numerical differentiation
- write program to find numerical integration

13.1 INTRODUCTION

In this section, we will implement few basic algorithms for searching, sorting, computing roots of an equation, numerically computing differentiation and integration of a function.

13.2 SEARCHING ALGORITHMS

Searching is the process of finding the location of given element in an array. The search is said to be successful if the given element is found, i.e., the element does exists in the array; otherwise unsuccessful.

There are two approaches to search operation:

- Linear search
- Binary search

The algorithm that one chooses generally depends on organization of the array elements. If the elements are in random order, then one have to use linear search technique, and if the array elements are sorted, then it is preferable to use binary search technique. These two search techniques are described in the next sections.

13.2.1 Linear Search

Given no information about the array *a*, the only way to search for given element *item* is to compare *item* with each element of *a* one by one. This method, which traverses *a* sequentially to locate *item* is called *linear search* or *sequential search*.

Listing 13.1

```
/*
 *   Program to demonstrate the use of linear search to search
 *   a given element in an un-sorted array
 */

#include <stdio.h>

int main()
{
   int a[50], i, n, item, flag;
   printf("\nEnter size of array : " );
   scanf("%d", &n );
   printf("\nEnter %d elements of array\n", n);
   for ( i = 0; i < n; i++ )
      scanf( "%d", &a[i] );
   printf( "\nEnter element to search : " );
   scanf( "%d", &item );
   flag = 0;
```

```
   for ( i = 0; i < n; i++ ) {
      if( item == a[i] )        /* match found   */
      {
          flag = 1;
          break;
      }
   }
  if ( flag == -1 )
     printf( "\nElement found at index: %d\n", i );
  else
     printf( "\nElement not found...\n" );
  return 0;
}
```

Test Run 1

```
Enter size of array : 10
Enter 10 elements of array
12
5
18
9
11
10
25
36
22
100
Enter element to search : 11
Element found at index: 4
```

Test Run 2

```
Enter size of array : 10
Enter 10 elements of array
12
5
18
9
11
10
25
36
22
100
Enter element to search : 55
Element not found...
```

Complexity Analysis

In the best possible case, the *item* may occur at first position. In this case, the search operation terminates in success with just one comparison. However, the worst case occurs when either the item is present at last position or missing from the array. In the former case, the search terminates in success with n comparisons. In the later case, the search terminates in a failure with n comparisons. Thus, we find that in worst case the linear search is $O(n)$ operations.

13.2.2 Binary Search

Suppose the elements of the array A are sorted in ascending order (if the elements are numbers) or dictionary order (if the elements are strings). The best searching algorithm, called *binary search,* is used to find the location of the given element. We do use this approach in our daily life. For example, suppose we want to find the meaning of the term *modem* in a computer dictionary. Obviously, we don't search page by page. We open the dictionary in the middle (roughly) to determine which half contains the term being sought. Then for the subsequent search one half is discarded, and we search in the other half. This process is continued till either we have located the required term or that term is missing from the dictionary, which will indicated by the fact that at the end we will be left with only one page.

Example 13.1:

To illustrate the working of the binary search technique, consider the following sorted array A with 7 elements

3, 10, 15, 20, 35, 40, 60

and we want to search element 15.

Solution:

	$a[0]$	$a[1]$	$a[2]$	$a[3]$	$a[4]$	$a[5]$	$a[6]$
Given Array *a*	3	10	15	20	35	40	60

To start with, we take $beg = 0$, $end = 6$, and compute location of middle element as

$$mid = (beg + end) / 2 = (0 + 6) / 2 = 3$$

Since $a[mid]$, *i.e.*, $a[3] \neq 15$, and $beg < end$. We start next iteration.

As $a[mid] = 20 > 15$, therefore, we take $end = mid - 1 = 3 - 1 = 2$, where as beg remains unchanged. Thus

$$mid = (beg + end) / 2 = (0 + 2) / 2 = 1$$

Since $a[mid]$, *i.e.*, $a[1] \neq 15$, and $beg < end$. We start next iteration.

As $a[mid] = 10 < 15$, therefore, we take $beg = mid + 1 = 1 + 1 = 2$, where as *end* remains unchanged.

Since $beg = end$, again compute location of the middle element as

$$mid = (beg + end)\,/\,2 = (\,2 + 2\,)\,/\,2 = 2$$

Since $a[mid]$, *i.e.*, $a[2] = 15$, the search terminates on success.

The element is found at index 2.

Listing 13.2

```
/*
 *   Program to demonstrate the use of linear search to search
 *   a given element in a sorted array
 */

#include <stdio.h>

int main()
{
    int a[50], i, n, item, beg, end, mid, flag;
    printf("\nEnter size of array : " );
    scanf("%d", &n );
    printf("\nEnter %d elements of array in ascending order\n", n);
    for ( i = 0; i < n; i++ )
       scanf( "%d", &a[i] );
    printf( "\nEnter element to search : " );
    scanf( "%d", &item );
    flag = 0;
    beg = 0;
    end = n - 1;
    while ( beg < end )
    {
       mid = ( beg + end ) / 2;
       if( item == a[mid] )       /* match found  */
       {
          flag = 1;
          break;
       }
       if( item < a[mid] )
          end = mid - 1;
       else
          beg = mid + 1;
    }
   if ( flag == 1 )
      printf( "\nElement found at index: %d\n", mid );
   else
      printf( "\nElement not found...\n" );
   return 0;
}
```

Test Run 1

```
Enter size of array : 10
Enter 10 elements of array in ascending order
5
9
10
11
12
18
25
36
44
100
Enter element to search : 44
Element found at index: 8
```

Test Run 2

```
Enter size of array : 10
Enter 10 elements of array in ascending order
5
9
10
11
12
18
25
36
44
100
Enter element to search : 35
Element not found...
```

Complexity Analysis

In each iteration, the search is reduced to one half of the array. Therefore, for n elements in the array, there will be $\log_2 n$ iterations or recursive calls. Thus, the complexity of binary search is $O(\log_2 n)$. This complexity will be same irrespective of the position of the element, even if it is not present in the array.

13.3 SORTING ALGORITHMS

Sorting is the process of arranging the elements in some logical order. This logical order may be ascending or descending in case of numeric values or dictionary order in case of alphanumeric values.

We do, almost, use this process daily in our routine activities. For example, we do arrange our class notes in increasing order of date in order to refer them quickly later on. Like this there are many situations, which you can enumerate.

In this section, we sill discuss following sorting algorithms:

- Bubble sort
- Insertion sort
- Selection sort

13.3.1 Bubble Sort

The Bubble sort method requires $(n-1)$ pass to sort an array. In each pass every element $a[i]$ is compared with $a[i+1]$, for $i = 0$ to $(n-k)$, where k is the pass number and if they are out of order, *i.e.*, if $a[i] > a[i+1]$, they are swapped. This will cause the largest element move or bubble up.

Thus, after the end of the first pass the largest element in the array will be placed in nth position, and on each successive pass, the next largest element is placed at position $(n-1)$, $(n-2)$, ..., 2, respectively.

For more clarity, carefully examine the following steps.

Pass 1:

Step 1. If $a[0] > a[1]$ then swap $a[0]$ and $a[1]$.
Step 2. If $a[1] > a[2]$ then swap $a[1]$ and $a[2]$.
⋮
Step $n-1$. If $a[n-2] > a[n-1]$ then swap $a[n-2]$ and $a[n-1]$.

Pass 2:

Step 1. If $a[0] > a[1]$ then swap $a[0]$ and $a[1]$.
Step 2. If $a[1] > a[2]$ then swap $a[1]$ and $a[2]$.
⋮
Step $n-2$. If $a[n-3] > a[n-2]$ then swap $a[n-3]$ and $a[n-2]$.

⋮

Pass k:

Step 1. If $a[0] > a[1]$ then swap $a[0]$ and $a[1]$.
Step 2. If $a[1] > a[2]$ then swap $a[1]$ and $a[2]$.
⋮
Step $n-k$. If $a[n-k+1] > a[n-k]$ then swap $a[n-k+1]$ and $a[n-k]$.

⋮

Pass $n-1$:

Step 1. If $a[0] > a[1]$ then swap $a[0]$ and $a[1]$.

After $(n-1)$ passes, the array will be sorted in ascending order.

Example 13.2:

To illustrate the working of bubble sort method, consider the sorting of the following array in ascending order.

12 40 3 2 15

Solution: Note that, the output of a given pass becomes the input for the next pass. The sorting process is self explanatory. In each pass, one element, shown as shaded, reaches to its final position. Given array can be shown as

a[0]	*a*[1]	*a*[2]	*a*[3]	*a*[4]
12	40	3	2	15

Pass-1:

a[0]	*a*[1]	*a*[2]	*a*[3]	*a*[4]
(12)	(40)	3	2	15

(*a*) Compare $a[0]$ and $a[1]$. Since $a[0] < a[1]$ $(12 < 40)$, no action is taken.

a[0]	*a*[1]	*a*[2]	*a*[3]	*a*[4]
12	(40)	(3)	2	15

(*b*) Compare $a[1]$ and $a[2]$. Since $a[1] > a[2]$ $(40 > 3)$, swap these elements.

a[0]	*a*[1]	*a*[2]	*a*[3]	*a*[4]
12	3	(40)	(2)	15

(*c*) Compare $a[2]$ and $a[3]$. Since $a[2] > a[3]$ $(40 > 2)$, swap these elements.

a[0]	*a*[1]	*a*[2]	*a*[3]	*a*[4]
12	3	2	(40)	(15)

(*d*) Compare $a[3]$ and $a[4]$. Since $a[3] > a[4]$ $(40 > 15)$, swap these elements.

a[0]	*a*[1]	*a*[2]	*a*[3]	*a*[4]
12	3	2	15	40

Thus, after first pass, the largest element, 40, has moved to its final position. However, the rest of the numbers, which may have changed their positions, are yet to be sorted. The shaded part shows the elements that have been sorted.

For the remaining passes, only comparisons and swaps, if required, are shown.

Pass-2:

a[0]	*a*[1]	*a*[2]	*a*[3]	*a*[4]	Action
(12)	(3)	2	15	40	Swap
3	(12)	(2)	15	40	Swap
3	2	(12)	(15)	40	No swap
3	2	12	15	40	

After second pass, the second largest element, 15, has moved to its final position.

Pass-3:

a[0]	*a*[1]	*a*[2]	*a*[3]	*a*[4]	Action
(3)	(2)	12	15	40	Swap
2	(3)	(12)	15	40	No swap
2	3	12	15	40	

After third pass, the third largest element, 12, has moved to its final position.

Pass-4:

a[0]	*a*[1]	*a*[2]	*a*[3]	*a*[4]	Action
(2)	(3)	12	15	40	No swap
2	3	12	15	40	

After fourth pass, the fourth largest element, 3, has moved to its final position. Thus, the array is completely sorted in 4 passes.

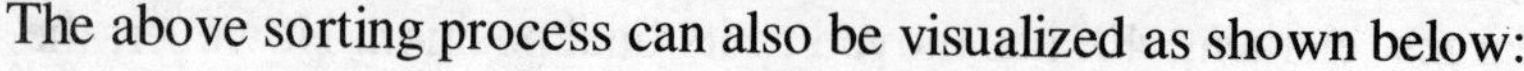

The above sorting process can also be visualized as shown below:

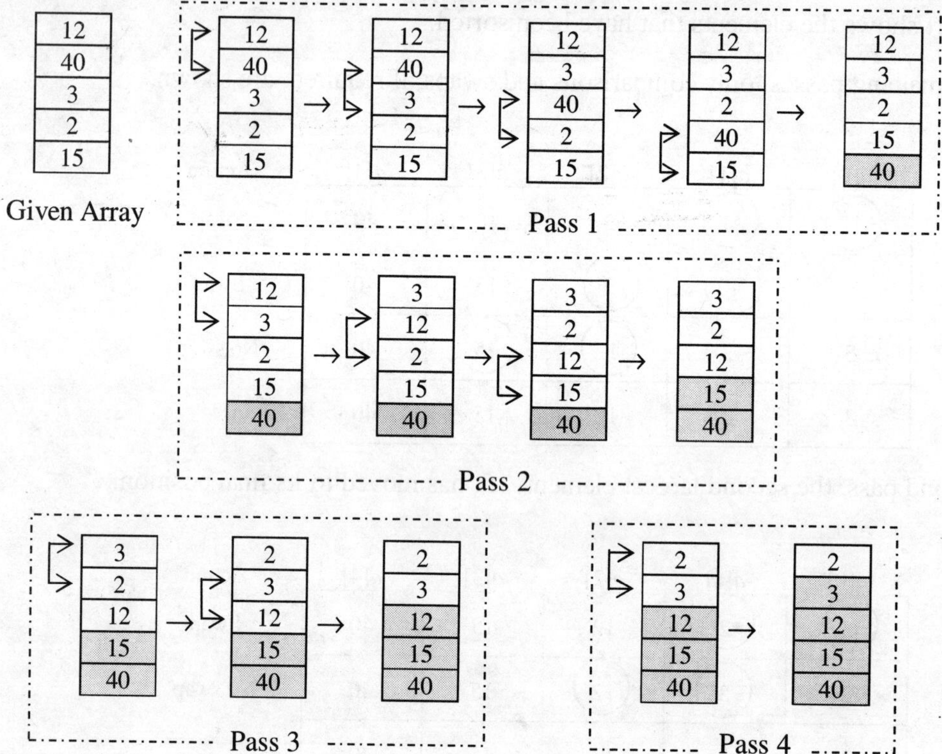

Figure 13.1: Illustration of Bubble sort method

Complexity Analysis

After $(n-1)$ passes, the array will be sorted in ascending order. As you must have noticed, the first pass requires $(n-1)$ comparisons, the second pass requires $(n-2)$,..., kth pass requires $(n-k)$, and the last pass requires only one comparison. Therefore, total comparisons are

$$f(n) = (n-1) + (n-2) + (n-3) + \ldots + (n-k) + \ldots + 3 + 2 + 1 = n(n-1)/2 = O(n^2)$$

Listing 13.3

```
/*
*    Program to demonstrate the use of Bubble sort method to sort a
*    a given array in ascending order
*/

#include <stdio.h>

int main()
```

```
{
   int a[50], i, j, n, temp;
   printf("\nEnter size of array : " );
   scanf("%d", &n );
   printf("\nEnter %d elements of array\n", n);
   for ( i = 0; i < n; i++ )
      scanf( "%d", &a[i] );
   for ( i = 0; i < n-1; i++ ) {
      for ( j = 0; j < n-i-1; j++ ) {
         if ( a[j] > a[j+1] ) {
             temp = a[j];
             a[j] = a[j+1];
             a[j+1] = temp;
         }
      }
   }
   printf( "\nArray after sorting...\n\n" );
   for ( i = 0; i < n; i++ )
       printf( "%d ", a[i] );
   printf( "\n" );
   return 0;
}
```

Test Run

```
Enter size of array : 10

Enter 10 elements of array
5
12
10
15
22
18
2
-10
7
16

Array after sorting...

-10 2 5 7 10 12 15 16 18 22
```

13.3.2 Selection Sort

Selection sort method also requires (n–1) pass to sort an array. In the first pass, find the smallest element from elements a[0], a[1], a[2], . . ., a[n–1] and swap with the first element, *i.e*, a[0]. In the second pass, find the smallest element from elements a[1], a[2], a[3], . . ., a[n–1] and swap with a[1]. And so on.

For more clarity, carefully examine the following steps.

Pass 1:

- Find the location *loc* of the smallest element in the entire array, *i.e.*, *a*[0], *a*[1], *a*[2],..., *a*[*n*−1].
- Interchange *a*[0] & *a*[*loc*]. Then *a*[0] is trivially sorted.

Pass 2:

- Find the location *loc* of the smallest element in the sub array *a*[1], *a*[2], *a*[3],. . ., *a*[*n*−1].
- Interchange *a*[1] & *a*[*loc*]. Then elements *a*[0] and *a*[1] are sorted, since *a*[0] ≤ *a*[1].

⋮

Pass *k*:

- Find the location *loc* of the smallest element in the sub array *a*[*k*], *a*[*k*+1], *a*[*k*+2],. . ., *a*[*n*−1].
- Interchange *a*[*k*] & *a*[*loc*]. Then elements *a*[0], *a*[1], *a*[2], . . ., *a*[*k*] are sorted.

⋮

Pass *n*−1:

- Find the location *loc* of the smaller of the elements *a*[*n*−2], *a*[*n*−1].
- Interchange *a*[*n*−2] & *a*[*loc*]. Then elements *a*[0], *a*[1], *a*[2], . . ., *a*[*n*−1] are sorted.

After (*n*−1) passes, the array will be sorted in ascending order.

Example 13.3:

To illustrate the working of the selection sort method, consider the following array *a* with 7 elements as

20, 35, 40, 100, 3, 10, 15

Solution: In each iteration *i*, we find the location *loc* of the smallest element in the unsorted part of the array. If *loc* ≠ *i* then element at *i* and *loc* are swapped.

	a[0]	*a*[1]	*a*[2]	*a*[3]	*a*[4]	*a*[5]	*a*[6]
Given Array *a*	20	35	40	100	3	10	15

	a[0]	*a*[1]	*a*[2]	*a*[3]	*a*[4]	*a*[5]	*a*[6]	
Pass 1:	20	35	40	100	3	10	15	*i* = 0 *loc* = 4

Interchange elements *a*[0] & *a*[4], *i.e.*, 20 & 3 to obtain following array.

Pass 2:

a[0]	a[1]	a[2]	a[3]	a[4]	a[5]	a[6]
3	35	40	100	20	10	15

$i = 1$
$loc = 5$

Interchange elements $a[1]$ & $a[5]$, *i.e.*, 35 & 10 to obtain following array.

Pass 3:

a[0]	a[1]	a[2]	a[3]	a[4]	a[5]	a[6]
3	10	40	100	20	35	15

$i = 2$
$loc = 6$

Interchange elements $a[2]$ & $a[6]$, *i.e.*, 40 & 15 to obtain following array.

Pass 4:

a[0]	a[1]	a[2]	a[3]	a[4]	a[5]	a[6]
3	10	15	100	20	35	40

$i = 3$
$loc = 4$

Interchange elements $a[3]$ & $a[4]$, *i.e.*, 100 & 20 to obtain following array.

Pass 5:

a[0]	a[1]	a[2]	a[3]	a[4]	a[5]	a[6]
3	10	15	20	100	35	40

$i = 4$
$loc = 5$

Interchange elements $a[4]$ & $a[5]$, *i.e.*, 100 & 35 to obtain following array.

Pass 6:

a[0]	a[1]	a[2]	a[3]	a[4]	a[5]	a[6]
3	10	15	20	35	100	40

$i = 5$
$loc = 6$

Interchange elements $a[5]$ & $a[6]$, *i.e.*,100 & 40 to obtain following sorted array.

a[0]	a[1]	a[2]	a[3]	a[4]	a[5]	a[6]
3	10	15	20	35	40	100

Figure 13.2: Successive passes of selection sort method

The shaded part shows the part of the array sorted so for after each iteration. In each iteration, one element is added on the right of the sorted part.

To implement the selection sort algorithm, we need a routine to find the location *loc* of the smallest element among the elements $a[k-1]$, $a[k+1]$, $a[k+2]$,. . ., $a[n-1]$, during kth pass.

Listing 13.4

```
/*
*   Program to demonstrate the use of selection sort method to sort a
*   a given array in ascending order
*/
#include <stdio.h>
int main()
{
   int a[50], i, j, n, temp, min, loc;
```

```
    printf("\nEnter size of array : " );
    scanf("%d", &n );
    printf("\nEnter %d elements of array\n", n);
    for ( i = 0; i < n; i++ )
       scanf( "%d", &a[i] );
    for ( i = 0; i < n-1; i++ ) {
       min = a[i];
       loc = i;
       for ( j = i+1; j < n; j++ ) {
          if ( a[j] < min ) {
              min = a[j];
              loc = j;
          }
       }
       if ( loc != i ) {
          temp = a[i];
          a[i] = a[loc];
          a[loc] = temp;
       }
    }
    printf( "\nArray after sorting...\n\n" );
    for ( i = 0; i < n; i++ )
        printf( "%d ", a[i] );
    printf( "\n" );
    return 0;
}
```

Test Run

```
Enter size of array : 6
Enter 6 elements of array
12
5
10
15
22
18
Array after sorting...
5 10 12 15 18 22
```

Complexity Analysis

As you must have noticed, the first pass requires $(n-1)$ comparisons to find the location *loc* of smallest element, the second pass requires $(n-2)$, ..., kth pass requires $(n-k)$, and the last pass requires only one comparison. Therefore total comparisons are

$$f(n) = (n-1) + (n-2) + (n-3) + \ldots +(n-k) + \ldots + 3 + 2 + 1$$
$$= n(n-1)/2 = O(n^2)$$

13.3.4 Insertion Sort

This algorithm is very popular with bridge players when they first sort their cards. In this procedure, we pick up a particular value and then insert it at the appropriate place in the sorted sub list, *i.e.*, during *k*th iteration the element *a*[*k*] is inserted in its proper place in the sorted sub array *a*[1], *a*[2], *a*[3], . . ., *a*[*k*–1].

This task is accomplished by comparing *a*[*k*] with *a*[*k*–1], *a*[*k*–2], *a*[*k*–3], and so on until the first element *a*[*j*] such that $a[j] \le a[k]$ is found. Then each of the elements *a*[*k*–1], *a*[*k*–2], . . ., *a*[*j*+1] are moved one position up, and then element *a*[*k*] is inserted in (*j*+1)st position in the array.

For more clarity, carefully examine the following steps.

Pass 1: *a*[1] is inserted either before or after *a*[0] so that *a*[0] and *a*[1] are sorted.

Pass 2: *a*[2] is inserted either before *a*[0] or between *a*[0] and *a*[1] or after *a*[1] so that the elements *a*[0], *a*[1], *a*[2] are sorted.

Pass 3: *a*[3] is inserted either before *a*[0] or between *a*[0] and *a*[1] or between *a*[1] and *a*[2] or after *a*[2] so that the elements *a*[0], *a*[1], *a*[2], *a*[3] are sorted.

⋮

Pass *k*: *a*[*k*] is inserted in proper place in the sorted sub array *a*[0], *a*[1], *a*[2], . . ., *a*[*k*–1] so that after insertion, the elements *a*[0], *a*[1], *a*[2], . . ., *a*[*k*–1], *a*[*k*] are sorted.

⋮

Pass *n*–1: *a*[*n*–1] is inserted in proper place in the sorted sub array *a*[0], *a*[1], *a*[2], . . ., *a*[*n*–2], so that after insertion, the elements *a*[0], *a*[1], *a*[2], . . ., *a*[*n*–1] are sorted.

Thus, after (*n*–1) passes, the array will be sorted in ascending order.

Example 13.4:

To illustrate the working of the insertion sort method, consider the following array *a* with 7 elements as

35, 20, 40, 100, 3, 10, 15

Solution: Given array *a*

a[0]	*a*[1]	*a*[2]	*a*[3]	*a*[4]	*a*[5]	*a*[6]
35	20	40	100	3	10	15

Pass 1:

a[0]	*a*[1]	*a*[2]	*a*[3]	*a*[4]	*a*[5]	*a*[6]
35	20	40	100	3	10	15

Since *a*[1] < *a*[0], insert element *a*[1] before *a*[0] giving the following array.

Pass 2:

a[0]	a[1]	a[2]	a[3]	a[4]	a[5]	a[6]
20	35	40	100	3	10	15

Since *a*[2] > *a*[1], no action is performed.

Pass 3:

a[0]	a[1]	a[2]	a[3]	a[4]	a[5]	a[6]
20	35	40	100	3	10	15

Since *a*[3] > *a*[2], again no action is performed.

Pass 4:

a[0]	a[1]	a[2]	a[3]	a[4]	a[5]	a[6]
20	35	40	100	3	10	15

Since *a*[4] is less than *a*[3], *a*[2], *a*[1] as well as *a*[0], therefore insert *a*[4] before *a*[0], giving the following array.

Pass 5:

a[0]	a[1]	a[2]	a[3]	a[4]	a[5]	a[6]
3	20	35	40	100	10	15

Since *a*[5] is less than *a*[4], *a*[3], *a*[2], and *a*[1], therefore insert *a*[5] before *a*[1], giving the following array.

Pass 6:

a[0]	a[1]	a[2]	a[3]	a[4]	a[5]	a[6]
3	10	20	35	40	100	15

Since *a*[6] is less than *a*[5], *a*[4], *a*[3], and *a*[2], therefore insert *a*[6] before *a*[2], giving the following sorted array.

a[0]	a[1]	a[2]	a[3]	a[4]	a[5]	a[6]
3	10	15	20	35	40	100

Figure 13.3: Successive passes of insertion sort method

Listing 13.5

```
/*
*   Program to demonstrate the use of insertion sort method to sort a
*   a given array in ascending order
*/
#include <stdio.h>
int main()
{
   int a[50], i, j, k, n, temp, min, loc;
   printf("\nEnter size of array : " );
   scanf("%d", &n );
   printf("\nEnter %d elements of array\n", n);
   for ( i = 0; i < n; i++ )
```

```
        scanf( "%d", &a[i] );
    for ( k = 1; k < n; k++ ) {
        temp = a[k];
        j = k - 1;
        while ( ( temp < a[j] ) && ( j >= 0 ) ) {
            a[j+1] = a[j];
            j--;
        }
        a[j+1] = temp;
    }
    printf( "\nArray after sorting...\n\n" );
    for ( i = 0; i < n; i++ )
        printf( "%d ", a[i] );
    printf( "\n" );
    return 0;
}
```

Test Run

```
Enter size of array : 7
Enter 7 elements of array
5
12
10
15
22
18
16
Array after sorting...
5 10 12 15 16 18 22
```

13.3.4 Merge Sort

Merge sort is a sorting algorithm that uses the idea of *divide and conquers*. This algorithm divides the array into two halves, sorts them separately, and then merges them. This procedure is recursive, with the base criteria — the number of elements in the array are not more than 1.

Suppose variable *beg* and *end* represents the index of the first and last element of the array respectively, the merge sort can be defined recursively as

```
If ( beg < end ) then
   Divide the list into two halves
   Mergesort the left half
   Mergesort the right half
   Merge the two-sorted halves into one sorted list
Endif
```

Example 13.5:

To illustrate the working of the merge sort method, consider the following array *a* with 7 elements as

33, 26, 35, 29, 18, 10, 24

Solution: The following figure demonstrates successive steps of merge sort.

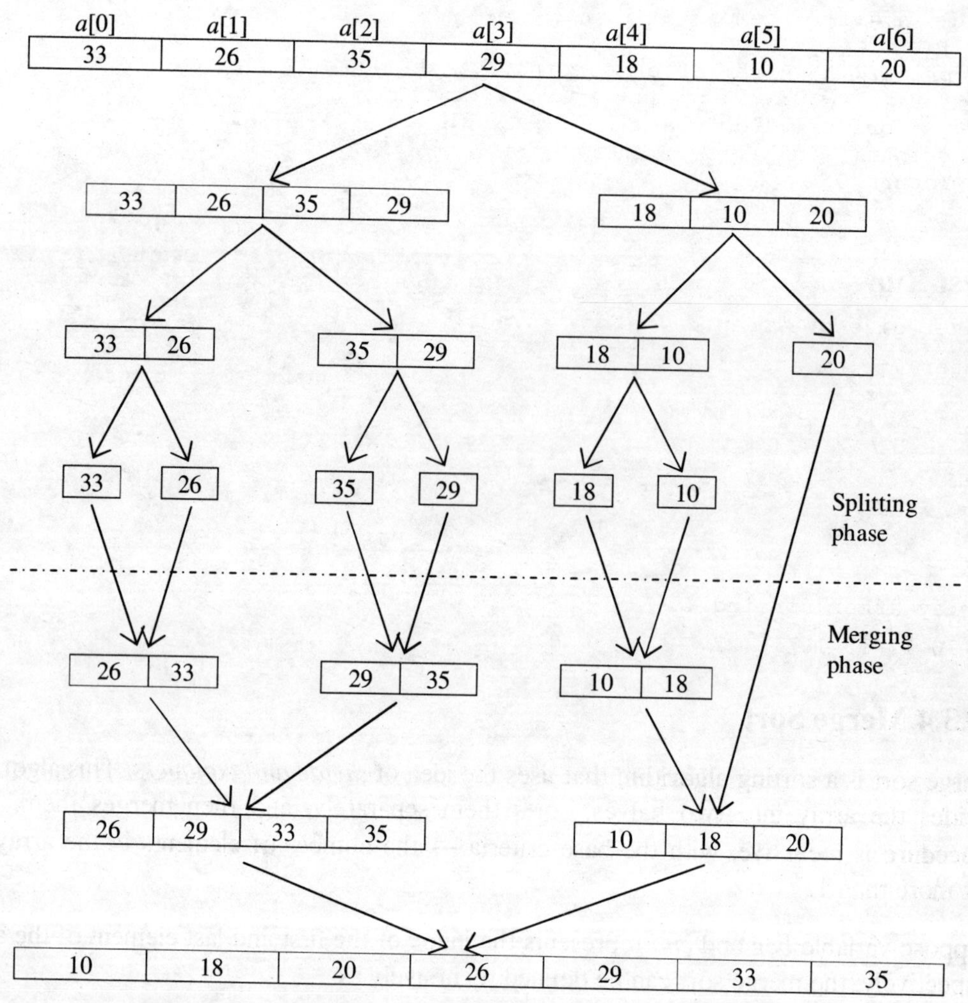

Figure 13.4: Illustration of successive steps of Merge sort

Complexity Analysis

The major work is done in the merge procedure, which is an O(n) operation. The merge procedure is called from merge-sort procedure after the array is divided into two halves, and each half has been sorted. In each of the recursive calls, one for left half and one for right half, the array is divided into halves, thus dividing the array into four segments. At each level, the number of segments doubles. Therefore, the total divisions are $\log_2 n$.

Hence, total number of comparisons

$$f(n) = n \times \log_2 n = O(n\log_2 n)$$

Listing 13.6

```
/*
*   Program to demonstrate the use of merge sort method to sort a
*   a given array in ascending order
*/
#include <stdio.h>
void mergeSortMethod( int a[], int beg, int end );
void mergingSortedSubArrays(int a[50],int lb,int lr,int rb,int rr);
int main()
{
   int i, n, a[50];
   printf( "\nEnter size of array : " );
   scanf( "%d", &n );
   printf( "\nEnter %d elements of array\n\n", n );
   for ( i = 0; i < n; i++ )
      scanf( "%d", &a[i] );
   mergeSortMethod( a, 0, n-1 );
   printf( "\nArray after sorting...\n\n" );
   for ( i = 0; i < n; i++ )
       printf( "%d ", a[i] );
   printf( "\n" );
   return 0;
}
void mergeSortMethod( int a[], int beg, int end )
{
   int mid;
   if ( beg < end )   {
      mid = ( beg + end ) / 2;
      mergeSortMethod( a, beg, mid );
      mergeSortMethod( a, mid+1, end );
      mergingSortedSubArrays( a, beg, mid, mid+1, end );
   }
}
void mergingSortedSubArrays(int a[50],int lb,int lr,int rb,int rr)
{
   int na, nb, nc, k, c[50];
   na = lb;
   nb = rb;
   nc = lb;
   while ( ( na <= lr ) && ( nb <= rr ) ) {
      if ( a[na] < a[nb] )
         c[nc] = a[na++];
      else
```

```
         c[nc] = a[nb++];
      nc++;
   }
   if ( na > lr )
   {
      while ( nb <= rr )
         c[nc++] = a[nb++];
   } else {
      while ( na <= lr )
         c[nc++] = a[na++];
   }
   for ( k = lb; k <= rr; k++ )
     a[k] = c[k];
}
```

Test Run

```
Enter size of array : 6
Enter 6 elements of array
33
26
29
18
10
24
Array after sorting...
10 18 24 26 29 33
```

13.3.5 Quick Sort

Quicksort is a sorting algorithm that also, like merge sort, uses the idea of *divide and conquer*. This algorithm finds the element, called *pivot*, that partitions the array into two halves in such a way that the elements in the left sub array are less than and the elements in the right sub array are greater than the partitioning element. Then these two sub arrays are sorted separately. This procedure is recursive in nature with the base criteria – the number of elements in the array are not more than 1.

Suppose variable *beg* and *end* represents the index of the first and last element of the array respectively, the quick sort can be defined recursively as

```
If ( beg < end ) then
   Find the location of the pivot such that it partitions the
   array into two halves
   Quicksort the left half
   Quicksort the right half
Endif
```

Example 13.6:

To illustrate the above procedure, consider the array

25 10 30 15 20 28

Solution: The following figure demonstrates successive steps of quick sort.

a[0]	*a*[1]	*a*[2]	*a*[3]	*a*[4]	*a*[5]
25	10	30	15	20	28
20	10	30	25	30	28
15	10	20	25	28	30
10	15	20	25	28	30
10	15	20	25	28	30

Figure 13.5: Illustration of successive steps of Quick sort, here circled element is the partitioning element (also called *pivot* element)

Complexity Analysis

To find the location of the element that splits the array into two sections is an O(n) operation, because every element in the array is compared to the dividing element.

After the division, each section is examined separately. If the array is split approximately in half (which is not usually), then there will be $\log_2 n$ splits.

Therefore, the total comparisons are

$$f(n) = n \times \log_2 n = O(n \log_2 n)$$

Quick sort is sensitive to the order of the input data. And it gives the worst case performance when the elements are already in the ascending order. Then it divides the array into sections of 1 and (n–1) elements in each call. Thus, there will be (n–1) partitions, in all.

Therefore, in this case, the total number of comparisons

$$f(n) = n \times (n - 1) = O(n^2)$$

The efficiency of quick Sort is affected by the initial order of elements.

Listing 13.7

```
/* Program to demonstrate the use of quick sort method to sort a
*  a given array in ascending order */
#include <stdio.h>
typedef enum { false, true } boolean;
int partitionArray( int a[], int beg, int end );
void quickSortRecursive( int a[], int lb, int ub );
int main()
{
   int i, n, a[50];
   printf( "\nEnter size of array : " );
   scanf( "%d", &n );
   printf( "\nEnter %d elements of array\n\n", n );
   for ( i = 0; i < n; i++ )
      scanf( "%d", &a[i] );
   quickSortRecursive( a, 0, n-1 );
   printf( "\nArray after sorting...\n\n" );
   for ( i = 0; i < n; i++ )
      printf( "%d ", a[i] );
   printf( "\n" );
   return 0;
}
void quickSortRecursive(  int a[], int lb, int ub )
{
    int loc;
    if ( lb < ub ) {
         loc = partitionArray( a, lb, ub );
         quickSortRecursive( a, lb, loc-1 );
         quickSortRecursive( a, loc+1, ub );
    }
}
int partitionArray( int a[], int beg, int end )
{
    int left, right, temp, loc;
    boolean done;
    left = loc = beg;
    right = end;
    done = false;
    while ( !done ) {
         while ( ( a[loc] < a[right] ) && ( loc != right ) )
              right--;
         if ( loc == right )
            done = true;
         else {
            temp = a[loc];
              a[loc] = a[right];
              a[right] = temp;
              left = loc + 1;
              loc = right;
         }
         if ( !done ) {
              while ( ( a[loc] > a[left] ) && ( loc != left ) )
                   left++;
              if ( loc == left )
```

```
                done = true;
            else {
                temp = a[loc];
                 a[loc] = a[left];
                 a[left] = temp;
                 right = loc - 1;
                 loc = left;
            }
        }
    }
    return loc;
}
```

Test Run

```
Enter size of array : 6
Enter 6 elements of array
25
10
30
15
20
28
Array after sorting...
10 15 20 25 28 30
```

13.4 FINDING ROOTS OF AN EQUATION

In general, there are two kinds of methods to find roots of an equations. These are

- **Direct methods**

Direct methods give the roots of non-linear equations in a finite number of steps. In addition, these methods are capable of giving all the roots at the same time.

For example, the roots of the quadratic equation

$$ax^2 + bx + c = 0 \qquad \text{where } a \neq 0$$

are given by

$$x_{1,2} = \frac{-b \pm \sqrt{b^2 - 4ac}}{2a}$$

- **Iterative methods**

Iterative methods, also known as *trial and error* methods, are based on the idea of successive approximations. They start with one or more initial approximations to the root and obtain a sequence of approximations by repeating a fixed sequence of steps till the solution with reasonable accuracy is obtained. Iterative methods, generally, give one root at a time.

Iterative methods are very cumbersome and time-consuming for solving equations manually. However, they are best suited for use on computers, due to following reasons:

1. Iterative methods can be concisely expressed as computational algorithms.
2. It is possible to formulate algorithms that can handle class of similar problems. For example, an algorithm can be developed to solve a polynomial equation of degree n.
3. Round-off errors are negligible in iterative methods as compared to direct methods.

The following are popular iterative methods to find roots of an equation.

- o Bisection Method
- o Regula-falsi method
- o secant method
- o Newton-Raphson method
- o Method of Successive approximations
- o

We will learn about Bisection method to find the roots of an equation of type

$$f(x) = 0$$

in this section.

Bisection method is one of the simplest iterative methods. To start with, two initial approximations, say x_1 and x_2 such that $f(x_1)\times f(x_2) < 0$ which ensures that root lies between x_1 and x_2, are taken. Next x-value, say x_3, as mid point of interval $[x_1, x_2]$ is computed.

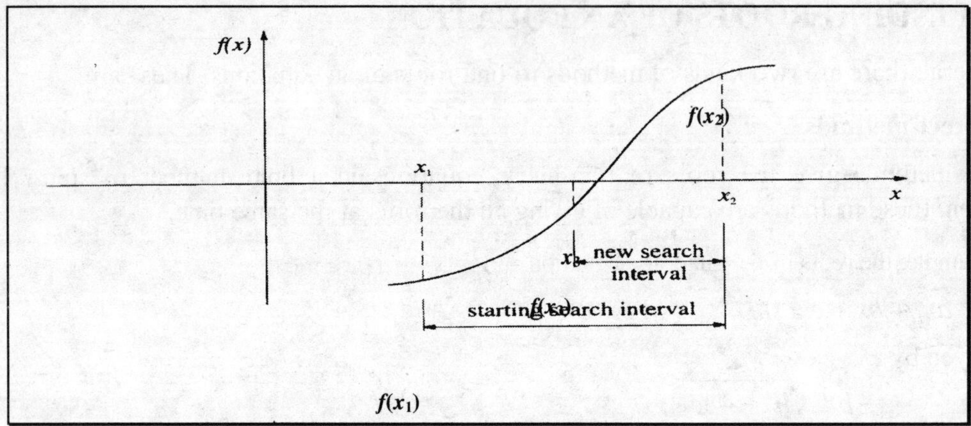

Figure 13.6: Root approximation by Bisection method

There are three possibilities that can arise:

i) If $f(x_3) = 0$, then we have a root at x_3.

ii) If $f(x_1)$ and $f(x_3)$ are of opposite sign, then the root lies in the interval (x_1, x_3). Thus x_2 is replaced by x_3, and the new interval, which is half of the current interval, is again bisected.

iii) If $f(x_1)$ and $f(x_3)$ are of same sign, then the root lies in the interval (x_3, x_2). Thus x_1 is replaced by x_3, and the new interval is again bisected.

Therefore by repeating this interval bisection procedure, we keep enclosing the root in a new search interval, which is halved in each iteration. This iterative cycle is terminated when the search interval becomes smaller than the prescribed tolerance. Hence, if *epsilon* is the prescribed tolerance in the required root, then the iterative cycle terminates when the absolute error becomes less than or equal to *epsilon*, i.e.,

$$|x_1 - x_2| \leq epsilon$$

After repeating the bisection process n times, the search interval is reduced to length $\frac{x_2 - x_1}{2^n}$ that contains the required root. We take the mid point of the last search interval as the desired approximation to the root.

Listing 13.8

```
/*
 *   Program to implement Bisection method to find one of the
 *   root of equation x^3 - 4x - 9 = 0
 */
#include<stdio.h>
#include<stdlib.h>
#include<math.h>
double f( double x )
{
   return pow((double)x,(double)3.0)-4*x-9;
}
int main()
{
   float x1, x2, epsilon, x3;
   printf("Enter first point of the search interval : ");
   scanf("%f", &x1);
   printf("Enter second point of the search interval : ");
   scanf("%f", &x2);
   if ( ( f(x1) * f(x2) ) > 0 ) {
      printf("\nInitial approximations are unsuitable\n");
      return 1;
   }
   printf("Enter prescribed tolerance : ");
   scanf("%f", &epsilon);
   do {
      x3 = (x1+x2)/2;
      if ( f(x1) * f(x3) < 0 )
         x2 = x3;
      else
         x1 = x3;
   }
   while( fabs((double)(x1-x2)) > epsilon);
```

```
    printf("\nApproximate root = %8.4f\n", x3);
    return 0;
}
```

Test Run 1

```
Enter first point of the search interval : 2.5
Enter second point of the search interval : 2.6
Initial approximations are unsuitable
```

Test Run 2

```
Enter first point of the search interval : 2.6
Enter second point of the search interval : 2.8
Enter prescribed tolerance : 0.0001
Approximate root = 2.7065
```

13.5 FINDING NUMERICAL DIFFERENTIATION OF A FUNCTION

Many problems in science and engineering involve the use of differentiation of various types of functions. If a function is expressed in mathematical form, its derivative can be easily obtained by analytical methods.

The first order derivative of a function $f(x)$ is defined as

$$f^1(x) = \frac{df(x)}{dx} = \lim_{\delta x \to 0} \frac{f(x+\delta x) - f(x)}{\delta x}$$

so if the derivative is desired at the point $x = x_0$, then we have to compute the ratio

$$\frac{f(x_0 + \delta x) - f(x_0)}{\delta x} \qquad \text{for small value of } \delta x.$$

But in many situations, the values of the independent variable x and the corresponding values of the dependent variable y are available either in graphic form or tabular form.

Consider the situation where the distance covered by an athlete as a function of time during his/her run for a 100-meter race is given in the following table:

Time (Secs.) :	0	1	2	3	4	5	6	7	8	9	10
Distance (Mts.) :	0	2.5	10	20	30.5	50	54	65.5	77.2	88.5	100

Here many questions can be asked, for example:

1. What was the speed of the athlete after 5 seconds?
2. What was the speed of the athlete as he approached the tape?
3. What was the acceleration of the athlete after 88 seconds?

Normally, speed and acceleration are calculated analytically. Suppose y represents the distance traveled by the athlete in x seconds, then

$$\text{Speed} = \frac{dy}{dx} \qquad \text{Acceleration} = \frac{d^2y}{dx^2}$$

But the mathematical relationship between y and x is not known in the above example. Therefore, it is not possible to use analytical methods. However, we can use the data given in the table to approximate the values of $\frac{dy}{dx}$ and $\frac{d^2y}{dx^2}$. Technique, which performs such calculations, is known as *numerical differentiation*.

The general formula for computer numerical value of first derivative at one of tabulated points is

$$\left.\frac{dy}{dx}\right|_{x=x_k} = \frac{1}{h}\sum_{j=1}^{n-k}\left[(-1)^{j+1}\frac{d_{kj}}{j}\right]$$

where d_{kj} represents Δ_k^j (jth order forward difference at tabulated point $x = x_k$) and is the element of the forward difference table represented by a matrix D of order $(n-1)\times(n-1)$ for a function tabulated at n points.

Example 13.7:

Given the following table

x :	0.50	0.75	1.00	1.25	1.50
$y = f(x)$:	0.13	0.42	1.00	1.95	2.35

Find $f^1(0.75)$.

Solution: The forward difference table for the given data is

i	x_i	y_i	Δy_i	$\Delta^2 y_i$	$\Delta^3 y_i$	$\Delta^4 y_i$
1	0.50	0.13	0.29	0.29	0.08	–1.00
2	0.75	0.42	0.58	0.37	–0.92	
3	1.00	1.00	0.95	–0.55		
4	1.25	1.95	0.40			
5	1.50	2.35				

Since $h = 0.25$, and the derivative is desired at the $x = 0.75$ (i.e. $k = 2$). Expanding the formula up to third term, we get

$$\left.\frac{dy}{dx}\right|_{x=0.75} = \frac{1}{h}\left[d_{21} - \frac{d_{22}}{2} + \frac{d_{23}}{3}\right]$$

$$= \frac{1}{0.25}\left[0.58 - \frac{0.37}{2} + \frac{-0.92}{3}\right] = \frac{1}{0.25}[0.58 - 0.185 - 0.307] = 0.352$$

Listing 13.9

```
/*
*  Program to compute first derivative of the tabulated function
*/
#include<stdio.h>
#include<stdlib.h>
int main()
{
   float x[10], y[10], d[10][10], a, sum, derivative, h, term;
   int i, j, k, n, sign;
   printf("Enter number of table points : ");
   scanf("%d", &n);
   printf("Enter interval size : ");
   scanf("%f", &h);
   printf("Enter %d values for (x,y)\n", n);
   for ( i = 1; i <= n; i++ )
     scanf("%f,%f", &x[i], &y[i]);
   printf("Enter tabulated point where to find derivative : ");
   scanf("%f", &a);
   if ( (a < x[1]) || (a > x[n]) ) {
       printf("\nValue lies outside range\n");
       return 1;
   }
   i = 1;
   while ( a != x[i] )
       i++;
   k = i;
   for ( j = 1; j <= (n-1); j++ ) {
      for ( i = 1; i <= (n-j); i++ ) {
         if ( j == 1 )
            d[i][j] = y[i+1] - y[i];
         else
            d[i][j] = d[i+1][j-1] - d[i][j-1];
      }
   }
   sum = 0.0;
   sign = 1;
   for ( j = 1; j <= (n-k); j++ ) {
      term =  sign * d[k][j] / j;
      sum = sum + term;
      sign = - sign;
   }
   derivative = (1.0/h) * sum;
   printf("\nValue of derivative = %8.2f\n", derivative);
   return 0;
}
```

Test Run

```
Enter number of table points : 5
Enter interval size : 0.25
```

```
Enter 5 values for (x,y)
0.5,0.13
0.75,0.42
1.0,1.0
1.25,1.95
1.5,2.35
Enter tabulated point where to find derivative : 0.75
Value of derivative = 0.35
```

13.6 FINDING NUMERICAL INTEGRATION OF A FUNCTION

Numerical integration is the process of computing the value of a definite integral from a set of numerical values of the function. If a function is defined as a mathematical expression, then its integral is usually determined using the technique of calculus, such solutions are called *closed form solutions.*

We usually encounter three kinds of problems in numerical integration:

1. Certain functions do not possess closed form solutions. For example, the integral of $\frac{\sin x}{x}$ cannot be expressed in a closed form.
2. Closed form solutions do exist, but these solutions are too complex and difficult to use for computations.
3. Functions that are available in the form of tables and no mathematical relationship between the variables are known.

In all such situations, values of the integral can be obtained by numerical technique whose aim is to provide effective procedures for approximate evaluation of definite integrals.

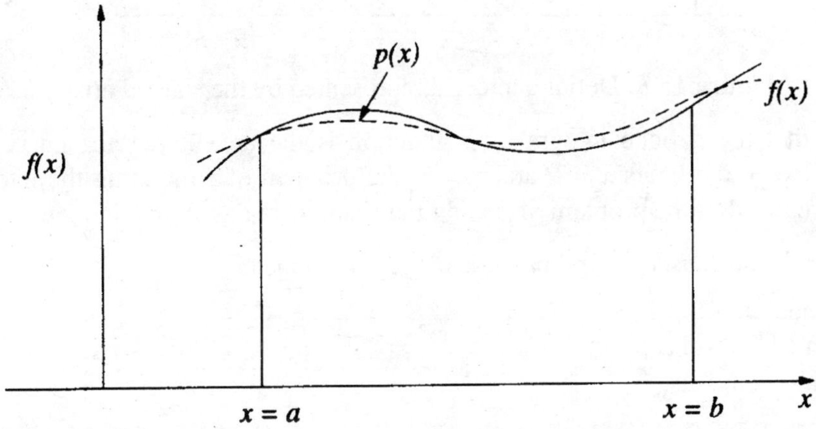

Figure 13.7: Illustrating approximating polynomial $p(x)$ for function $f(x)$

In practice, given set of values for a function $f(x)$, the following table of data

x :	a	x_1	x_2	x_3	...	b
$f(x)$:	$f(a)$	$f(x_1)$	$f(x_2)$	$f(x_3)$	...	$f(b)$

is used to compute the value of the integral $\int_a^b f(x)dx$.

The principal idea behind all these techniques is:

(i) Replace the function to be integrated $f(x)$ by approximating polynomial $p(x)$, and

(ii) Integrate $p(x)$ and take $\int_a^b p(x)dx$ to be the required approximation of $\int_a^b f(x)dx$.

The value of the definite integral of a function $f(x)$, which is a continuous function of x in the interval $[a,b]$, is given by

$$I = \int_a^b f(x)dx = F(b) - F(a)$$

where $F(x)$ is the anti-derivative of $f(x)$.

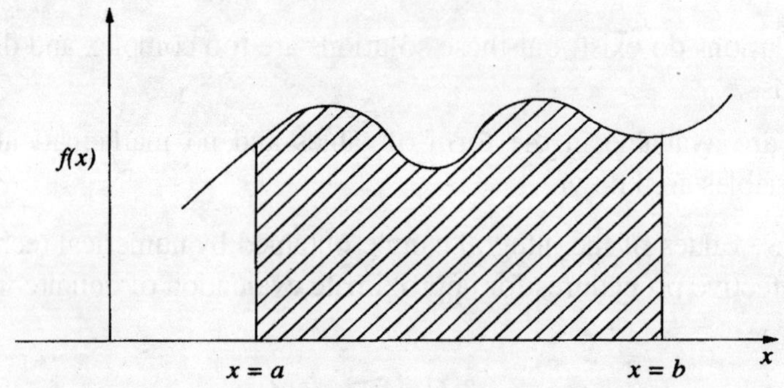

Figure 13.8: Definite integral represented by the shaded area

Remember that the definite integral of a function is the area under the curve $y = f(x)$ enclosed between the limits $x = a$ and $x = b$, the problem of computing the integral of a function is reduced to the problem of finding the shaded area as shown in Figure 13.8.

The popular methods used to find numerical integration include:

- Trapezoidal rule
- Simpson's 1/3rd rule
- Simpson's 3/8th Rule

We will learn about Trapezoidal rule as an example to find the numerical integration of a function.

Trapezoidal Rule

The *trapezoidal rule* approximates the area under a curve by connecting successive points on the curve to form trapezoids of uniform width, and then summing the area under these trapezoids to obtain the approximate area under the curve.

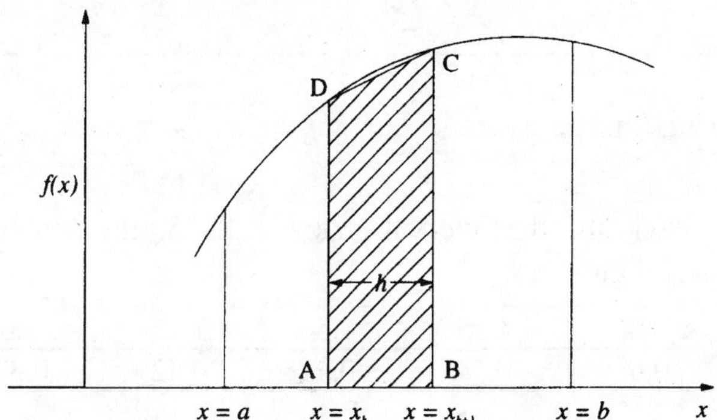

Figure 13.9: Approximation of area by Trapezoidal rule

Consider the function $f(x)$, whose graph between $x = a$ and $x = b$ is shown in Figure 13.9. An approximation to the area under the curve is obtained by dividing the interval $[a, b]$ into n strips of width h each, and approximating the area of each strip by that of a trapezoid as shown by the shaded area.

Formula for trapezoid rule is

$$I = \frac{h}{2}\left[y_1 + 2y_2 + 2y_3 + 2y_4 + .. + 2y_n + y_{n+1}\right]$$

assuming that function $f(x)$ is given in the following form

x	x_1	x_1+h	x_1+2h	...	x_1+nh
$y = f(x)$	y_1	y_2	y_3	...	y_{n+1}

Example 13.8:

The function $f(x)$ is given as follows

x	0	0.1	0.2	0.3	0.4	0.5	0.6	0.7	0.8	0.9	1.0
y	1	1.2	1.4	1.6	1.8	2.0	2.2	2.4	2.6	2.8	3.0

Compute the integral of $f(x)$ between $x = 0$ and $x =1.0$.

Solution: Given $h = 0.1$ and $n = 10$

The formula for Trapezoidal rule is

$$I = \frac{h}{2}\left[y_1 + 2(y_2 + y_3 + y_4 + y_5 + y_6 + y_7 + y_8 + y_9 + y_{10}) + y_{11}\right]$$

Substituting the values of y_i's and h, we get

$$I = \frac{0.1}{2}[1+2\times(1.2+1.4+1.6+1.8+2.0+2.2+2.4+2.6+2.8)+3.0] = 2.00$$

Example 13.9:

Evaluate $\int_1^2 e^{-\frac{1}{2}x} dx$ using four intervals.

Solution: With four intervals, the interval size h = 0.25, the function is tabulated as (rounded to two decimal digits)

x	1	1.25	1.50	1.75	2.0
$f(x)$	0.61	0.54	0.47	0.42	0.37

Substituting these values, we get

$$I = \frac{h}{2}[y_1 + 2(y_2 + y_3 + y_4) + y_5] = \frac{0.25}{2}[0.607 + 2(0.535 + 0.472 + 0.417) + 0.368]$$

$= 0.48$ (rounded to two decimal places)

Listing 13.10

```
/*  Program to implement Trapezoidal rule for tabulated function  */
#include<stdio.h>
int main()
{
   int i, n;
   float x[20], y[20], h, sum, integral;
   printf("Enter number of intervals : ");
   scanf("%d", &n);
   printf("Enter size of interval : ");
   scanf("%f", &h);
   printf("Enter %d pair of (x, y)\n", n+1);
   for ( i = 1; i <= (n+1); i++ )
       scanf("%f,%f", &x[i], &y[i]);
   sum = ( y[1] + y[n+1] )/2;
   for ( i = 2; i <= n; i++ )
       sum = sum + y[i];
   integral = h * sum;
   printf("\nValue of the integral = %7.2f\n", integral);
   return 0;
}
```

Test Run

```
Enter number of intervals : 10

Enter size of interval : 0.1
```

```
Enter 11 pair of (x,y)
0,1
0.1,1.2
0.2,1.4
0.3,1.6
0.4,2.0
0.5,2.2
0.6,2.4
0.7,2.6
0.8,2.8
0.9,3.0
1.0,1.2
Value of the integral = 2.00
```

Listing 13.11

```
/*  Program to implement Trapezoidal rule for known function*/
#include<stdio.h>
#include<math.h>
float f(float x)
{
   return exp(-0.5*x);
}
int main()
{
   int i, n;
   float a, b, h, sum, integral;
   printf("Enter lower limit of integration : ");
   scanf("%f", &a);
   printf("Enter upper limit of integration : ");
   scanf("%f", &b);
   printf("Enter number of intervals : ");
   scanf("%d", &n);
   h = (b - a)/n;
   sum = (f(a)+f(b))/2.0;
   for ( i = 1; i <= (n-1); i++ )
       sum = sum + f(a+i*h);
   integral = h * sum;
   printf("\nValue of the integral = %7.2f\n", integral);
   return 0;
}
```

Test Run

```
Enter lower limit of integration : 1
Enter upper limit of integration : 2
Enter number of intervals : 4
Value of the integral = 0.48
```

❑ ❑ ❑

Chapter 14

Structures

Learning Objectives

After reading this chapter, students will be able to

- explain the concept of structure
- explain how a structure is different from an array
- declare , initialize and do input/output of structures
- explain the way array of structures are handled
- explain the way structures are passed as arguments to functions
- write efficient programs using structures to solve variety of problems

14.1 INTRODUCTION

We have seen that arrays can be used to represent a group of data items that belong to same data type, such as *int* or *float*. However, if data items in a group belong to different data types, then we can not use array.

The C language supports a structured data type called *structure* that has the capability to represent a group of data items that belong to different data types. A *structure* is a convenient to handling a group of logically related data items, which of course can belong to different data types.

The concept of a *structure* is analogous to that of a *record*. For example, a record of a student may comprise *roll number*, *name*, *father's name*, *grade*, etc.

Few examples of structures are

Name of Structure	Probable Constituent Data Items
Date	day, month, year
Time	hours, minutes, seconds
Book	title, author, publisher, price
Address	name, house number, locality, city, state, pincode
Student	roll number, name, father's name, grade
Customer	name, address, mobile no
Inventory	item code, description, quantity, unit price
Employee	employee id, name, address, mobile no

Note that a structure is type defined by the users as per their requirements. This way a user creates a new data type. These newly created data type is known as *user-defined data type*. Structures can be used to organize complex data in a more meaningful way.

This chapter describes various aspects of structures.

14.2 DEFINING A STRUCTURE

The syntax for defining a structure is

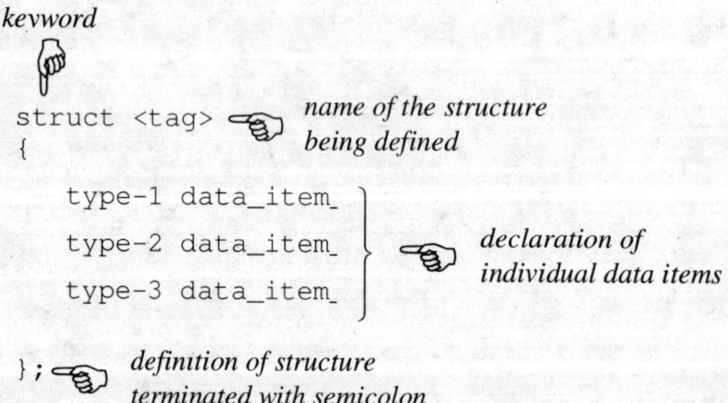

The definition starts with the keyword *struct*.

The next element in the definition is *tag*. The tag is the identifier for the structure, and will be used to declare variables later on in the program.

The declaration statements inside the braces such as *type-1 data_item_1*, *type-2 data_item_2*, *type-3 data_item_3*, ..., etc., declare the individual data members of that make up the structure.

The individual data members are also known as *fields*.

The class definition ends with a semicolon.

Following are few examples of definitions of structures:

```
struct Date
{
  int day;
  int month;
  int year;
};

struct Time
{
  int hours;
  int minutes;
  int seconds;
};

struct Book
{
  char title[25];
  char author[25];
  char publisher[15];
  float price;
};

struct Customer
{
  char name[25];
  char address[80];
  long mobile_no;
};

struct Inventory
{
  char item_code[25];
  char desc[25];
  int qty;
  float unit_price;
};

struct Address
{
  char name[25];
  int house_no;
  char locality[25];
  char city[15];
  char state[15];
  long pincode;
};

struct Employee
{
  int   code;
  char  name[25];
  char  deptt[15];
  float salary;
};

struct Student
{
  long roll_no;
  char name[25];
  char fname[25];
  char grade;
};
```

14.3 DECLARING STRUCTURE VARIABLES

Once a structure is defined, we can declare structure variables. Usually, the definition is placed in the global area of the program, *i.e.*, before the *main()* function, so that it is visible to all the functions in the program.

The variables, on the other hand, are usually declared in the local area of the functions or in the argument list in the functions headers.

The syntax for declaring a structure variable is

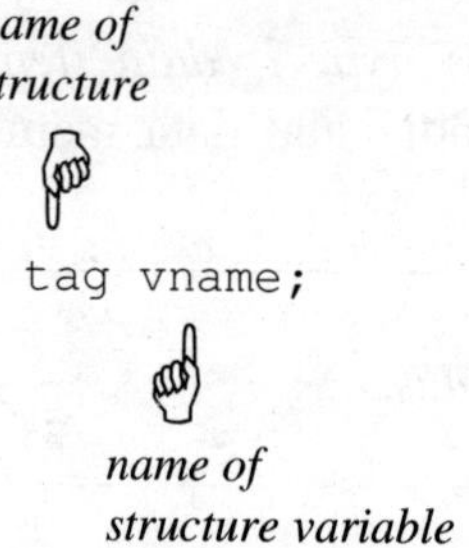

where *tag* is the name of the structure defined and *vname* is the name of the structure variable.

For example, for defined structure *Student*, its variable will be declared as

```
Student aStudent;
```

For other defined structures in previous section, the variables will be declared as

```
Date aDate;            Time aTime;            Book aBook;

Customer cust;         Inventory invt;        Address addr;

Employee emp;
```

The declaration of a structure variable can also be combined with definition of the structure as shown below:

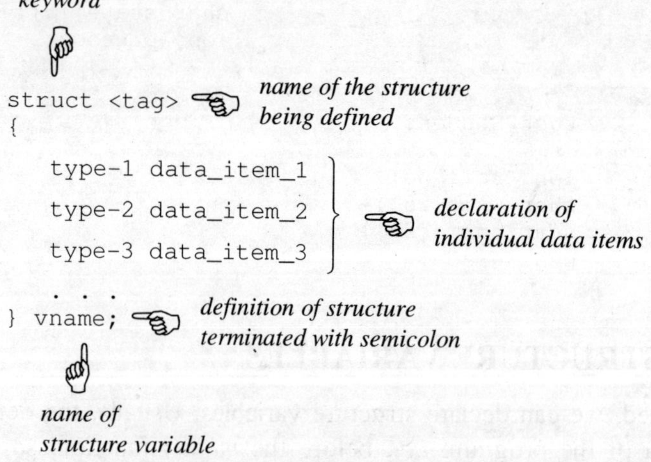

Note that the name of the structure variable appears between closing brace and semicolon. However, if we want to define more variables, they are, as usual, separated by comma.

Consider following code

```
struct Employee
{
   int   code;
   char  name[25];
   char  deptt[15];
   float salary;
} emp1;
```

It defines structure named *Employee* and declares *emp1* as its variable.

```
struct Employee
{
   int   code;
   char  name[25];
   char  deptt[15];
   float salary;
} emp1, emp2, emp3, emp4;
```

It defines structure named *Employee* and declares its variable three variables *emp1*, *emp2* and *emp3*.

Usually, this approach of declaring variables is not recommended, because of the following

1. Since structure declaration are placed in the global area, and so the variables will also be global.
2. In case we want to declare local variables using this approach, we may have to place the structure in local scope, which will make declaration of structure invisible to other functions.

14.4 INITIALIZING STRUCTURES

Like simple variables and arrays, structure variables can also be initialized at declaration time. The format used is quite similar to that used to initialize arrays.

The following segment illustrates this

```
typedef struct
{
  int   rollno;
  char  name[25];
  int   age;
  float height;
} STUDENT;

STUDENT aStudent = { 1000, "Surbhi", 18, 5.6 };
```

Like partially initialized arrays, if a structure variable is partially initialized, the remaining numeric fields will be initialized to zero and the string fields will be initialized to null.

14.5 ACCESSING STRUCTURE ELEMENTS

Individual structure elements of a structure variables can be accessed using the *dot operator* '.' This dot operator is also referred to as *membership operator*.

The syntax for accessing a structure element is as follows

name of structure variable

```
sname.vname;
```

name of structure element

Note that the structure elements are treated just like other variables.

Consider the following statements

```
struct Student
{
  int  rollno;
  char name[25];
  char fname[25];
  char grade;
};
Student aStudent;
```

The individual elements of structure variable *aStudent* will be accessed as shown below:

```
aStudent.rollno    // reference to element rollno
aStudent.name      // reference to element name
aStudent.fname     // reference to element fname
aStudent.grade     // reference to element grade
```

14.6 READING AND WRITING STRUCTURES

We can also read into and write data from a structure element in the same manner as we do with simple variables. For example, the elements of *aStudent* structure, we can read data, interactively, from the keyboard and place in the *aStudent* structure using following statements

```
printf("\nEnter roll number of the student : ");
scanf("%d", &aStudent.rollno);
printf("\nEnter name of the student : ");
scanf("%d", aStudent.name);
printf("\nEnter age of the student : ");
scanf("%d", &aStudent.age);
printf("\nEnter height of the student : ");
scanf("%d", &aStudent.height),
```

Note that in the *scanf()* function, the expression

```
&aStudent.rollno
```

is interpreted by the compiler as

```
&(aStudent.rollno)
```

because of higher precedence of direct selection operator over *addressof* operator (&), and that is what exactly is required.

Listing 14.1

```
/* Program to illustrate way data is entered into structures */
#include<stdio.h>
#include<sting.h>
struct EMPLOYEE
{
   int code;
   char name[25];
   char department[15];
   float salary;
};
int main()
{
   struct EMPLOYEE aEmployee;
   printf("Enter employee's code: " );
   scanf( "%d", &aEmployee.code );
   fflush(stdin);
   printf("Enter employee's name: " );
   gets( aEmployee.name );
   printf("Enter employee's department: " );
   gets( aEmployee.department );
   printf("Enter employee's salary: " );
   scanf("%f", &aEmployee.salary );
   printf("\n\nParticulars of employee as" );
   printf(" entered by user\n" );
   printf("\nEmployee's code: %d", aEmployee.code );
   printf("\nEmployee's name: %s", aEmployee.name );
   printf("\nEmployee's department: %s",aEmployee.department);
   printf("\nEmployee's salary: %.2f\n", aEmployee.salary );
   return 0;
}
```

Test Run

```
Enter employee's code: 826
Enter employee's name: Rajesh Kumar
Enter employee's department: Computer Science
Enter employee's salary: 20000
```

```
Particulars of employee as entered by user
Employee's code: 826
Employee's name: Rajesh Kumar
Employee's department: Computer Science
Employee's salary: 20000.00
```

Following is a program that uses structures and direct selection operator. It multiplies two fractions and prints the result. For example, if the fractions are 2/5 and 3/5, it prints the result as 6/25.

Listing 14.2

```
/*   Program to multiply two fractions      */
#include<stdio.h>
struct FRACTION
{
  int nom;          /*   nominator    */
  int denom;        /*   denominator */
};
int main()
{
   struct FRACTION aFraction, bFraction, cFraction;
   printf( "Enter first fraction as x/y : " );
   scanf( "%d%*c%d",&aFraction.nom, &aFraction.denom);
   printf( "Enter second fraction as x/y : " );
   scanf( "%d%*c%d",&bFraction.nom, &bFraction.denom);
   cFraction.nom = aFraction.nom * bFraction.nom;
   cFraction.denom = aFraction.denom * bFraction.denom;
   printf( "\nResult of (%d/%d) x (%d/%d) = (%d/%d)\n",
           aFraction.nom, aFraction.denom,
           bFraction.nom, bFraction.denom,
           cFraction.nom, cFraction.denom );
   return 0;
}
```

Test Run

```
Enter first fraction as x/y : 2/5
Enter second fraction also as x/y : 3/5
Result of (2/5) x (3/5) = (6/25)
```

14.7 ASSIGNING OF STRUCTURES

A structure is an entity that can be treated as a whole. There is only one operation that can be performed on the structure as a whole is that a structure can be assigned/copied into another structure of the same type using the assignment operator.

Again consider the following statements

```
typedef struct
{
  int   rollno;
  char  name[25];
  int   age;
  float height;
} STUDENT;
STUDENT aStudent, bStudent;
```

The following assignment statement

```
aStudent = bStudent;
```

assigns the contents of structure *bStudent* to *aStudent*.

It is a unique feature of structures as compared to arrays, where in order to copy one array to another array of same type, we have to set up a loop to copy element-by-element. This is rather an amazing capability when you think about it. When you assign one structure to another, all the values in the structure are assigned to corresponding structure elements. Simple assignment statement cannot be used this way for arrays. That is, to assign one array to another, we have to assign element by element.

14.8 ARRAYS OF STRUCTURES

In many practical situations, we need to create an array of structures. As an example, we need to create an array of students to work with a group of students in a class. By putting the data of students in an array of structures, we can quickly and efficiently process the student's data.

An array of structures to store the data of students will be declared as

```
STUDENT students[50];
```

14.8.1 Accessing Elements of Array of Structures

Individual elements of a structure in an array of structures are accessed by referring to structure variable name, followed by index, followed by direct selection operator, and ending with the structure element desired.

In our example of students of a class, the name of the ith student can be accessed as follows:

```
students[i].name;
```

14.8.2 Initializing Array of Structures

Like any other array, an array of structures can also be initialized. Since each element of array structures is a different structure, we need to include elements of each structure in a separate set of braces as shown:

```
STUDENT students[50] = { { 1000, "Monika",{56,76,85,69}, 'A' },
                         { 1001, "Ram", {50,66,70,60}, 'B' },
                                     :
                         { 1049, "Raju", {65,62,68,59}, 'B' },
                       };
```

Following program illustrates input, processing and output of array of structures.

Listing 14.3

```
/*
* Program to illustrate processing of array of structures by
*   storing list of students in memory, and computes their grades
*/
#include <stdio.h>
typedef struct
{
   int  rollno;
   char sname[25];
   int  marks[4];
   char grade;
} STUDENT;
int main()
{
   STUDENT students[50];
   int totalMarks, i, j, n;
   printf( "\n\nEnter number of students in a class : " );
   scanf( "%d", &n );
   for ( i = 0; i < n; i++ )
   {
      printf("\nParticulars of student #%d\n\n", i+1);
      printf( "Enter students' roll number : " );
      scanf("%d", &students[i].rollno );
      printf( "\nEnter students' name : " );
      gets( students[i].sname );
      printf( "\nEnter students marks in four subjects\n\n" );
      for ( j = 0; j < 4; j++ )
         scanf("%d", &students[i].marks[j] );
   }
   for ( i = 0; i < n; i++ )
   {
      totalMarks = 0;
      for ( j = 0; j < 4; j++ )
         totalMarks += students[i].marks[j];
      if ( totalMarks > 75 )
```

```
      students[i].grade = 'A';
   else if ( totalMarks > 60 )
      students[i].grade = 'B';
   else if ( totalMarks > 50 )
      students[i].grade = 'C';
   else if ( totalMarks > 40 )
      students[i].grade = 'D';
   else
      students[i].grade = 'F';
  }
  printf("\nPerformance of students\n\n");
  printf("%-10s", "Roll No.");
  printf("%-30s", "Name");
  printf("%6s\n", "Grade");
  for ( i = 0; i < n; i++ )
  {
     printf("%-10d", students[i].rollno);
     printf("%-30s", students[i].sname);
     printf("%4c\n", students[i].grade);
  )
  return 0;
}
```

Test Run

```
Enter number of students in a class : 3

Particulars of student #1

Enter students' roll number : 1000
Enter students' name : Ram Kumar
Enter students marks in four subjects
98 99 89 88

Particulars of student #2

Enter students' roll number : 1001
Enter students' name : Mohit Kumar
Enter students marks in four subjects
65 55 45 60

Particulars of student #3

Enter students' roll number : 1002
Enter students' name : Jaspreet Singh
Enter students marks in four subjects
41 44 45 50

Performance of students

SNo.          Student's Name     Grade
  1                    Sonu        A
  2                  bhollu        C
  3                jaspreet        D
```

14.9 STRUCTURES AND FUNCTIONS

In order to be fully useful, we must be able to pass structures to functions as arguments and returning them from functions.

```
typedef struct {
   int day;
   int month;
   int year;
} DATE;
void printDate(DATE);
void main()
{
   DATE aDate = { 10, 6, 2008 };
   int x;
   printDate(aDate);
   /*  more statements    */
}
```

```
/*  function definition   */
void printDate(DATE tDate )
{

   /*  local declarations */
   /*  other statements   */

}
```

Figure 14.4: Passing structure by value

Structure can be passed by value as well as by reference. In this section, we will consider passing a structure by value only. Passing structure by reference, we will consider in the *Chapter 15*.

Listing 14.4

```
/*  Program to illustrate passing of a structure by value   */
#include <stdio.h>
typedef struct {
   int day;
   int month;
   int year;
} DATE;
void printDate( DATE aDate );   /*  function declaration    */
void main()
{
   DATE tDate = { 10, 6, 2008 }; /* initialize a structure   */
   printDate( tDate );            /*  function call           */
}
void printDate( DATE aDate )
{
  printf( "\nDate in format dd/mm/yy: %02d/%02d/%2d\n",
          aDate.day, aDate.month, aDate.year );
}
```

Test Run

```
Date in format dd/mm/yy: 10/06/2008
```

A function can also return a value of structure type as well via *return* statement as illustrated below.

```
typedef struct
{
   int day;
   int month;
   int year;
} DATE;
DATE getDate(void);
void main()
{
   DATE aDate;
   int x;
   aDate = getDate();
   /*  more statement    */
}
```

```
/*  function definition    */
DATE getDate(void)
{
   DATE tDate;
   /*  local declarations */
   /*  more statements    */
   return tDate;
}
```

Figure 14.5: Function returning a structure

Listing 14.5

```
/* Program to illustrate function returning a structure  */
#include <stdio.h>
typedef struct
{
   int day;
   int month;
   int year;
} DATE;
DATE getDate( void );        /*  function declaration    */
void main()
{
   DATE tDate;
   printf( "Enter date in format dd/mm/yyyy : " );
   tDate = getDate();
   printf( "\nDate entered by you: %02d/%02d/%2d\n",
         tDate.day, tDate.month, tDate.year );
}
DATE getDate( void )
{
   DATE xDate;
   scanf( "%d/%d/%d", &xDate.day, &xDate.month, &xDate.year );
   return xDate;
}
```

Test Run

```
Enter date in format dd/mm/yy: 10/6/2008

Date entered by you: 10/06/2008
```

14.10 SUPPLEMENTARY PROBLEMS

Problem 14.1:

Given the following declaration

```
struct STUDENT {
  int  rollNo;
  char name[31];
  int   marks;
};
```

to represent the information of a student.

Using this structure, write a function that takes list of students, in the form of an array, as its argument, and sorts them in the descending order of the marks secured by the students.

Using the above structure and function, write a program that reads the data for *n* students and displays them in descending order of marks secure by the students.

Listing 14.6

```
/* Program to the given information of students in
*  descending order of the marks secured by them    */
typedef struct {
  int  rollno;
  char name[20];
  int  marks;
} STUDENT;
void arrangeBubble(STUDENT students[], int n);
int main()
{
  STUDENT students[50];
  int i, n;
  printf( "\n\nEnter number of students : " );
  scanf( "%d", &n );
  for ( i = 0; i < n; i++ )
  {
     printf("\nParticulars of student #%d\n\n", i+1);
     printf( "Enter students' roll number : " );
     scanf("%d", &students[i].rollno );
     printf( "Enter students' name : " );
     gets(students[i].name );
     printf( "Enter students' marks : " );
     scanf("%d", &students[i].marks );
  }
  arrangeBubble(students,n);     /*  function call   */
  printf("\nStudent's Information after sorting\n\n");
  printf("%-10s", "Roll No.");
  printf("%-20s", "Name");
  printf("%6s\n\n", "Marks");
  for ( i = 0; i < n; i++ )
  {
```

```
      printf("%-10d", students[i].rollno);
      printf("%-20s", students[i].name);
      printf("%4d\n", students[i].marks);
    }
    return 0;
}
void arrangeBubble(STUDENT st[], int n)
{
    int i, j, k;
    STUDENT temp;
    for ( i = 1; i < n; i++ )
    {
        k = n-i;
        for ( j = 0; j < k; j++ )
        {
            if ( st[j].marks < st[j+1].marks )
            {
                temp = students[j];
                st[j] = st[j+1];
                st[j+1] = temp;
            }
        }
    }
}
```

Test Run

```
Enter number of students : 5

Particulars of student #1

Enter students' roll number : 1000
Enter students' name : Ravi
Enter students' marks : 80

Particulars of student #2

Enter students' roll number : 1001
Enter students' name : Shankar
Enter students' marks : 79

Particulars of student #3

Enter students' roll number : 1002
Enter students' name : Ankit
Enter students' marks : 65

Particulars of student #4

Enter students' roll number : 1003
Enter students' name : Rupinder
Enter students' marks : 75

Particulars of student #5

Enter students' roll number : 1004
Enter students' name : Mehak
```

```
Enter students' marks : 88
Student's Information after sorting
Roll No.   Name                Marks
 1004      Mehak                88
 1000      Ravi                 80
 1001      Shankar              79
 1003      Rupinder             75
 1002      Ankita               65
```

Problem 14.2:

Use a structure to model a complex number. Using this structure write functions to accomplish the following tasks:

- Function that returns the structure read from the keyboard.
- Function that takes two structures using call be value mechanism as its arguments and return their sum.
- Function that takes single structure using call be value mechanism as its arguments and prints it.

Use these functions in the program to demonstrate their working.

Listing 14.7

```
/*  Program to demonstrate passing structure to a function using
 * call by value mechanism and function returning a structure   */
#include <stdio.h>
typedef struct
{
   float real;
   float imag;
} COMPLEX;
COMPLEX input(void);          /*  function declarations    */
void output(COMPLEX);
COMPLEX add(COMPLEX, COMPLEX);
COMPLEX multiply(COMPLEX, COMPLEX);
int main()
{
   COMPLEX n1, n2, n3, n4;
   printf("\nProgram to add two complex numbers\n\n");
   printf("\nEnter first complex number\n");
   n1 = input();
   printf("\nEnter second complex number\n");
   n2 = input();
   n3 = add(n1,n2);
   printf("\nSum of given complex numbers\n\n");
   output(n3);
   n4 = multiply(n1,n2);
   printf("\nProduct of given complex numbers\n\n");
   output(n4);
   return 0;
```

```
}
COMPLEX input(void)
{
   COMPLEX t;
   printf("\nEnter real part : ");
   scanf("%f", &t.real);
   printf("Enter imaginary part : ");
   scanf("%f", &t.imag);
   return t;
}
void output(COMPLEX t)
{
   printf("Real part : %.2f", t.real);
   printf("\nImaginary part : %.2f", t.imag);
}
COMPLEX add(COMPLEX a, COMPLEX b)
{
   COMPLEX t;
   t.real = a.real + b.real;
   t.imag = a.imag + b.imag;
   return t;
}
COMPLEX multiply(COMPLEX a, COMPLEX b)
{
   COMPLEX t;
   t.real = a.real * b.real - a.imag * b.imag;
   t.imag = a.real * b.imag + a.imag * b.real;
   return t;
}
```

Test Run

```
Program to add two complex numbers
Enter first complex number
Enter real part : 1.0
Enter imaginary part : 2.5
Enter second complex number
Enter real part : 2.5
Enter imaginary part : -1.5
Sum of given complex numbers
Real part : 3.50
Imaginary part : 1.00
Product of given complex numbers
Real part : 6.25
Imaginary part : 4.75
```

EXERCISE

1. What is the main reason for using structures?
2. How a structure is different from an array?
3. What is the structure tag and what is its purpose?
4. What are different ways of declaring a structure variable?
7. Is any there thing wrong with the following?

```
struct Time {
    int hrs;
    int mts;
    int secs;
}
time t1;
```

8. What is wrong with the following, if any?

```
struct Time {
    int hrs =10;
    int mts = 20;
    int secs = 35;
} t1, t2, t3;
```

9. Identify the errors, if any, in the following

```
struct {
    int hrs;
    int mts;
    int secs;
} time;
time t1, t2, t3;
```

10. Give the output of the following program:

```
struct Point {
    int X, Y;
};
void Show( Point P )
{
    printf("\n%d:%d\n", P.x, P.y);
}
     void main()
     {
         Point U = { 10, 20 }, V, W;
         V = U;
         V.Y -= 10;
         W = V;
         U.Y -= 5;
         U.X += 5;
         W.y -= 5;
         Show(U);
         Show(V);
         Show(W);
     }
```

11. Give the output of the following program:

```
#include <stdio.h>
struct MyBox {
    int Length, Breadth, Height;
};
void Dimension( MyBox M )
{
    printf("\n%d x %d x %d\n",M.Length,M.Breadth,M.Height);
}
void main()
{
    MyBox B1 = { 12, 20, 8 }, B2, B3;
    ++B1.Height;
    Dimension(B1);
    B3 = B1;
    ++B3.Length;
    B3.Breadth++;
    Dimension(B3);
    B2 = B3;
    B2.Height += 5;
    B2.Length--;
    Dimension(B2);
}
```

PROGRAMMING EXERCISE

1. Design a structure named *distance* to store a length in *yards*, *feets* and *inches*. Using this structure, write a program that accepts two measurements from the user as represented by these structures and prints the absolute difference between these measurements.
2. Design a structure named *student* to store data about a student which contains following elements — *rollno* of type *int*, *name* an array of type *char* of size 20, *college* an array of type *char* of size 40, and *score* of type *float*. Assume that there are not more than 100 students. Write a program to input the data about students, and output the stored data according to the merit of the students.
3. Consider the following declaration:

```
struct EMPLOYEE {
    int code;
    char name[31];
    float salary;
};
```

   Given that there are *n* (≤50) employees in an organization. Write a program that output the details of the employee having highest salary.

4. Create a structure named *Time* to model a time in 12 hour system having three fields as *hours*, *minutes* and *seconds*. Write a function called *elapsedTime* that takes two arguments, the start time and the end time. The function should return a *Time* structure containing the time elapsed between the two arguments. Write a program to test the above function.

5. A point in plane in Cartesian system can be represented by its coordinates *x* and *y*. We can create a structure to represent a point in plane as shown below:

```
typedef struct {
    int x;
    int y;
} POINT;
```

Write a function that accepts the structure representing a point and returns an integer value 1, 2, 3 or 4 indicating the quadrant in which the point is located. Write a program to test the above function.

6. A straight line is a geometric object connecting two points, therefore, it can be represented by a nested structure having two structures of POINT type

```
typedef struct {
    POINT beg;
    POINT end;
} LINE;
```

Write a function that accepts two argument of POINT type and returns a structure of type LINE representing the line connecting the two points Write a program to test the above function.

7. Write a function that accepts a structure type LINE as its argument and return an integer (1,2,3), where 1 means line is vertical, 2 means line is horizontal, and 3 means line is oblique. Write a program to test the above function.

[**Hint:** A vertical line is line whose *x*-coordinates are same. Horizontal line is a line whose *y*-coordinates are same. An oblique line is a line which is neither vertical nor horizontal]

8. Define a structure that contains three members – name of country, name of the capital, and per capita income. Using this structure, write a program to list the countries along with their capitals in the decreasing order of their per capita income.

9. Consider the following structure definition:

```
struct BOX {
    char make[25];
    float length, breadth, height;
};
```

Write a function that takes the address of the *BOX* structure and returns its volume.

10. Consider the following declaration:

```
struct EMPLOYEE {
    int code;
    char name[31];
    float salary;
};
```

Given that there are *n* (≤50) employees in an organization. Write a program, using pointer notation to access the data of an employee that output the details of the employee having highest salary.

❑ ❑ ❑

Chapter 15

Pointers and Dynamic Memory Management

Learning Objectives

After reading this chapter, students will be able to

- comprehend the world of pointers, one of the richest feature of C language
- explain how main memory is organized and addresses are assigned to each memory location
- declare , initialize and access through pointer
- explain the usefulness of pointers in passing arguments to a function
- explain the permissible operations on pointers
- explain the concept of memory allocation
- distinguish between static allocation and dynamic allocation
- comprehend and use various memory management functions for dynamic memory management
- explain what possible problems can occur while working with pointers
- write efficient programs using pointers to solve variety of problems

15.1 INTRODUCTION

Pointers are one of the most important features of C language. Pointers, by most people, are regarded as one of the most difficult topics in C. Let me tell you frankly, it is more a myth rather a fact. I would prefer to say that pointers are one of the most delicate aspects of C language, and you know delicate things need very careful handling. Therefore, pointers need very careful handling.

There are many reasons for using pointers, some of them are enumerated below:

- A pointer allows a function or a program to access a variable (better we say memory location) outside the preview of function or a program. In fact, using a pointer, your program can access any memory location in the computer's memory.
- Since using *return* statement, a function can only pass back a single value to the calling function, pointers allows a function to pass back more than one value by writing them into memory locations that are accessible to the calling function.
- Using pointers, arrays and structures can be handled in more efficient way.
- Without pointers, it will be impossible to create complex data structures, such as *linked lists*, *trees* and *graphs*.
- To communicate with operating system about memory. For example, the operator *new* returns the location of free memory block by using a pointer and the operator *delete* returns the memory block pointed to by a pointer to the operating system.

In totality, we can say that the real power of C language lies in the judicious use of pointers. Therefore, every reader of C must learn and master the art of using pointers.

In this chapter our goal is to explain the pointers as clearly as possible. In an attempt to achieve our goal, we ensure that the groundwork is laid carefully before we move on to use pointers in more advanced situations.

15.2 UNDERSTANDING POINTERS

Computer's memory is organized as a linear collection of bytes or words. For Intel processors, memory is byte-organized whereas for most of the non-Intel processors, memory is word-organized. In byte-organized memory, each memory location is of one byte, whereas in word-organized, each memory location is of one word. Each memory location is assigned a unique number called *location number* or *address*. Figure 15.1 shows the schematic of memory organization.

We know that one byte is equal to 8 bits, whereas one word may be made up of two or more bytes. A word is a measure of the capacity of processor in terms of the size of operands that it can process (*i.e.* add, subtract, multiply, divide, compare, etc.) in single operation. When we say that a processor is a 16-bit processor, it means that its word size is 16-bits (2 bytes) and it can process 16-bit operands in single operations. For large size operands, it needs more operations.

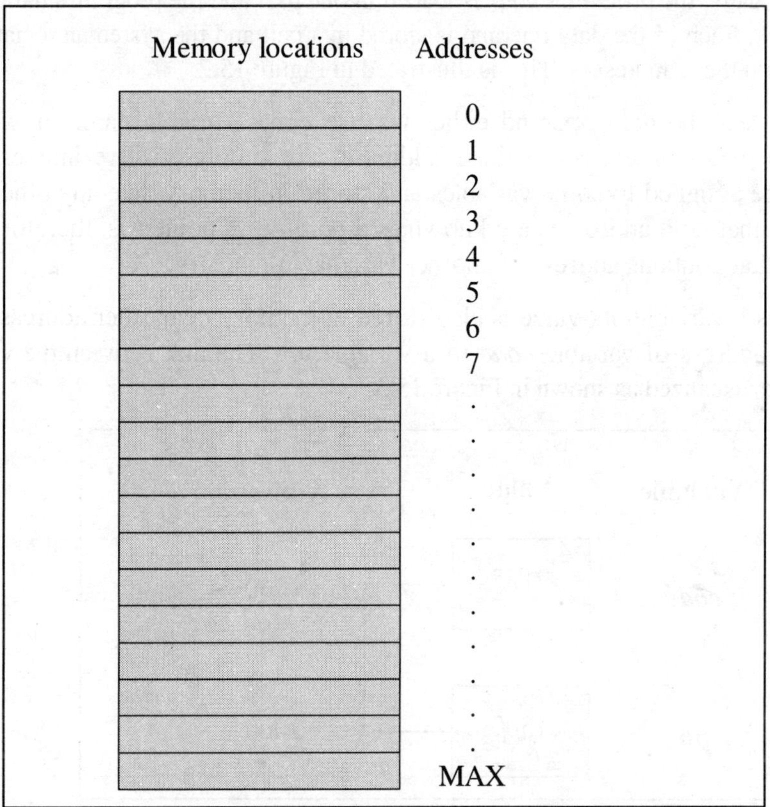

Figure 15.1: Memory Organization

A *memory cell* is either of one byte/word or more contiguous bytes/words. Each cell can store one value at a given time. The address of a cell is always the address of the first byte/word.

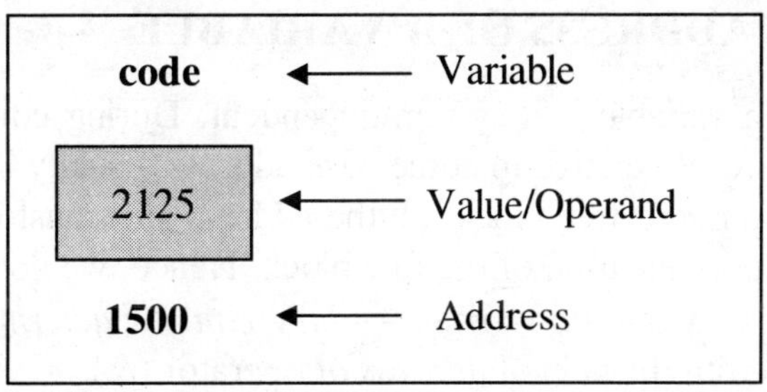

Figure 15.2: Representation of a Variable in Memory

When you give a command to run a program, the operating system first finds a free block of requisite size from computer (main) memory, and then loads the program into that block. Even in that block, usually, the program's code is loaded in one part and the program's data in another part of the block. Each of the data operand is stored in a cell and the system associates each of the variables with these addresses. This is illustrated in Figure 15.2.

In order to access the data operand either we use either variable name or we can use address of the memory cell. Since these addresses are simply positive integer numbers, they can also be assigned to some variables and stored in memory, like any other variable. Such variables that hold addresses are known as a *pointer*. A pointer is, therefore, nothing but a variable that contains address of another variable in memory.

Since pointer is a variable, its value is also stored in memory in another address. Suppose we assign the address of variable *code* to a variable *ptr*. The link between the variable *ptr* and *code* can be visualized as shown in Figure 15.3.

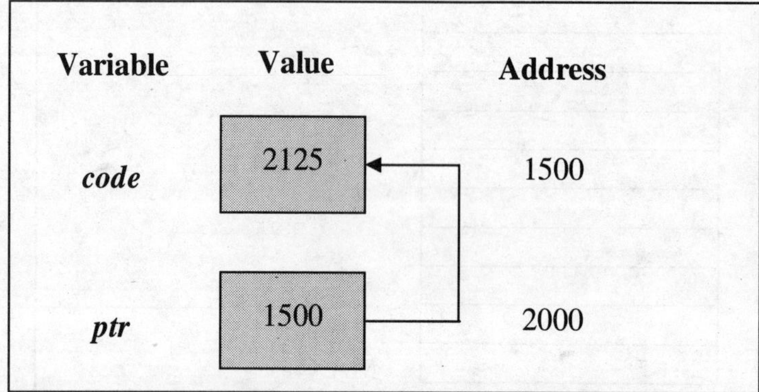

Figure 15.3: Pointer as a Variable

Since the value of the variable *ptr* is the address of the variable *code*, we can access the value of variable *code* by using the value of variable *ptr* and therefore, we say that the variable *ptr* points to the variable *code*, and hence *ptr* gets the name pointer.

15.3 ACCESSING ADDRESS OF A VARIABLE

The actual address of a variable is a system dependent. During compilation and linking, addresses are assumed to be relative to some base address, usually 0. When the operating system loads the program in a free block, all the address are transformed with relative to address of the first memory location of the free block. Hence, we do not know the address of a variable. Therefore, a question arises — *how can we determine the address of a variable*? This is done with the help of *address of* operator (&).

Consider the following statement

```
ptr = &code;
```

It will assign the number 1500 (address of variable *code*) to the variable *ptr*.

The following restrictions must be observed carefully:

1. The address of operator can only be used with variables or an array element. The following are illegal use of *address of* operator:

   (*a*) `&1200` (pointing at constant expression)
   (*b*) `&(a/b)` (pointing at expression)

2. Pointer variable can be initialized only with the use of *address of* operator or by assigning the value of another compatible pointer variable. The following way of initializing a pointer variable *ptr* is illegal:

   ```
   ptr = 1500;
   ```

   Though, the number 1500 happen to be the address of variable code.

15.4 DECLARING AND INITIALIZING POINTERS

Like other variables, the pointer variables are to be declared first in the declaration block to tell the compiler that to which kind of values these variables will be pointing. The syntax for declaring pointer variable is

```
type *ptr_name;
```

where *type* is a *pre-defined* or *user-defined* data types and indicates that the pointer will point to the variables of that specific data type, and character '*' indicates that variable is a pointer variable. For example, the statement

```
int *ptr1;
```

declares a pointer variable *ptr1* that can point to an integer type variable.

The pointer variable(s) declaration can also be combined with the declaration of other variables, provided they are of same type. For example, the statement

```
int x, *ptrX;
```

declares an integer variable *x* and a pointer variable *ptrX*.

Once a pointer has been declared, it must be initialized prior to its use. It is important to note here that like other variables, a pointer variable will take a garbage value, which can be an address of any storage location. Therefore, if not properly initialized, a pointer may point to any location in memory including those locations where operating system is running, and your system may hang-up i.e. stop responding. Such un-initialized pointers are sometimes referred to as *dangling/wild pointers.*

15.5 ACCESSING A VARIABLE THROUGH ITS POINTER

Once a pointer has been assigned the address of a variable, the question remains as how to access the value of the variable using the pointer. This is done using indirection operator (*). Consider the following statements

```
int *ptrX, x = 10, y;
ptrX = &x;
y = *ptrX;
printf("Value of variable x = %d\n", x );
printf("Value of variable pointed to by ptrX = %d\n",*ptrX );
printf("Address of variable x = %u\n", ptrX );
printf("Value of variable y  = %d\n",  y );
```

The declaration statement tells the compiler that *ptrX* is pointer variable that will point to an integer value, *x* is an integer variable and it also initializes the variable *x* with value 10, and *y* is another integer variable.

And suppose that during the execution of the above segment, a memory location with address 1098 is set aside for variable *x*.

The output of the above segment will look like:

```
Value of variable x = 10
Value of variable pointed to by ptrX = 10
Address of variable x = 1098
Value of variable y = 10
```

It is important to note that assignment of pointers and addresses is always done symbolically, by means of symbolic names. You cannot access the value stored at address 1098 by writing *1098. It will not work.

Listing 15.1

```
/* Program to illustrate use of addressof and indirection operators */
#include<stdio.h>
int main()
{
   int *ptrX, x = 10, y;
   ptrX = &x;
   y = *ptrX
   printf( "Value of variable x = %d\n", x );
   printf( "Value of variable pointed to by ptrX = %d\n", *ptrX );
   printf( "Address of variable x = %u\n", ptrX );
   printf( "Value of variable y  = %d\n",  y );
   return 0;
}
```

15.6 POINTER ARITHMETIC

The C language is very consistent in its approach to pointer arithmetic. The integration of pointers, arrays, and pointer arithmetic is one of the strengths of the C language. In this section, we will briefly describe the various operations permissible on pointers.

The following operations are permitted on pointers.

1. **Addition of a number to a pointer variable.**

   Suppose *p* is a pointer variable pointing to an element of integer type, then the statement

   ```
   p++;        or    ++p;
   ```

   increments the value of *p* by a factor of 2, so that it points to the next location that holds another value of integer type. This increment factor will be 1 for *character*, 4 for *long integer* and *float*, and 8 for *long float*. The statement

   ```
   p += i;
   ```

   where *i* is either a positive integer constant or an integer variable having positive value, increments *p* such that it points to the *i*th location beyond the location to which it is currently pointing.

2. **Subtraction of a number from a pointer variable.**

   Suppose *p* is a pointer variable pointing to an element of integer type, then the statement

   ```
   p—;        or    —p;
   ```

   decrements the value of *p* by a factor of 2, so that it now points to the location preceding the current location. The statement

   ```
   p -= i;
   ```

   where *i* is either a positive integer constant or an integer variable having positive value, decrements *p* such that it points to the *i*th location before the location to which it is currently pointing.

3. **Subtraction of one pointer variable from another.**

   One pointer variable can be subtracted from another provided both point to the same data type. The difference of the two indicates the number of bytes separating the corresponding elements.

In addition to these arithmetic operations, pointer variables can be compared with one another, provided they are compatible, *i.e.*, point to variables of same data type.

The following arithmetic operations on pointers are not permitted.

- Addition of two pointer variables.
- Multiplication of a pointer variable by a number.
- Division of a pointer variable by a number.

15.7 POINTER TO A POINTER

As mentioned, a pointer is variable that holds the address of another variable. This concept can be further extended. We can have a variable that hold an address of a variable that in turn holds an address of another variable. This type of variable will be known as *pointer to a pointer*. The underlying concept is known as *double indirection*. This concept can be further extended to triple level, fourth level, and so on.

A pointer to a pointer will be declared as

```
int **ptr;
```

The value pointed to by a pointer to another pointer will be accessed as

```
**ptr;
```

Listing 15.2

```
/*  Program to illustrate the use of double indirection  */
#include<stdio.h>
int main()
{
    int a = 5, *ptrA, **ptrPtrA;
    ptrA = &a;
    ptrPtrA = &ptrA;
    printf( "\nAddress of a = %u", &a );
    printf( "\nValue of a = %d", a );
    printf( "\nAddress of ptrA = %u", &ptrA );
    printf( "\nValue of ptrA = %u", ptrA );
    printf( "\nValue pointed to by ptrA = %d", *ptrA );
    printf( "\nAddress of ptrPtrA = %u", &ptrPtrA );
    printf( "\nValue of ptrPtrA = %u", ptrPtrA);
    printf( "\nValue pointed to by ptrPtrA = %d", **ptrPtrA);
    return 0;
}
```

Test Run

```
Address of a = 65524
Value of a = 5
Address of ptrA = 65522
Value of ptrA = 65524
Value pointed to by ptrA = 5
Address of ptrPtrA = 65520
Value of ptrPtrA = 65522
Value pointed to by ptrPtrA = 5
```

A practical example of using pointers to pointers is when pointers are passed by address to a calling function. The following skeleton of code demonstrates this:

```
void main()
{
   int *ptr1;
   // . . .
   func1( &ptr1, . . . );
   // . . .
}
void func1( int **ptr2, . . . )
{
   // . . .
   func2( &ptr2 );
   // . . .
}
void func2( int ***ptr3, . . .)
{
   // . . .
   // . . .
}
```

In the rest of the sections, we will extensively demonstrate the of use pointers. This is the area that is given a secondary treatment in most of the textbooks on C language. It is important to remember that pointers are the backbone of C language. Therefore every reader of C language must master them.

15.8 MEMORY ALLOCATION

It is important to note that anything that needs to be executed (programs) or processed (data) must be loaded into memory before it can be executed or processed. Therefore, for every program to be executed or data to be processed, some memory must be allocated for them. The memory allocation can be done in two ways – *statically* and *dynamically*. Let us look at both the ways.

15.8.1 Static Memory Allocation

When you give a command to run your program, the operating system allocates a block of memory for your program, loads it from the secondary storage (Floppy disk, hard disk, CD or DVD, etc.) into that block and then initiates its execution. When the program finishes its execution, the memory occupied by the program is automatically released. It means that the memory requirements are determined prior to execution of your program, and thereafter your program neither can acquire more memory nor can release the free memory, if not required.

The above situations depicts a situation where the amount of memory required is known before hand, and the compiler then can determine the memory requirements for the data as well as the instructions. In such a situation, memory allocation is known as *static memory allocation*.

15.8.2 Dynamic Memory Allocation

Further, it is important to note that the memory requirements for the instructions are always fixed. However, there may be situation when the exact memory requirements for the data may not be known in advance or the data requirements may vary from one program execution to another program execution, *i.e.*, memory requirements for the data are dynamic.

Therefore, when the amount of memory is not known before hand for a particular data item(s), then it is allocated at the execution time, *i.e.*, when the program is running. In such a situation, memory allocation is known as *dynamic memory allocation*.

15.8.3 Heap/Free Store

As mentioned earlier, every program is provided with a pool of unallocated memory that it can utilize during execution. This pool of unallocated memory is known as *heap* or *free store*. Therefore, whenever the memory of requisite size (amount) is required by the program, it is taken from the free store, and when the previously allocated memory is not required further, it is returned back to the free store.

The memory requirements for the instructions (program code) are always fixed, whereas the memory requirements for data may change when your program is dealing with dynamic structures.

15.9 DYNAMIC MEMORY MANAGEMENT

As mentioned earlier, when you give a command to run your program, the operating system allocates a block of memory for your program, loads it from the disk into that block and then initiates its execution. When the program finishes its execution, the memory occupied by the program is automatically released. It means that the memory requirements are determined prior to execution of your program, and there after your program can neither acquire more memory nor can release the free memory, if not required.

However, C language provides a set of library functions (listed in Table 15.1), called *dynamic memory management functions*, to allocate and de-allocate memory at execution time, *i.e.*, dynamically. By allocation, we mean that your program can obtain as much memory as required by your program even during execution of your program. By de-allocation, we mean that the memory acquired dynamically can be released at any time during your program execution. It is important to note that memory allocated dynamically, must be de-allocated before your program finishes its execution. Otherwise, even if your program terminates, memory allocated dynamically is never released automatically, and from operating system point of view that memory is still in use. Therefore, if you run the same program many times, many users are using your program concurrently, the operating system may run out of memory.

Table 15.1: Memory Management Functions

Function Name	Description
`malloc`	Allocates memory from heap.
`calloc`	Allocates memory from heap and initializes the allocated memory to zeroes.
`realloc`	Readjusts the existing block and copies the contents to the new location.
`free`	Deallocates a block allocated by *malloc*, *calloc* and *realloc* functions.
`coreleft`	Returns a measure of unused memory.

The *malloc()* function dynamically allocates memory from heap. The prototype for *malloc()* function is

```
void *malloc(size_t size);
```

It takes one argument that specifies the size of the block in bytes. The function returns a pointer to the allocated memory on success or a null pointer (0) in case of failure.

The *calloc()* function dynamically allocates memory and automatically initializes the memory to zeroes. The prototype for *calloc()* function is

```
void *calloc(size_t nitems, size_t size);
```

It takes two arguments. The first argument is the number of elements and the second argument is the size of each element. The function returns a pointer to the allocated memory on success or a null pointer (0) in case of failure.

The *realloc()* function changes the size of previously dynamically allocated memory with *malloc()*, *calloc()* or *realloc()* functions. The original contents held in the previously allocated memory are not changed provided the memory allocated is larger than the amount of memory previously allocated otherwise the contents are unchanged upto the size of new object. The prototype for *realloc()* function is

```
void *realloc(void *block, size_t size);
```

It takes two arguments. The first argument is the pointer to the original object and the second argument is the new size of the object.

Depending on the values of these arguments, following things can happen

- If the pointer to the original object is 0 (NULL), the *realloc()* function works identical to *malloc()* function.
- If size of new object is 0 and pointer is not 0, the memory of the object is freed.
- If the pointer is not 0 and the size of the new object is greater than zero, *realloc()* function tries to allocate new block of memory. If new space cannot be allocated, the object pointed to by the pointer is unchanged.

The *realloc()* function returns either a pointer to reallocated block or a null pointer.

The *free()* function deallocates a memory block previously allocated with *malloc()*, *calloc()* or *realloc()* functions. The prototype for *free()* function is

```
void free(void *block);
```

It takes one argument that specifies the pointer to the allocated block. But it is important to note that only the allocated block is deallocated, the pointer variable is not deleted.

The *coreleft()* function returns amount of free memory in the heap. Its protypes is

```
unsigned long coreleft(void);
```

15.10 POINTERS AND ARRAYS

When we declare an array, the compiler allocates a block of memory of appropriate size so that all the elements of an array can be stored in contiguous memory locations. The address of the first memory location (also the address of the first element of the array) of allocated block is known as the *base address*, and is assigned to the array name. Thus, array name behaves as a pointer variable.

15.10.1 Pointers and One-dimensional Arrays

Consider the following declaration statement

```
float a[9] = { 0, 1, 2, 3, 4, 5, 6, 7, 8 };
```

This statement set aside a contiguous block of 9 memory locations for the array named *a*. Here the array named *a* holds the address of the first element of the array i.e. base address of the array. The memory map of the array *a* is shown in Figure 15.4. By adding offset (index of the element) to this base address, the other elements of the array can also be accessed. For example, using pointer notation, elements of array *a* can be accessed as

```
*(a+0),  *(a+1),  *(a+2),  ...,  *(a+8)
```

999	1003	1007	1011	1015	1019	1023	1027	
0	1	2	3	4	5	6	7	8
a[0]	*a*[1]	*a*[2]	*a*[3]	*a*[4]	*a*[5]	*a*[6]	*a*[7]	*a*[8]

Figure 15.4: Memory map of one-dimensional array *a* with a base address 999

Listing 15.3

```
/* Program to demonstrate the way elements of one dimensional
 *  array are accessed using pointer notation
 */
#include<stdio.h>
int main()
{
   int arr[10]={12,15,20,17,25,50,11,10,8,13};
   int i, count, *ptr;
   float sum, average;
   ptr = arr;
   for ( sum = 0, i = 0; i < 10; i++ )
      sum += *(ptr+i);
   average = sum / 10;
   for ( count = 0, i = 0; i < 10; i++ ) {
      if ( *(ptr + i ) > average )
         count++;
   }
   printf( "\nNo. of elements > average = %d\n", count);
   return 0;
}
```

15.10.2 Pointers and Two-dimensional Arrays

Consider the following declaration statement

```
float a[3][3] = {{1,2,3},{4,6,9},{3,2,7}};
```

This statement set aside a contiguous block of 9 memory locations for the array named *a*. Here the array named *a* holds the address of the first element of the array, *i.e.*, base address of the array. As we know that there is no concept of rows and columns in memory. The elements of the array, irrespective of that whether it is one-dimensional, two-dimensional or three-dimensional, are stored in a continuous chain, *i.e.*, one after the other.

	Col #0	Col #1	Col #2
Row #0	1	2	3
Row #1	4	6	9
Row #2	3	2	7

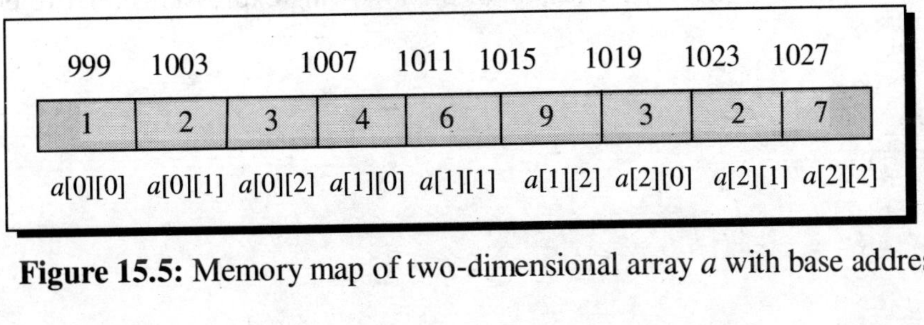

999	1003		1007	1011	1015	1019	1023	1027
1	2	3	4	6	9	3	2	7
a[0][0]	*a*[0][1]	*a*[0][2]	*a*[1][0]	*a*[1][1]	*a*[1][2]	*a*[2][0]	*a*[2][1]	*a*[2][2]

Figure 15.5: Memory map of two-dimensional array *a* with base address 999

Now let us see how we can access individual elements of the above two-dimensional array using pointers. The procedure is slightly difficult. As mentioned earlier that two-dimensional array can be treated as an array of arrays, where each element of the array is one-dimensional array. For example, above array can be visualized as

a[0]	1	2	3
a[1]	4	6	9
a[2]	3	2	7

Figure 15.6: Two-dimensional array *a* as array of one-dimensional arrays

We can refer to individual elements as *a*[0], *a*[1], and *a*[2]. More specifically, *a*[0] gives the address of the first one-dimensional array, *a*[1] gives the address of the second one-dimensional array, *a*[2] gives the address of the third one-dimensional array.

Listing 15.4

```
/*  Program to illustrate 2D array as array of 1D arrays  */
#include<stdio.h>
int main()
{
   int a[3][3] = { { 1, 2, 3 }, { 4, 6, 9 }, { 3, 2, 7 } };
   int i;
   for ( i = 0; i < 3; i++ )
   {
      printf("\nAddress of  1D array number %d = %u", i+1, a[i]);
   }
   printf( "\n" );
   return 0;
}
```

Now the question is — *how can we access the individual elements of these arrays*? Suppose we want to access the *j*th element of the *i*th row. We know that *a*[*i*] will give address of the *i*th one-dimensional array (i.e. *i*th row). And we also know from our knowledge of one-dimensional arrays that writing *a*[*i*] in subscript notation is equivalent to *(*a*+*i*). Further if *a*[*i*] is the address of the *i*th row, the address of the *j*th element of *i*th row will be (*a*[*i*]+*j*), and thus the element can be accessed as *(*a*[*i*]+*j*), which on replacing *a*[*i*] by *(*a*+*i*) becomes *(*(*a*+*i*)+*j*). Thus, all of the following expressions refer to element a_{ij}.

```
a[i][j]
*(a[i]+j)
*(*(a+i)+j)
```

Listing 15.5

```
/* Program to print elements of the 2D array using pointer notation */
#include<stdio.h>
int main()
{
   int a[3][3] = { { 1, 2, 3 }, { 4, 6, 9 }, { 3, 2, 7 } };
   int i, j;
   printf("\nElements of two-dimensional array are\n\n");
   for ( i = 0; i < 3; i++ ) {
      for ( j = 0; j < 3; j++ )
          printf ( "%4df\t", *(*(a+i)+j) );
      printf ( "\n" );
   }
   return 0;
}
```

15.10.3 Dynamic Arrays

The declaration of arrays at the compilation time (i.e. using subscripted notation) has one major limitation. The memory is allocated during the compilation time. If the number of actual data elements is very less as compared to the declared size, then a lot of memory is wasted. On the other hand, if the number of actual data elements is more than the declared size then we have to modify the source code. However, this limitation can be overcome if the memory is allocated at the execution time. The next program illustrates this concept.

Listing 15.6

```
/* Program to illustrate the allocation of memory
*  for one-dimensional array at execution time    */
#include<stdio.h>
#include<alloc.h>
int main()
{
   int  *a, n, i, big;
   printf( "Enter size of one-dimensional array: "  );
   scanf( "%d", &n );
   a = (int *) malloc(n*sizeof(int)); /* allocate memory for array */
   if ( a == NULL ) {
      printf ( "\nUnable to allocate memory\n" );
      return;
   }
   printf( "Enter %d elements of array\n", n );
   for ( i = 0 ; i < n ; i++)
      scanf( "%d", a+i );
   for ( big = *a, i = 1 ; i < n ; i++ ) {
      if ( *(a+i ) > big )
          big = *(a+i);
   }
   printf( "\nLargest element of the array = %d\n", big );
   free(a);    /* release the memory held by array */
   return 0;
}
```

15.11 POINTERS AND FUNCTIONS

15.11.1 Pointers as Function Arguments

If you remember, in *Chapter 11*, we had mentioned that the arguments to a function could be passed using either *call by value* or *call by address* mechanism. When we use call by value mechanism, the formal arguments of the function are declared as simple variable, and at execution time the values of the actual arguments are copied into formal arguments (formal arguments are local to the function), and the execution of the function begins.

However, when we use call by reference mechanism, the formal arguments are declared as pointers, and at execution time, the addresses of the actual arguments are copied into formal arguments and the execution of the function begins.

Listing 15.7

```
/*  Program to illustrate pointers as function arguments   */
#include<stdio.h>
int main()
{
   int a = 10, b = 20;
   void interchange( int *, int *);  /* function prototype */
   printf( "\nValue of a = %d and b = %d", a, b );
   printf( " before function call\n"  );
   interchange ( &a, &b);   /*   function call   */
   printf( "\nValue of a = %d and b = %d", a, b );
   printf( " after function call\n"  );
   return 0;
}
void interchange( int *x, int *y )  /* function definition */
{
  int temp;
  temp = *x;
  *x = *y;
  *y = temp;
}
```

Test Run

```
Value of a = 10 and b = 20 before function call
Value of a = 20 and b = 10 after function call
```

Consider the following program listing.

Listing 15.8

```
/* Program to illustrate non-pointer variables as function arguments */
#include<stdio.h>
int main()
{
   int a = 10, b = 20;
   void interchange( int, int );   /* function prototype */
```

```
    printf( "\nValue of a = %d and b = %d", a, b );
    printf( " before function call\n"  );
    interchange ( &a, &b);              /* function call        */
    printf( "\nValue of a = %d and b = %d", a, b );
    printf( " after function call\n"  );
    return 0;
}
void interchange ( int x, int y )   /* function definition */
{
    int temp;
    temp = x;
    x = y;
    y = temp;
}
```

Test Run

```
Value of a = 10 and b = 20 before function call
Value of a = 10 and b = 20 after function call
```

Why this version of the program could not complete the task of interchanging the values of the arguments. In this version, values of the *a* and *b* are copied into *x* and *y*, which act as local variables. Thus the values, in fact, of *x* and *y* are interchanged in the workspace of the *interchange()* function, but as soon as the function completes its execution, these variables are destroyed. Thus, the values of the variables remain un-effected. However, in the first version of the program, the addresses of variables *a* and *b* are copied into pointer variables *x* and *y*. These pointer variables, though local to the function *interchange()*, interchanges the values of *a* and *b* indirectly in the work space of the *main()* function, with the help of a local variable *temp*. When the function *interchange()* completes its execution, the variables *x*, and *y* along with temp are destroyed, but the task has been accomplished.

15.12 POINTERS AND STRINGS

As we know that a string is an array of characters, terminated with a null character '\0'. Therefore, like one-dimensional arrays, we can use individual characters in a string.

Listing 15.9

```
/* Program to illustrate access of individual characters in a string */
#include<stdio.h>
int main()
{
    char city[]= "Chandigarh is a beautiful city";
    char *ptr;
    ptr = city;
    printf( "Individual characters of the strings are" );
    printf( "\n\n" );
    while ( *ptr != '\0' )
    {
```

```
        printf ( "\n%c is stored is address %u", *ptr, ptr );
        ptr++;
    }
    printf ( "\n"  );
    return 0;
}
```

As mentioned earlier, storing a table of strings (list of strings) using a two-dimensional array is not an efficient way. We will take up that issue here again.

Consider the following declaration

```
char names[4][12] = { "Ram", "Inder Mohan", "Amanpreet", "Rajan" };
```

Where we have considered that each string can be of 20 characters, at maximum excluding the null character. This list of strings will be represented in memory as shown below:

R	a	m	‘\0’								
I	n	d	e	r		M	o	h	a	n	‘\0’
A	m	a	n	p	r	e	e	t	‘\0’		
R	a	j	a	n	‘\0’						

Total memory requirements are 48 bytes. However, if we count, first string requires 4 bytes, second string requires 12 bytes, third string requires 10 bytes, and the fourth string requires 6 bytes. Thus total memory requirements come out to be 32, wastage of 16 bytes. In practice, it has been shown that, on average, half of the allocated space is mere wastage.

However, this kind of representation of list of strings can be practical only if all strings are of equal length, but this happens rarely in practice.

Therefore, more practical and efficient way of storing a list of strings is using array of pointers to strings.

The following declaration illustrates this point

```
char *names[4] = { "Ram", "Inder Mohan", "Amanpreet", "Rajan" };
```

This will be represented in memory as

R	a	m	‘\0’								
I	n	d	e	r		M	o	h	a	n	‘\0’
A	m	a	n	p	r	e	e	t	‘\0’		
R	a	j	a	n	‘\0’						

This declaration allocates only 32 bytes of memory, *i.e.*, what is actually needed.

Listing 15.10

```
/* To illustrate I/O of strings represented using array of pointers */
#include<stdio.h>
#include<string.h>
int main()
{
   char *names[30];
   int i, n;
   printf( "\nEnter number of strings : " );
   scanf( "%d", &n);
   for ( i = 0; i < n; i++ ) {
      printf ( "\nEnter string #%d : ", i+1 );
      gets(names[i]);
   }
   printf( "\nYou have entered following strings\n\n" );
   for ( i = 0; i < n; i++ )
      puts(names[i]);
   return 0;
}
```

15.13 POINTERS AND STRUCTURES

As we can use pointers with other data types, we can also use pointers for structure variables. Consider the following declarations

```
typedef struct
{
   int code;
   char name[20];
   int  dept_code;
   float  salary;
} EMPLOYEE;
EMPLOYEE empl, *ptr;
```

These declarations create and user-defined data type and given it name *EMPLOYEE* and declares *empl* as variable of type employee and *ptr* as pointer variable to type employee.

Now the following statement

```
ptr = &empl;
```

can be used to assign the address of variable *empl* to pointer variable *ptr*. Now, we can access the members of the structure variable *empl* using pointer variable *ptr*. You may expect that the elements can be accessed as shown below:

```
*ptr.code     *ptr.name     *ptr.dept_code     *ptr.salary
```

But this approach will not work as the *dot operator* '.' has higher priority than the *indirection operator* '*'.

The correct way is to write as

```
(*ptr).code    (*ptr).name   (*ptr).dept_code   (*ptr).salary
```

There is another approach that is more elegant and simple. In this approach, the elements of structure are accessed using *arrow operator* '–>' which is a combination of two characters, *i.e.*, hyphen '–' and greater-than '>'. The syntax for accessing members of structure using arrow operator is:

```
ptr->vname
```

where *ptr is* pointer variable pointing to a structure, and *vname* is the name of element of the structure.

Using arrow operator, the elements of structure of type *employee* pointed to by pointer variable *ptr* can be accessed as

```
ptr->code     ptr->name     ptr->dept_code     ptr->salary
```

Listing 15.11

```
/*  Program to illustrate I/O of structure using pointers  */
#include<stdio.h>
#include<string.h>
typedef struct
{
   int code;
   char name[20];
   int dept_code;
   float salary;
} EMPLOYEE;
int main()
{
   EMPLOYEE empl, *ptr;
   ptr = &empl;
   printf("\nEnter employee code as integer number: ");
   scanf( "%d", &(ptr->code));
   printf( "\nEnter name of employee : " );
   gets(ptr->name);
   printf("\nEnter department code as integer number: ");
   scanf( "%d", &(ptr->dept_code) );
   printf( "\nEnter Salary: " );
   scanf( "%f", &(ptr->salary) );
   printf( "Particulars of employee as entered by" );
   printf( "you are\n\n" );
   printf( "\nEmployee code : %d", ptr->code );
   printf( "\nEmployee name : %s", ptr->name );
   printf( "\nDepartment code : %d", ptr->dept_code );
   printf( "\nEmployee salary : %.2f", ptr->salary );
   return 0;
}
```

15.13.1 Self-referential Structures

The self-referential structures are structures that include an element that is a pointer to another structure of the same type. These structures find their application in building complex data structure such as *linked lists*, *trees* and *graphs*.

Following are some examples of self-referential structures.

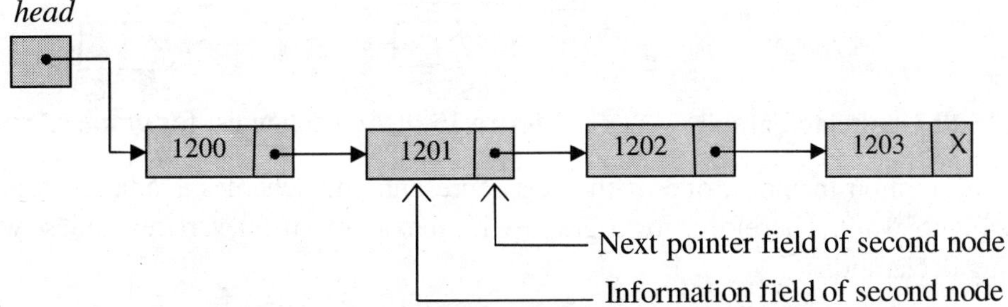

Figure 15.6: Linear linked list of integer values with nodes 4

To represent the above linear linked list in memory, we need following declarations

```
typedef struct nodeType
{
   int info;
   struct nodeType *next;
} NODE;
NODE *start;
```

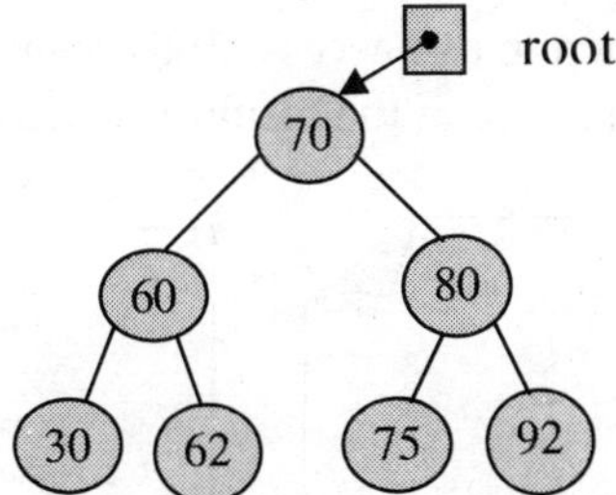

Figure 15.7: Binary tree

To represent a binary tree in memory, we need following declarations

```
typedef struct nodeType
{
   struct nodeType *left;
   int info;
   struct nodeType *right;
}  BNODE;
BNODE *root;
```

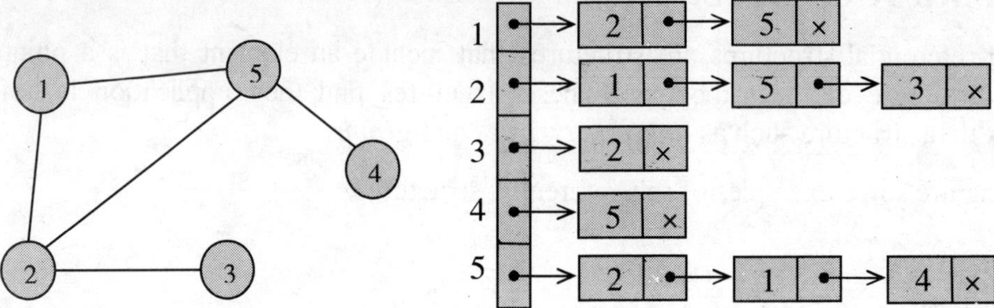

Figure 15.8: Undirected graph **Figure 15.9:** Adjacency list for graph

To represent a graph in memory, one of the best representation schemes is adjacency list as shown in Figure 15.9. Therefore, for a graph with maximum of 50 vertices/nodes, we need following declarations

```
#define MAX 50
typedef struct nodeType
{
   int vertex;
   struct nodeType *link;
} node;
node *adj[MAX];
```

15.13.2 Passing Structures by Reference to a Function

When we pass a structure by address, only address of the first byte of the structure is passed. Using this address, the called function can access all the elements of the structure, and thus the called function can process the structure in the memory space of the calling function.

```
typedef struct {
   int day;
   int month;
   int year;
} DATE;
void printDate(DATE *);
void main()
{
   DATE aDate = { 10, 6, 2008 };
   int x;
   printDate(&aDate);
   /*  more statements    */
}
```

```
/*  function definition    */
void printDate(DATE *tDate )
{

   /*  local declarations */
   /*  other statements   */

}
```

Figure 15.10: Passing entire structure by address

Listing 15.12

```
/* Program to illustrate the passing of a structure by address  */
#include <stdio.h>
typedef struct
{
   int day;
   int month;
   int year;
} DATE;
void printDate( DATE *aDate );      /* function declaration  */
int main()
{
   DATE tDate = { 10, 6, 2008 };   /* initialize a structure */
   printDate( &tDate );            /* function call          */
   return 0;
}
void printDate( DATE *aDate )
{
   printf( "\nDate in format dd/mm/yy: %02d/%02d/%2d\n",
           aDate->day, aDate->month, aDate.->year );
}
```

15.14 POSSIBLE PROBLEMS WITH THE USE OF POINTERS

Pointers can be the source of mysterious and catastrophic program bugs. Common bugs related to pointers and memory management is *dangling/wild pointers*, *memory leaks*, and *allocation failures*. Each of these problems is discussed next.

15.14.1 Problem of Dangling/Wild Pointers

The most common problem with pointers is that the programmer fails to initialize a pointer with a valid address. Such an initialized pointer, referred to as *dangling/wild pointer*, can end up pointing anywhere in memory that may include the program code itself or to the code of the operating system. If the programmer assign a value to such pointer, the value will overwrite the program or operating system instructions, and the computer program may show undesirable behaviour or may even crash, *i.e.*, stop responding. When the system stop responding, we say the system has hanged up and the only option left is to reboot the system. Therefore, care must be taken to initialize pointers with valid address.

15.14.2 Problem of Null Pointer Assignment

One particular situation that happens is when the pointer points to address 0, which is called NULL. For example, this may happen that if the pointer variable is declared as global since global variables are initialized to 0. Likewise, this can also happen for a local un-initialized pointer variable, particularly for local static variables, they are also initialized to 0. When it happens, and no catastrophic situations had occurred, then the system will display a message "*Null pointer assignment*" on termination of the program.

15.14.3 Problem of Memory Leak

Another very serious problem with pointers is that of *memory leak*. Memory leak is a situation where the programmer fails to release the memory allocated at run time in a module. Note that when memory is allocated, a pointer variable is used to hold the address of the allocated block, however, when the module completes its execution, the pointer variable goes out of scope and there will be no way to reach that memory block. Therefore, care must be taken to release the allocated memory block in a module where memory was allocated.

Listing 15.13

```
/*  Program to illustrate the cause of memory leak   */
#include<stdio.h>
int main()
{
   . . . . .
   fun(); //  invoke function named 'fun'
   . . . . .
}
void fun()
{
   int *intPtr;
   . . . . .
   /*  allocate memory for 'n' integer numbers
   intPtr = ( int * ) malloc(n*sizeof(int));
   /*   work on the allocated block    */
}
```

15.14.4 Problem of Allocation Failures

Allocation failure is a situation when the program through *malloc()*, *calloc()*, *realloc()*, function request for a block of memory, and the operating could not fulfill the request of the program because the sufficient memory may not be available in the free pool of memory. In that case, these functions return a NULL pointer indicating allocation failure.

Therefore, the programmer should take care of allocation failures and provide a safe exit in their programs on such failures.

Listing 15.14

```
/* Program to illustrates the allocation failure, and
*  the way it should be handled       */
#include<stdio.h>
void main()
{
   int *intPtr;
   . . . . .
   /*  allocate memory for 'n' integer numbers
   intPtr = ( int * ) malloc(n*sizeof(int));
```

```
    if ( intPtr == NULL ) {
        printf("\nUnable to allocate memory . . .\n");
        return;
    }
    /*   work on the allocated block    */
    . . . . .
    free(intPtr);    // release the memory
}
```

15.15 SUPPLEMENTARY PROBLEMS

Problem 15.1:

Write a program that takes a list of numbers as its command line arguments, and prints the sum of these numbers.

The procedure to be followed is as follows:

The command line arguments are received by the *main()* function as string. Since the command line arguments are just numbers, therefore the string are made up of only letters 0-9 and decimal point '.'. We use here a library function *atof()* to convert a string of representing a number to numeric value. Then we add these numeric values one by one after conversion. We need to include *stdlib.h* header file in order to use *atof()* library function.

Listing 15.15

```
/* Program to add list of integer numbers given as
*  command line arguments
*  filename : sum.c          */
# include <stdio.h>
# include <stdlib.h>
int main( int argc, char *argv[] )
{
    int i;
    float sum = 0;
    for ( i = 1; i < argc; i++ ) {
        sum += atof( argv[i] );
    }
    printf("\nSum of numbers on command line = %.2f\n", sum);
    return 0;
}
```

Test Run

```
>sum 1 2 3 4 5 6 7 8 9 10
Sum of numbers on command line = 55.00
```

Problem 15.2:

Consider the following declaration:

```
char *names[]={"Vimal", "Amit", "Anuj", "Rohit", "Abhijit"};
```

Write a program to produce the following output:

```
tijihbA, tihoR, junA, timA, lamiV
```

Listing 15.16

```
/*  Program to reverse each string of array of strings    */
# include <stdio.h>
# include <stdlib.h>
void reverseString(char *p);
int main()
{
   int i;
   char *names[] = {"Vimal", "Amit", "Anuj", "Rohit", "Abhijit"};
   printf( "\n" );
   for ( i = 4; i >= 1; i-- )
   {
       reverseString(names[i]);
       printf( "%s,", names[i]);
   }
   reverseString(names[i]);
   printf( "%s,", names[i]);
   printf( "\n" );
   return 0;
}
void reverseString(char *p)
{
   char t;
   char *sStr, *eStr;
   sStr = p;
   eStr = p + strlen(p) - 1;
   while ( eStr > sStr )
   {
       t = *sStr;
       *sStr = *eStr;
       *eStr = t;
       sStr++;
       eStr--;
   }
}
```

Test Run

```
tijihbA, tihoR, junA, timA, lamiV
```

Problem 15.3:

Write a function that takes an array as its argument and returns the largest, smallest and range of its elements. Using this function, write a program using pointers to find the largest, smallest and range of elements of the array.

Listing 15.17

```
/* Program to find the largest, smallest, and range of elements
*  using pointer notation only */
#include<stdio.h>
#include<alloc.h>
void compute(int *,int,int *,int *,int); /*function declaration*/
int main()
{
   int *a, i, n, largest, smallest, range;
   printf( "\nEnter size of array: "  );
   scanf( "%d", &n );
   a = (int *) malloc(n*sizeof(int)); /* allocate memory for array */
   if ( a == NULL ) {
      printf ( "\nUnable to allocate memory\n" );
      return;
   }
   printf( "\nEnter %d elements of array\n\n", n );
   for ( i = 0 ; i < n ; i++ )
      scanf( "%d", a+i );
   compute(a, n, &largest, &smallest, &range); /*function call*/
   printf( "\nLargest element of the array    = %d", largest );
   printf( "\nSmallest element of the array   = %d", smallest );
   printf( "\nRange of elements of the array = %d\n", range );
   free ( a );        /* release the memory held by array */
   return 0;
}
void compute(int *a, int n, int *big, int *small, int *range)
{
   int i;
   *big = *small = *a;
   for ( i = 1; i < n; i++ ) {
      if ( *(a+i) > *big ) *big = *(a+i);
      if ( *(a+i) < *small ) *small = *(a+i);
   }
   *range = *big - *small;
}
```

Test Run

```
Enter size of array: 10
Enter 10 elements of array
12 30 21 34 9 59 70 54 44 33
Largest element of the array    = 70
Smallest element of the array   = 9
Range of elements of the array = 61
```

EXERCISE

1. How can we get the address of a variable?
2. What is a pointer variable?
3. How is a pointer variable declared?
4. How can the values pointed to by a pointer variable be accessed?
5. What are the various types of pointers?
6. Pointers are double-edged weapons. Comment.
7. What are the operations permissible on pointers?
8. What are the operations, which are not permissible on pointers?
9. What is the difference between *static* and *dynamic* memory allocation?
10. What do you mean by a *dangling/wild pointer*? What type of problems it may cause?
11. What is a NULL pointer assignment?
12. What is a memory leak? What can be the possible reason for it? How can memory leaks be avoided?
13. What is an allocation failure?

PROGRAMMING EXERCISE

1. Write a program that dynamically allocates memory for an array of size *n*, reads elements of array and sorts them in ascending order.
2. Write a function *substr()* whose prototype is given as

```
char *substr(char *str1, char *str2);
```

   that scan the first string for the occurrence of a second string, and returns a pointer to the element in the first string where the second string begins. However, if the second string does not occur in the first string, the function should return NULL. Write a program to test the above function.

3. Write a function *replace()* whose prototype is given as

```
int replace(char *str, char c1, char c2);
```

   that replace every occurrence of character c1 with character c2, and returns the total replacements made. Write a program to test the above function.

4. Consider the following structure definition:

```
struct BOX {
   char make[25];
   float length, breadth, height;
};
```

   Write a function that takes address of the *BOX* structure and returns its volume.

5. Consider the following declaration:

```
struct EMPLOYEE {
   int code;
   char name[31];
   float salary;
};
```

Given that there are *n* (≤50) employees in an organization. Write a program, using pointer notation to access the data of an employee that output the details of the employee having highest salary.

6. Write a function *substr()* whose prototype is given as

```
char *substr(char *str1, char *str2);
```

that scan the first string for the occurrence of a second string, and returns a pointer to the element in the first string where the second string begins. However, if the second string does not occur in the first string, the function should return NULL. Write a program to test the above function.

7. Write a function *replace()* whose prototype is given as

```
int replace(char *str, char c1, char c2);
```

that replace every occurrence of character c1 with character c2, and returns the total replacements made. Write a program to test the above function.

❑ ❑ ❑

Chapter 16

File Handling

Learning Objectives

After reading this chapter, students will be able to

- comprehend the concept of data file and its usefulness
- explain the different steps in processing a file
- explain the opening, reading and writing of files
- describe the variety of library functions available for doing input/output on files
- write efficient programs for file handling

16.1 INTRODUCTION

The programs described so far, accepts the input data from the keyboard at the time of execution. The main limitation of this approach is that it is very difficult to handle large volume of data. As an example, suppose there are about 100 data items to enter. Some of the problems that may arise are enumerated below:

- It takes lot of time to enter the entire data.
- If the user makes a mistake while entering the data, he has to start from the beginning.
- If the same data is to be processed again at some later stage, again we have to enter it again. That is, for every program run, we have to enter the same data again and again.

Therefore, if the data is entered in computer's memory, checked for its correctness, and finally stored in a disk file, a program can read it directly from the disk and that too at very high speed.

In addition, the output of one program may become input for another program. In such a situation, it is more efficient to store the output of a program in a disk file, which can subsequently be read by other program(s).

A program developed in C language can read and write files in a variety of ways. Each of these ways is described in this chapter in a very simple manner and illustrated with well-designed programming examples.

16.2 STEPS IN PROCESSING A FILE

The processing of a file involves following steps:

1. **Opening a file** — First step in file processing is to open the file in appropriate mode. If you want to read from a file in your program, the file must be opened in the read/input mode. Similarly, if you want to write the output of your program to a file, the file must be opened in the write/output mode. However, there may be cases when you want to read from and also write onto the same file, then file must be opened in read-write mode.
2. **Reading from or writing onto a file** — Once a file is opened successfully, data can be read from a file or written to a file in a variety of ways that are described in next sections.
3. **Closing the file** — This is the final step in file processing. Once we have completed the reading and writing of the files, each file must be closed.

16.2.1 Opening a File

Before a program can write to a file or read from a file, the program must open it. Opening a file establishes an understanding between the program and the operating system. This provides the operating system with the *name* of the file and the *mode* in which the file is to be opened, *i.e.*, whether for reading or writing and that too in text mode or binary mode. Communication areas are set up between the file and the program. One of these areas is a structure of type *FILE*, declared in header file named *stdio.h* that holds information about the file.

For example, the statement

```
fptr = fopen( "test.dat", "w" );
```

request the operating system to open a file named *test.dat* in text mode and prepare it for writing.

Table 16.1: File Opening Modes

Mode	Purpose
r	Open a file for reading. The file must already exist.
w	Open a file for writing. If the file already exists, its contents will be discarded. If it does not exist, it will be created.
a	Open a file for extending. Data will be added to the end of the existing file, if file already exists. If it does not exist, it will be created.
r	Open a file for both reading and writing. The file must already exist.
w+	Open a file for both reading and writing. If it does not exist, it will be created.
a+	Open a file for both reading and appending. If the file does not exist, it will be created.

When the program makes a request to open a file, it receives back a pointer to this particular structure, if the request is granted; otherwise it receives a sentinel value, such as a *NULL* value defined *stdio.h*. Each file opened will have its own *FILE* structure, with a pointer to it. Any program can open any number of files.

Possible Trouble with Opening a File

As mentioned earlier, the request for opening a file may be granted or rejected. In case of rejection, the program will not run and will terminate abnormally. There may be many reasons for the rejection of program request.

For example

- Trying to open a file for reading that does not exist.
- Trying to open a file for writing, but sufficient space is not available on the disk.
- Trying to open a file that has been corrupted, etc.

Thus, it is important for the program that uses a disk file to check whether a file has been opened successfully before trying to read from or write onto the file. If the file cannot be opened, *fopen()* function returns a NULL value.

Therefore, a program can check the value returned by the *fopen()* function to determine whether the file is opened successfully or not. Hence, it is always better to write program segment responsible for opening a file as in next code segment.

```
fptr = fopen ( "test.dat", "w" );
if ( fptr == NULL )
{
   printf( "\nCan't open file test.dat.\n" );
   return 1;
}
```

16.2.2 Closing a File

When a program has finished with reading/writing of a file, it must be closed. This task is carried out by using *fclose()* library function, whose syntax is

```
fclose( fptr );
```

where *fptr* is a file pointer associated with a file which is to be closed.

Closing a file explicitly has two effects. These are

- Any data remaining in the buffer is written to the file. It may be noted that the buffer used is invisible to the programmer.
- Frees the communication areas used by the particular file so that they are available for other files. These areas include the *FILE* structure and the buffer itself.

For all possible ways of reading & writing, way of opening and closing a file is same.

Why buffer is required?

A *buffer* is a temporary storage area in main memory. A buffer is necessary even if it is invisible. To visualize its importance, let us consider a particular example. Suppose our program accesses the disk to read/write one character at a time. The disk system takes some time to position the head on the correct track and then further waits for the correct sector of the track to come around.

For every read/write operation, the motor that rotates the disk actually has to start from a stand still. If you type several characters repeatedly, and each one requires a separate disk access, some of the characters would probably be lost. So this approach will be inefficient. To solve this problem, the buffer is used.

When a program writes data to a file, it is actually stored in a buffer rather than being written immediately to the disk. When the buffer is full, its contents are written to the disk all at once, and subsequent writes continue onto the buffer. Similarly, when a program reads data from a file, a block of data, equal to the size of buffer except the last block, is read from the disk file and is placed in the buffer. The input functions subsequently read data from a buffer. When a program attempts to read a data item that is not in buffer, it forces to read another block of data containing the requested data item.

16.2.3 Reading and Writing of Files

There is a variety of ways of reading data from a file and writing data to a file. These are enumerated below:

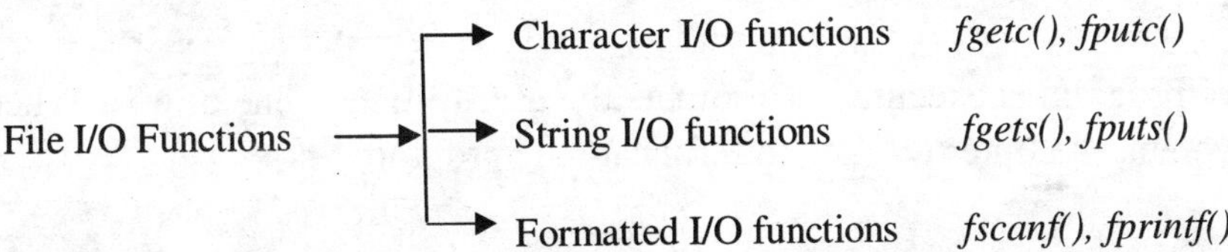

16.3.3.1 Reading and Writing using Character I/O Functions

Using character I/O functions, data can be read or written one character at a time. This is analogous to the way functions *putchar()* and *getchar()* write data to screen and read data from the keyboard.

Writing to a file

Once the program has established a line of communication with a particular file by opening it, then it can write to the file. The syntax of function that writes one character at a time is

```
fputc( ch, fptr );
```

where *ch* is a character variable or constant, and *fptr* is a file pointer.

The *fputc()* function is similar to *putchar()* function, the only difference is that a *putchar()* function always writes to screen unless redirection is employed. The following listing shows the example of a program that accepts a line of text from keyboard, one character at a time, and writes into disk file named *file1.dat*.

Listing 16.1

```
/*
*  Program to demonstrate writing of one character at a time to file
*/
#include<stdio.h>
int main()
{
   FILE *fptr;
   char ch;
   fptr = fopen( "file1.dat", "w" );
   if ( fptr == NULL )
   {
      printf( "\nUnable to open file1.dat\n" );
      return 1;
   }
   printf( "\nType a line of text, when finished" );
   printf( ", when finished hit Enter key\n" );
   while ( ( ch = getche() ) != '\r' )
      fputc ( ch, fptr );
   fclose( fptr );
   return 0;
}
```

When the above program is executed, it prompts the user to type a line of text. When you have finished, you hit the Enter (↵) key to terminate the program.

Test Run

```
C is a powerful procedural language. It provides both low-level as well
as high level features. ↵
```

Reading from a file

If the program can write to a file, it should also be able to read from a file. The syntax of the function that reads and returns one character at a time is

```
ch = fgetc( fptr );
```

where *ch* is a character variable, and *fptr* is a file pointer.

The *fgetc()* function returns the character read from the file or the end-of-file (EOF) character if it has reached the end of the file. The *fgetc()* function is similar to *getchar()* function, the only difference is that the later functions always read from the keyboard unless redirection is employed. The following listing shows the example of a program that reads one character at a time from file, and writes onto the screen.

Listing 16.2

```
/*
*   Program to demonstrate reading of character at a time from a file
*/
#include<stdio.h>
#include<stdlib.h>
int main()
{
   FILE *fptr;
   char ch;
   fptr = fopen( "file1.dat", "r" );
   if ( fptr == NULL )
   {
      printf( "\nUnable to open file1.dat\n" );
      return 1;
   }
   printf( "\nContens of file are:\n\n" );
   while ( ( ch = fgetc (fptr) ) != EOF )
      putchar( ch );
   fclose( fptr );
   return 0;
}
```

When the above program is executed, it reads the contents of file *file1.dat*, one character at a time and writes onto screen till it encounters the end-of-file (EOF).

Test Run

```
Contents of file are:
C is a powerful procedural language. It provides both low-level as well
as high level features.
```

16.3.3.2 Reading and Writing using String I/O functions

Using string I/O functions, data can be read or written in the form of string of characters. Reading and writing strings of characters is as easy as individual characters. This is analogous to *puts()* and *gets()* functions that write data to screen and read data from the keyboard.

Writing to a file

The syntax of the function that writes a string of characters at a time is

```
fputs( str, fptr );
```

where *str* is a array of characters or a string constant, and *fptr* is a file pointer.

The *fputs()* function is similar to *puts()* function, the only difference is that the *puts()* function always writes to the screen unless redirection is employed.

The following listing shows the example of a program that accepts a series of strings from keyboard, and writes them onto a disk file.

Listing 16.3

```
/*
 *    Program to demonstrate writing of strings to a file
 */
#include<stdio.h>
#include<string.h>
int main()
{
    FILE *fptr;
    char str[81];
    fptr = fopen( "file2.dat", "w" );
    if ( fptr == NULL )
    {
        printf( "\nUnable to open file2.dat\n" );
        return 1;
    }
    printf( "\nEnter a set of strings, press just" );
    printf( " Enter key to finish\n" );
    while ( strlen( gets( str ) ) > 0 )
    {
        fputs( str, fptr );
        fputs( "\n", fptr );
    }
    fclose( fptr );
    return 0;
}
```

Test Run

```
C is a powerful procedural language.↵
It is a middle level language.↵
All Programs are tested using Turbo C Compiler.↵
↵
```

When the above program is executed, it accepts set of strings terminated by hitting *Enter* key. When you have finished, hit the *Enter* key in the beginning without entering anything, which is taken as string of length 0, *i.e.*, *null string*, to terminate the program.

In the above program, we have set up an array of characters to store the string. The *fputs()* function then writes the contents of the array to the disk. Since *fputs()* function does not add a *newline* character automatically to the end of the string, we must do this explicitly to make it easier to read the string back from the file.

Reading from a file

The syntax of the function that reads strings from a file is

```
fgets( str, n, fptr );
```

where *str* is an array of characters and specifies the address where the string is to be stored, *n* is the maximum length of the input string, and *fptr* is a file pointer.

The *fgets()* function is similar to *gets()* function, the only difference is that the *gets()* function always reads from keyboard unless redirection is employed. The *fgets()* function returns a *NULL* value when it reads end-of-file *EOF*. Following listing shows example of a program that reads one string at a time from a file, and writes onto the screen.

Listing 16.4

```
/*
*   Program to demonstrate reading of strings from a file
*/
#include<stdio.h>
#include<string.h>
int main()
{
   FILE *fptr;
   char str[81];
   fptr = fopen( "file2.dat", "r" );
   if ( fptr == NULL )
   {
      printf( "\nUnable to open file2.dat\n" );
      return 1;
   }
   printf( "\nContens of file are:\n\n" );
   while ( fgets( str, 80, fptr ) != NULL )
   {
      puts( str );
   }
   fclose( fptr );
   return 0;
}
```

When the above program is executed, it reads the contents of *file3.dat* one string at a time and writes them onto the screen till it encounters EOF.

Test Run

```
Contents of file are:

C is a powerful procedural language.
It is a middle level language.
All Programs are tested using Turbo C Compiler.
```

16.3.3.3 Reading and Writing using Formatted I/O functions

So far we have considered reading and writing of characters, strings, and integer numbers. *What about the real numbers*? and *What about the mixed type of data*? For example, suppose that we want to store information about an agent comprising his name (a string), code number (an integer number), and height (a real number). We want to create a data file for a given list of agents. This can be done using formatted I/O functions.

Writing to a file

The syntax of the function that writes formatted data to a file is

```
fprintf( fptr, "format-string" , ditems );
```

where *fptr* is a file pointer, and *ditems* is a lists of variables to be written to a file. The *fprintf()* is similar to *printf()* function, the only difference is that *printf()* function writes formatted data onto the screen.

Listing 16.5

```
/*
*  Program to demonstrate writing of formatted data to a file
*/
#include<stdio.h>
int main()
{
   FILE *fptr;
   char yes_no;
   char name[41];
   int code;
   float height;
   fptr = fopen( "file3.dat", "w" );
   if ( fptr == NULL ) {
      printf( "\nUnable to open file3.dat\n" );
      return 1;
   }
   while(1)
   {
      printf( "\nEnter name, code number, height" );
      scanf( "%s,%d,%f", name, &code, &height );
      fprintf( fptr,"%s,%d,%f", name, code, height );
      printf( "Any more input y/n?: " );
      yes_no = tolower( getche() );
      fflush ( stdin );
      if ( yes_no == 'n' )
         break;
   }
   fclose( fptr );
   return 0;
}
```

Test Run

```
Enter name, code number, height
Geetu, 10, 160.25
Any more input y/n?: y
Enter name, code number, height
Shivani, 11, 158.5
Any more input y/n?: y
Enter name, code number, height
Vijay, 12, 165.5
Any more input y/n?: y
Enter name, code number, height
Gurpreet, 13, 166.25
Any more input y/n?: n
```

The above information is now in a file named *file3.dat*. If we attempt to look at it using TYPE command, the entire output will be on the same line as there are no *newlines* in the data. To format the output more conveniently, we can write a program specifically to read the above file using formatted input.

Reading from a file

The syntax of the function that reads formatted data to a file is

```
fscanf( fptr, "format-string" , ditems );
```

where *fptr* is a file pointer, and *ditems* is a lists of address where the values read from a file are to be stored.

The *fscanf()* is similar to *scanf()* function, the only difference is that *scanf()* function reads formatted data from the keyboard.

Listing 16.6

```
/*
*  Program to demonstrate writing of formatted from a file
*/
#include<stdio.h>
int main()
{
   FILE *fptr;
   char yes_no;
   char name[41];
   int code;
   float height;
   fptr = fopen( "file3.dat", "r" );
   if ( fptr == NULL )
   {
      printf( "\nUnable to open file3.dat\n" );
      return 1;
```

```
    }
    printf( "\nContens of file are:\n\n" );
    while(fscanf(fptr,"%s,%d,%f", name, &code, &height) != EOF)
    {
        printf( "%s %d %f\n", name, code, height );
    }
    fclose( fptr );
    return 0;
}
```

Test Run

```
Contents of file are:

Geetu 10 160.25
Shivani 11 158.5
Vijay 12 165.5
Gurpreet 13 166.25
```

16.3 FILE STATUS FUNCTIONS

The C language provides following three functions to handle file status queries:

- Function *eof()* to test end of file.
- Function *ferror()* to test error.
- Function *clearerr()* to clear error.

16.3.1 Test End of File: *feof()* Function

The *feof()* function is used to check if the end of file has been reached. If the file pointer is at the end, *i.e.*, all data have been read, the function returns 1. If the end of file is not reached, it returns value 0. The prototype for *feof()* is

```
int feof(FILE *stream);
```

where *stream* is a file pointer for the currently opened file.

16.3.2 Test Error: *ferror()* Function

The *ferror()* function is used to test the error status of file. As mentioned earlier, errors can be created for many reasons, ranging from bad media (disk, CD, etc.) to illegal operations such as trying to read a file in the write state. If the *ferror()* function returns 1 if an error has occurred after a file operation. If no error has occurred, the file ferror() returns value 0. The prototype for *ferror()* is

```
int ferror(FILE *stream);
```

where *stream* is a file pointer for the currently opened file.

It is important to note here that testing for an error does not reset the error condition. Once an error has occurred, it can only return to normal read or write state after clearing the error state using *clearer()* function, described next.

16.3.3 Clear Error: *clearerr()* Function

When an error occurs, the subsequent calls to the *ferror()* function return 1, until the error status of the file is reset. The *clearerr()* function is used for this purpose. The prototype for *clearerr()* is

```
void clearerr(FILE *stream);
```

where *stream* is a file pointer for the currently opened file.

It is important to note here that even though we have cleared the error, we have not necessarily cured the problem. We may find that subsequent read or write operation may return to error state.

16.4 FILE POSITIONING FUNCTIONS

The C language provides following three functions to handle file positioning operations:

- Function *rewind()* to set the file pointer to the beginning of the file.
- Function *ftell()* to know the current position of the file pointer in the file.
- Function *seek()* to change the position of the file pointer in the file.

16.4.1 Rewind File: *rewind()* Function

One way of positioning the file pointer to the beginning of the file is to close the file and then re-open it again. However, we can accomplish the same task without closing the file using *rewind()* function. This function positions the file pointer in the beginning of the file. This function sounds very much like rewinding the audio or video cassette in order to listen or watch the cassette from the beginning.

The prototype of *rewind()* function is

```
void rewind(FILE *stream);
```

where *stream* is a file pointer for the currently opened file.

16.4.2 Current Location: *ftell()* Function

In some situations, it may be required to find the current location of the file pointer within the file. The *ftell()* function lets us know the current position of the file pointer.

The prototype of the *ftell()* function is

```
long int ftell(FILE *stream);
```

where *stream* is a file pointer for the currently opened file. Note that the *ftell()* function returns a long integer. This is necessary because many files may have more that 32, 767 bytes of data.

Recall that the C I/O system considers files as streams of bytes of data. It measures the position in the file by the number of bytes, relative to zero, *i.e.*, from the beginning of the file. When file pointer is at the beginning of the file, the *ftell()* function returns 0. If the file pointer is at the second byte, the *ftell()* function returns value 1.

16.4.3 Set Position: *fseek()* Function

In order to read a data item from anywhere in a file, we have to move the file pointer to the beginning of that data item. To accomplish this task, we can use *fseek()* function.

The prototype of using *fseek()* function is

```
int fseek(file *stream, long offset, int wherefrom );
```

The *fseek()* function takes three arguments, where the first argument *stream* is a file pointer, the second argument *offset* is variable of type *long integer* that specifies the number of bytes by which file pointer is to moved, and third argument *wherefrom* specifies from which position the *offset* is measured. The various values for argument *wherefrom* are listed in Table 16.2.

Table 16.2: Various Values of *wherefrom* for *fseek()* function

Mode	Offset is measured from
0	Beginning of the file
1	Current position of the file
2	End of the file

Table 16.3: Some examples illustrating the use of *fseek()* functions

Seek Call	Action performed
`fseek(fptr, 0, 0);`	Moves the file pointer *fptr* to the beginning of the file. If file pointer is currently at beginning of file, it results in no action.
`fseek(fptr, n, 0);`	Moves the file pointer *fptr* forward by *n* bytes, *i.e.*, move the file pointer to (*n*+1)th bytes in the file.
`fseek(fptr, -n, 1);`	Moves the file pointer *fptr* backward by *n* bytes from current position.
`fseek(fptr, 0, 2);`	Moves the file pointer *fptr* to the end of the file. If file pointer is currently at end of file, it results in no action.

`fseek(fptr, 0, 2);`	Moves the file pointer *fptr* to the end of the file. If file pointer is currently at end of file, it results in no action.
`fseek(fptr, n, 1);`	Moves the file pointer *fptr* forward by *n* bytes from current position.
`fseek(fptr, 1, 1);`	Moves the file pointer *fptr* to the next byte.
`fseek(fptr, -1, 1);`	Moves the file pointer *fptr* to the previous byte.
`fseek(fptr, m, 2);`	Moves the file pointer *fptr* backward by *m* bytes from end of file.

16.5 SUPPLEMENTARY PROBLEMS

Problem 16.1:

Program to find the size of a given file, where the name of the file is given as the command-line argument.

To know the seize of the specified file, position the file pointer at the end of the file using *fseek()* function, and access the value of the file pointer using *ftell()* function that gives the size of the file.

Listing 16.7

```
/*
* Program to find the size of a given file
*   filename : fsize.c
*/
#include <stdio.h>
int main ( int argc, char *argv[] )
{
    FILE *fptr;
    fptr = fopen(argv[1], "r");
    if (!fptr) {
        printf("\nFile %s does not exist\n",   argv[1]);
        return 1;
    }
    fseek(fptr, 0L, 2);
    printf("\nSize of file = %ld bytes.\n", ftell(fptr));
    fclose(fptr);
    return 0;
}
```

Test Run

```
>fszie fsize.c↵
Size of file = 387 bytes.
```

The above test run shows that the size of the program file (source code) created in Listing 16.7 is 387 bytes.

Problem 16.2:

Write a program that read some text from the keyboard and write it into a file named TEXT. Program then reads this file and displays its contents on screen.

Listing 16.8

```
/*
* Program that creates a file and then reads its contents
* and display them on the computer screen
*/
#include <stdio.h>
int main()
{
   char ch;
   FILE *fp1;
   fp1 = fopen("TEXT", "w");     /*  open file for writing  */
   if ( fp1 == NULL )
   {
      printf("\nUnable to open file TEXT for writing\n");
      return 1;
   }
   printf("\nType some text and terminate");
   printf(" the input by Enter key\n\n");
   while ( ( ch = getche() ) != '\r' )
      fputc(ch, fp1);
   fclose(fp1);    /*  close file  */
   fp1 = fopen("TEXT", "r");     /*  open file for reading  */
   if ( fp1 == NULL ) {
      printf("\nUnable to open file TEXT for reading\n");
      return;
   }
   printf("\n\nContents of file TEXT are\n\n");
   while ( !feof(fp1) ) {
      ch = fgetc(fp1);
      putchar(ch);
   }
   fclose(fp1);
   return 0;
}
```

Test Run

```
Type some text and terminate the input by Enter key

Don't do any thing with others which you wish other should not
do with you.↵

Contents of file TEXT are

Don't do any thing with others which you wish other should not
do with you.
```

Problem 16.3:

Write a program to copy the contents of one file to another file byte-by-byte. The names of the files are taken as command line arguments.

Listing 16.9

```
/*
 *   Program to copy the contents of a given file to another file.
 *   filename : kopy1.c
 */
#include <stdio.h>
int main(int argc, char *argv[])
{
    char ch;
    FILE *fp1, *fp2;
    fp1 = fopen(argv[1], "r");
    if ( fp1 == NULL )
    {
        printf("\nUnable to open file: %s for reading\n", argv[1]);
        return 1;
    }
    fp2 = fopen(argv[2], "w");
    if ( fp2 == NULL )
    {
        printf("\nUnable to open file: %s for writing\n", argv[2]);
        return 1;
    }
    while ( !feof(fp1) )
    {
        ch = fgetc(fp1);
        fputc(ch, fp2);
    }
    printf("\nFile copied successfully...\n");
    fclose(fp1);
    fclose(fp2);
    return 0;
}
```

Test Run

```
>kopy1 kopy1.c kk
File copied successfully...
>
```

You can verify that the contents of file *kk* will be same as that of *kopy1.c*.

Problem 16.4:

Write a C program to reverse the first *n* characters in a file. The *file name* and *n* are specified on the command line.

Listing 16.10

```
/*
*   Program to copy contents of a given file to another file
*   filename : kopy2.c
*/
#include <stdio.h>
int main(int argc, char *argv[])
{
   char *str, ch;
   int i, n;
   FILE *fp1;
   fp1 = fopen(argv[1], "r+");
   if ( fp1 == NULL )
   {
      printf("\nUnable to open file: %s for reading\n", argv[1]);
      return 1;
   }
   i = 0;
   n = atoi(argv[2]);
   str = ( char * ) malloc ( n * sizeof(char) );
   while ( ( !feof(fp1) ) && ( i < n ) )
   {
      ch = fgetc(fp1);
      str[i] = ch;
      i++;
   }
   rewind(fp1); /* reposition the file pointer to the beginning */
   i = n-1;

   while ( i >= 0 ) {
      fputc( str[i], fp1);
      i--;
   }
   fclose(fp1);
   return 0;
}
```

Test Run

```
Original Contents of file test.dat
1234567890abcdefghijklmnopqrstuvwxyz
>kopy2 test.dat 5
>
New Contents of file test.dat
5432167890abcdefghijklmnopqrstuvwxyz
```

You can verify that the contents of the file after program execution by using type command on the command prompt.

In the above program, first the given file is opened in read/write mode. Next, first *n* bytes of the file are copied in dynamically allocated character array. Next we rewind the given file, *i.e.*, reposition the file pointer at the beginning of the file. Finally, we write the contents of the character array in reverse order onto the file. Thus, we are able to accomplish the desired task.

EXERCISE

1. Name the various systems for performing file I/O in C.
2. Is it is advisable to close a file explicitly opened for writing?
3. Name the function to close a file.
4. What information system gets by opening a file?
5. What you mean by a *file pointer*?
6. How a file opened with *fopen()* function is referred to in a program?
7. Suppose a program wants to examine every byte of a file, which mode will be more appropriate?
8. What do you mean by term *offset* in reference to a file?
9. What is the task performed by the *fseek()* function?
10. What is the task performed by the *ftell()* function?
11. Which value is returned by the *fopen()* if some error occurs in opening a file?
12. What is the difference between *w+* and *r+* modes?
13. What a *rewind()* function does?

PROGRAMMING EXERCISE

1. Given a text file containing some text. Write a program that prompts the user to input name of a text file, reads this file and outputs the number of vowels and number of words in the text.
2. Given a text file containing some text. Write a program that prompts the user to input name of a text file, reads this file and replaces each occurrence of character 'x' with uppercase 'X'.
3. A beginner to the C language has typed the entire program in uppercase letter. As you know that the normal convention in C language is to type the source code using lowercase letters only except for macros and defined constants. Write a program that converts the source code into lowercase letter. Comments should be left unchanged.

❑ ❑ ❑

Appendix **A**

Precedence & Associativity of Operators

Table A.1 summarizes the rules for precedence and associativity of all operators. Operators in the same row have the same precedence and rows are in order of decreasing precedence.

Table A.1: Precedence and Associativity of Operators

Operator	Description	Precedence Level (Rank)	Associativity
() [] -> .	Function call Array element reference Structure operator used with pointer to a structure Structure operator used with structure variable	1	Left-to-right
! ~ ++ — + – * & (type) sizeof	Logical NOT operator 1's complement Increment Decrement Unary plus Unary minus Pointer reference (indirection) Address of Type cast Size of an operand	2	Right-to-left
* / %	Multiplication Division Modulus (remainder)	3	Left-to-right

Table A.1: Precedence and Associativity of Operators ***Contd.***

Operator	Description	Precedence Level (Rank)	Associativity
+	Addition	4	Left-to-right
–	Subtraction		
<<	Left shift	5	Left-to-right
>>	Right shift		
<	Less than	6	Left-to-right
<=	Less than or equal to		
>	Greater than		
>=	Greater than or equal to		
==	Equal to	7	Left-to-right
!=	Not equal to		
&	Bitwise AND	8	Left-to-right
^	Bitwise exclusive OR	9	Left-to-right
|	Bitwise inclusive OR	10	Left-to-right
&&	Logical AND	11	Left-to-right
||	Logical OR	12	Left-to-right
?:	Condition (ternary)	13	Right-to-left
= += –= *= /= %= &= ^= != <<= >>=	Assignment operators	14	Right-to-left
,	Comma	15	Left-to-right

❑ ❑ ❑

Appendix **B**

FAQs for Oral Examination

Question #1

Whether C language is *low-level*, *high-level*, or *middle-level* language?

Answer

The C language is a *middle-level* language. It is called a *middle- level* language because it has features of *high-level* language as well as *low-level* language.

Question #2

List the key characteristics of C language.

Answer

The C language was and will remain as one of the popular programming languages. Some of the key characteristics that add to its popularity are:

- It is a general purpose programming language, and therefore, can be used to solve vide variety of problems.
- It is supports structuring programming, and therefore, programs developed in it can easily be understood.

- It is free form, *i.e.*, no rigid format for writing programs. Any instruction can start from anywhere and end anywhere. In addition, a single instruction can span (can be written in) many lines.
- It is case sensitive. It distinguishes between lowercase (small) and uppercase (capital) alphabets.
- It was the first language to provide rich set of operators.
- It allows you, through pointers, to access any storage location and the devices connected to your computer through your program.
- It allows you to manipulate internal processor registers, and thus it is very useful for low-level programming.
- It is portable, that means any program written in it can be used on any computer without or with little modification(s).
- It allows you to develop your own library of functions that can be linked to your any program like standard library functions.

Question #3

What are various forms that *main()* function can take?

Answer

The *main()* function is a part of every C program. The C language permits following forms of *main()* function:

- `main()`
- `main(void)`
- `void main()`
- `int main()`
- `void main(void)`
- `int main(void)`

- The empty pair of parenthesis indicates that the *main()* function takes no arguments. This may be explicitly indicated by using the keyword *void* inside the parenthesis.
- We may also specify the keyword *void* or *int* before the word main.
- When the keyword *void* is used, it indicates that the function *main()* does not return any value to the operating system.
- When the keyword *int* is used, it indicates that the function *main()* will return an integer value to the operating system. Value 0 is returned to the operating system to indicate that the program terminated on completion of its intended task whereas the value 1 is used to indicate that the program terminated prematurely (could not complete its intended task).

Question #4

The output produced by a C compiler is an object code, *i.e.*, machine code, but not in a form that can be executed. Why?

Answer

Recall that a program can contain calls to library function as well as user-defined functions that are in other disk files and are not included using *file inclusion* pre-processor directive (*#include*).

The compiler doesn't have access to the definitions of these functions, and hence can't bind the function calls to function definitions. Hence, function calls are left unresolved. In addition, some more information is required by the operating system to run the program.

Question #5

Basically, what does the header files contain?

Answer

The header files contain declarations of library functions (prototypes of library functions) and useful enumerations and macros for the convenience of the programmers.

Question #6

What is the need of having large number of header files? Why not just one?

Answer

Note that header files are read by the compiler, which helps it in the process of compilation of the program. If all header files are combined into a single header file, this file will become very large and lot of compiler's time will be wasted. Further, note that in a program, we are not going to use diverse library functions in a single program, hence relevant declarations are put in different header files and relevant and meaningful names are given to these header files that show its intent.

Question #7

What is the difference between #include <...> and # include "..."?

Answer

There are two ways to include a header file:

```
#include <stdio.h>      and      #include "stdio.h"
```

The first form directs the preprocessor to include the header file from the standard directory while the second form directs the preprocessor to look for the specified header file in the user directory.

Question #8

What happens during linking?

Answer

The next step after compilation is linking, *i.e.*, to resolve the unresolved references to functions. This task is accomplished by another program known as *linker*. The linker takes object code(s) as its inputs and searches for unresolved references. For every unresolved reference, it searches libraries for their definitions and adds them to the end of final code being generated and fills its address at point of call. If search of any function is unsuccessful, the linker will generate a message like unresolved references and also gives name of the function called. Output of a linker is a machine language program that is in executable form better known as executable code or run file.

Question #9

What is the difference between declaration and definition of a variable?

Answer

Declaration only identifies the data type of a variable whereas definition causes the space to be reserved for the variable.

Thus, declaration is a place where the nature of the variable is stated but no storage is allocated whereas definition is the place where the variable is created or assigned storage.

Question #10

What is the difference between the following statements?

```
extern int k;     and     int k;
```

Answer

The first is a declaration indicated that *k* is a variable of type *int* and is defined externally, *i.e.*, in some another source file. The second is a definition and causes 2-bytes to be reserved for it.

Question #11

What is the restriction on the declarations and/or definitions of variables?

Answer

The restriction on the declarations and/or definitions is that they must come before the executable statements in a block, and hence they appear in the beginning of a block.

Question #12

Suppose a global variable and a local variable have the same name. Is it possible to access a global variable from a block where local variable is defined?

Answer

No. It is not possible in C. It is always the most local variable that gets preference.

Question #13

Write a "hello world" program in C without using a semicolon.

Answer

```
#include<stdio.h>
void main()
{
    if ( printf("hello world\n") ) { }
}
```

Explanation: The *printf*() is a function that returns the number of characters it is able to print. This return value can be used in the *if* conditional expression. With this combination, we can print the required string without using a semicolon.

Question #14

What is the difference between *static* and *global* variables?

Answer

While the life of an object determines whether the object is still in the memory (of the process), scope of the object decides whether the variable can be accessed at that point in the program. Static variables are local in scope to the block or file in which they are defined, but their lifespan is throughout the program. For instance, a static variable inside a function cannot be called from outside the function (because it's not in the scope) but is alive and exists in the memory. It retains its old value between function calls.

Global variables persist throughout the program; scope is also throughout the program. It means that global variables can be accessed from any function, any file (unless declared static) in the program.

Question #15

What is the use of *register* keyword in the context of variables?

Answer

The register keyword specifies that the variable is to be stored in the CPU register, if possible. Variables are usually stored in stack and passed to and from the computer processor, as and when required, the speed the data is sent at is pretty but can be improved on. Almost all computer processors contain CPU registers, these are memory slots on the actual processors, and storing data there gets rid of the overhead of the retrieving data from the stack. This memory (in registers) is quite small compared to normal memory, therefore, only a few variables can be stored there. Having a register keyword for variables and parameters also reduces code size, which is important in embedded systems. The number of available CPU registers is strictly dependent on the architectural design of the CPU itself. The number of CPU registers is 32 in most cases.

Question #16

How do we make a global variable accessible across files? Explain the *extern* keyword.

Answer

If a variable is declared (with global scope) in one file but referenced in other, the extern keyword is used to inform the compiler of variable's existence. Note that the keyword extern is for declarations, not definitions. An extern declaration does not create any storage. Variable initializations should not be done with extern.

Question #17

What is a function prototype?

Answer

A function prototype is a declaration similar to variable declarations. Function declarations are generally placed in header files. Specifically, it tells the compiler

- The name of the function
- The type of the output returned by the function.
- The number of types of inputs (called arguments), if any, the function expects to receive and the order in which it expects to receive them.

Question #18

What is the difference between declaration and definition of a function?

Answer

Like variables, declaration of a function only identifies the return type of the function and the type of format arguments. The declaration of a function is usually referred as a *function prototype*. On the other hand, definition of a function contains the statements to accomplish the intended task. Like variables, functions also have an address associated with its name.

Question #19

Is the name of the formal arguments in a function prototype mandatory?

Answer

No. Only data type is mandatory. However, the name of formal arguments can be useful to know the kind of arguments that a function will be taking. This is explained with the help of the following example:

The *displayAt()*function accepts three arguments: row number, column number, and a string. It display the string starting from the given row and column.

The prototype of this function can be

```
void displayAt(int, int, char *);
```

But from this prototype, it is not clear whether row is to passed as first argument or column is to be passed as first argument. However, if its prototype is taken as

```
void displayAt(int row, int col, char *charPtr);
```

then it is clear that first argument will be row while the second will be column.

Question #20

What is the significance of storage class?

Answer

The storage class, in general, determines the scope and lifetime of a variable, which in turn helps to economize the memory usage.

Question #21

What is a dangling pointer?

Answer

It is a pointer that is not initialized with a valid address. Such a pointer can end up pointing anywhere in memory that may include the program code itself or to the code of the operating system. The use of such pointer can lead to undesirable results. Therefore, care must be taken to initialize pointers with valid address before use.

Question #22

What is a memory leak?

Answer

It is a situation where the programmer fails to release the memory allocated at run time in a module. Remember that when memory is allocated, a pointer variable is used to hold the address of the allocated block, however, when the module completes its execution, the pointer variable goes out of scope and there will be no way to reach that memory block. Therefore, care must be taken to release the allocated memory block in a module where memory was allocated.

Question #23

What do you mean by *Lvalue* and *Rvalue*?

Answer

There are two values associated with a variable:

1. Its data value that is stored at some memory address. This sometimes referred to as variable's *Rvalue* (pronounced as "are-value"). We may think *Rvalue* as meaning *read value*. Both a literal constant and a variable can serve as *rvalue*.
2. Its address value that is its address in memory within which its data value is stored. This sometimes referred to as variable's *Lvalue* (pronounced as "ell-value"). We may think *Lvalue* as meaning *location value*. Only a variable can serve as *Lvalue*.

Question #24

Cite some cases where *switch* statement cannot be used?

Answer

The *switch* statement cannot be used when the variable or expression is not of integral type (*int*, *long* or *char*). The other situation is where conditions are of type that does not require exact match, such *amount* <= 1200.

Question #25

Among *gets()* and *fgets()* functions, which function is safe to use?

Answer

fgets() is safe to use. This is illustrated below. The prototype of *gets()* functions is

```
char *gets(char *s);
```

It reads a string of characters terminated by newline characters from *stdin* and stores in *s*. As there is no way to tell the size of the string there is always a possibility of overflow.

The prototype of *fgets()* functions is

```
char *gets(char *s, int n, FILE *stream);
```

It reads a string of characters from *stream* and stores in *s*. It stops when either it reads (*n*-1) characters or a newline character, whichever comes first. So overflow condition never occurs.

Question #26

What would be the consequence if the function prototypes are local to *main()* function?

Answer

If any other function calls these functions, the compiler will flag an error message, as these prototypes are not available in that function, hence the compiler may not be able to compile the program properly.

Question #27

When should the function prototypes be made global?

Answer

When the functions can be called from more than one function.

Question #28

Is the following nested comments are acceptable?

```
/* Outer comment /* Nested comments */ allowed/not allowed */
```

Answer

No. Note that anything that lies between /* and */ is treated as comment. Therefore, in the above case, from word *Outer* to word *comments* everything is treated as comment including /*. Hence the string "allowed/not allowed */" does not lie in the comment.

Thus, it is being improper statement the compiler will flag an error.

Question #29

When should we pass arguments by reference (address)?

Answer

Argument passing by reference (address) is useful in following situations:

- When we intend to change the values of actual arguments.
- When we want to save the memory by preventing the creation of large array and/or structure variables being passed to the function.

Question #30

Given a choice, would you prefer to use *const* over *#define* in order to use a constant?

Answer

Using *const* is always a better choice because we can control its scope, which is not possible with *#define*.

Question #31

Passing arguments by reference (address), we can prevent the creation of large array and/or structure variables in the called function. Here the called function can change the values of array and/or structure variables. Is there any way to prevent the called function from doing so?

Answer

Yes, by prefixing the formal argument by keyword *const* as shown in the following example

```
void fName(const int *a)
{
   /*   some statements   */
}
```

Question #32

In how many ways can we pass arguments to a function?

Answer

There are two ways in which we can pass arguments to a function:

- By value

```
void f(int, int)  /* declaration  */
f(a, b);          /*  call    */
```

- By reference (address)

```
void f(int *, int *)  /* declaration   */
f(&a, &b);            /*  call   */
```

Question #33

Differentiate between call by value and call by reference (address).

Answer

Call by Value	Call by Reference (Address)
1. The actual arguments can be constants, variables, or expressions.	1. The actual arguments can only be variables.
2. The values of actual arguments are substituted in formal arguments which are ordinary variables.	2. The addresses of the actual arguments are substituted in formal arguments which are pointer variable.
3. Any change made to the formal arguments will have no effect on actual arguments, since the function will only be using the local copy of the arguments.	3. Any change made to the formal arguments will have immediate effect on actual arguments, since the function will be working on actual arguments through pointers.

Question #34

What is the main difference between *malloc()* and *calloc()*?

Answer

The main difference between *malloc()* and *calloc()* is that *malloc()* function just allocates the memory whereas the *malloc()* function also initializes the memory to zeros.

Question #35

What is free store/heap?

Answer

Free store/heap is area of memory from where memory is allocated at runtime using *malloc()* or *calloc()* functions.

Question #36

Recall that when we use *free()* function to deallocate the block, we only pass pointer to the block, then how *free()* function know how many bytes it should deallocate?

Answer

When operating system allocates memory, on call to *malloc()*, *calloc()* or *realloc()* function, to a program from its free pool of memory (also called free store), it keeps track of the address of the block and the size of the block. Therefore, when the memory needs to be deallocated, program need only to tell the address of block to the operating system.

Question #37

What is a void/generic pointer?

Answer

When a variable is declared as being a pointer to a variable of type void it is known as a generic pointer. Since we cannot have a variable of type void, the pointer will not point to any data and therefore cannot be de-referenced. It is still a pointer though; to use it we have to cast it to another kind of pointer first. Hence, the term generic pointer. It is very useful when you want a pointer to point to data of different types at different times.

Question #38

Why arithmetic operation can't be performed on a void/generic pointer?

Answer

The C language doesn't allow pointer arithmetic on void pointers. The argument being that we don't know the size of what's being pointed to with a void *and therefore can't know how far to seek the pointer to get to the next valid address.

Question #39

How do you access command line arguments?

Answer

A program is started by the operating system by calling a program's *main*() function. The *main*() function is the only function in C that can be defined in multiple ways. It can take no arguments, two arguments, or three arguments. The two and three argument forms allow it to receive arguments from the shell. The two arguments takes an int and an array of strings. When defining *main*() function any name can be given but it is convention to call them *argc* and *argv*[]. The first argument (*argc*) holds a count of how many elements there are in the array of strings passed as the second argument (*argv*). The array is always null terminated so *argv* [*argc*] = null.

Here's short program demonstrating the use:

```
int main (int argc, char *argv[])
{
   int i;
   for( i = 0; i < argc; i++ ) {
      printf("argv[%d] == %s\n", i, argv[i]);
   }
   return 0;
}
```

The integer *argc* is argument count (hence *argc*). It is the number of arguments passed into program from the command line, including the name of the program.

The array of character pointers is the listing of all the arguments. The *argv*[0] is the name of the program. After that every element number less than *argc* is command line arguments. You can use each *argv* element just like a string, or *argv* as a 2D array.

Question #40

What is the value of the expression 5["CONQUER"]?

Answer

```
E
```

The string literal "CONQUER" is an array, and the expression is equivalent to "CONQUER"[5]. The inside-out expression is equivalent because *a*[*b*] is equivalent to *(*a*+*b*) which is equivalent to *(*b*+*a*) which is equivalent to *b*[*a*].

Question #41

What is a self-referential structure?

Answer

If a structure contains a member that is a pointer to the same structure, then the structure is called self- referential structure.

```
struct list
{
    int nodedata;
    struct list *next;
};
```

Question #42

Write a recursive function to find sum of elements of an array named *a* with *n* elements.

Answer

```
int sum(int a[], int n)
{
    if ( n == 0 )
        return a[0];
    else
        return ( a[n-1] + sum(a,n-1) );
}
```

Question #43

What are library functions? Where are they stored?

Answer

Library functions are a collection of predefined functions. They are stored in files with extension *lib*. These functions are shipped with the compiler for the convenience of the programmers.

❑ ❑ ❑

Appendix C

Solution of Selected Programming Exercises

Chapter 9

1. Given three numbers, determine whether they can form sides of a triangle.

   Note that by the triangle inequality, in order for three line segments to make a triangle, the sum of the lengths of any two line segments must exceed the length of the third line segment.

Listing C.1

```
#include <stdio.h>
int main()
{
   int a, b, c;
   printf("\nEnter value for side AB : ");
   scanf("%d", &a);
   printf("Enter value for side BC : ");
   scanf("%d", &b);
   printf("Enter value for side CA : ");
   scanf("%d", &c);
   if ( ( (a+b) > c ) && ( (b+c) > a ) && ( (c+a) > b ) )
       printf("\nYes, triangle can be made with these sides\n");
   else
       printf("\nNo, triangle cannot be made with these sides\n");
   return 0;
}
```

Test Run 1

```
Enter value for side AB : 2
Enter value for side BC : 3
Enter value for side CA : 5

No, triangle cannot be made with these sides
```

Test Run 2

```
Enter value for side AB : 5
Enter value for side BC : 6
Enter value for side CA : 9
Yes, triangle can be made with these sides
```

5. Given three points $A(x_1, y_1)$, $B(x_2, y_2)$ and $C(x_3, y_3)$, determine whether they are collinear, *i.e.*, lie on the same line.

Note that three points are collinear if they lie on a line. This condition can be checked by following any of the following criteria:

(*a*) area of the triangle formed by these points is zero.
(*b*) slope of the line joining any two pair of points is same.

We will implement second criteria,

Listing C.2

```
#include <stdio.h>
int main()
{
    int x1, y1, x2, y2, x3, y3;
    float m1, m2;
    printf("\nEnter point A(x1,y1)  : ");
    scanf("%d,%d", &x1, &y1);
    printf("\nEnter point B(x2,y2)  : ");
    scanf("%d,%d", &x2, &y2);
    printf("\nEnter point C(x3,y3)  : ");
    scanf("%d,%d", &x3, &y3);

    /*  slope of line segment  AB  */
    if ( (x2-x1) != 0 )
        m1 = (float) (y2-y1)/(x2-x1);
    else
    {
        printf("\nSlope of line segment AB is infinity\n");
        return 1;
    }

    /*  slope of line segment  BC  */
    if ( (x2-x1) != 0 )
        m2 = (float) (y3-y2)/(x3-x2);
    else
    {
        printf("\nSlope of line segment AB is infinity\n");
        return 1;
    }
    /*  compare slopes of line segments AB & BC  */
    if ( m1 == m2 )
        printf("\nPoints A, B, C are collinear\n");
    else
        printf("\nPoints A, B, C are not collinear\n");
```

```
    return 0;
}
```

Test Run 1

```
Enter point A(x1,y1) : 5,5
Enter point B(x2,y2) : 9,9
Enter point C(x3,y3) : 11,11
Points A, B, C are collinear
```

Test Run 2

```
Enter point A(x1,y1) : 5,5
Enter point B(x2,y2) : 6,9
Enter point C(x3,y3) : 10,7
Points A, B, C are not collinear
```

Chapter 10

1. Two prime are said to be twin prime numbers if they differ by 2, such as 11 and 13, 17 and 19, etc. Write a program to print first *n* pairs of twin prime numbers.

Listing C.3

```
#include <stdio.h>
#include <math.h>
int main()
{
    int n, cprime = 2, flag, nprime, k, m, num = 3, count = 0;
    printf("\nHow many pair of twin prime numbers to print : ");
    scanf("%d", &n);
    while ( count < n )
    {
        if ( (num >> 2) && (num%2==0) ) {
            num++;
            continue;
        } else {
            m = sqrt(num);
            flag = 1;
            for ( k = 3; k <= m; k++ ) {
                if ( num % k == 0 ) {
                    flag = 0;
                    break;
                }
            }
            if ( flag == 1 ) {
                nprime = num;
                if ( nprime - cprime == 2 ) {
                    count++;
                    printf("(%d,%d)   ", cprime, nprime);
            }
            cprime = nprime;
```

```
        }
        num++;
        }
    }
    printf("\n");
    return 0;
}
```

Test Run

```
How many pair of twin prime numbers to print : 5
(3,5)  (5,7)  (11,13)  (17,19)  (29,31)
```

4. A factorial chart from 1 to 5 looks like the following:

1! = 1
2! = 1×2
3! = 1×2×3
4! = 1×2×3×4
5! = 1×2×3×4×5

Write a program that will generate a factorial chart from 1 to *n* for any ≤ 9.

Listing C.4

```
#include <stdio.h>
#include <math.h>
int main()
{
    int i, j, n;
    printf("\nEnter value for n (<=9) : ");
    scanf("%d", &n);
    for ( i = 1; i <= n; i++ )
    {
       printf("\n%d! = 1", i);
       for ( j = 2; j <= i; j++ )
           printf("x%d", j);
    }
    printf("\n");
    return 0;
}
```

Test Run

```
Enter value for n (<=9) : ;
```

1! = 1
2! = 1×2
3! = 1×2×3
4! = 1×2×3×4
5! = 1×2×3×4×5

8. A positive integer number IJK is said to be *well-ordered* if I < J < K. For example, number 138 is called *well-ordered* because the digits in the number increase from left to right, *i.e.*, 1 < 3 < 8. Number 365 is not *well-ordered* because 6 is larger than 5. Write a program that displays all possible three digit *well-ordered* numbers.

Listing C.5

```
#include <stdio.h>
int main()
{
    int i, d1, d2, d3, t;
    printf("\n\nThree digit well-ordered numbers\n\n");
    for ( i = 100; i <= 999; i++ )
    {
        t = i;
        d3 = t % 10;
        t = t / 10;
        d2 = t % 10;
        t = t / 10;
        d1 = t % 10;
        if( (d1 < d2) && (d2 < d3) )
        {
            printf("%d  ", i);
        }
    }
    printf("\n");
    return 0;
}
```

Test Run

```
Three digit well-ordered numbers

123 124 125 126 127 128 129 134 135 136 137 138 139 145 146 147
148 149 156 157 158 159 167 168 169 178 179 189 234 235 236 237
238 239 245 246 247 248 249 256 257 258 259 267 268 269 278 279
289 345 346 347 348 349 356 357 358 359 367 368 369 378 379 389
456 457 458 459 467 468 469 478 479 489 567 568 569 578 579 589
678 679 689 789
```

12. You know that an even number is a number which is divisible by 2. However there is another approach that can be used to check whether the given number is even or not. The approach is by inspecting the unit digit - *if the unit digit is 0, 2, 4, 6, or 8, the number is even.* So you are required to write a program to check whether the given number is even or not without performing the division by 2.

Listing C.6

```
#include <stdio.h>
int main()
{
```

```
    int num, udigit;
    printf("\n\nEnter any whole  number : ");
    scanf("%d", &num);
    udigit = num % 10;
    switch (udigit)
    {
        case 0:
        case 2:
        case 4:
        case 6:
        case 8: printf("\n%d is even number\n", num);
                break;
        default; printf("\n%d is odd number\n", num);
    }
    return 0;
}
```

Test Run 1

```
Enter any whole  number : 204
204 is even number
```

Test Run 2

```
Enter any whole  number : 155
155 is odd number
```

Chapter 12

6. Given a matrix *A* of order *m*×*n*, write a program to find the row having the maximum number of elements which are even.

Listing C.7

```
#include<stdio.h>
int main()
{
    int a[30], i, j, k, n;
    printf("\nHow many elements? : ");
    scanf("%d", &n);
    printf("\nEnter %d elements of array\n", n);
    for ( i = 0; i < n; ++i )
    scanf("%d", &a[i]);
    for( i = 0; i < n; ++i )
    {
        for( j = i+1;j < n;)
        {
            if(a[i]==a[j])
            {
                for( k = j; k < n-1;++k )
```

```
                    {
                        a[k]=a[k+1];
                    }
                    --n;
                }
                else
                {
                    ++j;
                }
            }
        }
        printf("\nArray elements after removing duplicate elements\n");
        for ( i = 0; i < n; ++i )
            printf("%d  ", a[i]);
        return 0;
}
```

Test Run

```
How many elements? 10
Enter 10 elements of array
11,11,22,33,22,56,67,33,99,100
Array elements after removing duplicate elements
11 22 33 56 67 99 100
```

7. Given a matrix *A* of order *m*×*n*, write a program to find the row having the maximum number of elements which are even.

Listing C.7

```
#include <stdio.h>
int main()
{
    int a[10][10], count[10], i, m, n, j, max, loc;
    printf("\nEnter size of matrix as m,n : ");
    scanf("%d,%d", &m, &n);
    printf("\nEnter %d elements of matrix row-wise\n", m*n);
    for ( i = 0; i < m; i++ )
    {
        for ( j = 0; j < n; j++ )
        {
            scanf("%d", &a[i][j] )
        }
    }
    for ( i = 0; i < m; i++ )
    {
        count[i] = 0;
        for ( j = 0; j < n; j++ )
        {
            if ( a[i][j] % 2 == 0 )
                count[i]++;
        }
    }
```

```
    max = count[0];
    loc = 0;
    for ( i = 1; i < m; i++ )
    {
        if ( count[i] > max )
        {
            max = count[i];
            loc = i;
        }
    }
    printf("\nRow having maximum number of even elements = %d\n",loc+1);
    return 0;
}
```

Test Run

```
Enter size of matrix as m,n : 4,4
Enter 16 elements of matrix row-wise
5 4 3 2
6 4 5 10
5 3 1 9
1 5 6 3
Row having maximum number of even elements = 2
```

8. A square matrix *A* of size *nxn* is said to be symmetric if element $a_{ij} = a_{ji}$ for all values of *i* and *j*. Write a function, say *int isSymmetric(int a[][], int n)* that returns value 1 if the input matrix is symmetric else returns value 0.

Listing C.8

```
#include <stdio.h>
int main()
{
   int a[10][10], i, j, n;
   printf("\nEnter size of square matrix : ");
   scanf("%d", &n);
   printf("\nEnter %d elements of matrix row-wise\n", n*n);
   for ( i = 0; i < n; i++ )
   {
        for ( j = 0; j < n; j++ )
        {
            scanf("%d", &a[i][j] );
        }
   }
   for ( i = 0; i < n; i++ )
   {
        for ( j = i+1; j < n; j++ )
        {
            if ( a[i][j] != a[i][j] )
            {
                printf("\nGiven matrix is not symmetric\n");
                return 1;
```

```
            }
        }
    }
    printf("\nGiven matrix is symmetric\n");
    return 0;
}
```

Test Run 1

```
Enter size of square matrix : 3
Enter 16 elements of matrix row-wise
5 4 3
6 4 5
5 3 1
Given matrix is not symmetric
```

Test Run 2

```
Enter size of square matrix : 3
Enter 16 elements of matrix row-wise
1 2 3
2 1 4
3 4 1
Given matrix is symmetric
```

10. Given a matrix *A* of order *m*×*n*, write a program to sort the even rows in ascending order and odd rows in descending order

Listing C.9

```
#include <stdio.h>
int main()
{
    int a[10][10], count[10], i, m, n, j, k, t;
    printf("\nEnter size of matrix as m,n : ");
    scanf("%d,%d", &m, &n);
    printf("\nEnter %d elements of matrix row-wise\n", m*n);
    for ( i = 0; i < m; i++ )
    {
        for ( j = 0; j < n; j++ )
        {
            scanf("%d", &a[i][j] );
        }
    }
    for ( i = 0; i < m; i++ )
    {
        if ( i % 2 == 0 )       /* even row */
        {
            for ( k = 0; k < n-1; k++ )
            {
                for ( j = 0; j < n-k-1; j++ )
```

```
                {
                        if ( a[i][j] > a[i][j+1] )
                        {
                           t = a[i][j];
                           a[i][j] = a[i][j+1];
                           a[i][j+1] = t;
                        }
                }
            }
        } else {                /* odd row */
            for ( k = 0; k < n-1; k++ )
            {
                for ( j = 0; j < n-k-1; j++ )
                {
                    if ( a[i][j] < a[i][j+1] )
                    {
                        t = a[i][j];
                        a[i][j] = a[i][j+1];
                        a[i][j+1] = t;
                    }
                }
            }
        }
    }
    printf("\nMatrix after sorting\n\n");
    for ( i = 0; i < m; i++ )
    {
        for ( j = 0; j < n; j++ )
        {
            printf("%3d", a[i][j]);
        }
        printf("\n");

    }
    return 0;
}
```

Test Run

```
Enter size of matrix as m,n : 4,4
Enter 16 elements of matrix row-wise
5 4 3 2
6 4 5 10
5 3 1 9
1 5 6 3
Matrix after sorting
 2  3  4  5
10  6  5  4
 1  3  5  9
 6  5  3  1
```

❑ ❑ ❑

Index

A

B

C

O

P

Q

R

S

❑ ❑ ❑

AICTE RECOMMENDED BOOKS BY THE SAME AUTHOR

DATA STRUCTURES

RS Salaria

CONTENTS

Chapter 1: Introduction to Data Structures; Chapter 2: Introduction to Algorithms; Chapter 3: Arrays; Chapter 4: Linked Lists; Chapter 5: Stacks; Chapter 6: Queues; Chapter 7: Trees; Chapter 8: Heaps; Chapter 9: Graphs; Chapter 10: Hashing and Hash Tables; Chapter 11: Sorting Algorithms

Edition : Latest **ISBN : 9789386173966** **Pages (Approx.) : 498**

MASTERING OBJECT-ORIENTED PROGRAMMING IN C++

RS Salaria

CONTENTS

Chapter 1: Introduction to Object-Oriented Programming; Chapter 2: Migrating form C to C++; Chapter 3: Standard Input/Output; Chapter 4: Classes and Objects; Chapter 5: Pointers and Dynamic Memory Management; Chapter 6: Constructors and Destructors; Chapter 7: Overloading and Type Conversion; Chapter 8: Inheritance; Chapter 9: Virtual Functions and Polymorphism; Chapter 10: Exception Handling; Chapter 11: Templates and Generic Programming; Chapter 12: File Handling; Chapter 13: Introduction to Standard Template Library (STL)

Edition : Latest **ISBN : 9789382609391** **Pages (Approx.) : 488**

COMPUTER ORIENTED NUMERICAL METHODS

RS Salaria

CONTENTS

Chapter 1: Preamble; Chapter 2: Data Representation & Computer Arithmetic; Chapter 3: Solution of Non-Linear Equations; Chapter 4: Matrices and Determinants; Chapter 5: Solution of System of Linear Equations; Chapter 6: Interpolation and Approximation; Chapter 7: Curve Fitting & Method of Least Squares; Chapter 8: Numerical Differentiation; Chapter 9: Numerical Integration; Chapter 10: Solution of Ordinary Differential Equations

Edition : Latest **ISBN : 9789381068489** **Pages (Approx.) : 488**

COMPUTER CONCEPTS AND PROGRAMMING IN C

PROF. R. S. SALARIA

FEEDBACK FORM

1. Which topics from your examination point of view are inadequately or not covered in this book?

____

____

2. Is there any misprints/ mistakes/ factual inaccuracy in this book? If so, please specify.

____

____

3. What is your assessment of this book as regards the presentation of the subject-matter, expression, precision and price in relation to the other recommended books available on this subject?

____

____

4. Which competing books you regard as better than this? Please mention their author and publishers.

____

____

5. Any further suggestions/comments you would like to make for the improvement of the book?

____

____

PS: If needed, please attach a separate sheet.

Name : ______________________

College : ______________________

Address : ______________________

Email : ______________________

Mobile : ______________________

Please mail the feedback form at:

KHANNA BOOK PUBLISHING CO. (P) LTD.

4C/4344, Ansari Road, Daryaganj, New Delhi-110002

You can also email this feedback form at contact@khannabooks.com or Whatsapp at +91 – 99109 09320

BEST FEEDBACK WILL BE REWARDED SUITABLY

[illegible]

Which topics in your [illegible]

Have any major [illegible] please [illegible]

What is [illegible] of this book [illegible]

Which comments [illegible] author and publisher [illegible]

Any [illegible]

Name [illegible]

College [illegible]

Address [illegible]

Email [illegible]

Mobile [illegible]

[illegible]

KHANNA [illegible]

[illegible]